BANGLADESH

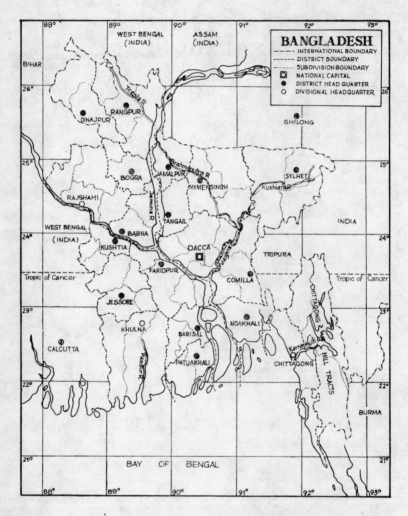

Map reproduced with the permission of Dr. A.K.M. Ghulam Rabbani, Secretary, Statistics Division, Ministry of Planning and Director-General, Bangladesh Bureau of Statistics. Source: *Statistical Pocket Book of Bangladesh*, 1979.

BANGLADESH
THE
FIRST
DECADE

MARCUS FRANDA

South Asian Publishers Pvt Ltd
New Delhi, Madras

in association with

Universities Field Staff International
Hanover, New Hampshire

South Asian Publishers Pvt Ltd
36 Netaji Subhash Marg, Daryaganj, New Delhi 110002
177 Avvai Shanmugham Salai, Madras 600086

Universities Field Staff International
4 West Wheelock Street, P.O. Box 150, Hanover, NH 03755

Library of Congress Cataloging in Publication Data

Franda, Marcus F.
    Bangladesh, the first decade.

    Bibliography: p.
    Includes indexes.
    1. Bangladesh—Politics and government—
1971–   .   I. Title.
DS395.5.F69   954.9′205   81-19639
ISBN   0–88333–006–7   (Universities Field Staff
                        International)   AACR2

Published by South Asian Publishers Pvt Ltd
New Delhi and printed in India at Prabhat Press, Meerut.

To

CHARLIE

whose generation may live
to see the revitalization of
BANGLADESH

PREFACE

The essays in this book were written over the past decade, as part of my reporting for Universities Field Staff International, a consortium of 17 academic institutions that supports scholarly journalists who cover contemporary affairs around the world. Formerly known as the American Universities Field Staff—until it went international in 1981—UFSI espouses no causes, promotes no ideology, aligns with no political group, has no governmental connections, and favors no particular social science theory. As a Fieldstaff Associate since 1971, my principal charge has been to write readable and balanced short articles (called Fieldstaff Reports) on events of significance for an international audience. The Fieldstaff—based in Hanover, New Hampshire and associated with both the Development Feature Service and the Institute of World Affairs in Salisbury Connecticut—makes educational films, prepares television documentaries, and hosts conferences. It is funded in part by the 17 universities and educational institutions that sponsor it, in part by the sale of its books, articles, films and television programs, and in part by grants from Foundations, private corporations and individuals interested in the study of world affairs.[1]

My interest in Bangladesh began in 1959, when I first started studying the Bengali language at the University of Chicago. It has

1. The 17 member institutions of Universities Field Staff International are: University of Alabama at Birmingham; University of Alabama at Tuscaloosa; Brown University; California State University at Fullerton; California State University at Northridge; Dartmouth College; East-West Center; University of Hawaii; Indiana University; Institute for Shipboard Education; University of Kansas; Michigan State University; University of Missouri; University of Pittsburgh; Ramapo College of New Jersey; Utah State University; University of Wisconsin System.

grown steadily during the past two decades. Since my first research trip to Dacca in 1963, I have visited the territory that is now Bangladesh (formerly East Pakistan) at least once every year, with the exception of only two years. During this period, the government has changed hands six times, the country has witnessed the only successful civil war in this century, and the economy has been in a state of almost steady turmoil and decline. As is clear from the last few essays in this volume, there are many positive features as one looks at the Bangladesh landscape in the 1980s, but the overwhelming picture is still one of unprecedented challenge rather than unlimited opportunity.

The essays in this volume are divided into four sections: (1) The liberation war and its aftermath; (2) Indo-Bangladesh relations; (3) population and resources; and (4) Ziaur Rahman's Bangladesh. These are categories that suggested themselves by the topics of the essays as originally written. Within each section, essays have been arranged in chronological order, with the latest essays coming in the later sections of the book. The result is that the essays can be read to provide a topical account of the major political, economic and social factors affecting Bangladesh, or, by skipping from Part I to Part IV, as a chronological account of the volatile politics of Bangladesh in the 1970s and early 1980s.

This collection brings out dramatically the changes that took place among the leaders of the Bangladesh liberation movement once they achieved office. In the first essay, Mujibur Rahman's government is correctly labelled "one of the most popular elected governments in the world" while, Mujib and his colleagues are said to have "consistently supported parliamentary democracy" as "someone who shies away from formal ceremonies and protocol." These observations were based on years of Mujib-watching in the 1960s, as he rose from the cacaphonic lairs of Awami League politics to become *Bangabandhu* ("friend of Bengal") and Father of the Nation.

From a personal perspective, nothing was more shocking to me than to see the upright and courageous people around Mujib turn from their concern with issues and principals having to do with justice, freedom and independence to matters of patronage, spoils and pay-offs almost immediately after the liberation of the country. With unprecedented support to begin with, the popularity of Mujib's government plummeted very quickly—much more rapidly than I or anyone else had predicted. Mujib himself not only got rid of his shyness but even came to depend on the adulation and fawning of his colleagues for sustenance. By the end of his life he had given up his consistent support for democratic institutions and had made of his great movement a petty one-party regime much like those of other Third World leaders who have failed.

My own feeling is that the blame for this lies primarily with the international development establishment, which moved into Bangladesh in great numbers and with huge amounts of money immediately after the liberation. Unfortunately, these outsiders—some of them extremely well-meaning—were able to buy Ministers, establish elaborate homes and offices and institutions for themselves and their organizations, and provide contracts for the sale of milk powder, nutritional biscuits, foodgrain, waterworks, ferries, and a host of other items of international aid, but they were unable to develop Bangladesh, or, with some few exceptions, to get development going in anything resembling a promising manner. This book details some of those failures, and discusses some of the massive problems that have been exacerbated by an international relief and development effort that has, for the most part, been misdirected.[2]

The present government is convinced that ever larger amounts of international aid are necessary for Bangladesh's development, even though Ziaur Rahman admitted before his death that there was undoubtedly more corruption at that time than there was when he took over in 1975. Zia was also convinced that the principal source of corruption was the massive infusion of foreign funds. One is tempted to compare Ziaur Rahman and his regime to the military-bureaucratic complex built with foreign funds by Ayub Khan in the 1960s, but there were clearly differences between Zia and Ayub. Zia was not nearly as aloof as Ayub Khan. He mixed easily with people from all walks of life and made it a point to get out into the

---

2. For more detailed discussions of Bangladesh's aid-dependence see my article, "The Moral Implications of Bangladesh," *Asia* (Journal of the Asia Society), Supplement No. 1 (Fall 1974), pp. 43–67. See also my testimony in "Political Trends in India and Bangladesh," *Hearing Before the Subcommittee on the Near East and South Asia of the Committee on Foreign Affairs, House of Representatives, Ninety-Third Congress, First Session (October 31, 1973)*, (Washington, D.C.: U.S. Government Printing Office, 1973).

countryside to learn what was happening. Unlike Ayub, Zia enjoyed politics and was somewhat skilled at political maneuvering.

But Zia had problems. He was forced on a number of occasions to put down rebellions and attempted coups in the army with brutal force, yet he still made little headway in building a solid party organization or in de-bureaucratizing the administration. He had grand plans and targets for population control, but there was virtually no progress whatsoever on that all-important front during his 5-1/2 years in power. Bountiful food harvests offered some respite from traditional shortages, providing some hope for the development of a long-term rational food policy that might attack gnawing problems of equity and periodic acute shortage. The concluding chapters in this book make clear, however, that the evolution of such a food policy—and other aspects of development as well—are highly dependent on cooperative relationships with India. Cooperation with India is in turn dependent on the resolution of a number of outstanding issues in Indo-Bangladesh relations (see Section II), on the elaboration of Ziaur Rahman's concept of Bangladeshi nationalism (Section IV), and on a harmonious succession (last chapter).

Perhaps the most positive features of Bangladesh stem from the effectiveness of Zia's government, which was the first effective government that Bangladesh ever had, and the enthusiasm that Zia generated for development activities. A hopeful scenario would have these as Zia's legacies for the future. More than likely, however, neither law and order nor enthusiasm, nor a combination of both at once, will be sufficient to tide Bangladesh neatly over the tumultous days that lie ahead. There is enormous factionalism in the post-Zia Bangladesh, and even greater disenchantment with the degrading conditions under which Bangladeshis have been forced to live in the last few decades. While Zia was alive, the opposition parties were unable to muster sufficient support to present any kind of threat to Ziaur Rahman's Bangladesh National Party (BNP), but the history of political movements in Bangladesh would not allow for complacency because of that. At key points in the past, opposition has mushroomed from out of nowhere, amid awe-inspiring spurts of violence and martyrdom, toppling leaders and governments along the way. Equally unpredictable have been the coups and attempted coups within the army, which have led to the last four changes of government in Bangladesh.

One is almost forced to conclude that the most important variables abroad in Bangladesh are the aspirations behind Ziaur Rahman's nationalism, rather than the obvious inability of Bangladeshis to immediately realize them. To paraphrase from the next-to-last essay in this volume: Governmental leaders want people to feel strongly and emotionally that they are Bangladeshis; they want people to be enthusiastic about building up the country; they want Bangladeshis to be vigilant and prepared to resist, militarily if necessary, pressures from outside; they want people to have confidence that they can grow things themselves and do things themselves, without relying on foreigners; they want the Bangladesh people to take pride in their religion, and to have no problems with minority communities. None of these things are yet there, nor are they likely to be there in the next decade. But these aspirations—which are essentially the aspirations of Ziaur Rahman's Bangladeshi nationalism—could well be the nascent beginnings of a set of ideals which will eventually guide Bangladesh, as a nation, into the future.

In a book like this, there are literally hundreds of people who are involved, including all of those who granted interviews over the years and all of those who spent time in discussion, hammering out particular points. Among those people, a few stand out. Professor Talukder Maniruzzaman of Dacca University has been my principal mentor on Bangladesh through the years; he and his wife, Ruby, have also been the closest of personal friends. I have benefited immeasurably from the affectionate fellowship of "Munnibhai" (Q.S. Shamsuzzaman) and his family, and, more recently, from the warmth of the Centre for Policy Research at Dacca University, directed by Dr. Ataur Rahman. Mrs. Soundara Raghavan deserves special mention for so ably typing most of these manuscripts in first-draft form, as does Ms. Manon Spitzer, Field-staff editor and Associate, who has edited portions of all of these essays. My wife, Vonnie, has been proofreader and companion, the discoverer of "Munnibhai," and a most valuable critic. Whatever merit there is in this volume is due more to these and others than to me. The errors and mistakes in judgement are not their fault, they are mine.

New Delhi   MARCUS FRANDA
16 December, 1981

CONTENTS

PART I

THE LIBERATION WAR AND ITS AFTERMATH

Some measure of the tragedy that has overtaken Bangladesh in the last decade is the fact that it has become trite and a truism to say that the nation was born in one of the bloodiest civil wars in history. Much has been written on the war itself, the aid-dependence it engendered, and the war's aftermath. The essays in this first section, written in 1972 and 1975, poignantly demonstrate that the problems encountered by Bangladesh during its first decade of existence were quite visible from the beginning. The essays also lay some of the historical background necessary for an understanding of the thorny issues of Indo-Bangladesh relations, population growth and use of resources, all of which are explored more fully in later sections of the present volume.

THE BEGINNINGS OF BANGLADESH (1972)

The new nation of Bangladesh, which achieved its Independence with the help of the Indian military in December 1971. is now the world's eighth most highly populated country. It is the third most populous of the new nations to come into being since World War II (only India and Indonesia being larger), and it represents the largest successful secessionist movement in the history of the nation-state system. The birth of Bangladesh has already had an impact on international power alignments in South Asia, and its pattern of future development promises to have continuing international repercussions. For all of these reasons, the creation of Bangladesh must be considered among the more significant events to take place in Asia in this century.

But perhaps more important than the international political position of Bangladesh is the challenge that it presents in terms of human values. During the past 18 months this relatively small geographic area (it is slightly larger in land size than Ohio) has witnessed massive natural disasters, innumerable human atrocities, the unprecedented movement of 10 million international refugees, and finally the horrors of a quick but brutal war. While everyone hopes that human tragedy on the same scale will not continue into the immediate post-Independence period, enormous political, social, and economic problems nevertheless remain. It is the magnitude of these problems that leads one to question the capacity of mankind ever to come to grips with the realities of life in Bangladesh.

Many of Asia's problems are carried to their extremes in Bangladesh. Paramount among these is a heavy and rapidly increasing population pressure, reflected in unusually high man/land and man/natural resource ratios. Bangladesh, for example, is about three times as crowded as India, its population density in 1970 being 1,360 people per square mile while the comparable figure for India was only 460 people per square mile. Moreover, Bangladesh does not have the abundance of natural resources that one finds in India, and it has virtually no industrial base. The principal resources of Bangladesh are its magnificent if uncontrolled rivers, its fertile deltaic land, and its untapped reserves of natural gas, but it has no known quantities of minerals, ore, coal, petroleum, cement, or any of the other numerous resources needed to pursue a policy of industrialization. The economy of Bangladesh is, therefore, an agricultural peasant economy, with 90 per cent of the population living in rural areas and over 80 per cent engaged in agriculture. During the period when Bangladesh was part of Pakistan (1947–1971), agriculture generated about 60 per cent of gross product and over 90 per cent of the exports of the territory now included in Bangladesh.

Under these circumstances it is little wonder that the economy of Bangladesh has been forged in the classic colonial pattern, with agricultural produce being exported in return for the products of industry. In the seventeenth and eighteenth centuries the British developed and established control over the indigo, jute, and tea that was grown in East Bengal (the area that is now Bangladesh), and it shipped these products either to Calcutta or to England to be processed. This meant that British-Indian Managing Agents— centered either in Calcutta or London—in many ways controlled the destinies of the people of East Bengal, and such control increasingly led to feelings of exploitation on the part of East Bengalis In response to British "exploitation," the people of East Bengal quickly moved to the forefront of the Indian nationalist movement in the nineteenth century, and eventually chose to side with Pakistan after 1947, only to find that they had merely substituted "one colonialism for another." The result, of course, was the recent upsurge of Bangladesh nationalism against the colonialist Pakistanis.

Now that the people of East Bengal have attained complete legal sovereignty over their territory for the first time, there is renewed hope that genuine cooperative economic relationships can be worked out between Bangladesh, India, and the rest of the world, in such a manner as to end exploitation of the Bangladesh economy by non-Bengalis. The Prime Minister of Bangladesh, Sheikh Mujibur Rahman, has stated that his goal is to make Bangladesh "The Switzerland of the East," by pursuing a neutralist foreign policy and

engaging in widespread trade and commercial ventures while at
the same time raising the standard of living of his countrymen. In
pursuit of this goal, Sheikh Mujib has declared his adherence to
precisely those values that India's national leadership has tried to
advance since 1947, i.e., secularism, socialism, and democracy.

The task that Sheikh Mujib has set for the political leadership
of Bangladesh is imposing, not only because there is overpopulation
and underdevelopment, but also because of the inheritance of
cultural and psychological problems from the past. During the
past 14 years the people of East Bengal have lived under a military
regime that was trying to construct an "Islamic Republic" without
even token gestures to socialism, which means that Sheikh Mujibur
Rahman and his followers are now going to have to establish
"secularism, socialism, and democracy" in the absence of all but
rudimentary legacies from the past. Moreover, since West Pakistan
so thoroughly dominated the governmental, police, and military
structures of East Bengal during the period when it was part of
Pakistan, the new leaders of Bangladesh will now have to struggle
to maintain governmental stability and effectiveness, in an atmosphere where the bulk of the population is highly politicized. In
these respects too one could argue that Bangladesh exemplifies the
problems of new Asian nations carried to their extremes.

When I arrived in Bangladesh a few weeks ago, shortly after the
surrender of Pakistani troops to the Indian army, the atmosphere
was such that one could easily forget the massive long-range
problems of this war-ravaged new nation. The emphasis almost
everywhere was on short-term reconstruction, and the mood of the
country was decidedly optimistic. People talked freely about the
atrocities that the Pakistan army had perpetrated on the Bengali
population, and they expressed their bitterness, disbelief, and sense
of tragic loss for friends and relatives who had been killed during
the army crackdown and the war. But all of this merely provided
a backdrop for the prevailing discussion of plans for a brighter
Bengali future. Perhaps more important, one could witness
considerable activity being directed toward the tasks of reconstruction, with new temporary shelters being built, fields being planted,
airstrips being repaired, the dead being buried, and the wounded
and the sick at least temporarily cared for.

In sharp contrast to my previous visits to East Bengal, I was
overwhelmed this time by the way in which freedom was being

relished in Bangladesh. Ministers, MNAs (Members of the National Assembly), and especially the Prime Minister, moved about without military or police protection, people talked openly about their past experiences and present concerns, and there was little evidence that anyone was being involuntarily constrained. Especially striking was the constant movement of young *mukti bahini* (freedom fighters) who were trying to find a substitute for their recent guerrilla activities. Some were attempting to repair bridges and roads, some were guarding the minority communities that had sided with the Pakistanis, and some were continuing to train themselves for a future role in the military and police services. Many of them simply roamed about the cities or the countryside, with their guerrilla caps, beards, and guns, occasionally shouting "*Joi Bangla*," or discharging their weapons into the air in jubilant exultation. In the midst of such celebration, it was painfully obvious to everyone in Bangladesh—and especially to the new Bangladesh government—that the prevailing optimism in the country could easily lead to frustration, and that freedom could quickly degenerate into chaos and disorder. But this made it all the more surprising that people could speak so optimistically and openly, while at the same time busying themselves with reconstruction.

RECONSTRUCTION AND REHABILITATION

It would be difficult to overstate the massive relief and rehabilitation effort that will be necessary to restore some sense of economic order to Bangladesh. Many parts of the country are still trying to recover from the cyclones and floods that ravaged East Bengal in November 1970, and virtually every city and village was somehow affected by the army crackdown and the war in 1971. The most obvious extensive damage still visible is the partial destruction of innumerable bridges in the countryside (the government estimates that 318 road bridges and 247 rail bridges are either partially or wholly damaged), most of which resulted from *mukti bahini* sabotage efforts intended to disrupt the flow of Pakistani men and material. Temporary diversions have been built around these bridges, down into the dried-up river beds, so that it is still possible in most places to move trucks and cars with considerable delay and inconvenience. However, when the monsoons come later this year these diversions will have to be replaced by temporary pontoon bridges and ferries, with a further loss in transportation efficiency.

Transportation becomes especially crucial because of the need to move large amounts of food, clothing, medicine, and building materials to areas that have been especially hard-hit. In an effort to dampen the enthusiasm of the *mukti bahini*, the Pakistan army pursued a deliberate policy of retribution for guerrilla activities, with the result that a number of villages and neighborhoods have been completely leveled or burned. In those areas where the *mukti* were able to maintain undisputed control, physical damage is less severe and crops are growing nicely, but in areas where there were sustained struggles between the *mukti* and the Pakistanis one finds considerable physical damage and a paucity of agricultural produce. The problem for the Bangladesh administration at present is to move relief supplies into areas of scarcity, while at the same time sustaining the relative self-sufficiency of the more affluent areas.

Transportation problems would be less severe if all of the ports were functioning at full capacity, but unfortunately this is not the case. The major port at Chittagong still has a number of sunken ships blocking the harbor, parts of the channel have apparently been mined (no one knows quite where or by whom), and damage to docks and warehouses is such that Chittagong's handling capacity has been reduced to something like 70,000 tons per month, far below the government's estimated requirements of 550,000 tons of imported relief supplies per month for the next year. The smaller ports at Chalna and Khulna have never figured very prominently in the international economy as it relates to East Bengal, and they too have now been severely disrupted, so that one clearly cannot expect adequate relief supplies to be moved to Bangladesh by sea.

Because of its transportation bottlenecks, the Bangladesh government has attempted to secure as many planes and helicopters as possible, to be used to move relief supplies during the period that bridges, roads, and port facilities are being repaired. The six major airports in Bangladesh have already been restored to working order, and the presence of Indian army, United Nations, and Red Cross air transport has thus far provided valuable communication and transport links between areas that would otherwise not have contact with one another. Unfortunately, however, a number of legal "snafus," resulting primarily from the confused pattern of recognition of Bangladesh, have prevented international relief agencies from moving as quickly as they would have wished.

Perhaps the most tragic part of all of this is that communications are so poor that no one can really find out what is needed where, for how long, or in what quantities. Public telegraph and telephone communications between different parts of the country, never good, have all but closed down for the time being, while mail service is wildly sporadic at best (in Dacca, for example, different branches of the post office could not even agree in February on the price of postage stamps or the cost of letters). Much of the communications system has been co-opted by international and domestic "tracing services" that attempt to find out who is missing and who is dead, while other communications facilities are being used by the army and the government to facilitate the movement of 10 million refugees returning from India. Since it is so difficult to repair telephone lines or telegraph equipment in the present condition of the country, the most effective means of communication has proven to be the short-wave radio, operated from temporary and makeshift stations scattered throughout the country.

In this atmosphere it is difficult to assess the exact needs of Bangladesh over the next few years, but the tentative figures that have been drawn up by the Bangladesh government seem realistic, if not modest. These include 200,000 to 250,000 tons of food grains per month, 100,000 tons of cement, 50,000 tons of corrugated iron sheets for building homes, 50,000 tons of timber, and 100,000 tons of other commodities, including medicines and industrial supplies. According to Mr. A.H.M. Kamruzzaman, Minister of Relief and Rehabilitation, maintenance of supplies at these levels every month for the next 12 months, if coupled with removal of transportation bottlenecks, would enable the Bangladesh government to reconstruct port facilities, airports, roads, bridges, railway lines, and factories damaged during the army crackdown and the war, while it would also provide satisfactory accommodation for those refugees whose homes, businesses, tools, and agricultural implements were destroyed. In addition, of course, Bangladesh will need foreign exchange in large amounts, since it received none of its share of Pakistan's foreign exchange reserves after the war, and it will also need considerable technical assistance to replace those among its intellectuals who were killed or murdered. Since the total cost of rebuilding the damaged Bangladesh economy is estimated by the Bangladesh government at approximately US $3 billion—about eight times the total annual revenue of East Bengal in 1969–70—it is obvious that reconstruction is going to require substantial external assistance if more major human disasters are going to be avoided in the future.

THE SEARCH FOR EXTERNAL ASSISTANCE

Thus far the bulk of the external assistance that has been promised to Bangladesh has come from India, which is seriously straining its own resources to help Bangladesh as much as it possibly can. The Indian government has already allocated about 50 crores of rupees (US $67 million) worth of food grains for relief purposes, along with the promise of more food grain allocations for Bangladesh later this year. In addition, India has given Bangladesh a general purpose grant of Rs. 30 crores (US $40 million) to buy essential goods from India during the coming year. Smaller grants for reconstruction of the transportation system (10 crores), a foreign exchange loan (9.5 crores), and an allocation for refugee rehabilitation (Rs. 18.58 crores), when coupled with a grant of two ships and several aircraft (worth approximately 10 crores) brings India's total assistance thus far to Rs. 128 crores (US $180 million), a figure that is woefully inadequate to meet the needs of Bangladesh but an obvious sacrifice for poor India. It is likely that India will somehow find even more resources that can be allocated for reconstruction and rehabilitation needs in Bangladesh during the next year, but the most one could hope for would be an aid effort of US $500 million (Rs. 350 crores), which would strain India's resources as much as anyone could expect.

For this reason, and for others that will be detailed later, the new government in Bangladesh has attempted to cart its net as widely as possible in its search for foreign assistance. Sheikh Mujib himself has met with officials and representatives of every major government (including Senators Stevenson and Kennedy from the United States), and has made clear to each of them his hope that aid will be forthcoming from a variety of international sources. Clearly the new government does not want to be overly dependent on either India or the Soviet Union—the two nations that were instrumental in bringing about the liberation of Bangladesh—but if other nations fail to provide substantial external assistance, the new government will have little choice. It is also uncertain at this point that the Soviets would be willing to offer Bangladesh the kinds of resources that are needed, but more will be known about this when Sheikh Mujib travels to the Soviet Union in early March.

The principal hurdles that stand in the way of a massive international aid effort for Bangladesh revolve around questions concerning debt repayment by Bangladesh and relations with the United States. The Bangladesh government has thus far taken the stand that it is not a successor government and should not, therefore, be burdened with Pakistan's debts, a posture that creates obvious problems for the standing of Bangladesh in the world community. After a recent visit to Dacca, World Bank President Robert McNamara personally requested Sheikh Mujib to enact legislation enabling Bangladesh to join the International Monetary Fund and International Bank for Reconstruction and Development, but at the same time it was made clear that some alteration of the present Bangladesh position regarding debt repayment would have to be forthcoming before membership could be granted (at present the IBRD has outstanding credits to the erstwhile East Pakistan government totaling $145.9 million for both completed and ongoing projects).

Most observers are convinced that Sheikh Mujib is flexible enough that some solution can be found for the problem of debt repayment but at this point no one that I have talked with in Bangladesh or India is sanguine about the position of the Nixon administration regarding recognition and American aid. In his annual foreign policy message to the American Congress in early February, President Nixon stated that he had "never been hostile to Bengali aspirations," that the United States "relief effort in East Bengal will continue," and that he had "no intentions of ignoring these 70 million people." At the same time, National Security Advisor Henry Kissinger told newsmen that the "juridical basis" of United States relations with Bangladesh was "under active review." However, both Kissinger and Nixon continued to insist that they would have preferred an arrangement in which the people of East Bengal were given "complete autonomy" within a Pakistan federation, rather than complete independence from Pakistan, a choice that runs directly against the overwhelming nationalist sentiment of the East Bengalis.

Perhaps more important, political leaders in both India and Bangladesh are bothered by the propensity of the Nixon administration to deal with South Asia solely in terms of big power conflicts. While no one is certain about all of the implications of President

Nixon's new foreign policy initiatives, there is consensus among political leaders, both in India and Bangladesh that the Nixon administration will most likely continue its attempts to "restrain" the Soviet Union in South Asia while being generally supportive of China's interests in Pakistan. Under these circumstances neither India nor Bangladesh seems willing to move toward open confrontation with the Nixon administration, but leaders in both governments are preparing for the possibility that substantial new economic aid programs between America, India, and Bangladesh may not materialize for some time to come. Indian Prime Minister Indira Gandhi has recently placed an extremely heavy emphasis on self-reliance in future economic planning, and has reportedly instructed all of the Ministries in New Delhi "to plan on the basis that the country will have to do without United States economic aid for the foreseeable future." The Bangladesh government, which is not in as strong an economic position as India, has nevertheless indicated that any American aid that is forthcoming will have to be channeled through the United Nations or other international agencies, and Finance Minister Tajuddin Ahmed has launched a study within his own Ministry to "determine ways that the Bangladesh government can slice down our programmes of economic reconstruction and depend more heavily on our own resources."

Barring a sudden change in American policy, the failure of the Nixon administration to build relationships of confidence with Bangladesh is likely to hamper attempts by the World Bank and the United Nations to provide massive assistance, and this in turn could deprive the Bangladesh government of the large amounts of external assistance that are within the capabilities of America's citizenry. It is conceivable that some of the European nations, or possibly Japan, might pick up at least a portion of the slack felt by the absence of American aid programs, but if this is not the case one either looks to the Soviet Union or searches in vain. Paradoxically, America's efforts to "restrain" the Soviet Union in South Asia may have created extremely favorable conditions for future Soviet foreign policy interests.

SHEIKH MUJIB AND GOVERNMENTAL AUTHORITY

For the moment, at least, Bangladesh is fortunate in having one of the most popular elected governments in the world, united behind a single truly charismatic figure, Sheikh Mujibur Rahman. "Sheikh Mujib" was born in 1920 in the village of Tongipara in Faridpur district (just south of Dacca), a relatively poor rural area frequently visited by floods and storms, and dominated until 1947 by Hindu landlords. Mujib was the eldest son (he has two older sisters) of a landed Muslim *Serastadar* (civil court clerk), described by Mujib himself as being "just middle class, neither lower nor upper." At the age of seven he was moved to the small district town of Gopal-ganj, where he attended a private school, until he contracted an eye ailment at the age of 14. This forced him out of school for three years, but during this time he was tutored privately at home and was therefore able to gain entrance to the Christian mission school from which he was matriculated in 1942.

At the early age of 13 Mujib had his first encounter with the British police, while observing a political meeting that was considered illegal. Resentful of British high-handedness in dispersing the meeting, Mujib and some of his classmates chose to stone the local police station, as a result of which they received a lecture (but no judicial action) from the officer-in-charge. Five years later (in 1939) Mujib was sent to jail for seven days, because of his role in organizing a meeting for Muslim nationalist leaders A.K. Fazlul Haq and H.S. Suhrawardy during a visit to Gopalganj. In Mujib's own words, "My boyhood seemed to end on the day I went to jail."

After his matriculation in 1942, Mujib traveled to Calcutta to study at Islamia College, where he joined Suhrawardy's Muslim League, then championing the cause of Pakistan. In 1946 he was personally designated by Suhrawardy as principal organizer of Faridpur district, but was able to return to Calcutta in time to graduate from Islamia College just before the partition of 1947. After partition he was enrolled as a law student at Dacca University, from which he was soon expelled because of his participation in the Bengali language movement against the West Pakistan government. In 1948 he founded the East Pakistan Muslim Students League, and in 1949 was a cofounder of his present political party, the Awami League

The Awami League was one of a number of small political parties in East Pakistan that banded together in 1954 to rout the Muslim League in the East Pakistan provincial elections, largely on the basis of Bengali regional sentiment directed against West

Pakistan. As cofounder and General Secretary of the Awami League, Mujib was elected to the provincial legislature in 1954 and was twice named a Minister in the numerous provincial cabinets that tried to govern East Bengal after the 1954 elections. His longest tenure as Minister lasted for a period of seven months in 1956, when he headed the Ministry of Commerce and Industries. During this period he was still struggling to establish his own reputation as a political leader, while at the same time maneuvering his party through the seemingly interminable maze of Bengali factional politics.

After 1958, when Ayub Khan banned political party activity and instituted rule by the military, Sheikh Mujib spent most of his time either in covert political activity or in jail. His enormous popularity in East Bengal dates from 1966, when he formulated his "six-point program" for regional autonomy and was subsequently jailed in what has come to be known as the Agartala conspiracy case. Mujib's "six-point program" called for "regional autonomy," to be brought about by 1) a parliamentary federal government for Pakistan, elected by universal adult franchise; 2) a division of powers that would leave only defense and foreign affairs in the hands of the central government, with all other powers (including residual powers) vested in provincial units; 3) two separate but convertible currencies for the two wings of Pakistan; 4) powers of taxation and revenue collection only in the hands of the provincial units; 5) separate foreign exchange accounts for the two wings of Pakistan, with each wing establishing its own trade and commercial relations with foreign countries; and 6) the formation of a militia or paramilitary force for East Pakistan.

While Sheikh Mujib consistently contended that he "never believed in unconstitutional politics," and while his advocacy of the "six-points" was clearly within the legal bounds of the Pakistan constitution, he and 34 other members of his party were charged in the Agartala conspiracy case with an elaborate plot to bring about the dismemberment of Pakistan. According to the Ayub Khan government, Mujib's representatives met with Indian representatives on July 12, 1967, in the city of Agartala (in India), for the purpose of securing arms, ammunition, and funds for a massive conspiracy. In the Agartala case, the Pakistan government charged that Mujib and his men had attempted to enlist Bengali soldiers from the Pakistan armed forces, along with ex-service men and civilians, into commando style military units, which would eventually be supported with Indian arms and funds. Mujib's commandos, it was alleged, would try to "create general political disaffection by propaganda," and would eventually try to "seize power in East Pakistan by means of an armed revolt."

When massive rioting and violence broke out in East Bengal in early 1969 – in response to the demand for Sheikh Mujib's release, revocation of the Agartala conspiracy case, and adoption of the "six points"—the Ayub Khan government at first tried to rally support by calling a Round-Table Conference of all political parties, but when this failed Ayub himself decided to step down and the charges against Sheikh Mujib were dropped. On February 21, 1969, in a broadcast to the nation, Ayub Khan stated that he would not be a candidate for the next Presidential elections; within a month he was succeeded in office by General Yahya Khan.

The enormous popularity of Mujib and his "six-point program" was confirmed in the elections of December 1970, when the Awami League gained more than 80 per cent of the vote and 167 of 169 seats in East Pakistan. Perhaps because of his popularity, perhaps by sheer chance, Sheikh Mujib was merely arrested (rather than killed) when the Pakistan army brutally cracked down on the East Bengal population on March 25, 1971. Mujib himself has stated that the Pakistani soldiers who arrested him on the night of March 25 tried to force him to flee from his house, in which case they could have killed him for resisting arrest, but his refusal to leave the house made it necessary that they arrest and protect him. Mujib is also convinced that orders had been given by Yahya Khan to hang him just before the surrender of Pakistani troops in December 1971, while he was imprisoned in the Mianwali jail in West Pakistan. President Nixon has insisted that he (Nixon) received assurances from Yahya Khan that Sheikh Mujib would not be executed, but President Z. A. Bhutto (Yahya Khan's successor as President of Pakistan) has said that Yahya's last request to him was to "finish Sheikh Mujib". According to Mujib's own account, a grave was dug for him in his jail compound at Mianwali just before the surrender of Pakistan; but a prison warden with whom Mujib had established a close friendship chose to shelter Mujib instead of executing him. When Yahya Khan was replaced by Bhutto, four days after the surrender of Pakistan troops on December 16, the order for Mujib's execution was reported (again by Mujib himself) to have been rescinded. On January 8, 1972, Sheikh Mujib was released.

Mujib's present popularity in Bangladesh stems primarily from his daredevil ability to resist the Pakistanis and escape death, but it is also clear that he is an extremely skillful politician who is capable of inspiring people, either in small groups or in crowds. He lives in a relatively modest home in Dacca, shies away from formal ceremonies and protocol, and seems to have a boundless reserve of energy that he prefers to expend in political activity. He describes himself as "neither a rightist nor a leftist," but as someone who has "a passion for politics." He has consistently supported parliamentary democracy on the British model, and his adherence to socialism is reminiscent of the general fascination among South Asian intellectuals of his generation for the Labour party and Fabian socialists who were so supportive of the Indian Independence movement. Having entered politics to champion the movement for Pakistan, Mujib quickly found himself in opposition to those who conceived of Pakistan exclusively in terms of a religious state, although he chose not to stress his adherence to secularism so long as Pakistan ruled East Bengal. Perhaps the best indication of his general outlook on life is provided by a list of the authors and public figures that he most admires, among whom he lists Nazrul Islam (a Muslim Bengali poet), Rabindranath Tagore (a Hindu Bengali poet), Bernard Shaw, Harold Laski, John F. Kennedy, Bertrand Russell, and Mao Tse-tung.

In the present Bangladesh government Sheikh Mujib has chosen to surround himself with those people who have been closest to him during his political career, rather than seek a broader representation of Bangladesh political forces. Sheikh Mujib himself is Prime Minister, holding four Cabinet portfolios (Defense, Home, Information and Broadcasting, and Cabinet Affairs). All of the other 14 Ministers in the Cabinet are from the Awami League, and 12 of the 14 have been with the Awami League since the early 1950s. The youngest member of the Cabinet is Dr. Kamal Hossain (35), Minister of Law, Parliamentary Affairs, and Constitution-making, who has acted as Mujib's principal political advisor since 1966. The oldest member of the Cabinet—and the only Hindu—is Phani Mazumdar (70), Minister of Food and Civil Supplies. The average age of the Ministers is 51, precisely the same age as Sheikh Mujib himself. Of the 15 members of the Cabinet, nine are trained lawyers, two former business executives, one a teacher, one a trade union leader, and two (including Sheikh Mujib) professional politicians.

Despite the revolutionary elan that its principal leader has acquired, the new Bangladesh government is decidedly moderate, composed of professional people and businessmen, dedicated to secularism, democracy, and a vague socialism, and supported by a broad spectrum of the population. Unfortunately, most of the members of the Cabinet, like Sheikh Mujib himself, have little direct experience with governance, and within their Ministries they have not been able to draw on a very large pool of highly-experienced civil servants. The Pakistan government did make an attempt in the 1960s to recruit more and more Bengalis for administrative positions in East Pakistan, so that almost all of the secretaries in the East Pakistan secretariat, and most of the 61 district commissioners and their deputies were Bengalis when civil war erupted in March 1971. But the most senior all-Pakistan civil service cadre was always drawn from among West Pakistanis, and Bengalis who were recruited to the civil service in the 1960s were appointed much too late to gain a great deal of experience under a stable government. The result is an obvious lack of experienced senior administrative personnel in the new Bangladesh.

Some members of the Bangladesh Cabinet have argued that their lack of governmental and administrative experience could be an enormous advantage, particularly if they are able to maintain popular support among students and other influential political groups. This is an argument that is especially appealing to those who are interested in administrative reforms, or in other changes (such as reform of the educational system) that might be prevented or delayed in a highly bureaucratized political system. Four of the five Cabinet members that I talked to, for example, argued that they were going to try to resist the temptation to expand the size of their Ministries, and all of them agreed that the relatively small size of the Cabinet was an advantage for a government that is trying to do a great deal in a hurry. Three of them stressed the fact that Bangladesh has a low technology agricultural economy that has historically functioned without a large governmental infrastructure.

However, if only because of the massive reconstruction effort that is going to be required, the administrative skills of the Bangladesh government are going to be severely tested during the next few months. In this atmosphere there may be little time for administrative or educational reforms, and there are likely to be a number of problems associated with the attempt to maintain law and order. Moreover, it is clear that there will be significant opposition to the present government, and, as is usually the case in Bengal, the opposition is likely to be both radical and factionalized. These are all factors that will tax the capacities of the infant administrative and governmental network presently being established.

PROBLEMS OF LAW AND ORDER

The most serious law and order problems that Bangladesh is likely to experience in the next few months are those that result from the continued presence of a large number of Bihari Muslims (the term "Bihari Muslims" is widely and inaccurately used to describe those Muslims who came to East Pakistan from a variety of different non-Bengali areas, including Bihar, after the partition of 1947). As is characteristic of immigrant communities elsewhere, the Muslim Biharis have chosen to group themselves into rather tightly-knit communities in urban areas, and they have gained a reputation for their aggressiveness in business and commercial ventures. Many of them have in the past been rather fanatical supporters of the concept of Pakistan. While the majority of the Biharis are non-skilled laborers or very poor shopkeepers, the most well known among them are successful businessmen that experienced social and economic mobility under the Pakistan government.

It is difficult to accurately determine the size of the Bihari community in Bangladesh, but a reasonable estimate would place their numbers at 700,000 to 800,000. The largest groupings are found in the cities of Saidpur, Dinajpur, Ishurdi, Khulna, Narayanganj, Chittagong, and Dacca, with the largest single concentration being the adjoining Dacca suburbs of Mirpur (250,000) and Mohammadpur (50,000). Before the civil war of last year the Bihari Muslims lived in these neighborhoods in relative isolation from the Bengali population, with their own schools, hospitals, and other community service organizations. After the army crackdown, however, a number of them moved out of their neighborhoods to assist the Pakistan army with its attempted repression of the Bengali population, and, as a result, the entire Bihari community has now acquired the stigma of criminal collaboration with Pakistan atrocities.

Since the surrender of Pakistani troops to the Indian army in December 1971, there have been a number of clashes involving communal conflict between the Biharis and the local Bengali population, and many of these have resulted in violence. The Bangladesh government has thus far prevented large-scale reprisals by using the Indian army to cordon off Bihari neighborhoods, and in some instances has moved the Biharis into prisons or camps in order to give them better protection. Allegations have occasionally been made that the Biharis were starving because the local population was preventing food from being sent into Bihari areas, but these charges have been denied by the international Red Cross and other agencies that have been supplying relief assistance to the Biharis. During my recent stay in Bangladesh I was impressed with the determined effort being made to afford protection to the Bihari community.

While temporarily under control, the "Bihari problem" in Bangladesh will become much more severe once the Indian army withdraws from Bangladesh (total withdrawal was scheduled for completion by March 25, 1972). Sheikh Mujib has promised that everyone who is guilty of collaboration with Pakistan will be brought to trial and punished, but he has also cautioned people "against the urge to take justice into your own hands." In an attempt to defuse the Bihari issue he has sought to use his infant army and police in a thorough cordon and search operation in Bihari neighborhoods, designed to disarm Bihari militants, and he is also exploring the possibility of exchanging the Bihari community in Bangladesh for those Bengalis who are still in Pakistan. The danger is that disarmament of both the Bihari and Bengali populations is likely to be less than complete, and animosity between Biharis and Bengalis is such that even Sheikh Mujib's massive personal popularity may be insufficient to prevent a blood bath. Since it is highly unlikely that Pakistan would be willing to absorb the Bihari Muslim community (Pakistan would prefer an exchange of captured Pakistan soldiers for the Bengalis presently in Pakistan), it would appear that the Bihari problem is likely to be an irritant for the Bangladesh administration for some years to come.

THE POTENTIAL FOR OPPOSITION

If the organizational effectiveness of the Bangladesh government is problematic, the same must be said for the political party apparatus on which the government is based.   To be sure, Mujib's Awami League did secure an overwhelming victory in the December 1970 elections, but that electoral victory was not the result of a grassroots organization so much as it was a response to Mujib's personal popularity, the acceptance of his "six-points," and an upsurge of Bangladesh nationalism against the West Pakistan military regime. Moreover, during the period of civil war the organizational activities of the Awami League were preempted by various *mukti bahini* guerrilla forces—while most of the Awami League leaders fled to Calcutta, Europe, or America—with the result that the present Awami League organization must now reach some sort of political accommodation with a variety of guerrillas with different factional interests and heightened expectations.

Organizational accommodation of the guerrillas by the Awami League has become even more difficult as a result of Mujib's decision to form a government composed exclusively of his old and trusted colleagues.   This action is consistent with Mujib's previous policy, dating from the early 1950s, that Awami League membership be restricted to manageable numbers, but under the new circumstances his refusal to bring into his government and party any of the new heroes of the liberation struggle has created some tension and misunderstanding. Mujib has invited the guerrilla fighters to join the new Bangladesh army and the police force and many of them have enthusiastically accepted his invitation to do so, but among those who are politically inclined the invitation to join military or police units (which are intended to be subordinate to the civilian government and administration) has little appeal.

To complicate matters, some of the liberation heroes have now gained a local following that could in the long run be a potential challenge to Mujib and his government.   The most outstanding example of this is 26-year-old Abdul Qadr Siddiqui (popularly known as the "Tiger of Tangail"), who has established himself as somewhat of a local warlord in Tangail district, just north of Dacca. Prior to the civil war, Siddiqui was a marine commando in the Pakistan army, but he quickly defected to the *mukti bahini* after the army crackdown on East Bengal in March 1971. Using the skills he had developed as a result of his training, Siddiqui captured two Pakistan barges loaded with weapons and ammunition (he reportedly set off a charge underneath the boats that was "loud enough to scare the hell out of the Paks, but not strong enough to do any damage," causing the Pakistanis to flee without their cargo). Using his captured weapons as an inducement, Siddiqui then invited every family in Tangail to provide one adult recruit for his liberation army, which soon grew to over 50,000 men. During the civil war these men obtained training (and additional arms) from India, and they were tested in battle during their innumerable forays against the Pakistan army.

As I traveled through Tangail about a month after the surrender of Pakistani troops, it was evident that Siddiqui was the darling of the local populace, and that there was good reason for the almost universal admiration and respect that he had acquired. In contrast to many other parts of Bangladesh, Tangail had been secured and held by the liberation forces for a considerable portion of the nine-month civil war, with the result that fields and crops had been planted, there was plenty of food in the market, and reconstruction problems after the surrender were minimal. Siddiqui himself claimed in February that he still had 12,000 loyal "crack guerrilla fighters," another 17,000 men that "were in need of training," and a "future force" (*babhashut bahini*) of more than 70,000 boys between the ages of eight and 16. Siddiqui's "office" in the city of Tangail was obviously as crowded as any government or party office anywhere in Bangladesh. Young men with guerrilla caps and beards were much in evidence throughout Tangail district, as were small units of the "future force," armed with guns carved from bamboo, marching across the fields, crawling under barbed wire fences, and otherwise reliving the heroic events of the past nine or ten months.

For the present at least, Siddiqui (and others like him) have sworn their allegiance to Sheikh Mujibur Rahman, and have verbally agreed to surrender their arms to the national militia. However, at a ceremonial "laying down of arms" in late January, when Mujib himself traveled to Tangail to receive the weapons and ammunition that Siddiqui had collected, only 3,000–5,000 arms were surrendered and Siddiqui was ominously silent about Mujib's invitation to join the Bangladesh army or the police force, This means that Siddiqui, despite his oaths of allegiance to Sheikh Mujib, will most likely retain an independent political and military position, without organizational attachments to the Awami League, the Bangladesh government or the military. Should he choose to use his considerable influence in Tangail at some point in the future, he will certainly be something of a force to be reckoned with

Many of the small leftist parties that dot the political landscape in Bengal are confident that local warlords like Siddiqui will eventually be allies of the left in opposition to the government, but, in addition, many of the leftists are reportedly accumulating their own weapons and ammunition for future "struggles." Thus far the three major leftist parties—the National Awami Party (NAP) of Maulana Bhashani, the Bangladesh National Awami Party (BNAP) of Professor Muzaffar Ahmed, and the Communist Party of Bangladesh (CPB)—have all pledged their support to Sheikh Mujib and the government, arguing that the enormous tasks of reconstruction require at least temporary political unity and cooperation. However, each of the three leftist parties is also attempting to stake out new tactical and strategic positions independent of the government and the Awami League, in response to both international and domestic political changes.

While the leftists would appear to be quite weak in comparison to the Awami League, they have nevertheless interpreted the events of the last year as being favorable to their growth and development. They do not expect to suffer the rigorous suppression that they had become accustomed to under Pakistan's military regime. They should have an easier time resolving the "contradictions" between "nationalist" and "class struggles" now that Independence has been achieved. Almost all of them did participate in the liberation movement, which means that they have established their nationalist bona fides. And finally, the factionalism that has accompanied Sino-Soviet ideological conflict should now be minimized, since a pro-Peking position has been so thoroughly discredited in Bangladesh by the events of the past year.

Some of the issues that the leftists will try to exploit in the future have already surfaced, while others will depend on the actions of the Awami League government. Muzaffar Ahmed, President of BNAP, has indicated that his party will oppose United States aid to Bangladesh "under any circumstances," and will work for a close alliance between the Soviet Union and Bangladesh. Despite Maulana Bhashani's pledge of complete cooperation with the Mujib government, some of Bhashani's supporters have leveled charges of corruption at the Cabinet (in the words of one NAP correspondent, writing in a Bengali newspaper, "jobs are being handed down like precious little giveaways with somewhat misplaced magnanimity"). NAP supporters are also particularly distressed that Mujib has failed to find a place in his government for *mukti bahini* heroes, and Bhashani himself has promised NAP student leaders that he would personally lead a massive movement against the government "if students continue to be frustrated in their search for jobs." The CPB has announced that its organizational focus in the future will be landless and poor peasants, who are increasingly being disadvantaged by the new agricultural technology, and almost all of the leftists have expressed their concern that the present Bangladesh government may become too closely linked with the "bourgeois" Indian government and Indian business interests.

CONCLUSIONS

The attention that has been focused on political realignments in Bangladesh and South Asia during the past year has tended to obscure the fact that an unprecedented human condition has made possible an unparalleled series of human tragedies. The cyclones that ravaged East Bengal in the autumn of 1970 were important politically when they exacerbated tensions between East Bengal and West Pakistan, but they took the lives of more than 500,000 people primarily because population pressure had forced these people to live in the lower Bengal delta, in areas that were considered unfit for human habitation until this century. The ten million refugees traveling to India in 1971 undoubtedly were moved by a combination of terror and scarcity that was brought about by political repression, but perhaps the real significance of a refugee movement of this size lies in the fact that there are so many peasants in East Bengal that can be so quickly uprooted from their overpopulated villages. The one million estimated deaths that can be traced to the army crackdown and the war in 1971 were for the most part politically-inspired, but murder on such a grand scale has been known to take place only under conditions of dense overcrowding and technological underdevelopment (the only comparable phenomenon is the Indonesian anti-Communist massacre of 1966).

If politics has been a necessary but not a sufficient cause of human tragedy in East Bengal these past few years, then we would delude ourselves if we searched solely for political solutions to the problem of restoring human dignity in the future Bangladesh. No matter how great Sheikh Mujib's commitment to parliamentary democracy, he will have a difficult time preserving it if the bulk of his people continue to lack shelter, food, and protection from annual floods and storms. Despite Maulana Bhashani's determined effort to promote cooperation between the opposition and the government, Bhashani's supporters will desert him for one of the radical millenarian movements that are so characteristic of Bengal if the Bangladesh economy continues to decline precipitously relative to other parts of the world. In the event of further human tragedy within the borders of Bangladesh, it is not unlikely that large-scale refugee movements could again be set in motion (indeed, less restricted travel between Bangladesh and India might encourage migration). In short, new political forms, realignments, and structures in Bangladesh will eventually produce greater stability and a better life for the people only if they are accompanied by a series of developments that make it possible for so many people to live in such a small geographic area with a modicum of satisfaction.

Viewed in this way, the requirements of Bangladesh are technological rather than political. Unprecedented engineering projects are needed to construct dams and embankments sophisticated enough to control the floodwaters from the Himalayas that ravage an average of 60 per cent of the cultivable land area of Bangladesh each year. Development of a new "floating rice," which would produce high yields even under flood conditions that destroy existing rice strains, might produce enough food to feed a population that is growing at the rate of three per cent compounded annually. Even then, massive irrigation systems, and a network of roads, railways and reliable water routes will be needed to solve the problems of distribution that have plagued Bengal in the past. Unfortunately, the people of Bangladesh presently lack the technology that would enable them to gain greater control of their future destiny, and their political leaders are only fighting against time if they fail to secure new technological inputs from outside their borders.

Mrs. Gandhi and the Indian government, as well as the leadership of Bangladesh, are well aware of all of this. But India also lacks technology and resources in sufficient quantities to cope with the enormous requirements of East Bengal all by itself. It is in this sense that Bangladesh presents a challenge to the human values of those of us who live in nations that are in a position to provide resources and technical assistance.

TWO

AID-DEPENDENCE AND THE MANY FUTURES OF BANGLADESH (1972)

In September and October—when the monsoons are finished, the rice crop is up and growing, and the innumerable wide and powerful rivers of Bangladesh are deliciously full but not overflowing—this country has some of the most beautiful natural scenery imaginable anywhere. You look at the paddy that grows right down to the very edge of the rivers, and at the innumerable trees filled with lush ripening fruit, and wonder how Bangladesh could possibly have a larger food deficit than any other nation. When you listen to a Tagore song or a love poem by Nazrul Islam, sung by beautiful young Bengali girls in a little village hut at the edge of a tropical forest, you can easily disbelieve the extent of human misery that undoubtedly exists in Bangladesh. Stand at the top of one of the many hills just outside Chittagong and look down toward Burma at one of the widest, largest, and most magnificent beaches in the world, stretching on for miles past gorgeous ocean scenery, and try to figure out why fishermen who live in this idyllic natural setting have become more and more willing to band together with their fellow countrymen in political movements that have virtually ruined the economy of Bangladesh.

People in Bangladesh will tell you that their ancestors once lived in Sonar Bangla, a beautiful Bengal where there was almost always a food surplus, where human misery was no greater than anywhere else and much less than in most places, and where cultural and artistic genius seemed to sprout as readily as a seed that falls on fertile deltaic soil. The Bengalis have never tried to conquer anyone else, they have used their ocean ports for trade and commerce and for export of their cultural genius, and they have in the past been satisfied—some would say even arrogant—in the knowledge that they live in a beautiful part of the world. They almost universally explain their present condition by telling you about British colonial exploitation, Pakistani military domination, and a variety of other "conspiracies against Bengal," led by a whole host of foreigners who would like to exploit their land, their rivers, and their people.

Whatever else they did in Bangladesh, there is no doubt that the British and the Pakistanis failed to develop the economy as fast as the rate of population growth. During the past two hundred years, and particularly in this century, death rates have come down much faster than birthrates, a common modern phenomenon that has had more severe consequences in Bengal than anywhere else. Bangladesh is now so poor, so crowded, and so incapable of affording its citizens the possibility of even minimal human dignity that intelligent men the world over seriously question the likelihood of any widely accepted societal values being realized in Bangladesh. There are certainly other poor nations in the world, but the larger among them (India or Indonesia, for example) have far more land and natural resources relative to population than does Bangladesh while the smaller poor nations are confronted with more manageable political and economic problems if only because of their size. With regard to any single matter having to do with poverty, crowding, and human dignity, Bangladesh almost always represents the extreme point on a continuum; it is the combination of a long series of such extremes that leads one to describe the difference between Bangladesh and other poor nations as a difference in kind rather than degree.

No one knows how many people there are in Bangladesh. The last census that was attempted (in 1961, when Bangladesh was the Eastern Province of Pakistan) registered a total population of 50.8 million but everyone concerned now agrees that this figure erred significantly on the low side. Most people in Bangladesh argue that the Ayub Khan government willfully understated the Bengali population in 1961 in an attempt to balance the two wings of the erstwhile Pakistan for purposes of electoral representation and economic distribution. Demographers and politicians in West Pakistan, on the other hand, claimed that they simply used faulty census techniques in the East, in response to their own ignorance of an alien culture and the massive problems associated with census-taking in a crowded deltaic region. Whatever the reason for the underestimate, it was consistently pointed out by international agencies in the 1960s that the population of East Bengal was greater than was indicated in the 1961 census, and every available sample survey in East Bengal since 1961 has confirmed this judgment. By 1970 both the World Bank and the Pakistan government were working with figures that assumed an East Bengal population of 71–73 million (living on a piece of land that is about half the size of Great Britain and Northern Ireland). The present Bangladesh government has proclaimed on one of its first postage stamps that it represents a nation of 75 million people in 1972.

During the past few years Bangladesh has witnessed a series of unprecedented tragedies that have shocked the world, including a massive popular revolt against the Ayub Khan regime in 1969, major cyclones and floods in 1970, a series of atrocities inspired by political and military considerations in 1971, and severe dislocations associated with the reconstruction effort following the achievement of independence. While no official figures are available, the ruling party of Bangladesh (the Awami League) claims on the basis of its own surveys that more than a million people lost their lives in the 1970 cyclones, and that more than 3 million died as a result of the Pakistan army crackdown in 1971. Moreover, many opposition leaders claim that the death rate in Bangladesh at present is rising fairly rapidly, as a result of ineffective relief efforts on the part of the present government. If this were the case one might look for a reduction of the population of Bangladesh, or at least a levelling off of population growth rates in the future. However, all available evidence contradicts the casualty claims of the Awami League, and most observers (including both those who are sympathetic and those in opposition to the Awami League) admit privately that figures on deaths are almost always exaggerated by politicians in their attempts to discredit Pakistan, to attract the support of aid donors, and to embarrass the present government.

Without minimizing the extent of the human tragedies that have befallen East Bengal during the past few years, it is most likely that the tragedies have not significantly affected the size of the population or its growth rate. National figures are obviously unavailable but one can gain some idea of what has happened by looking at small geographical areas where fairly reliable population estimates are available. One such area is the island of Hatia, a sandy piece of land jutting out of the Bay of Bengal, which was considered uninhabitable in the earlier part of this century because of the frequency of cyclones and floods. With increased pressure on land elsewhere, Bengalis began to settle Hatia in the 1930s, and settlement has taken place in such numbers since that there are now an estimated 270,000 people on the island. The Japanese Red Cross team that has been distributing relief on the island since 1970 has attempted to maintain accurate records for its own purposes, and according to its estimates a little more than 2,000 people from the island lost their lives during the cyclones. However, since the cyclone casualties were primarily from the older age groups—from among those who were too old and infirm to be moved from the island during and before the cyclones—neither the birthrate nor the size of the population among men and women of present and future reproductive ages was altered downward. Indeed, there is some evidence to indicate that the birthrate on Hatia actually spurted upward for a short period nine to twelve months after the 1970 cyclones.

In addition, it is most likely that the rapid response of international relief and charitable agencies to the cyclones of 1970 prevented any sharp rise in the death rate during the period of recovery. Certainly this is the argument of the international organizations (USAID estimates that Bangladesh lost a little more than one month of population growth as a result of the cyclones) and the relevant ministries in the present Bangladesh government confirm this opinion on the basis of their information. The overall impression, therefore, is one of relatively stable birth and death rates, with short jumps in each at particular moments, but with an increasingly youthful population that continues to grow at a crude overall rate (subtracting deaths from births) of more than 3 per cent per year. This demographic picture is duplicated elsewhere and is consistent with those few reliable studies that have been done in a variety of other local regions in Bangladesh.

In a somewhat similar manner, there is every reason to doubt the Awami League (AL) figures of three million deaths during the 1971 army crackdown, since random checks at the local level invariably show that actual figures have been inflated by anywhere from three to ten times by party personnel. Again, while no detailed reliable studies are available (several are under way), one gets the impression from talking to families that most of the deaths in 1971 were from among the older generations who could not readily move from one geographical area to another to escape army terror or hostilities, even though there is no reason to doubt that a number of brutal atrocities were committed against people from the younger generations as well. There is also clear evidence that the population of almost ten million people who came to India as refugees in 1971 had both lower death rates and higher birthrates during their stay in India than they had experienced prior to 1971 in East Bengal. Approximately 6.7 million refugees stayed in camps, where complete medical facilities were provided, and only a little more than 7,000 of these 6.7 million died in the camps. This means that the death rate in the camps was as low as one per thousand (as compared with the approximately 20 per thousand figure that is usually given for ordinary times in East Bengal). During my conversations with medical personnel in the refugee camps in early 1972 every single doctor and nurse told me that birthrates were also considerably higher than usual in the camps, owing largely to the nature of camp life (no one in the camps was allowed to be employed, people lived in closer proximity to one another than usual, and contraceptives were not distributed in the camps because it was thought that this would "offend sensitivities").

Since the liberation of Bangladesh the country has been invaded by one of the largest contingents of international relief personnel that any nation has ever witnessed, and this has also prevented a rise in the death rate. The United States alone has already committed $287 million of reconstruction and relief aid, and USAID administrators in Dacca are projecting an annual American commitment of $190 million ($90 million in food and $100 million in grants) for at least the next two fiscal years. More than 50 other relief agencies (some from other nations, some international, and some private) account for a pool of supplies and funds that totals another $560 million at present. While many of these organizations expect the size of their contributions to diminish over time, most of them also plan to be in Bangladesh for a number of years in the future (the United Nations Relief Organization in Dacca, or UNROD, hopes to be out of Bangladesh within a year but it also expects to be replaced by the United Nations Development Program). In sharp contrast to the 1960s, therefore, one finds the international airport at Dacca constantly packed with a cosmopolitan crowd of Swedes and Swiss, Canadians and Czechs, and well-intentioned men and women relief workers from almost every other developed nation one can imagine.

The two luxury hotels in downtown Dacca are almost always filled with relief workers (a few years ago they had a less than 20 per cent occupancy rate), with the result that the relief agencies have now rented almost every space available in the two large residential colonies of Dacca that have Western-style facilities, for their homes, hostels, and offices. The Americans are now discussing the possibility of constructing their own new buildings and a new community swimming pool, while enlarging the American International School in Dacca. The port of Chittagong has a 114,000-ton American ship anchored 47 miles outside harbor, to serve as a storage area for foodgrains from ships of other nations until they can be transferred into jeeps, planes, helicopters, mini-bulkers, and country boats for shipment into the interior. Meanwhile, 11 Russian warships are busy clearing Chittagong harbor of mines and wreckage while a variety of other Soviet personnel are engaged at the port in other occupations intended to make Chittagong fully operational. The six small airports in Bangladesh witness the frequent comings and goings of a variety of helicopters, skyvans, C-130s and small cargo planes, most of them operated by UNROD or the various chapters of the Red Cross. One can hardly drive through the Bangladesh countryside these days without passing the innumerable jeeps, trucks, minibuses, and small imported cars that provide the principal form of transportation for the relief workers and their supplies.

One result of this massive relief effort is that food and supplies are getting through to virtually every part of the new nation, even though there are continual bottlenecks, tensions and anxieties. Competition and lack of coordination between relief agencies, conflicts between the relief agencies and the government, disconnected and faulty scheduling of relief supplies to particular regions are all part of the daily scene for most agency administrators in Dacca, but one has to conclude, nevertheless, that the food, the medicines, and the material for rebuilding Bangladesh are at least temporarily keeping people alive. Almost all of the charges and countercharges one hears—concerning shortages in some areas, misappropriation and corruption in other areas, and administrative bungling throughout—can be traced to three prominent factors: (1) a wide variety of political and administrative factions attempting to discredit or embarrass others in order to secure more for what they conceive to be their own interests; (2) a broad cultural gap between donors and recipients, which frequently leads to serious misunderstandings on both sides as to the purpose of the relief that is being provided; and (3) the sheer massiveness of this relief endeavor.

STRAINS IN THE RELIEF EFFORT

Some idea of the kinds of problems encountered in providing relief to the people of Bangladesh can be gained by looking at foodgrain production in Bangladesh, current food relief measures, and plans for feeding the population in the future. According to World Bank figures, foodgrains imports into Bangladesh averaged about one million tons a year during the five-year period 1965-1969, increasing to 1.7 million tons in 1969-70 and 1970-71. During 1971-72 pressure on foodgrains was relieved somewhat by the exodus of 10 million refugees to India, where they were fed in the relief camps, but this year the Bangladesh government has calculated that it will need more than three million tons of foodgrains from foreign countries. In short, East Bengal would have been in serious difficulty on the foodgrains front even without the great tragedies of the last few years, but as a result of those tragedies its situation is now verging on the calamitous. Next fiscal year Bangladesh expects to have a shortfall of two million tons of foodgrains.

Recognizing the severity of the problems facing Bangladesh, international relief agencies have by now committed approximately 2.7 million tons of foodgrains for the current year, with the promise of more to come in the future. From the point of view of the international agencies this has been a herculean effort, exceeding any previous relief enterprise anywhere in the world. And yet, both the Bangladesh government and the opposition have kept up a constant barrage of criticism of the relief effort, and Bangladesh society in general has assumed an attitude toward relief that strikes most Westerners there as being unproductively uncooperative.

In any relief program of this size, and particularly one involving people from two such diverse cultural backgrounds, one would expect some conflicts and tensions. Since major complaints are so salient and so frequent on both sides, however, one is led to conclude that the vast majority of people involved are seriously unhappy with the way in which the relief effort is being conducted. Bengalis believe, for example, that the quality of foodgrains being imported is inferior—the rice does not taste as good and does not have the same texture as that to which they are accustomed, most of the foodgrains have come in the form of wheat (which has never been prominent in the Bengali diet), and some of the foodgrains have reached the people in an adulterated or rotting condition. There is a widely-held assumption—stated almost daily in the Bengali papers and in the speeches of opposition politicians and echoed by almost every single villager one talks with—that the foreigners are either sending their waste products or trying to bolster their own food processing industries by sending poor quality wheat or rice, and such unfamiliar things as high protein foods and nutritional biscuits, to Bangladesh.

Particularly among students and urban residents one frequently hears the charge that the foreigners have come to Bangladesh in such numbers only because they are interested in living well—they stay in the big hotels and live in the better residential areas, or if they live elsewhere they regularly frequent those areas. The foreigners import liquor, European cigarettes, have plush carpets, air-conditioning, servants, swimming pools, cars, jeeps, and other symbols of luxury; they eat the best rice, the finest fish, only quality fruits and vegetables, and in general are thought to live better in Bangladesh than they would live in their own countries. Foreign aircraft being used in Bangladesh have received especially harsh criticism because they are manned exclusively by foreign crews and usually carry only foreign personnel. A number of articles in Bangali newspapers—some in progovernment dailies—have argued that foreign relief planes are commonly used to carry foreigners unconnected with relief operations, to provide pleasure trips and weekends on the beach for foreign wives and girl friends, or to smuggle into Bangladesh supplies of liquor, cigarettes, chocolates, perfumes, and similar items that would otherwise be subject to heavy customs duty.

One cannot talk to many people in Bangladesh without hearing recurring stories about alleged collusion between foreigners, big businessmen, and the upper classes of Bengali society. According to these reports the Indians are smuggling relief supplies across the border to be sold for profits; the Americans and Russians are cooperating with hoarders, smugglers, and black marketeers, as well as with government and party leaders, in order to establish *dalals* (agents) in the country; the United Nations is being "duped" by the government and interested groups that want to use the relief effort for personal and party gains; and all foreigners, it is commonly thought, exchange their currency on the black market. Administrators in the relief agencies admit that some of the relief supplies have found their way into the hands of hoarders and smugglers, although they argue that much of this was largely the result of a Bangladesh government decision to distribute relief primarily through committees staffed by Awami League party personnel. Government leaders also admit that some relief materials have gone to smugglers and hoarders, but they see this as inevitable, granted the higher price structure in India as compared with Bangladesh and the massive size of the emergency relief effort. With the public censure of 19 Awami League Members of the National Assembly in mid-September (all 19 members were dropped from the party) the Bangladesh government now feels that it may have control of the situation, and that it will be able to check illicit practices in the future.

From the government's perspective, the major problems associated with the relief effort have stemmed from the unresponsiveness of foreign agencies to what the government considers its real needs. Bangladesh officials have been especially critical of a six-month charter of the *S.S. Manhatten* to serve as a "floating silo" for storage of foodgrains, as a result of which a private American firm received $4,075,000. An expenditure of $3.5 million (which might be reduced downward after adjustments) for airborne relief, and other expenditures on transportation totaling $28 million, have also been considered wasteful. The Bangladesh government would have preferred that foreign agencies direct more of their efforts toward rebuilding damaged transport links, constructing new ones, and buying more jeeps, trucks, cars, and river transport that would remain permanently in Bangladesh. Every government official that I talked to agreed that Bangladesh would like to have relief aid continue, but with far fewer foreign personnel and with decision-making about relief needs determined almost exclusively by the government.

Both government leaders and Awami League politicians have been irritated by what they see as the foreign relief worker's inflated notion of his importance. The relief workers are said to be constantly hounding top government officials for visas, permits, adjustments on import duty, income tax clearance, and other matters that are ordinarily dealt with at lower levels. Some foreign relief workers have been accused of attempts to take over relief committees, or to engage in factionalism within the committees, and some problems have been encountered because a few foreign relief workers were reportedly on drugs. Most government officials resent the way in which young foreigners—many of them fresh out of university—have occupied better housing than most government personnel can obtain.

The relief situation has been further complicated by the factionalism that has taken place within the Awami League government, and by the radical proclivities of the opposition in Bangladesh. Most of the public charges against the relief agencies have come from radical political leaders attempting to embarrass the government, and a number of attempts have been made to involve foreign personnel in incidents that might gain wide publicity for the opposition. As a result of these kinds of maneuvers most foreign relief workers out in the countryside have been subjected to some harassment, three foreigners have been murdered, and at least 19 foreign relief workers have been injured or molested in confrontations with Bengali militants. Those government leaders who have condemned such acts have chosen to do so privately, since they fear being identified with "foreign interests." One therefore finds no public statements in praise of the relief effort (or even in condemnation of attacks on foreign relief personnel), and several factional leaders within the Awami League have continually denigrated the role of relief workers in their public utterances. At a government-sponsored "protest day" meeting on September 10—held to protest the Chinese veto of Bangladesh membership in the United Nations—more than 200,000 people in Dacca heard Finance Minister Tajuddin Ahmad discuss what he called "the dirty game" and the "nefarious activities" of the United States in Bangladesh, while acting Prime Minister Syed Nazrul Islam (in the absence of Sheikh Mujibur Rahman, who was in Europe recuperating from surgery and fatigue) told the assembled multitude that "we shall not allow any outside interference in our international affairs, be it from Indian, Russian, American, or any other agents."

Perhaps the speeches and behavior of the governmental leaders of Bangladesh are understandable, since they must necessarily act as go-betweens for both their own impoverished people and their principal sources of international funds, food, and supplies. On the one hand, they must present themselves to "the people" as leaders who can secure necessary relief without being overly servile or dependent on the developed nations, and particularly on those nations that have in the past failed to support Bengali causes. In their interaction with relief agencies and foreign governments, on the other hand, they must try to bargain for more relief and development aid while channelling the existing aid in ways that are politically beneficial to their own domestic interests. The easiest way to reconcile these two conflicting imperatives is to take shelter in extreme nationalist rhetoric, since nationalism has proven itself as both a rallying cry for the masses and a source of leverage that can be used by Asian nations for a variety of purposes when they are dealing with the developed Western world.

The relief agencies from the West have an entirely different set of problems. As most of them conceive of their task, they are not in Bangladesh to prop up a particular government or set of interests, even though they cannot help but favor some and deprive others. Their first concern must be their own constituents and patrons back home, who are likely to cut off funds if there is a major scandal or a shocking failure. The men who lead these agencies fear most the possibility that things may go sour, so they tend to be close-mouthed and blandly optimistic while refusing to talk publicly about particulars. UNROD, the largest of the relief agencies in Bangladesh, has so consciously adopted this style that it now allows only its public relations officers to speak to newsmen, whether they be foreign or indigenous.

Relief workers inside the various agencies (who cannot help but talk to newsmen, since they move so frequently in the same circles) overwhelmingly feel that they have knocked themselves out for Bangladesh. At a time when both rice and wheat are relatively scarce in the world (because of a series of poor harvests almost everywhere), they have been able to talk a variety of nations into supplying an unprecedented gift of foodgrains to Bangladesh. This has been done at the cost of considerable time and energy on their part, most of whom are not directly connected with the foreign policy establishments in their host countries but who are nevertheless linked in the minds of the Bengalis with the foreign policy "designs and interests" of the Western world.

Workers in the relief agencies are also frustrated by the conflicts between Western values and those of the people of Bangladesh. A group of 22 Irish medical workers, for example, said they were constantly losing their tempers with the Bengali authorities in the hospitals and clinics because the Bengalis would consistently refuse admission (even when there were empty beds) to members of the Bihari minority community and lower class landless labourers. UNICEF workers complain bitterly that government officials will deny them available transport for their high protein foods and nutritional biscuits for weeks, in the expectation that a shipment of rice might be coming from somewhere. A number of misunderstandings have resulted from the combined Bengali unwillingness to engage in manual labor and the Westerners disdain for such a custom (for example, a truckload of rice will arrive at a needy village and the Bengalis will expect the Europeans to arrange for the unloading of the shipment, while children are scampering all over the bags of rice, cutting them open and stuffing rice grains into their pockets and knapsacks). The seeming disorganization and passivity of Bengal's social life—the crowds of people everywhere, the constant and frequently bothersome close family ties, the relaxed style of living—these smack of inefficiency, nepotism, and laziness to many people reared with Western values, even though they may have been cautioned in orientation sessions not to think this way.

Most of the foreign relief workers in Bangladesh will tell you that they are "fed up" with charges that they are engaging in corruption and high living. Among them Bangladesh is often described as "the end of the earth," and because most of them are young and (by Western standards) poorly paid volunteers from upper middle-class American and European families, they usually consider their presence in Bangladesh somewhat of a personal sacrifice. They generally work long and frustrating hours, the men miss the female companionship that is lacking in a fairly rigid Muslim society, and the few women feel (in the words of a German girl) that they are being "visually raped a thousand times a day." Most of them do not resent the loneliness of their jobs or the fact that so many impoverished people are constantly staring at them as much as they resent the charge that their motives are misplaced. In their eyes, they are the ones who try to prevent relief supplies going to black marketeers, hoarders, and smugglers, and the fact that this continues despite their best efforts is only proof that "the society is shot through with corruption," that "every

crooked man has a relative in the ministries," and that they themselves either have to frequently turn their supplies over to people
whose motives they question or else risk censure from someone
who is influential enough to kick up a fuss back in their Western-
based headquarters.

Among the leaders of the relief agencies, not one that I talked
to thought that the relief effort was going as well as they had
expected, granted the massive commitment involved. Comparisons
by those who were involved in relief for Biafra and Bihar, for
example, indicated uniformly that those operations were much more
manageable and satisfactory than the current Bangladesh effort,
even considering differences in scale.   Many of the leaders of the
relief agencies are now trying to plan ahead for the day when they
can withdraw from Bangladesh, and some well-placed people have
argued that all agencies should get out as soon as possible, even
by the end of this year.   It is all too apparent, however, that
significant withdrawal would certainly result in a rapid escalation
of the death rate—by starvation, by disease, and most likely by
slaughter.   In the words of one high-ranking relief coordinator,
"We are going to have to remain here for some time, simply
because we refuse to pull out and allow people to die—even though
there is little we can do but keep people barely alive."

AID-DEPENDENCE

It would be difficult to overstate the extent to which Bangladesh
will be dependent on external resources, both for the relief and
rehabilitation effort in the short run and for long-range development programs.   The only known natural resources that Bangladesh has in abundance are its fertile deltaic land, its magnificent but
uncontrolled rivers, and some untapped reserves of natural gas.
It has no known quantities of minerals, fossil fuels, petroleum, or
any of the other numerous resources needed to pursue a policy of
industrialization.   The Planning Commission is assuming that raw
jute and jute textiles will account for almost 90 per cent of exports
for the next few years (earning about $400 million per year), and
there is little hope of developing anything else for export in significant volume except in the very long run.   In the absence of
external assistance the foreign exchange that Bangladesh earns from
jute would be used up in the purchase of crude and industrial

petroleum (which no nation will give to Bangladesh as external assistance in any case), for machinery and other imported facilities to keep the jute mills running, in transportation networks that could move the jute to port, and for consular and trade legations abroad. This means that every other industry in Bangladesh (and perhaps even jute), will be aid-dependent, as will be any significant inputs for a "green revolution" that might narrow the food deficit.

On the domestic side, the current national budget projects a total estimated revenue of $391 million, of which $171 million (44 per cent) comes from customs duties on goods and materials imported primarily under external assistance programs. Another $124 million (31 per cent of total revenue) comes from excise and corporation taxes and receipts from nationalized industries, or in other words from industries that are in very large measure sustained by external assistance. Bangladesh realizes only $5 million (1.2 per cent of total domestic revenue) in annual land taxes, and only $11 million (2.5 per cent of total revenue) from its income tax, the rest of the revenue budget being made up by a sales tax, sale of stamps, and a series of other small miscellaneous items. In short, without external assistance even the domestic revenue of the Bangladesh government would have to be cut to less than half the present level, despite the fact that it now allows for only a little more than $5 per capita per year ($391 million is divided among 75 million people). Indeed, without an external assistance program much of the huge administrative staff that makes up the government of Bangladesh (now estimated at 300,000 people) would simply not be able to draw salaries, and virtually all central government funds for research and higher education, family planning, hydroelectric development, transportation, communications, shipping, water and flood control, public housing, health, and social welfare (not to mention relief and rehabilitation) would cease to exist.

Aid-dependence is not confined to budgetary and trade matters, but extends to the kinds of attitudes and predispositions one finds in the bureaucracy. As a result of the long experience with colonial regimes, people in authority in Bangladesh have been conditioned to think of social problems in a paternalistic manner, and to structure administrative programs hierarchically. In present day Bangladesh this phenomenon extends all the way up to the Prime Minister, Sheikh Mujibur Rahman (popularly known as Bangabandhu or "Father of the Nation"), who consciously refers to the land, people, and produce of Bangladesh in the first person possessive (my people, my peasants, my laborers, my party workers, my villages, my jute, and so forth). As part of this style leaders will seldom go out to mix with "their people" but will instead "entertain requests" and "consider demands" in their offices and their drawing rooms. Both relief and development programs are then "granted" to certain areas and groups, while being denied to others, usually on the basis of a wide network of personal, family, and factional ties. As has been pointed out many times, such a system discourages innovation, risk-taking, and a smooth flow of transactions (both at the top and at the bottom of the administrative hierarchy), and it therefore increases dependence on external "agents" that can be convinced of the need to attempt innovation from the outside when things go wrong When things do go wrong and external assistance enters the picture it invariably reinforces the positions of those at the top.

Immediately after the liberation of Bangladesh it was hoped that the new government would break this mold, if only because most of the leaders of the Awami League were men with little administrative background. At the very least, since even the upper echelons of the administrative cadre were extremely thin on experience, many observers had hoped that the new administration might come to be dominated by younger and less tradition-bound civil servants. Unfortunately, none of this has come to pass. Sheikh Mujib has been so idolized by "his people" and "his ministers" that they have left virtually every major decision (as well as many minor ones) entirely up to him. He has been seeing anywhere from 200–500 people in his office or his home almost every day that he has been in Bangladesh (there are countless numbers of stories current in Dacca about how people will follow Mujib everywhere—even into his bathroom—in order to get decisions or favors). After seven months of this harried schedule, it is little wonder that Sheikh Mujib suffered what one of his ministers called "a near-nervous breakdown," just before he went off to Europe for a six-week stay in August and September (during which time he had a gall bladder and appendicitis operation that was apparently not entirely successful). In Mujib's absence the government almost ground to a dead halt, prices soared to an average of two and three times their previous levels, and law and order became a problem of the first magnitude. Consequently, Mujib found it necessary to resume a round-the-clock schedule (again seeing 200–500 people a day) upon his return to Bangladesh in mid-September.

To be sure, some individuals and groups have tried to move away from a paternalistic pattern of decision-making in order to get things done. In most cases, however, such attempts have produced only factionalism, frustration, and backbiting. Many of the foreign relief agencies, for example, have tried to work in local villages and neighborhoods without getting constant clearance from the upper echelons of the various ministries (some agencies are even operating merely on the basis of a letter of intent or a verbal agreement while their requests for contract approval are being passed from one ministry to the other), but this procedure has exposed them to charges that their presence is "unauthorized." Some ministers and politicians have tried to tour the districts and the constituencies in order to mediate disputes and facilitate decision-making down below, yet this too has often resulted only in an intensification of political factionalism and, in some cases, in political murder (Awami League leaders estimate that more than 100 of their party members have been killed in Bangladesh since liberation). Entry to the Central Secretariat in Dacca has now been denied prior to 1:00 P.M. for all but Secretariat employees, in an effort to decongest the offices and corridors of petitioners and favor-seekers. The action has raised great resentment even though it has not been effectively implemented.

In this atmosphere it is not surprising that people at the bottom of the social and administrative hierarchy have found it impossible to take initiative, and that much of the euphoria for nation-building that was so evident in the early months after liberation is now noticeably lacking. People who in January were trying to reconstruct roads and bridges on their own initiative have found that they cannot get building materials or permits without going to the upper echelons of the ministries in Dacca. Young men who were seriously considering the establishment of primary schools in the countryside have been told that their buildings, teachers, and books must all be licensed and appointed by the Education Ministry in the Central Secretariat (all primary schools in Bangladesh have been "nationalized" since liberation). Faced with these kinds of hurdles, many enthusiasts have already given up the attempt to do something useful, while others have joined the opposition. Those who remain loyal to the present regime either articulate the hope that Sheikh Mujib will somehow change all of this, or they have busied themselves with the attempt to gain access to high places in order to assure their positions in a system that is now being played according to old and familiar rules. The difficulty for the government, of course, is that this perpetuates the dependence of local leaders on national leaders, which in turn prevents a spontaneous increase in indigenous production that might lessen the nation's dependence on external assistance. Lacking an ability to get development going at the local level, the nation becomes even more dependent than before on external assistance, and the vicious circle of under-development continues.

FUTURE SCENARIOS

Almost everyone in authority in Bangladesh has his or her own solution to the problem of aid-dependence, although not many people have given the matter a great deal of thought. Both relief administrators and government officials have been too involved with the exigencies of the moment to take a serious look at the long-range implications of what they are doing, with the result that actions to date derive largely from emotional and personalistic responses to crisis events, or from immediate administrative and political considerations. Some funds have been allocated for evaluative studies of the external assistance effort (USAID, for example, has budgeted $50,000 to International Voluntary Services for an examination of possible future programs; the Bangladesh government has set up a variety of evaluative and inspectorate agencies). Because such research is being undertaken by people who are beyond even the peripheries of power, their findings are unlikely to carry much weight in the future. Moreover, many alternative courses of action—the possibility of pulling external assistance out of Bangladesh to take the most obvious example—are unlikely to be seriously considered by men whose careers are dependent upon aid programs.

The people who are presently involved in external assistance justify their existence in a variety of ways. Most of them admit that they are doing little more than keeping people alive without attacking basic problems, but they express a hope, and in some cases a conviction, that the situation will change in the future. Perhaps the most common expressions of optimism come from Western technical personnel and scientifically-oriented Bengalis who argue that Western technology will somehow be absorbed into Bangladesh in such a way as to bring about future "break-throughs." Perhaps new contraceptives will be invented that will restrain the birthrate in a relatively short space of time. Perhaps new agricultural techniques will enable the people of Bangladesh to eliminate their food deficits so that the nation can concentrate more of its energy on endeavors rather than merely feeding itself. Perhaps there will be new discoveries of valuable resources that will earn foreign exchange in quantities large enough to provide relative self-sufficiency to Bangladesh in the future.

It is also clear, however, that while Western technology is already far enough advanced to have solved many of the physical problems of Bangladesh in other contexts—we know how to construct highly sophisticated dams and embankments, we know how to build bridges and roads, we already have high-yielding seeds and chemical fertilizers that could increase yields enormously—there are a myriad of problems involved in the attempt to get these things to Bengalis at the local level. USAID, for example, would like to do as much as it can to increase agricultural production in Bangladesh. It is also well aware of the many sensitivities and obstacles that must be overcome if new agricultural techniques are to be widely and effectively used; there are negative legacies from the past Pakistani program, in which the United States was heavily involved; there are administrative constraints that limit the speed with which programs can be pursued; there are conflicts within the Bangladesh government as to what should be done first, where projects should be undertaken, and what kinds of things should be done at all. It is with these kinds of limitations in mind that many observers seriously question the very possibility of effectively transferring Western technology to Bangladesh through external assistance programs, or argue that the mere attempt to introduce Western technology on a large scale may again intensify rather than solve agricultural problems.

On the basis of this kind of reasoning, almost everyone concerned with future development programs in Bangladesh has emphasized the need for social and cultural change at the local level, to the point that this idea has taken on the character of a near-slogan with both Bengali and foreign administrators. The family planning ministry believes that it can bring about population control by focusing on changes in village attitudes about health and hygiene, as well as through mass education programs. The entire agricultural development effort that is being projected will revolve around cooperative societies that will do agricultural extension work at the level of the village and the *thana* (the *thana* is an administrative unit containing on the average 175,000 people). However, while everyone will agree that social and cultural change at the local level is necessary, there is still an air of unreality abou the schemes that are being projected to bring about such change. Bangladesh has made no significant progress in extending effective literacy beyond 20 per cent in the last 25 years, and yet policy-makers concerned with mass education are talking about abolishing illiteracy in the next decade. Agricultural cooperatives are being planned on the model of the highly successful Comilla experiments of the 1960s, but those experiments have attained their reputation largely from the benefits that have accrued to portions of only one district (Comilla), in which the impressive Academy for Rural Development has been working with massive funds from a variety of international sources since May 1959. Some of the ideas from Comilla have recently been tried in Bogra, Rajshahi, Chittagong, and Noakhali districts—with considerably less success than in Comilla—and in the 13 other districts of Bangladesh there has been no cooperative movement that would even begin to compare with the Comilla experience. This being the case, many fear that the attempt by the new Bangladesh government to rapidly establish cooperatives on a mass scale throughout Bangladesh (the government plans to blanket the entire country by 1976) will only lead to the discrediting of the more selective Comilla experiments, doing little or nothing to foster local initiative.

The predominant feeling within the government is that external assistance should continue to be granted to Bangladesh by Western nations, but that it should be unaccompanied by foreign personnel and restrictions, and that it should not be target-oriented. The reasoning here is that much of the haste with which development programs are pursued can be traced to the presence of energetic foreign advisors, and to the Western penchant for wanting tangible results in short periods of time from aid investments. Moreover, foreigners often serve only as scapegoats (for both the government and the opposition) and in most field situations tend to dominate affairs no matter how hard they try to remain in the background. Bangladesh government leaders readily admit that in the absence of foreign advisors they might make even more mistakes than at present, but they also argue that the nation will never be able to stand on its own feet so long as development programs are guided by experts from other nations.

This recommended style of aid-giving has in fact been assiduously pursued by India, which is giving large quantities of external assistance to Bangladesh, but is trying to do so with the lowest profile possible. To be sure, a number of Indian officials and bureaucrats have been in Bangladesh during the ten months since liberation, but they have stayed for short periods of time, have not made many public appearances, and have generally confined their contacts to the highest levels of government. For India this style of operation is almost essential, since it is *the* large neighbor that surrounds Bangladesh territorially and is, therefore, even more vulnerable to opposition criticism than the developed nations of the West. Then too, India's present leadership would like to establish a pattern of external assistance for itself in which Western nations would supply funds for development without foreign resident personnel and without "strings." It is only fitting that India should try to "practice what it preaches" in Bangladesh.

Among non-Indian foreign donors in Bangladesh there is considerable interest in the "Indian model" of external assistance, even though most aid donors do not see it as a viable solution to the problems which they and the Bangladesh government are confronting. To begin with, most of the aid-giving agencies in Bangladesh have long-established institutional structures that require the stationing of personnel in host countries, and most of them also have a list of criteria for aid-eligibility. Indeed, the most coveted types of external assistance usually come to an aid-recipient nation in the form of loans rather than outright gifts, and such loans are subject to the scrutiny of men who stand in the tradition of cost-conscious bankers and merchants. This means that even if an agency administrator in Dacca would like to change the pattern of external assistance that prevails at present, he would have to change institutional structures, modes of thinking, and in many cases the raison d'etre for aid programs in his own head-quarters. Nevertheless, a number of agencies are attempting to accommodate some of the demands of the Bangladesh government—

USAID, for example, is trying to operate in Bangladesh with fewer personnel than usual and has made some grants that do not require purchases in the United States—but to go further than this will at best take considerable time (granted institutional lags in the United States) and at worst will be offensive to the people whose tax dollars support USAID. Much the same can be said for the position of the United Nations and some of the other large aid organizations.

A second major problem involved in trying to work the "Indian model" is that many external assistance programs necessarily require the presence of foreign technicians when indigenous skills are unavailable. The Russian experts that are reportedly prospecting for oil in the southern delta, for example, are there only because Bengalis cannot prospect for oil with anywhere near the same degree of sophistication. British bridgebuilders have been called in to rebuild the huge Hardinge, Teesta, and King George VI bridges in response to a situation where indigenous engineers do not have a sufficient grasp of the necessary technical knowledge. If Bangladesh is going to maximize its gains from the new technology in agriculture fairly quickly, it is going to have to accommodate men and women from other countries who can apply that technology in the countryside, at least until such time as more Bengalis themselves become familiar with the complexities of the new technology.

Finally, it is difficult to see the "Indian model" being widely adopted in Bangladesh if only because of the wider foreign policy considerations of the larger donor nations, which ultimately control the bulk of the resources that are so desperately needed. Because the British (and perhaps the Common Market) still have a fair interest in jute and tea, they can be expected to use their external assistance in Bangladesh in a manner that promotes those interests, and this will undoubtedly require the presence of some Englishmen in Bangladesh as well as some attempts by the British to influence the priorities of the Bangladesh government. If the Russians should discover oil in Bangladesh they would obviously want to have first crack at any collaborative agreements that would provide for the exploitation of petroleum resources and their distribution in the rest of the world, and these kinds of considerations also require that the Soviets be more than passive spectators for the present. Most foreign policy analysts—even many of the more perceptive ones in New Delhi—argue that the Indians themselves will be unable to maintain their present low-profile posture in Bangladesh, since they obviously have a number of economic and strategic interests that will most likely remain controversial, front-page issues for a long time. Indeed, despite India's present posture, there is no question that Mrs. Gandhi's government has already come in for sharper criticism from the Bangladesh opposition than any other nation.

A number of other development scenarios are being discussed in Dacca these days, and there are countless variations on those described above. For the most part, however, the major issues have already been stated. Perhaps the only other significant pattern of development that is being advocated is the familiar Russian model, which entails barter agreements, state control of trading, education of large numbers of Bengali youth in the U.S.S.R., fairly tight Bangladesh links to Russian technology, and the exclusion of non-Soviet bloc personnel. While the pro-Moscow opposition parties in Bangladesh are ardent advocates of this pattern, and while it conforms in many ways to the aid-relationship being advocated by India, most Bengalis see it as lacking viability in the future, if only because neither India nor the Soviet Union would seem to have sufficient surplus resources to satisfy the needs of Bangladesh. Moreover, as a number of people in the present Bangladesh government have pointed out, Bangladesh is likely to continue to be receptive to aid from Western nations (including the United States) in order to balance Russian and Indian influence in the affairs of the nation.

The more formidable opposition in Bangladesh is expected to come from a large number of small terrorist and radical political groups that are at once anti-Soviet, anti-West, anti-Indian, and anti-government. Many of these groups trace their origins to the small bands of Maoists that were active in East Bengal during the latter years of Pakistani rule, but the new groups now resent any attempt to link them with the anti-Bengali nationalist stance currently being pursued by Peking. The principal public spokesman of these groups is still Maulana Bhashani, the 90-year-old veteran of a variety of radical left movements in the past, but a number of new younger leaders are also emerging. Perhaps the most popular hero of the radical left at present is A.M.S. Abdur Rab, a 28-year-old law graduate of Dacca University and a former vice-president of the powerful Dacca University Central Students

Union (DUCSU). Earlier this year Rab and Shahjahan Siraj (a 26-year-old associate) managed to split the Awami League's important student wing (the Chhatra League), and later managed to decisively defeat the pro-Mujib faction of the Chhatra League in a series of important student union elections. The Rab-Siraj group has since been advocating a society based on "scientific socialism," while at the same time denigrating "Mujibism" and protesting Awami League ineptitude. Physical attacks on Rab by irate pro-Mujib Awami Leaguers has only enhanced the young man's popularit .

The solution to the problem of aid-dependence being advocated by members of the Rab-Siraj group is by far the most radical one being proposed anywhere. They would simply have all foreigners withdraw from Bangladesh, regardless of the disastrous economic, political, and social consequences. Standing in the tradition of Bengali nihilists, they have refused to pay much attention to organizational detail, arguing that what is needed in Bengal is a long period of unorganized chaos, which they see as being necessary to bring about the massive changes in society that they desire. Their future scenario is one in which radical political groups would bring about a paralysis of government machinery (regardless of who was operating it), to be followed by a glorious bloodbath in which millons and millons of people would be killed, after which a leadership would presumably emerge to construct a self-sufficient and labor-intensive economy that sounds vaguely akin to what is being attempted in China. Surprisingly, one can even find some people in the present government who are seriously considering the likelihood of just this kind of scenario, at the same time that they are working on present development programs. At a recent seminar in Dacca, for example, the Secretary of the Rural Development and Cooperative Program of the Bangladesh government, a young man who has just returned from two years in China, speculated on the probability that his schemes for the establishment of cooperatives might not work. In his words:

...time is running out. Can we do enough in a short enough time while the remnants of euphoria last? Maybe what will be inevitable in Bangladesh is an anarchic situation, which would at least hold out the hope of completely changing the society. Maybe democracy is too slow. Maybe we need something else.

CONCLUSIONS

The tragedy of Bangladesh is that none of the scenarios being tossed around at present seem to have much chance of working out. Western technology has accomplished great things in the past, and it does hold out some promise of future greatness, but Bangladesh would seem to be a test case in the attempt to make Western technology relevant in the underdeveloped world. Judged on the basis of past experience, it could well be that the technologists will find their gadgets and discoveries inappropriate for export to Bangladesh. Both development theory and the inherent genius of many Bengalis, who now have considerable development expertise, may be sufficient to find solutions to unprecedented challenges to man's capacity for human management and coordination, but it is also possible that the development theorists, foreign and indigenous, might find themselves powerless when confronted with the enormous tasks ahead. The radical students may have their orgies of terrorism and violence, but they will almost certainly find that what Mao did in China was the result of a wide variety of factors that are simply not operative in Bengal. In Bangladesh these days one cannot help but be impressed by the way in which Western technology, the enormous administrative and managerial expertise of both Bengalis and Westerners, as well as the pent-up enthusiasm of youthful political aspirants, are working at cross-purposes, with no apparent end in sight.

The intersection of three great forces of our time—nationalism, the penchant for international development, and the urge for violent revolution—present only a challenge and a series of nagging questions when they are seen in their extreme forms, operating on the ground in Bangladesh. How much of the massive aid that is and will be going into Bangladesh will contribute to a better life for the Bengali people? To what extent can the activities of the international organizations, the government, and the opposition be directed toward any kind of fundamental attack on the real problems of Bangladesh? Will the burgeoning population of Bangladesh ever be controlled, or will it simply continue to grow because relief aid will keep it barely alive and healthy enough to merely exist? Will the majority of the Bengali people ever be able to live in a society where they can engage in productive and rewarding activity, and will production ever be raised to the level where people will not only be able to eat and survive but also to live decently? Will the Bengalis ever be able to hold their heads as high as those Bengalis who appear in their history books, their literature, and their dreams?

THREE

THE BANGLADESH
COUP (1975)

Political processes in the Indian subcontinent have frequently been subject to unpredictable events, often brought about by relatively unknown people or groups. Some of the most critical events of recent history fit this description—the assassinations of Gandhi, Liaquat Ali Khan, and Bandaranaike, the two major coups in Pakistan, the developments in March 1971 that led to the Bangladesh liberation war—and the Bangladesh coup d'etat of August 15, 1975 was no exception.

One might argue that the the potential for such events is ever-present, given the complexity of South Asian politics, the size of the political arenas, and the innumerable factions that must be accommodated. In addition, there is the inadequacy of institutionalized authority structures for realizing the far-reaching goals that South Asian leaders occasionally set for themselves and their nations, and a series of fundamental cleavages over the legitimacy of such structures as do exist. While many facets of sub-continental politics are perhaps better established than their counterparts in Africa or Latin America, there is at the same time a millenarian streak in almost every South Asian political actor which leads to forays in utopian problem-solving and, in turn, to the unpredictable events described above.

The Bangladesh coup provides a classic example of the way in which the most significant changes in government can be brought about by a very small group of people. From all the available evidence, the coup was conceived and commanded by 12 to 20 military and ex-military men, none of them above the rank of major, and perhaps with the tacit approval of two politicians. The four key figures in the coup (i.e., the only ones who apparently were aware of all planned activities) were Majors Farooq Rehman and Khondkar Abdul Rasheed, related to one another as brother-in-laws, and ex-Majors Shamsul Islam Noor and Shafiquer Rahman Dalim, both of whom had been dismissed from military service more than a year prior to the coup.

Rehman and Rasheed were the key figures in the military structure that made the coup possible because, between them, they commanded all the tanks and all the artillery of the Bangladesh Army. Noor and Dalim were crucial because the intense grudge they bore against President Mujibur Rahman, his family, and his government, enabled them either to order, or actually to shoot, the President himself and 14 members of his family.

The ineffectiveness of the infantry and Mujibur Rahman's security force (the Rakhi Bahini) in the face of the insurgent force was compounded by their ignorance of the overthrow plot, and by the early assassination of their leader. Although the sorting out process would drag on for months if not years, the coup was all but over in less than an hour, with a total of 46 people killed.

If the success of the coup was dependent on men with personal grudges and key military positions, the people's acquiescence can be traced to more general and complex social and political forces that have been building up in Bangladesh during the last three and a half years. At their core was the widespread belief that Sheikh Mujibur Rahman was attempting to create a family-centered political dynasty in Bangladesh for the benefit of his relatives and closest associates, at the expense of almost everyone else. As the unquestioned hero of the Bangladesh liberation movement, "Mujib" had been proclaimed "Bangabandhu" (the friend of Bengal) and "Father of the Nation" upon his return from a Pakistani prison in January 1972. As numerous observers have pointed out, sentiment gradually shifted: in 1972 and 1973 people blamed Mujib's associates for the ills of Bangladesh but by late 1974 Mujib himself was often described as the principal villain.

The charge that Mujib was building a family fortune and a family-centered dynasty seems well substantiated, and, more important, is almost universally believed in Bangladesh. Sheikh Abu Nasser, Mujib's only brother (who was in his late 40s when he was killed in the coup) had risen from a position of near poverty in 1971 to become perhaps the largest contractor in Khulna district by 1975. Nasser's wealth was enhanced by his alleged control of a two-way trade network, in which he exchanged Bangladesh jute in India for consumer goods, alcoholic beverages, cigarettes, and drugs for sale in Bangladesh, often in violation of trade agreements that had been signed by his brother. While many reports about the extent of Nasser's wealth are unquestionably exaggerated, his reputation for having gained quick and illicit affluence was enhanced by his increasingly ostentatious life style. He owned two Mercedes Benz cars and two luxurious homes, and shuttled frequently back and forth between Dacca and London. At least some leaders of the August coup were willing to participate because they had been demoted or dismissed by Mujib when they alleged they had traced to Sheikh Nasser illegal shipments of jute to India.

In addition to his brothers's family, four sisters were believed to have benefited excessively from their ties of kinship. The husband of one of Mujib's sisters, A.T.M. Syed Hossain, was a section officer (an intermediate clerk) in the Establishment Division (personnel) of the bureaucracy before the liberation of Bangladesh. Having served in West Pakistan during 1971, Syed Hossain returned to Bangladesh after the liberation war and was quickly promoted to Joint Secretary of the Establishment Division, a position that enabled him, by virtue of his kinship with Mujib, to control most appointments, transfers, and promotions within the administration. Only five days before the coup, Syed Hossain was made an Additional Secretary, a title ordinarily conferred on a bureaucrat after 13 or 14 years of experience. Syed Hossain was arrested during the coup.

While Abdul Rab Serneabad, another of Mujib's brothers-in-law, enjoyed a reputation for relative personal honesty and integrity, his son, Abul Hasnat, was widely condemned for his political activities in Barisal. As a consequence, Serneabad's position as a Minister (and potential Prime Minister in Mujib's eyes) was widely resented. Hasnat, in his early 30s when he escaped arrest during the August coup, had become secretary of Mujib's Jubbo (Youth) League in Barisal shortly after the liberation of Bangladesh. As a Youth League Leader Abul Hasnat organized what amounted to his own private army, intimidated political opponents, and was elected Chairman of the Barisal Municipality in elections that were almost universally described as unfair. As Chairman of the municipality and nephew of Mujib, Abul Hasnat was creating a fairly strong political base for himself in Barisal on the strength of his powers to grant licenses and permits, and he too had amassed considerable personal wealth, as indicated by his possession of several automobiles and homes in Barisal.

By far the worst reputation among Mujib's relatives was gained by Sheikh Fazlul Huque Moni, commonly known as "nephew of the nation," the son of another of Mujib's four sisters. Moni, who was 36 when he was killed in the coup, graduated last in his class from Dacca University in the 1960s with a B.A., third class, in political science. He then joined the ranks of the educated un-employed for a few years before securing a job as a newspaper reporter (at a salary of Taka 275, or $55 per month) in 1970. After the liberation of Bangladesh, Moni built a network of youth organizations as head of his uncle's national Jubbo (Youth) League, members of which were allowed by Mujib to carry arms. On the basis of his political connections and his control of this militant Youth League, Moni took over the Pasban Press and the Pasban Building in the Motijheel commercial section of Dacca and began publishing newspapers and magazines. He also controlled a num-ber of the agents and firms that import relief goods into Bangla-desh, primarily through permits and licenses, and this enabled him to accumulate considerable personal wealth, including several cars and two homes in one of the better residential areas of Dacca.

In terms of public reputation, Moni's position was rivaled by Sheikh Sahidul Islam, the son of Mujib's fourth sister. At age 24, he was given the rank of a government minister just five days prior to the coup. (Fifteen people had ministerial rank under Mujib's one-party system and four of them were relatives; one of the 15, of course, was Mujib himself). Unlike Moni, Sahidul Islam was considered an excellent student, having secured a B.A., first class, in chemistry as an undergraduate at Dacca University. Neverthe-less, his elevation to the position of Secretary of Mujib's party and his promotion to the rank of a government minister at such a young age, clearly caused young and old alike to bristle. Sahidul Islam's reputation in Bangladesh was also tarnished by persistent rumors that he had been intimately involved in a bank robbery and scandal in 1972 and in the assassination of seven Dacca University students in 1974.

Also involved in the 1972 scandal were Mujib's sons, Jamal and Kamal, aged 20 and 22 respectively. Kamal had even suffered bullet wounds in a shoot-out at the scene of the crime. In 1973 Jamal was sent to Sandhurst for military training, with the idea, as Mujib frequently expressed it, that "he will be head of my army some day." At the time of the coup the two sons were living in Mujib's house, both having been married in lavish ceremonies the previous week: Jamal, Kamal, and their new brides, as well as Mujib's 12-year-old son, Russell—named after Bertrand Russell—were all killed in the same bursts of gunfire that took Mujib's life.

If Mujib's tendency to grant political and financial favors to his relatives was unpopular in Bangladesh, so was his proclivity to arrogate personalistic and authoritarian powers to himself and his closest associates. When he first returned from a Pakistan prison in early 1972, Mujib was content to assume the position of Prime Minister under a constitution modeled after the Westminister Parliamentary system. However, he quickly began to disappoint political supporters, and to alienate opponents, when he created his personal Rakhi Bahini (Security Force), an organization of 10,000–12,000 men that was employed in intelligence and para-military activities designed primarily to protect Mujib, his family, and his associates.

After Mujib's Awami League won 307 of 315 parliamentary seats in elections in 1973 (the elections were usually described as blatantly and unnecessarily rigged), violent attacks against Awami Leaguers and government officials became commonplace. In 1974 at least six members of the Bangladesh parliament were killed by unknown assailants, and Mujib himself estimated that more than 3,000 members of his Awami League had been slain during the year. Arson, looting, and bombings were almost everyday occurrences in Bangladesh in 1974.

With the Bangladesh economy deteriorating rapidly, in part a result of floods and famines in 1974 but also because of the break-down of administrative authority, Mujib declared a state of emergency in December 1974. The emergency provided for special powers of arrest, all vested in Mujib, and curtailed those freedoms usually associated with the courts and the press. All political meetings, demonstrations, strikes and lockouts were banned. On January 25, 1975 Parliament amended the 1972 constitution, changing Mujib's title from Prime Minister to President. In the January 1975 amendment, which was passed in one hour and without debate (the vote was 294-0 and Members of Parliament were given copies of the amendment only after they had entered the halls of

Parliament), Mujib was vested with all executive powers and authorized to declare Bangladesh a one-party state. In subsequent months he abolished all opposition political parties, stripped the supreme court of its powers to enforce fundamental rights, created special courts and tribunals directly answerable to him, and closed down all but four daily newspapers (two in English and two in Bengali). All four of the newspapers that were allowed to exist were either government-or-party-owned.

On June 7, 1975 Mujib announced an entirely new regime, reminiscent of Nyerere's Tanzania, in which the entire government was to be merged with his single political party, the Bangladesh Krishak Sramic Awami League (BAKSHAL). BAKSHAL was headed by a 15-member national executive, consisting of four of Mujib's relatives, ten of his closest associates, and Mujib himself. Organizationally subordinate to the executive was a 115-member central committee representing various segments of society, including the military. No one was allowed to serve in the government without becoming a member of BAKSHAL, and almost everyone of any consequence was required to seek membership in BAKSHAL lest they be charged with being antinational. By mid-June Mujib's party men has begun to move into offices in the central secretariat, ousting bureaucratic officials, and plans were launched for expanding the number of districts in Bangladesh from 19 to 61. Just before the coup, governors of the 61 new districts were named, most of them political friends and associates of Mujib rather than old bureaucratic hands (only one retired military officer was granted a governorship).

Mujib had clearly stepped on many toes when instituting his BAKSHAL scheme, which he and his supporters described as a "second revolution." He further alienated various sectors of the population by other related actions. Early in 1975 he ordered the gates of the government secretariat locked at 10 A.M., so that latecomers to the office could not enter. By presidential proclamation he assumed powers to dismiss any member of the bureaucracy without giving reason. At the same time he moved more than 200,000 beggars and pavement dwellers out of the city of Dacca to nearby camps and had *bustees* (slums) bulldozed to make room for building projects. In April 1975 he demonetized 100-taka notes in an effort to flush out "black money," but the project was so poorly administered that it worked primarily to the detriment of the middle classes rather than the rich. At the insistence of international donors Mujib devalued the Bangladesh taka in mid-1975, thereby maintaining an inflation rate already in excess of 30 per cent. His constant shuffling of military personnel added salt to the wounds of soldiers already piqued by their subordination to the Rakhi Bahini.

In this atmosphere it is little wonder that most people in Bangladesh accepted Mujib's death on August 15, 1975 with little regret. Things had come to such a state that a middle-level clerk in a Bengali office could tell me the day before the coup—in loud and audible language and with more than two dozen other Bengalis present—that "they are trying to create a kingship here, and they will pay for it." That same clerk, a week after the coup, was not exactly joyous, but he expressed no feeling of remorse at the death of Sheikh Mujibur Rahman. In the month after the coup, every student and faculty member at Dacca University with whom I talked told me that they had been "terrified" by the coercive measures that Mujib had employed in an effort to register all university personnel as BAKSHAL members. (On the day of the coup Mujib was scheduled to appear at Dacca University where he was to receive applications for BAKSHAL membership from all university faculty members, to be presented in a silver basket by the Vice-Chancellor of the University.)

This is not to argue that Mujibur Rahman will go down in Bengali history books as a mere tyrant. Mujib has often been and still is described by Bengalis as a complex man who always seemed larger than life itself. After the coup Bengalis from all walks of life and all political factions still talked of him as being ebullient, garrulous, bold, courageous, emotional, and in many ways well-meaning. His ability to charm audiences while fracturing both the Bengali and English languages is often recalled with amusement and nostalgia. His promulgation of simple slogans, a talent that so ably served the cause of the Bangladesh liberation struggle, as well as his daring exploits and fearless challenges in the face of Pakistan's military authorities during the old East Pakistan days, evoke memories tinged with real respect and pride. Representative of Bengalis' ambivalent attitude toward Mujib is the statement by one of his most prominent opponents, who told me ten days after the coup: "I had learned to hate him, but I still smile when I think of his charm—and, without knowing why, I feel his absence very much."

Perhaps the most that one can say is that many of the traits and characteristics that served Mujib so well during the liberation struggle and the events leading up to it were precisely the same features of his personality that led to his increasing unpopularity as a government leader. His intense loyalty to his closest associates, for example, enabled him to build a political party that could serve as an effective nucleus for the promulgation of national slogans once he had roused Bengali sentiment against the Pakistan government. As Prime Minister and President of Bangladesh, however, this same loyalty to old associates led to a personalistic patronage system similar to that of traditional monarchial regimes. When some of his advisers and foreign relief officials told him that he should discipline relatives or friends who were taking advantage of their personal connections with him, Mujib would usually admit that some disciplinary action was in order, but he would also wax eloquent about his long-standing ties with a particular individual and his feeling that close friends should not be "betrayed."

In a similar manner, Mujib's distrust of those whom he saw as "enemies" was conducive to the building of solidarity within his own organization—and between his organization and political allies—during the liberation struggle. By simplifying issues and sharpening cleavages between people in West and East Pakistan, Mujib created an atmosphere of confrontation that helped to rally his countrymen around him. After the liberation, however, Mujib's continued use of confrontation politics, simplistic slogans, and his propensity to divide the political world into camps of friends and enemies only served to heighten tensions. To those who were predisposed to resist him, the only options were submitting entirely to Mujib's will or opposing it unreservedly.

Granted Mujib's importance to the growth of Bengali nationalism, and the ambivalent feelings of most Bengalis about him, it is perhaps appropriate that he was buried with "full honors" in his family's burial ground in Tangipara village in Faridpur district. Historians will have to sort out the meaning of the absence of mourners at his grave—people in Tangipara explained it as being the result of a combination of fear of reprisal and mixed emotions. Future generations will also have to pass judgment on the decision to bury Mujib's family members in wooden boxes rather than shrouds, in an area just outside the Dacca cantonment.

KHONDKAR MUSHTAQUE AHMED: THE NEW GOVERNMENT

If Mujib's regime had exacerbated tensions and cleavages within Bangladesh, these were not immediately mitigated by the August 15 coup. To be sure, the coup leaders eliminated the possibility of a future political dynasty built around Mujib. In doing so, however, they severed channels for communication between Mujib's most ardent supporters and the opposition. Moreover, they were faced with the immediate tasks of restoring lines of command within the army, articulating the future pattern of relationships between the military and civilian politicians, and sorting out factionalism among a variety of political parties. At the same time, they were highly conscious of the need for support from foreign governments, for Bang'adesh is as heavily dependent on international assistance as any other nation in the world.

Granted the enormous problems of Bangladesh in a world without so forceful a personality as Sheikh Mujibur Rahman, the post-coup government was perhaps the strongest among many possibilities that could be imagined. Shortly after the first announcement of the coup by ex-Major Dalim—at 6 AM. on the morning of August 15—Bangladesh Radio declared that Mr. Khondkar Mushtaque Ahmed had agreed to form a new government, with himself as President. The role of the majors who staged the coup was still unclear, but executive authority was lodged in the hands of the most highly respected of those few Bangladesh government leaders who had successfully dared to differ with Mujib in the past.

Khondkar Mushtaque Ahmed, popularly known as "Mushtaque," was born in 1918, two years earlier than Mujib, in Dashpara village, Comilla district of East Bengal. Trained as a lawyer at Dacca University, Mushtaque joined Mujib as a founding member of the Awami League (AL) Party in 1949 and was instrumental in building the party's legislative and ministerial wings during the late 1960s. When Mujib was imprisoned in 1971, Mushtaque Ahmed was one of four AL leaders included in the cabinet of the Bangladesh goverment-in-exile in Calcutta. After that government returned to Dacca with Mujib in January 1972, following the liberation of Bangladesh, Mushtaque was assigned two portfolios in succession—Water and Power Development, and Commerce and Trade—over the course of the next three and a half years. Mushtaque gained considerable respect from a number of Awami Leaguers and others because of his refusal to live as ostentatiously as most of the ministers and party leaders around Mujib. He is also respected for his commitment of Islam (his father was a Muslim *pir*, or religious leader), his reputation as a family centered person who has not bestowed undeserved favors on family members, and for his political acumen.

Shortly after the 1975 coup, Mujib's most ardent supporters argued that Mushtaque had, from the very beginning, been involved in the conspiracy that took Mujib's life. Mushtaque, his relatives, and his supporters were equivocal about the charge. While there is no concrete evidence, several things in Mushtaque's background support the complicity theory: he is distantly related through the first of his two wives to Major Rasheed, one of the four principal leaders of the coup; his position in Mujib's government had deteriorated and was threatened further by the new BAKSHAL scheme; and he had fairly consistently opposed other Awami League leaders on fundamental issues associated with both the conduct of the liberation war and the structure and functioning of Mujib's government. Mushtaque is also known to be anticommunist and pro-West, inclined against both Mujib's Soviet-backed one-party system and Mujib's policy of increasing dependence on India. At least one of Mushtaque's closest associates suggested that while Mushtaque was certainly not involved in the planning of the coup he may well have been informed about it. If informed about it, according to this interpretation, Mushtaque would not have been inclined to expose or resist it.

The only other major politician who has been repeatedly implicated in the coup—again primarily by Mujib's staunchest supporters—is Taheruddin Thakur, Minister of State for Information and Broadcasting under Mujib and subsequently under Mushtaque Ahmed. Thakur, it is alleged, agreed in advance to hand over the radio station to the coup leaders on the morning of August 15. This charge has been given considerable credence because of the importance that Thakur appears to have assumed in the new government, and because of the prominence given to Thakur's role in an account of the coup by Lewis Simons in the *Washington*

Post. As is frequently the case in a country that thrives on gossip, mention of a rumor in an authoritative manner in the Western press contributes greatly to its acceptance among Bengali intellectuals.

Thakur, 36, has an M. A. degree from Dacca University, where he was a leader of the AL's Student League in the 1960s. After his graduation from Dacca University in 1965, Thakur became a chief reporter for *Ittefaque*, a leading Bengali daily, and quickly gained a reputation for wielding a powerful pen. When Mujib was looking for bright young candidates for the National Assembly in 1970, Thakur was given an Awami League ticket, and his subsequent election to the Assembly in 1970 and to the Bangladesh parliament in 1973 provided the base for his nomination as state Minister in Mujib's cabinet. According to many of his supporters, when Thakur was taken into the ministry in 1973 his colleagues at *Ittefaque* became jealous, accusing him of being overly ambitious. Thakur's supporters now argue that petty jealousy has inspired the rumors of complicity. On the other hand, Mujib's supporters speak of Thakur as a "Brutus," noting that Thakur gave Mujib every indication of support for the BAKSHAL scheme in the months before the coup, then reversed his position completely as soon as the coup took place. If Taheruddin Thakur is eventually implicated in the coup, his position could become highly controversial.

Whether or not Mushtaque and Taheruddin Thakur were involved in planning the coup, it is clear they have since become two of the leading figures in a government that rejects Mujib's "second revolution" absolutely. Most observers have been impressed by the way the new government has moved, surely yet cautiously, in dealing with the domestic and international imbroglios aroused by the assassination of Mujib, thus increasing their chance of survival beyond what anyone thought imaginable in the first few days following the coup. It was often argued that Mujib was the only leader who could promise some semblance of stability in Bangladesh, yet the new government has exhibited a surprising degree of confidence.

REORGANIZING THE ARMY

Perhaps the most important factor contributing to the stability of the new government has been its effort to resolve conflicts within the military. During the first week of the coup, it was widely rumored that a number of army leaders were either maneuvering for position or planning countercoups For at least a week, most informed observers expected fighting among different segments of the army at any time. The atmosphere was all the more con- ductive to rumors of intrigue because the majors and captains who had led the coup were holed up in Bangabhavan, the old hotel- like official residence that Mujib had built for himself (but had only used for official purposes—he was killed in his smaller private residence in Dhanmondi), while most of the senior officers who were at various times reported being opposed to the coup were with their troops in the cantonment. In addition, during the first ten days after the coup neither the newspapers nor radio broadcasts made reference to anything involving the military, yet there were tanks stationed at key points throughout Dacca and truckloads of military personnel regularly patrolled the city. Visitors to Banga- bhavan—where Mushtaque and his government (including many of their family members) had also taken up permanent residence— reported the comings and goings of senior military officers, obviously engaged in negotiations with coup leaders.

On August 25, ten days after the coup, Mushtaque finally announced that he was appointing General M.A.G. Osmany his Defense Advisor, a new position apparently created to facilitate coordination between the military and the new civilian government. General Osmany had been Commander-in-Chief of the Bangladesh Armed Forces during the liberation struggle, being at that time the most senior Bengali officer in the Pakistan army who had defected to the liberation movement. As a consequence, Osmany was respected by those Bengali soldiers who had fought in Bangladesh during 1971, including many members of Mujib's Rakhi Bahini. In addition, Osmany was considered by those Bengali soldiers who had remained in Pakistan during the 1971 struggle (commonly known as "repatriates") to be a good officer, in the finest British- South Asian military tradition. Eccentric but well liked by almost everyone, Osmany had agreed to serve in Mujib's government as a Minister, but had been dumped unceremoniously by Mujib in early 1975 when he refused to go along with the BAKSHAL scheme. Having retired to gardening and home-building, Osmany was obviously not involved in the coup, but his willingness to serve as

Mushtaque's Defense Advisor signaled his approval, and his appointment was a positive factor in reconciling diverse military factional interests.

A second series of military appointments followed within 24 hours of Osmany's assumption of office. The key features of this reorganization were the willingness of Major-General K Shafiullah to resign as Chief of the Army Staff in favor of Major-General Ziaur Rahman, and the elevation of three military repatriates— Major-General M. Khalilur Rahman, Brigadier H.M. Ershad, and Brigadier Quazi Golam Dastgir—within the army hierarchy. (In 1972, Mujlb had by-passed Ziaur Rahman, who had seniority, to appoint Shafiullah, a move that rankled other military leaders. Because he had become identified with Mujib, Shaffiullah reportedly suggested that he be replaced as Chief of the Army Staff after the coup, arguing that his retirement from the position was due soon in any case. On the day of his exit he delivered a speech to his troops, calling on them to carry on in the best military tradition. He has since "been placed at the disposal of the Ministry of Foreign Affairs," according to an official announcement, and is apparently being considered for an appointment as ambassador to one of the oil-rich nations of the Persian Gulf.

Ziaur Rahman had distinguished himself in March 1971 when he rebelled against the Pakistan army while in command of the Eighth East Bengal Regiment in Chittagong, being the first to announce the formation of a Bangladesh government. An ambitious man, he also declared himself president of the new Bangladesh government, later retracting his self-appointment in deference to Sheikh Mujibur Rahman. The incident, however, created bitter animosity between the two men, which was intensified by Mujib's decision to by-pass Ziaur Rahman in favor of Shafiullah.

Equal in importance to the appointment of Osmany and the reorganization of military leaders following Shafiullah's retirement was the resolve of the majors and captains that had led the coup to either resume their positions within the military hierarchy or to play a subordinate role as individuals in the political process. All were in their late 20s and early 30s and none of them were repatriates from Pakistan. It is generally agreed that a decision by the coup leaders to form their own Revolutionary Council would have met bitter resistance from both senior military leaders and civilian politicians, and set in motion a series of events that would inevitably have produced considerable bloodshed. Military personnel believed that, in acting as they did, the coup leaders prevented both fratricidal killing within the army and widespread public violence.

Analysts and military leaders are also agreed that the coup was popular within the army, for a variety of reasons. First, Mujib had given much greater prominence and perquisites to his Rakhi Bahini than he had to the military, and had further alienated army leaders by constantly shuffling them around for political reasons. Mujib had also insisted that his Rakhi Bahini be trained by the Indian military, against the wishes of senior Bangladesh officers. Finally, most of the officers and soldiers who had returned from Pakistan more than a year after the end of the liberation war had felt discriminated against by Mujib, perhaps because Mujib had associated them with the Pakistani military regime that had jailed him 11 times in his career. Many senior military leaders believe Mujib should have promoted unity within the army by seeking to reconcile his India-trained troops with the Pakistan-trained troops and officers, who easily constitute a majority within the army. Instead, Mujib seemed bent on driving a wedge between the two, and the widespread feeling that he was doing so created considerable enmity.

Having resolved factional differences within the army, at least temporarily, one of the first tasks the new government set for itself was the integration of all military personnel under one command. General Osmany's general popularity among the military, including the Rakhi Bahini, together with the reported leadership skills of Ziaur Rahman and the officers around him, could facilitate such integration.

Perhaps the most difficult shift contemplated by the new government is to diminish India's role in training Bangladesh military personnel. Indian leaders might see this shift as adverse to their interests, particularly if Pakistan and China become involved in training troops or supplying weapons. The matter will have to be handled with great sensitivity. However, the Bangladesh army cannot possibly be considered a military threat to India in the near future, and training by both Pakistan and India could conceivably promote beneficial communication among military leaders of the three major nations of the subcontinent. It might be possible, therefore, to devise a cooperative arrangement that would meet

Bangladesh's domestic needs without alarming India   Both Indian and Bangladesh officials have argued that India's principal interest lies in stabilizing the Bangladesh political process, and a strong military could well be conducive to such stabilization. Another possibility being discussed is British training and supplies for the Bangladesh army, perhaps being funded by the oil-rich Islamic nations of the Persian Gulf.

IMPLICATIONS FOR INDO-BANGLADESH RELATIONS

Mention of India in post-coup Bangladesh raises a hornet's nest of international issues. For several days after the coup, diplomats were preparing for heightened international tension, since Pakistan, on the day of the coup, became the first nation to recognize the new regime and Pakistan Radio stated that the new government in Dacca had changed the name of the country from "The People's Republic of Bangladesh" to the "Islamic Republic of Bangladesh." With telephone communications between Dacca and New Delhi cut off and the Indian High Commissioner to Bangladesh in Delhi for consultations, India was unable to communicate with the new government for three days. Meanwhile, journalists in India were unable to get to Dacca because air links had been suspended, and they therefore tended to emphasize, largely on the basis of specu- lation, the post-coup possibilities for Indo-Bangladesh confronta- tion. It should be pointed out that such speculation was encouraged by the rigid press censorship rules then operative in India, which prohibited the kind of free and open discussion necessary for more balanced reporting.

That the new regime in Dacca was predisposed toward Pakistan was evident from broadcasts heard over Bangladesh radio in Calcutta. These consisted almost exclusively of curt announce- ments about curfews, and music—often martial in character— associated with Islam and Pakistan. The noticeable absence of Tagore songs and readings from the *Bhagavad Gita*—introduced after 1971 when Mujib proclaimed Bangladesh a secular state— coupled with Pakistan's announcement that Bangladesh now was an "Islamic Republic," convinced most observers that the subcontinent was in for a period of esclating, communally inspired confrontation. Understandably enough, India's Prime Minister Indira Gandhi quickly enlarged Border Security Forces around Bangladesh, attempting to seal the border against a mass exodus of Bangladesh refugees such as entered India during the liberation war.

When communications between India and Bangladesh were re-established on August 18 the new government quickly dispelled New Delhi's worst fears. The Foreign Ministry informed New Delhi that the name of the country had not been changed, and President Mushtaque Ahmed stated in an official note to the Indian Deputy High Commissioner in Dacca (communicated to New Delhi by telephone) that Bangladesh would "honor all bilateral agreements and obligations," presumably including a 25-year Treaty of Friendship signed by Mujib and Mrs. Gandhi in 1972. India's Foreign Secretary, Mr. Kewal Singh, then called on the Bangladesh High Commissioner in New Delhi, expressing his wish for "success and prosperity to the people of Bangladesh." Twelve days after the coup India became the 39th nation to recognize the new regime. (India has been criticized for delaying recognition of the new government for several days after most other major nations—including the United States, Japan, Iran, and the Soviet Union—had done so).

One of the coup's many ironies was that it occurred on India's Independence Day. The decision to move on the morning of August 15 is thought to be less symbolic than practical, although some must have derived a special pleasure from the coincidence. The coup leaders were more concerned with the presence in Dacca of most of Mujib's relatives and close associates and the scheduled speech by Mujib at Dacca University. They used the pretext that Dacca University students might cause trouble to station their forces outside the cantonment on the morning of the coup.

The coup was especially regrettable for Indians, who feel they have already invested so much in the future of Bangladesh. Indian soldiers in particular believe they contributed decisively toward liberating Bangladesh from Pakistan less than four years ago. Bangladesh army officers, however, insist they could have liberated the country without India's help and Mushtaque Ahmed in 1971 had opposed Awami League plans to liberate Bangladesh with the assistance of Indian troops.[1] He argued then and afterward that

1. In 1971, when Mushtaque explored the alternative of reconciliation with Pakistan through United States mediation, he earned Mrs. Gandhi's dis-

India's active involvement would result later in unrestrainable influence in Bangladesh affairs. In addition, most people in Bangladesh have long felt a vague but deep distrust of India. Mujib seemed to show no sensitivity to this anti-Indian sentiment, which Mushtaque can be expected to capitalize upon. In short, the coup leaders' clear bias against India is testimony to the failure to resolve these tensions in Indo-Bangladesh relations, particularly in the military, over the three and one-half year period of Sheikh Mujibur Rahman's government.

Mushtaque can also be expected to gain some support because of his constant opposition to Mujib's BAKSHAL scheme, which was openly championed by both India and the Soviet Union. In a secret poll of Awami League MPs, conducted by Mujib a week before his death, only 117 of 315 supported the BAKSHAL scheme. These dissenters can be expected to rally around Mushtaque Ahmed. Since the most ardent supporters of BAKSHAL have either been killed or imprisoned, or have reversed their stands, Awami League opposition to Mushtaque Ahmed is expected to be containable, so long as it is not supported by India.

Sorting out relationships with India will surely be the major task of the new government for as long as it lasts. If only because a desperately poor Bangladesh is surrounded on three sides by a much more affluent India, Bangladesh cannot escape the need for economic cooperation with its gaint neighbor. India must in turn take an interest in the communal and political tensions in Bangladesh, since they invariably affect India's domestic politics, the most extreme case of this being the 1971 exodus of 9.7 million Bangladesh refugees into West Bengal and India's northeastern states.

Ideally, India and Bangladesh would both benefit from cooperative agreements; their economies are complementary in many respects, and international development funds for transnational projects such as dams and flood control schemes would go a long

---

trust and the disapproval of his fellow ministers in the Bangladesh government-in-exile. As a result, he was not included in the Bangladesh delegation that went to the United Nations in 1971 at India's invitation. He was also barred from travelling to the United States later the same year, even though he was the government-in-exile's Foreign Minister. When Mujib returned from a Pakistan prison in January 1972 Mushtaque was relieved of his portfolio and his political position deteriorated steadily thereafter.

way toward alleviating the desperate poverty of this portion of the subcontinent. While Mujibur Rahman escalated the rhetoric for such close and friendly ties between Bangladesh and India to romantic heights, he lacked the vision and political control, even over his own relatives, necessary for promoting true cooperation.

Bangladesh and India would have had difficulties in establishing cooperative relationship after 1971 even without Mujib's hamhandedness. The rising prices of both manufactured goods and agricultural commodities in India after the liberation were bound to cause inflation in Bangladesh. To retard the inflation, Mujib banned all private trade between India and Bangladesh. At the same time, however, he allowed his relatives to engage in private trade with his unofficial blessings As the hypocrisy of his position became the primary subject of scandal in Bangladesh, and as the economy deteriorated for a host of other reasons, it was understandable that the people of Bangladesh would blame both Mujib and India for what was happening By mid–1975, shortly after the coup, a number of Bengalis who had previously advocated close ties with New Delhi began to argue, in the words of a Dacca University professor, that "We would prefer the old arrangement with Pakistan to this arrangement with India."

No one expects Bangladesh to return to its old relationship with Pakistan. Bengali nationalist sentiment is too strong for that; it is also too strong to tolerate a high level of Indian influence in Bangladesh affairs. Accordingly, the new government seeks to avoid confrontation with India, preferring "realistic ties, based on mutual respect for one another's interests." In practice, Bangladesh may attempt to move closer to Pakistan in terms of economic relations and perhaps for military training. It may look for closer trade and cultural links with China, which has already recognized the new government. It may pay greater attention to suggestions by Western nations with regard to aid and relief programs, and simultaneously cultivate closer ties with the Islamic nations of the Persian Gulf and Middle East. The large-scale presence of both the Soviet Union and India in Bangladesh may well be reduced, and Soviet recommendations for the domestic economic and political systems will receive less attention. In the words of a leading official in the Ministry of External Affairs, "We are not asking the Soviets and Indians to pack up and leave, but we are hoping to establish a more balanced foreign policy by moving closer to those nations outside the Soviet sphere of influence."

Mrs. Gandhi's response is difficult to gauge. Her belated recognition of Bangladesh and her tolerance for the Communist Party of India'e (CPI) public diatribes that attribute responsibility for the Bangladesh coup to the CIA (almost every other public statement about the coup has been banned in India), would indicate a mood of confrontation. Many Indian leaders worry that past animosities between Mrs. Gandhi and Mushtaque Ahmed will prevent the two from having cordial relations, and Mrs. Gandhi has made it known that she seriously disapproved the assassination of Mujibur Rahman and his family. Granted her recent penchant for intervention in the Indian states and neighboring territories, one might expect the Indian Prime Minister to seek a degree of control in Dacca that could lead to a serious and senseless clash.

For the time being, however, Mrs. Gandhi has maintained a studied silence. While she has allowed the CPI to brand Mushtaque "a lackey of America," she herself has made no charges about CIA involvement in the coup. Considering the severity of her own domestic problems, most observers argue that she would be well-advised to lessen her involvement with Bangladesh. Others maintain, however, that diminished Indian influence in Bangladesh would be intolerable in the event the new regime in Dacca unravels.

BANGLADESH FACTIONALISM

To say that the present regime is perhaps the strongest that could be put together without Mujib is not to discount the possibility that it could become unravelled. Bangladesh's economic problems are legendary, as are the factional splits in politics, the military, and the bureaucracy. It is almost unnecessary to mention that the population juggernaut rolls on.

The new government has made bureaucratic changes, in addition to the military reorganization described previously, designed to diminish factionalism. While most have been popular, they have by no means created a unified and efficient administrative structure, nor could they be expected to. Bangladesh will inevitably be plagued by a disorderly political process for some time, regardless of the government, if only because of the intense competition for scarce resources.

Personnel changes were first on the new government's list of priorities. It arrested A.T.M. Syed Hossain, Mujib's brother-in-law, who had played such a prominent role in the hiring, firing, and promotion of personnel during the previous three years, and replaced Gazi Gholam Mustafa, Chairman of the Bangladesh Red Cross, with B.A. Siddiqui. Mustafa had been Chairman of the Dacca city Awami League since 1949, when the party was founded, and has used the position to control vice and crime rackets in Dacca, from which he derived a substantial income. When Mujib appointed Mustafa head of the Bangladesh Red Cross after the liberation, he used the new position to build his own chain of drugstores, a private army of thugs, and an expanded underworld network. Red Cross officials and some of Mujib's associates objected to Mustafa's behavior, but Mujib argued that he could not "abandon" him for he had sustained Mujib's family during the many years he languished in jail in Pakistan. At least one of the coup leaders—ex-major Dalim—had acquired his motive for participating in the coup when, in the early summer of 1974, Mustafa had publicly insulted Dalim's wife after Dalim had tried to expose Mustafa's underground activities, and Mujib has dismissed Dalim from military service for his zeal.

Mr. B.A. Siddiqui is a former Chief Justice of the High Court. He had become identified with Pakistan in March 1971 when he administered the oath of office to the much-hated General Tikka Khan (Tikka Khan served as Governor of Bengal during the last months of Pakistan rule). Mujib dismissed Siddiqui after the liberation of Bangladesh, even though Siddiqui was generally considered to be a man of ability and integrity.

A number of other men and women who had been similarly identified with Pakistan have been brought back from retirement by the new government. One of the most prominent is Mr. S.M. Shafiul Azam, who served Pakistan as Chief Secretary in East Bengal throughout 1971. Two weeks after the coup, Shafiul Azam was appointed Secretary of the Cabinet Division of the new ministry, a position that should enable him to play a major role in the reorganization of the bureaucracy. The new government is clearly determined to resurrect a number of such capable administrators. In addition, many repatriate bureaucrats (i.e., those who had been detained in Pakistan for more than a year after liberation) have been restored to favor, and many of them have now secured jobs. Perhaps more important, in an effort to restore considerations of merit in administrative appointments, the government has established a seven-member committee under Shafiul Azam to name top-level bureaucrats.

A week after the coup the government arrested 26 of Mujib's political cronies and relatives on charges of corruption. Among the 26 were Syed Nazrul Islam, Mujib's Vice-President, and former Ministers A.H.M. Kamaruzzaman, Abdus Samad Azad, Sheikh Abdul Aziz, Tajuddin Ahmed, Korban Ali, and Mansoor Ali, Mujib's Prime Minister, who was originally reported in the Western press as being among those assassinated on the morning of the coup. Also arrested were a businessman, Abidur Rahman, and a Member of Parliament, Ashabula Huq, known to be close to Mushtaque—and one of Mushtaque's relatives, Nurudin Ahmed. Special martial law courts have been established to try the 26 and others accused of corruption. Bank accounts have been frozen and penalties ranging from ten years in prison to death have been prescribed if they are convicted.

The new cabinet is considered to be fairly representative of diverse interests and remarkably well balanced between supporters and detractors of Mujib's regime. Included within the new 21–man cabinet are four members of Mujib's 15–man BAKSHAL executive committee (the other 11 have either been killed or arrested) and a number of other Mujib supporters known to have been dissatisfied with the coup. Also included are two Hindus (Hindus account for at least 10 per cent of the population of Bangladesh), at least two men that are generally considered to be pro-India, and two more that are said to be pro-Russian, as well as three repatriates from Pakistan and a number of people thought to be pro-West. Finally, some of the cabinet appointments are felt to be based on merit rather than pure political considerations. Interestingly, the military is not represented, the theory being that the (now considerable) influence of the military should be channeled directly to President Mushtaque Ahmed through General Osmany, his military adviser.

The new cabinet's composition is consistent with the government's intention to scrap the BAKSHAL idea and the 61–district scheme and restore the constitution of 1971. While no mention has yet been made of such things as the restoration of electoral democracy and parliament, the new martial law regime has said that it will restore the position of the courts and has issued proclamations allowing for judical activities abolished during Mujib's last year in office. All political parties have temporarily been banned. The new government has also rescinded Presidential Order Number 9, which permitted Mujib to dismiss any civil servant without giving reason, and it has restored two nationalized newspapers (*Ittefaque* and *Sangbad*) to their original owners. The government has also released a number of political prisoners, including some from pro-Peking political parties, and has asked Enayetullah Khan, the pro-Peking editor of *Holiday*, who had been jailed by Mujib, to become editor of the government-owned *Bangladesh Times*.

Problems do remain. A number of potentially important leaders are resisting commitment to the new regime. Among the first to give his blessings to the new order was Maulana Bhashani, the 93–year old leader of the pro-Peking faction of the National Awami Party (NAP), who had wavered between cool support for Mujib and opposition. The leaders of the pro-Soviet faction of NAP and the pro-Soviet Communist Party of Bangladesh, on the other hand, have declared their opposition to the new government and they are reportedly trying to build peasant armies in the countryside. Some of Mujib's most ardent supporters, thought to be relatively few in number, are vowing revenge and attempting to rally support in the countryside behind the private armies of Sheikh Moni, Gazi Gholam Mustafa, Abu Hasnat, Qadr ("Tiger") Siddiqui, and other previously powerful BAKSHAL leaders. On the other side of the political fence, members of the Sharbahara party are trying to find and kill Mujib's staunchest supporters, seeking to avenge the death of their leader (Siraj Sikdar), allegedly killed by Mujib's party people in early 1975. This does not necessarily mean that the Sharbahara party is supporting the present government, but it does indicate the way in which small factional groups like Sharbahara have attempted to take advantage of the change of governments in Dacca to settle old scores.

There are a number of other political groups in Bangladesh that have gone into opposition to the new government, in most cases because of differences over ideology or personal leadership, These include the Bengal Communist Party (Leninist). a pro-Peking faction that recently split from Bhashani's NAP; the Jatiyo Samajtantrik Dal (National Socialist Party or JSD), which is extremely popular among Bangladesh students; the East Pakistan Communist Party of Abdul Huque, which wants reunification with Pakistan; the Bangladesh Communist Party of Mohammed Toaha; and the Bangladesh Communist Party (Marxist-Leninist) of Matin and Alauddin. None of these small groups, many of them Trotskyite and nihilist-terrorist, are given much chance of accumulating a strong enough following to challenge the present government, but their internecine warfare could cause considerable turbulence, particularly on the campuses and in the countryside.

Granted the extreme factionalism in Bangladesh and the weakness of institutionalized authority, such as the military or the bureaucracy, Mushtaque Ahmed has set as one of his first goals the elimination of arms in the hands of both private armies and individuals in the countryside. Observers have often argued that Mujib made a major mistake in not devoting more attention to this problem, the explanation for neglect usually being that Mujib wanted his own poliitcal party supporters to have arms. The new regime will give the Bangladesh army a monopoly of arms. Whether the policy can be implemented is open to doubt, particularly when one considers the cost of such a domestic military operation in a country where the army is already underfed and ill-housed, lacking either training or equipment appropriate to the task.

Similarly, the post-coup government has pledged itself to eliminate corruption in the bureaucracy and the army. It is recommending a simplified bureaucratic structure that systematically rewards efficiency and loyalty. Although these policies have been announced without the hooplah usually associated with South Asian political processes, and while the government still seems sincere in its intentions, the obstacles cannot be overstated. In a society as deprived of resources and managerial talent as Bangladesh is, the temptation for a bureaucrat or military officer to promote personal or family interests at the expense of society is usually overwhelming. Moreover, modes of corruption are already well established and based on social forces that seem stronger than the will to overcome them. The arrest and conviction of people engaging in blatant corruption will most certainly be commonplace in Bangladesh. The difficulty in getting beyond that stage, which still is seen as politically inspired tokenism, will come when action must be taken against government supporters in cases that are less clear cut. In

Bangladesh, as elsewhere, drawing a sharp line between what is and is not corrupt is nearly impossible. Where is the line to be drawn? Harshness can offend supporters and bring down the government as surely as laxity in pursuing corruption can destroy credibility. This problem, familiar in Bengal and Asia, becomes the more intense when machinery for implementation is as lacking as it is in Bangladesh, and when the economy is as badly off as this one surely is.

Estimates of the present government's viability vary. Because of the overwhelming number of forces working against it, most observers are convinced it will be lucky to survive a year. It might succeed *if* the army can remain united and support itself without draining the treasury; *if* both India and Pakistan will cooperate with the new regime; *if* international assistance is forthcoming and can be used in a more constructive manner than in the past; *if* factionalism can be contained. Perhaps the major positive factor favoring the present government is that most informed people in Bangladesh feel that its downfall could well bring chaos. In addition, there are prospects for a good rice crop (perhaps the best since liberation) and a leveling off of the rate of inflation, the last a delayed effect of international and domestic monetary policies and the promise of a good harvest.

Still, it is an atmosphere in which many people ask the question "What next?" A Dacca University student predicted a series of coups and countercoups like those in Vietnam after the fall of Diem; a college professor at Chittagong University suggested that Indian intervention, in response to disorder, was inevitable; an international development expert suggested that things will go on for the next three years in much the same way as they have in the past, with the government gradually losing its popularity, becoming more factionalized, and eventually being overthrown in another violent coup. Perhaps the most that one can say is that any and all of these scenarios are possible. Bangladesh politics remain unpredictable.

PART II

INDO-BANGLADESH
            RELATIONS

Nothing is more important to Bangladesh than its relationships
with India. While this is widely realized in Bangladesh, it is less
well-realized in India. Indians also tend to neglect the importance
of Bangladesh to the Indian economy and polity. The essays in
this second section, written in 1972 and 1975, detail the contributions of India to the Bangladesh liberation struggle and seek to
provide a balanced perspective on the many conflicts of interest
that have developed since 1971. Further discussion of some of the
issues introduced here, plus discussion of more recent issues in
Indo-Bangladesh relations, are contained in Parts III and IV.

FOUR

THE WAR, THE REFUGEES, AND THE INDIAN ECONOMY (1972)

Prime Minister Indira Gandhi of India seems to delight in confounding the experts. In late 1969 Mrs. Gandhi presided over a split in the ruling Congress party of India, despite admonitions from most political pundits that such a division of Congress would irrevocably divide the nation. After the split in 1969 Mrs. Gandhi constructed a series of precarious temporary national coalitions that kept her in office until March 1971, when she proceeded to secure an overwhelming majority (43 per cent of the popular vote and 350 of 518 seats) in the *Lok Sabha*, the lower house of the Indian Parliament. Later in 1971 her New Congress government waged a successful war against Pakistan in support of the Bangladesh independence movement, in the face of diplomatic opposition from both China and the United States and a lack of international support from almost every other nation except the Soviet Union and the Eastern bloc countries. Little wonder that when I arrived in New Delhi in December 1971, I was greeted by a series of billboards and posters expressing the kind of praise and admiration for Indira Gandhi that I was to hear from almost everyone I spoke with in the next few weeks. Representative of the message conveyed to me was one sign in Connaught Circus (the commercial hub of New Delhi), which read: "Her Father Had Glimpses of History. But SHE MAKES HISTORY."[1]

With national morale as high as it has ever been, Indira Gandhi's government now faces the challenge of making good its past accomplishments and delivering past promises. The New Congress fought the elections in 1971 on the basis of the slogan "*garibi hatao*" (eliminate poverty), and there were widespread expectations

---

1. The reference is to the book *Glimpses of World History*, written by Jawaharlal Nehru [Indira Gandhi's father], (New York: John Day, 1942).

immediately after the 1971 elections that new economic initiatives would lead to greater prosperity for almost all social classes in India. One of the most distinctive features of Indian politics in 1971 was the inability or unwillingness of Mrs. Gandhi to use her massive electoral victory for dramatic new advances in the economic sphere. As Professor David Bayley has pointed out, "New programs of economic development were not announced; the 1971-72 budget was a copy of the previous year's; and Cabinet changes were minor. The vast parliamentary majority of Mrs. Gandhi was mobilized in 1971 on only three measures. These were the constitutional amendments, and they were neither ideologically radical nor did they place new demands on the country."[2]

A lack of programmatic economic initiative in 1971 can be explained in several different ways. First, one could argue that the influx of almost ten million refugees into India, when coupled with the diplomatic international and domestic maneuvering that eventually led to war, was sufficient to divert attention from matters of economic development and social reform. Second, it is possible that Mrs. Gandhi was surprised at the extent of her election victory (although she has never admitted this), and she may have therefore been without new programs to implement, or the kinds of advisers who could generate them. Finally, Mrs. Gandhi's electoral victory in 1971 gave her an overwhelming majority in the national Parliament, but her political position in the states cannot be consolidated until state elections are held later this year. Her supporters now argue that it was politically wise to postpone economic and social reforms until the New Congress has secured its position in the state legislatures, and Mrs. Gandhi has already announced that her budget for next year will not be presented until the middle of March 1972 (a month later than usual and two weeks after the scheduled date of the state elections).

Whatever the explanation for India's economic policies in 1971, it is clear that 1972 will bring an unprecedented strain to the Indian economy. The 1971-72 budget, for example, originally called for a deficit of Rs. 227 crores (one crore equals ten million rupees which are currently being converted at the rate of Rs. 7.35=US$ 1.00), but by December 1971—midway through the budget year—

2. Quoted from a paper by David H. Bayley, "India: War and Political Assertion," *Asian Survey*, (January–February 1972).

the Indian government was estimating that this deficit would climb to more than Rs. 700 crores. Most observers now argue that even these projected figures are optimistic. For example, the 700 crore deficit that was announced in December projected a cost of Rs. 418.8 crores for eight million refugees for six months, but actual expenditures for 1971–72 will be more than this, if only because the bulk of the refugees will have stayed longer than six months and their numbers by December 1971 were already approaching ten million. Moreover, revised defense outlays in 1971–72 were put at Rs. 1,079 crores (almost a third of the total budget), but the defense bill is admittedly higher than this (in January) and is still climbing.

To cope with budgetary deficit the Indian government has cut nonplan expenditures by 5 per cent, enacted various emergency excise levies, established an income surtax on all companies, and increased import duties on some items. All of these measures taken together are expected to raise a mere Rs. 110 crores in the current fiscal year. In the absence of new sources of revenue, budgetary deficits will have to be met by printing more money, which will automatically levy a uniform and regressive tax on the entire Indian population through inflation, thus intensifying the poverty that Mrs. Gandhi is determined to alleviate. To quote Professor Bayley again, "the primary economic puzzle is why the Indian government has not moved more vigorously to mobilize additional revenue in order to reduce the deficit and dampen inflation. Mrs Gandhi came to power committed to a radical policy of reducing disparities in income and eliminating poverty, [and the Bangladesh crisis] represented an opportunity to udertake distasteful programs and cloak them in an appeal to patriotism. The failure to find an opportunity in crisis reinforces the impression that Mrs. Gandhi's government either lacks a coherent economic blueprint or is biding time until after next year's state elections."[3]

THE COSTS OF THE WAR AND THE REFUGEES

Even more astonishing than the present budgetary deficit, which would be sufficient to bring about severe economic hardship, is the way in which Mrs. Gandhi has eagerly taken on enormous new tasks. Having won a war with Pakistan to bring about an inde-

3. Ibid.

pendent Bangladesh, the Indian government is determined that it will find a way to return the bulk of the refugees to Bangladesh, rather than pay the higher price of rehabilitating the refugees within India. This means that India must play a large role in the reconstruction of the Bangladesh economy, if only to prevent future refugee movements of the same magnitude. Because of heightened international bitterness and animosity on the subcontinent, between India and Pakistan on the one hand and India and China on the other, Indian leaders are convinced that they must quickly re-equip their armed forces and fill strategic gaps in defense capabilities to protect India's western flank and northern borders. Finally, the unreliability of American aid programs, particularly as they were implemented in South Asia in 1971, has led Indian policy makers to a search for greater-self sufficiency.

In what has now come to be characteristic of her political style, Mrs. Gandhi has blithely asserted that India can return the bulk of the refugees, assist in the reconstruction of Bangladesh, regear the Indian armed forces, and lessen India's dependence on foreign aid but she has not announced any systematic new policies that would make it possible for the Indian economy to carry out these tasks. Her own public statements have thus far been vague and seemingly over-optimistic, reminiscent of her public rhetoric during the period preceding the split in the Congress, the 1971 elections, and the Indo-Pakistan war. Indeed, if it were not for her resounding success in coping with these three crises during the past three years, one would be inclined to discount her ability to deal with the economic problems that now loom on the horizon.

The magnitude of the burden that will be placed on India if it is to carry out the new tasks that Mrs. Gandhi has set is difficult to calculate, but the extent of the burden can hardly be overstated. A Mid-Term Appraisal of the Fourth Five-Year Plan (1969–1974) by the Planning Commission, completed in late 1971, has now been hopelessly overtaken by events, with the result that a second Mid-Term Appraisal is under way. Some idea of the costs of rehabilitation, reconstruction, rearmament, and self-sufficiency can be gleaned from the figures that already exist in the first Mid-Term Appraisal, but only if they are tempered with a judicious dose of tolerance for the margins.

In the Planning Commission's first Mid-Term Appraisal, an estimated additional Rs. 190 crores will be needed over the course of the next two years to move the refugees presently in India to Bangladesh, but this figure was apparently based on a much smaller number of refugees than there actually are, and it also assumes foreign assistance of Rs 70 crores per year. If Mrs. Gandhi is to carry out her pledge to rehabilitate the refugees with minimal foreign assistance, the aid figure given by the Planning Commission will have to be revised downward. Moreover, the total cost of rehabilitating the refugees is likely to be much higher than anticipated by the Commission, because Parliament has already had to pass a supplementary demand for Rs. 100 crores to cover the cost of the maintenance and rehabilitation of the refugees for only the month of January 1972.

The recent statement by the Bangladesh government in Dacca, that the "return, resettlement and rehabilitation of the refugees will begin in a big way on New Year's Day and will be completed within two months," is considered by almost everyone in Delhi to be wildly optimistic. It is generally agreed here that conditions in Dacca are fast returning to normal, and that most of the refugees seem anxious to return to their homes as quickly as possible. But the massive problems associated with repatriation are obvious. Transport facilities are likely to be the major hurdle to quick repatriation, since they are already scarce in the eastern region as a result of the many demands being made on them. In addition to the movement of refugees into Bangladesh, India has threatened to bring more than 100,000 Pakistani prisoners of war to India, and has promised to transport food, clothing, and other items of daily use to the war-ravaged districts of East Bengal. Moreover, the Indian government has decided to give returning refugees cash grants to help tide them over the initial period of their return to Bangladesh, and has also promised refugee centers in Bangladesh for those whose homes were destroyed. Under these circumstances, most observers argue that the cost of rehabilitation should be more realistically estimated at Rs. 600 crores at a minimum, with figures ranging upward to Rs. 2,000 crores or more.

Reconstruction within Bangladesh, to which India has also committed itself, will be at least as expensive as the rehabilitation of the refugees. The major items that will have to be provided are food grain imports (estimated by the government of Bangladesh at Rs. 300–400 crores) and repair costs for industrial, transportation, and government installations (estimated at Rs.

300–500 crores). None of these costs was included in the Mid-Term Appraisal of the Planning Commission, since that appraisal was conducted prior to the war with Pakistan, but reconstruction estimates will now have to be included in the second Mid-Term Appraisal. Given the low capacity for absorption of foreign assistance in Bangladesh, the Indian government might be wise to plan for minimal expenditures spaced over a considerable period of time, but nonetheless one can reasonably speak of a minimum of Rs. 600 crores and a maximum of Rs. 2,000 crores being spent on reconstruction in Bangladesh over the next two years. In a recent statement in Dacca, Bangladesh Prime Minister Tajuddin Ahmad estimated the total cost of both rehabilitation and reconstruction at Rs. 2, 000 crores.

When constrasted with the enormous resources needed for rehabilitation and reconstruction, anticipated expenditures on defense and self-sufficiency seem like minor budget items. The defense establishment in India has estimated that the additional defense burden in the next two years will be in the neighoorhood of Rs. 300 crores, but the Indian Defense Ministry (like its counterparts elsewhere) has a habit of escalating defense costs with each passing year. Moreover, there is already heightened discussion here about the possibility of India developing nuclear weapons in light of changing international circumstances in South Asia. Aid cuts (in pursuit of self-sufficiency) could go as high as Rs. 300–400 crores between now and 1973–74. Here again, the first Mid-Term Appraisal of the Planning Commission does not take into account either added defense expenditures or aid cuts.

Given only those costs listed above, one can forecast a need for unplanned resources totaling anywhere from Rs. 1,800 crores at a minimum to Rs. 4,700 crores at a maximum for the coming two year period, if India is to fully carry out the tasks that Indira Gandhi has set for the nation. This would mean that India would have to increase its revenues by a minimum of 25 per cent and 67 per cent maximum for each of the next two years, a feat which (to my knowledge) is unprecedented in the history of the world. That a nation like India, which already has a large budgetary deficit and a faltering economy, could come even close to performing the tasks set for it by Mrs. Gandhi seems unthinkable.

And yet, Mrs. Gandhi has made a number of speeches and statements like the following (quoted from a New Year's Day address to the nation):

> We are capable of meeting all of the needs of Bangladesh without asking anybody for help. If our industrialists, labourers, workmen, Government employees, dock workers and factory owners decide to meet the rising expectations of the nation, it is not a difficult task. If we decide to stand united and discipline ourselves the way we did during the 14 days of war, nothing is impossible for this nation. If we have this spirit for two years India can become self-sufficient.

To a certain extent, of course, Mrs. Gandhi's speeches can be dismissed as campaign rhetoric in an election year. In part they are exhortations of a leader who is trying to maintain a level of national mobilization associated with a crisis period. But past experience should teach us that the lady Prime Minister is not given to bluster. Assuming that she does intend to strive for the goals she has articulated, we might be well-advised to search for possible means by which the economy of India could be transformed. In the event that she does take drastic action, either before or after the state elections this year, we might then be better prepared to analyze the significance of such action.

THE PRESENT ECONOMY

Paradoxically, the one dominant stabilizing factor in the Indian economy at present is the bountiful food grain crop resulting from the new technology in agriculture. During the past four years, production of food grains has risen steadily each year, with output in 1970–71 totaling 107.8 million tons, an increase of 8.4 per cent over the previous year. During the current fiscal period (1971–72) the Ministry of Agriculture estimates that food grains production will rise to 113 million tons or more, giving India an unprecedented eight million tons of food grain stocks. It may be that the disruptions caused by the war in the border districts, when coupled with a drought in the Deccan, floods in the eastern region, and the Orissa cyclone, will bring output figures down to 110 or 111 million tons for the current fiscal year, but even if this is the case, production totals will still show a sizable increase over last year's bumper harvest.

India is not completely self-sufficient in food grains yet, since its surplus is not at a level necessary to tide it over a series of bad monsoons, but barring unforeseen disruptions to agriculture in the next few years it may succeed. The average growth rate in agriculture over the past two years has been 5.2 per cent, comfortably ahead of the planned target of 5 per cent, and recent increases in rice production indicate that some of the initial problems encountered with the use of high-yielding rice varieties may have been overcome. A pessimist would argue that India has simply been fortunate in having a series of good monsoons during the past few years, and that breakthroughs in agricultural technology have not affected production of some crops (principally fibers, pulses, and oilseeds), but most Indian agriculturalists are no longer inclined to pessimism. In a nation that has lived so long on the margins of survival because of a poor food crop and a burgeoning population, the new technology in agriculture has been enthusiastically received. Indeed, Mrs. Gandhi now seems to feel that she can contribute significantly to feeding the refugees who are returning to Bangladesh, and perhaps even supply food grains to Bangladesh on a continuing basis over the next few years, even though India has not yet made striking progress in its attempts to limit population growth.

India's cash crop production has not demonstrated the dramatic breakthroughs that one finds in the case of food grains, but, nevertheless, India's position in major cash crops seems comfortable, Raw cotton output in the current fiscal year promises modest improvements, with imports insuring more than adequate supplies. Oilseeds production has declined, but there is a large carry-over stock from previous years, and imports of oilseeds seem to be plentiful. Some idea of the difference between India's food grains and cash crop positions is indicated by the fact that the government of India has found it possible to stop wheat and rice imports under Public Law 480 agreements with the United States, but will still be relying on Public Law 480 concessional imports for both cotton and oilseeds during the next few years (at least to the extent that these are already in the pipeline). Domestic supplies of raw jute, tea, and sugar cane —all in plentiful supply already—are expected to receive an additional boost from increased trade with Bangladesh.

The problem area of the Indian economy at present is the

public and private industrial sector. From a rate of growth of 6.8 per cent in 1969–70, industrial production fell to 3.6 per cent in 1970–71, and to a miserable 1.5 per cent in the first half of 1971–72. The demands of increased military spending and the refugee influx, when coupled with lagging industrial production, have caused a sharp rise in prices for industrial products, which has only been partially offset by the maintenance of rather steady prices for food grains. To say that the government is disappointed in industrial production would be an understatement. Some slight improvement in industrial growth is forecast for the second half of the current fiscal year, but overall production increases for 1971–72 will most likely be on the order of 2 per cent. In light of the miserable showing of the industrial sector over the past two years, the Planning Commission has now abandoned hopes of achieving an anticipated industrial growth rate of 9.3 per cent for the Fourth Plan period (1969–1974).

Most frustrating for Indian planners and economists is their inability to identify precisely what is wrong with industry. Some government officials and politicians have argued that industrial production has actually grown much faster than the figures would lead one to believe, since the present industrial growth index gives undue weightage to older industries (like textiles) which have performed badly. According to this argument, most of the industrial growth during the past few years has been in newer industries and the small-scale sector, neither of which are adequately reflected in the computation of central statistics. But even if this is the case (and there is considerable debate about it among experts), it is at least clear that the older and most significant industries have grown at a shockingly low rate during the past few years. Again, more will be known about this aspect of the economy when the Planning Commission has completed its industry-by-industry studies, now under way.

On the balance of payments front, India's position during the past year has been relatively stable, but setbacks to exports as a result of the war, when coupled with a likelihood of stepped-up imports and uncertain foreign aid outlook, are expected to cause difficulties during the next few years. The Planning Commission forecasts that in the last two years of the Fourth Plan (1972–1974) foreign exchange requirements (i.e., imports, errors and omissions, and debt servicing charges) will add up to Rs. 5,700 crores.

During this same period exports are projected at Rs. 3,667 crores, with the balance being financed by international aid and credits. Suspension of aid by the United States, Belgium, and Japan during the war (Japan has since resumed its aid commitments) has thus far not been felt in the economy, largely because there is considerable aid in the pipeline and India was able to divert free foreign exchange resources to meet current requirements. However, if suspension of aid by the United States continues, the foreign exchange budget will have to be substantially revamped, since American aid now provides more than Rs. 200 crores per year toward the foreign exchange deficit.

Mrs. Gandhi has consistently argued since the war that India is now going to be much more discriminating when accepting foreign assistance for development purposes, with a view toward greater self-reliance. When asked at a press conference in January whether this meant that she would reject any offer by America to resume aid, Mrs. Gandhi paused for a noticeable period of time and then said that India's attitude would depend on "the main features of such a proposal." In her public statements, Mrs. Gandhi has expressed concern about the psychology of dependence that foreign aid encourages, and she has also been highly critical of the tendency on the part of some developed nations (particularly the United States) to use aid as an instrument of coercion in times of crisis. What clearly is evolving is an Indian policy of greater selectivity in acceptance of foreign aid, with multilateral assistance being preferable to bilateral, and greater receptivity being given to programs that cannot be used as political weapons. The obvious complement of this policy will be reductions in absolute levels of aid.

While India's foreign exchange problems continue to plague the economy, it is encouraging to note that the extent of India's dependence on foreign assistance has dwindled considerably. At one point in the mid-1960s foreign aid as a percentage of net domestic product was in excess of 8 per cent, but the same figure now is something like 1.3 per cent and is expected (by the Planning Commission) to decline to .9 per cent by 1973–74. The strains and tensions that would result from a continued suspension of American aid could be alleviated by resorting to a number of different measures. India can draw on foreign exchange reserves (Rs. 800 crores), or it could get credit from the International Monetary Fund (at present it has no outstanding IMF obligations).

If it chooses, India might also draw on the vast committed but unutilized assistance promised by the Soviet Union and Eastern Europe. Finally, of course, India can lessen its dependence on foreign aid if it is able to increase domestic savings, promote exports, or diminish imports, and in the long run, a balance between population growth and the growth of the domestic economy will be essential if India is to achieve self-sufficiency.

Problems of Resource Mobilization

Given the necessity to find untapped resources rather quickly, and given the determination of India's national leadership to accomplish the tasks that Mrs. Gandhi has set, one can expect significant economic changes in India during the course of the next few years. While it would be impossible to predict with certainty the exact nature of the economic policies that will eventually emerge from the Ministries in New Delhi, and barring the possibility that Mrs. Gandhi will choose to deal with economic crises in ways that have not been discussed thus far, it is possible to indicate those proposals that are being seriously advanced at present. Some of these proposals seem to be in the early stages of implementation already, others are widely anticipated in some form after the state elections are held in March (on the assumption that Mrs. Gandhi's New Congress will be victorious). Still others are merely being discussed by highly placed government officials and economists. Needless to say, there are partisans on many different sides of most economic issues, and ultimate policy decisions will result from the interaction of a variety of different political forces.

In an effort to free private industry from what *The Statesman* (a New Delhi and Calcutta daily) has called "the jungle of red tape and the glorious confusion of the Government's industrial policy," the Indian government announced on January 1, 1972, that licensing policy for 54 major industries would be "liberalized." This action was taken on the advice of Planning Minister C. Subramaniam and the Minister for Industrial Development, Moinul Haque Choudhury, both of whom have been arguing for some time that government licensing provisions were in a large part responsible for an underutilization of industrial capacity. Underutilization was in turn held to be largely responsible for economic slowdowns in the industrial sector, and for an overdependence on foreign assistance. To take the most glaring example, a Planning Commission study of 168 chemical and fertilizer companies (completed in early 1971) indicated that most of these firms were producing far below capacity because of government licensing procedures, and yet India has been spending more than Rs. 100 crores to import products that could otherwise be manufactured by these 168 companies.

Government licensing policy prior to January 1, 1972, allowed limited expansion by firms to an additional 25 per cent of their licensed capacity, but the new "liberalization" policy that was announced will now permit firms in 54 industries to raise their production to twice their licensed capacity without a new license. While private business circles in India generally praised liberalization measures as "a step in the right direction," they were also critical of the unwillingness of the government to take more drastic action. Of special concern to the business community was the government reservation that "liberalization" would not apply automatically to larger industrial houses and foreign majority firms, both of which will now have to submit applications to the government before contemplating expansion. A second reservation of the new policy is a government proviso that firms using indigenous raw materials will be granted licensing concessions more readily than those requiring imports, a matter of concern to those industries that manufacture trucks, synthetic fibres and drugs, which require imported equipment, parts, and materials. Government spokesmen have defended these reservations as necessary to prevent the growth of monopolies and to control foreign exchange, but most businessmen argue that such reservations may ultimately defeat the purpose of the liberalization policy itself. An editorial in the *Times of India*, for example, argued that:

> Larger industrial houses and foreign-majority firms account for a big chunk of the existing capacity in the 54 listed industries, and unless foreign exchange is granted and applications are cleared quickly the new liberalization measures may not have a sizable impact on industrial output.

From the point of view of the new Congress government it is difficult to make concessions to private industry in an election year, particularly for a government that is trying to co-opt the appeal of a number of other left of center socialist parties. If only for this reason, most business circles are expecting true "liberalization" to be delayed at least until the election results are in, with some token concessions being granted in the interim.

Political considerations have also weakened central government efforts to pressure the states into raising more resources during the next few years. To a greater degree than is true for the central government, most state governments in India are highly dependent on a series of political patronage networks. State planning efforts, therefore, are frequently responses to political considerations that make little sense to resource-minded administrators. For example, the Planning Commission has for years tried to pressure the states to impose "betterment levies" on landowners who have benefited from the extension of irrigation and power facilities, but most state governments have been reluctant to impose such levies on powerful rural interests that keep them in office. Since the enactment of such levies is reserved for the states in the Constitution, the central government is powerless to act without the cooperation of state governments, with the result that a major source of potential government revenue is not being collected.

In the latest in a long series of maneuvers by the central government, the Planning Commission has recently (January 1972) tried to exert greater pressure on the states by announcing that central government assistance will be cut considerably in 1972–73, while state overdrafts on central government reserves will no longer be automatically honored by the Reserve Bank. These measures are designed to encourage the state governments to mobilize sufficient means to balance reduced central assistance and prevent habitual overdrafts, but in the event that the state governments fail to mobilize enough resources there is little that the central government can do. Should the New Congress government decide to penalize a powerful state for failing to mobilize resources, it will immediately risk the possibility of losing party support in that state, and in many instances stronger states have been willing to come to the support of weaker ones in defense of "state's rights" and "interests." In recent pronouncements the Planning Commission has made concessions to some of the larger and more powerful Indian states, effecting central assistance cuts of only 3 per cent for those that have habitually had overdrafts, and 5 per cent cuts for all others.

The kind of political problems that the central government will face should it attempt to implement a policy of central assistance cuts can be illustrated by the reactions to the recent Planning Commission policy by Uttar Pradesh Chief Minister, Kamalapathi Tripathi, one of Indira Gandhi's most prominent supporters in India's largest state, who took strong exception to the manner in which central benefit cuts were applied by the Planning Commission. Tripathi, who heads a state government that is scheduled to receive 5 per cent less in central assistance because it has not habitually submitted overdrafts to the Reserve Bank, has argued that the present policy of the Planning Commission "penalizes those states that have exercised greater financial discipline." At the time this is being written, Mr. Tripathi's case is reportedly being given "a sympathetic hearing" in the Planning Commission.

Problems revolving around center-state relations are also involved in the failure thus far to maximize efforts to attain self-sufficiency by taking advantage of the new technology in agriculture. To take one example, since domestic wheat is priced at almost Rs. 30 per quintal (100 kilograms) more than Public Law 480 wheat, many state governments have tried to reverse the decision to stop wheat imports from the United States, fearing the consequences of both higher wheat prices and higher state budget deficits. Similarly, state governments have argued for political reasons that their power and irrigation projects should proceed as rapidly as possible, even if this means that foreign material and equipment will have to be imported, while the Planning Commission has advised that states should reorient their Plan programs and design their projects on the basis of indigenous material and equipment, even though this might cause delayed completion of projects. Finally, the Planning Commission has been urging the states to impose an agricultural income tax on those farmers who have benefited from the green revolution, but here again the power to levy an agicultural income tax lies with the states, and state political leaders have been reluctant to impose such a tax on the powerful political forces at home.

In addition to proposals for liberalized licensing procedures and disciplined state planning programs, a number of other proposals designed to mobilize resources are being considered. Most of these are intended to decrease India's dependence on foreign assistance, either by eliminating such assistance or by increasing domestic production. The most radical of such proposals would have India either postpone or permanently cancel debt repayments, particularly to the United States, a course of action that is especially appealing to left-wing intellectuals and politicians. Thus far there is no indication that a drastic measure of this kind has been seriously contemplated by the government, and the consequences of such an action for India's international position would be so severe that it seems most unlikely it will be considered. However, as a result of President Nixon's support of Pakistan during the recent war, Indo-American relations have now deteriorated to the point where almost any anti-American act is likely to receive substantial support in India.

Less drastic proposals for mobilizing greater resources within India have to do with selective government policies toward particular industries, use of emergency powers to prevent work stoppages, and controls on the manufacture of luxury and nonessential consumer goods. Those industries that are most frequently singled out for special attention are steel, copper, and fertilizers, all three of which have thus far been heavily dependent on imports and American assistance. (The Planning Commission estimates that India is presently spending Rs. 130 crores a year on imported steel, Rs. 40 crores on imported copper, and Rs. 195 crores on fertilizer imports.) Representative of the kind of selective policies toward these industries that the government is likely to pursue are those articulated for the steel industry by Iron and Steel Controller, S.S. Sidhu, in a January address to the All-India Iron and Steel Stockholders Federation. In his address, Mr. Sidhu stated that it was the intention of the government to use the emergency powers to resolve labor-management disputes, and to "take stringent action against those indulging in malpractices," in order that steel production coud be boosted. Moreover, Mr. Sidhu warned the steel industry that sale of steel within India should be confined to "essential" products rather than luxury items. In Mr. Sidhu's words, "If there are no voluntary checks by the trade on dealings in steel materials, Government will have to consider inclusion of a punitive clause against collusion in the Essential Commodities Act."

The problems confronting India's copper industry differ considerably from those of steel, if only because the copper industry has not grown at the same pace as steel over the past 20 years. In the case of steel, the major dilemma is that existing plants are not producing anywhere near capacity, but in the case of copper India simply does not have a large number of mines and processing units.

Although India does have some of the largest proven reserves of copper ore in the world, the annual output of copper produced within India has remained at a level of 10,000 tons for the last ten years. At the beginning of the Third Five-Year Plan (1962–1967), Indian planners accepted the Khetri copper project, which is eventually expected to produce 31,000 tons of copper per year. With the cost of copper on the world market presently pegged at Rs. 9,000 per ton, India stands to save a considerable amount of foreign exchange (and perhaps gain foreign exchange through export of copper) when the Khetri project is completed. During the past ten years, however, the project has been delayed by a series of successive changes in the Five-Year Plans and is currently scheduled to go into production in late 1973. In light of the new need for resources and foreign exchange, there is considerable pressure on government planners to move more quickly on the Khetri project.

ECONOMIC COOPERATION WITH BANGLADESH

The proposals mentioned above are measures being contemplated by the Indian government to mobilize new resources within the existing economy, but at least equally significant in the eyes of government planners are the new growth possibilities that are expected to flow from the recent transformation of the northeastern region of the Indian subcontinent. Indian planners are convinced that the new Bangladesh will act as an economic bridge between the Indian heartland and the isolated states and territories of the northeast. Plans for the integrated development of the Ganga-Brahmaputra basin are already under way. To facilitate greater administrative cooperation between the various ethnic and tribal groups in the Northeast, India created (in January 1972) the new state of Meghalaya and two new Union territories (Mizoram and Arunachal), all three being concessions to separatist tribal movements. The Governor of Assam has since been assigned to the governorship of Meghalaya, Manipur, and Tripura, while Mizoram will be under a lieutenant governor and Arunachal Pradesh under a chief commissioner. For development purposes, all of the northeastern states and territories will be participating in a reorganized North-Eastern Development Council, which will attempt to coordinate the economic activities of northeastern India and Bangladesh.

The emergence of Bangladesh as an independent nation friendly to India holds out the prospect of ending the post-1947 isolation of the Indian northeast. During the period when Bangladesh was part of Pakistan, road, rail, and other communication networks between the Indian heartland and the Brahmaputra valley had to proceed through a narrow strip of Indian territory (the Siliguri corridor, sandwiched between Nepal and East Pakistan) that at one point was less than 14 miles wide. During this period the Indian northeast was wedged between a hostile East Pakistan to the south and west and a hostile China to the north, denied access to the sea, and only tenuously linked to central India by a few air flights and a very difficult and inhospitable terrain. With the emergence of Bangladesh, India is now contemplating increased facilities for transit by road, rail, inland waterways, and air between the northeastern region and itself. Moreover, both India and Bangladesh are projecting the rapid growth of Chittagong as a port city capable of serving this vast hinterland, and a wide variety of schemes for regional cooperation between Nepal, Bhutan, Sikkim, Bangladesh, and the Indian states and territories of north-eastern India are now being discussed. Obviously, if planned cooperation can be sustained, there are a number of possibilities for greater economic development in this region.

In the short run, the most promising possibility is an increase in Indo-Bangladesh trade, which could be advantageous to both countries. Bangladesh has few natural resources other than a very fertile soil, mighty rivers, and some natural gas, while India has abundant reserves of coal, iron, ore, copper, and other minerals that are being developed for international markets. If customs arrangements can be worked out, India hopes to import newsprint, fish, vegetables, cotton, and other agricultural products from Bangladesh, and in return place valuable orders for coal, textiles, and light machinery. In the case of jute and tea—the two principal cash crops of Bangladesh—the Indians and East Bengalis will be competitors for international markets, but if joint planning is successful the two might be able to coordinate efforts to mutual advantage.

Successful long-term development of the potential resources in the Northeast will depend on the ability of India to work out satisfactory agreements with Bhutan, Sikkim, Nepal, and Bangladesh for the exploitation of the untapped hydroelectric potential of the region. India is hoping that Bangladesh will not try to use its natural gas reserves to produce electrical power, but will instead try to develop methods by which natural gas could be used as a feed stock for fertilizer and petro-chemicals. If the Bengalis can be convinced of the economic wisdom of this, India could then supply both hydroelectric and thermal power to Bangladesh, in return for chemical fertiliizers and petro-chemicals both in short supply throughout the subcontinent).

Exploitation of the vast hydroelectric potential of northeastern India would entail a series of projects that boggle the imagination. The largest mountains in the world are located just north of Bangladesh, and the area that lies at the base of these mountains is a patchwork of extremely powerful rivers that flow out of the Himalayas and are enhanced by the monsoons. The need for flood control, flood and cyclone warning systems, irrigation, and power makes it almost mandatory that the people living in this region seek greater cooperation in large-scale river development schemes, but the political and administrative problems involved are at least as formidable as the technical challenge. To fully harness the rivers of the Ganga-Brahmaputra basin would require a number of scientific and engineering feats of the first magnitude. Dams and water storage facilities would have to be built in places that are virtually inaccessible at present, while unprecedented drainage, coastal embankment, and polderization programs would simultaneously have to be developed. In the meantime, political and administrative priorities would have to be worked out between three states (India, Nepal, and Bangladesh), two states that are internally sovereign but closely tied to India in foreign affairs (Sikkim and Bhutan), and at least ten states and territories within India (Bihar, West Bengal, Orissa, Assam, Arunachal, Nagaland, Manipur, Tripura, Meghalaya, and Mizoram).

In the 1960s India did launch one large-scale river control project that affected Bangladesh, this being the controversial Farraka project (a series of installations located at Farraka in West Bengal), designed to divert the Ganges in such a way as to flush out the silted port of Calcutta further downstream. In addition, India has initiated discussions with Nepal for giant water storage projects to be located on Nepal's Karnali and Sharda Rivers, and is presently exploring other multipurpose hydroelectric projects in Nepal and Bhutan. However, political problems run rampant when contemplating any of these projects, simply because people in different nations and states disagree about the location of sites, the manner in which water should be diverted, the directions that power lines and irrigation channels should take, and the way in which labour and administrative personnel should be recruited. India's experience with multipurpose development schemes that cut across state boundaries within India would indicate that considerable political maneuvering will have to take place before Development Authorities can be established to the satisfaction of such a variety of different peoples, nations, and states as exists in India's Northeast.

When viewed from this perspective, one can expect greater economic cooperation between India and Bangladesh, but the prospects for large-scale economic development programs in the Northeast are extremely long-range. India and Bangladesh may be able to achieve some short-term economic gains by increasing trade between them, but during the next few years any such gains will be more than canceled out by the need to repatriate the refugees and reconstruct the Bangladesh economy. Finally, if India and Bangladesh are to exploit the economic potential of the Northeast, both political and economic resources will be needed on an unprecedented scale, which makes India's new tasks seem more, rather than less, formidable.

THE CHALLENGE TO MRS. GANDHI

The economic challenges that will confront the government of India during the next few years will, therefore, be severe. The economic costs of the war and the refugees by themselves have created severe budgetary problems, and Mrs. Gandhi's determined desire that India should play the major role in reconstructing Bangladesh, while at the same time achieving self-sufficiency, is likely to cause unprecedented economic strains and tensions. In the final analysis Mrs. Gandhi will most likely have to back down somewhat from her most optimistic and grand assertions, but few observers that I have talked to in New Delhi are discounting the possibility that she may still be able to move India some considerable distance toward her objective.

The most critical recently published comment on the Indian

economy that I have seen appeared in the January 7 issue of the *Eastern Economist*, a Delhi weekly that is generally predisposed to private business interests. The editorial thrust on this issue of the *Eastern Economist* was that, while Mrs. Gandhi had proved her political abilities, and had demonstrated her skillfulness in diplomacy and war, "it still remains to be shown that her intellectual processes are realistic and positive where her management of the nation's economic affairs are concerned." The advice of the *Eastern Economist* was that Mrs. Gandhi should "keep politics and economic management apart," on the theory that political management of the economy will "create avoidable troubles and difficulties." However, while one can certainly understand the penchant of Indian businessmen to divorce politics from economics, it may be that it is precisely Mrs. Gandhi's political acumen that will count most during the period of economic crisis that lurks ahead. Certainly, if Mrs. Gandhi is going to discipline state planning programs, free the industrial sector from unnecessary constraints, pacify labor, promote savings, tax agriculture, manipulate international aid and credits, risk food surpluses in Bangladesh, or perform any of the other economic feats that proved impossible for her predecessors, she is going to need all of the political clout that she can muster.

Moreover, Mrs. Gandhi's ability to cope with economic problems will depend to a considerable degree on political and diplomatic factors over which she has no direct control. Success in rehabilitating the refugees and reconstructing the Bangladesh economy, for example, will depend in a large part on the viability of the new Bangladesh government and its attitude towards India. Both the Bangladesh government and Mrs. Gandhi may eventually accept substantial international assistance in repatriating the refugees, since this kind of assistance would be time bound and would, therefore, not assume long-term dependence on the part of either India or Bangladesh, but it is also possible that Bangladesh may be willing to accept much more foreign assistance from non-Indian sources than is thought desirably by the Indian government. The tendency to view Bangladesh primarily as a new market and as a communications and transportation link to India's northeast is already evident in New Delhi, and such attitudes will not find favor in many circles in Dacca. East Bengalis have made it quite clear that they do not want to "exchange one set of colonial rules for another," aud they can therefore be expected to examine new trade and cooperation agreement with India quite carefully before committing themselves.

In the meantime, India must also worry about political instability within Bangladesh. It is widely believed in New Delhi that the return of Sheikh Mujibur Rahman by the West Pakistan government will bring sufficient euphoria to Dacca to see the new nation through the initial period of political development. However, many observers seriously doubt that even the organizational abilities of Sheikh "Mujib" can create an enduring government from among the cacophony of Bengali political factions and forces. It may be that no one could do so. The glaring fact of political life in Bangladesh is the lack of any institutionalized means for running the affairs of the nation, if only because 24 years of Pakistani rule have prevented the growth of an East Bengal administration, military, and political parties. Should political instability in the Northeast be the result of the emergence of Bangladesh, plans for economic development and cooperation might well have to be thrown out.

Increased trade between India and Bangladesh will also depend in large part on the smooth functioning of the West Bengal economy, which has suffered a precipitous decline over the past few years. In order to reverse this decline, the government of India announced a 16-point economic program for West Bengal in August 1971, and has since tried to restore some semblance of law and order to the confused political and administrative situation in the state (during the past nine months West Bengal has been under President's Rule). The government's 16-point economic program for West Bengal calls for a number of development projects in Calcutta and the new port of Haldia, with economic incentives being given to both new investors and established industries in the state. However, the 16-point program has thus far been implemented in meager piecemeal fashion, and development funds for West Bengal have not been allocated because of the war and the refugees. In the absence of a massive development effort in West Bengal, the economy of the state is unlikely to improve.

Perhaps even more foreboding is the prospect that continued neglect of West Bengal and Calcutta will leave the economy of the Bengali region in the hands of non-Bengalis (Marwaris, Gujaratis, Parsis, Jains, and others). Should this be the case, the political situation in West Bengal can be expected to deteriorate further creating a series of political convulsions that will be felt across the border in Bangladesh. Moreover, if increased trade between India and Bangladesh works primarily to the advantage of the non-Bengalis who presently control much of the economy of West Bengal, it will be increasingly difficult for both the Indian and Bangladesh governments to proceed with plans for the integrated development of the Northeast. The major rallying cry of Bengalis —East and West—has in this century been the charge that non-Bengalis have been exploiting Bengal economically, and there is now a heightened feeling of expectation in Bengal, that the new circumstances in South Asia will put an end to such exploitation. In the event that these expectations are not fulfilled, the Bengalis are sufficiently politicized to maintain a constant state of political disorder, threatening the legitimacy of anyone who tries to exert political authority in Bengal.

All of this places Mrs. Gandhi in somewhat of a dilemma with regard to the Bengali region. To the extent that India does play a major role in the reconstruction of Bangladesh, it maximizes the possibility that it will eventually be accused of doing so for its own economic and political advantage, or for the benefit of non-Bengalis. However, should it fail to meet the expectations of the Bangladeshis and West Bengalis regarding repatriation, reconstruction, and development costs, it will risk the possibility of greater cooperation in the future. Mrs. Gandhi may be able to walk the tightrope that falls between these two undesirable alternatives, but to do so will tax even her consummate political skills.

Another more important factor for India to consider at present is the possibility that it may not be able to raise sufficient resources to play a major role in rehabilitation, reconstruction, and development of the Bengali region. It is obviously in India's interest to do as much as it can, since there is economic potential in the Northeast, and since the maintenance of a friendly and stable Bangladesh is so important for India's international position. In the absence of either a hostile government or a serious law and order problem in Bengal, the Indian military will now be able to devote more attention to the Sino-Indian borders in the Northeast, and this in turn should lend greater credibility to India's efforts to defend itself against the Chinese. An unstable government in Dacca (and/or Calcutta), or a Bengali government that lacked confidence in India's willingness or ability to assist with development efforts, could easily upset these calculations. One of the more dreadful possibilities that might flow from continued instability or estrangement in the Bengali region is heightened separatist tendencies among India's states.

At the present time (less than a month after the conclusion of the war), almost everyone in India is still flushed with victory and confident about the future. Weak voices, warning that India faces its most difficult days in the months ahead, occasionally appear in the Indian press, but these are buried by the predominant feeling of confidence and optimism. There is a widespread expectation that Mrs. Gandhi will do something drastic, particularly if her New Congress wins the state elections in March by a wide margin. There is also an increasing recognition on the part of large numbers of people that Mrs. Gandhi will demand great sacrifices from almost everyone when the new budget is announced after the elections.

Whether or not Mrs. Gandhi can blend this mixture of sentiment and circumstance into a more purposeful economy remains to be seen. If she can use her massive support and her great political skills to mobilize enough untapped resources to even approximate her goals for the nation, her accomplishment will be greater than that of any of her predecessors, including her father. In many ways the opportunities for making dramatic new economic gains have never been greater, but then, neither has the challenge.

FIVE

REFUGEES AND MIGRATION PATTERNS IN NORTHEASTERN INDIA AND BANGLADESH (1972)

The movement of almost 10 million East Bengal refugees to India in 1971 was an event without precedent. If only because of the sheer scale of human tragedy involved, it has been difficult to fully comprehend how such a massive exodus could be possible, much less understand its future consequences. For people in the West, many of whom had barely heard of Bengal before 1971, but were now suddenly exposed to graphic newspaper and television photographs of countless numbers of Bengalis trekking through the monsoon mud, the "movement of ten million" was an event that frequently created (or reinforced) stereotypes like those forged by the partition of India a quarter-century ago. In this atmosphere it is essential that we try to place the refugee influx of 1971 in the perspective of previous refugee movements and migration patterns in South Asia.

PATTERNS PRIOR TO 1971

The nearly ten million refugees that came to India from East Bengal (now Bangladesh) in 1971 were not the first international refugees to travel to India. Beginning in 1947, when the subcontinent was partitioned between India and Pakistan, South Asians moved from their homes in increasing numbers, and many of them crossed international boundaries to seek asylum. It is especially striking, however, to compare the influx in India's Northeast with the movement of refugees in the western portion of India, where the problem has not lingered but has instead been stabilized by a quick and almost total exchange of minority communities.

The fact that there was an *exchange* of populations that took place in northwestern India in 1947 is usually traced to the determination of the Sikhs (a religious community that separated from Hinduism in the fifteenth century, but was also directed against Muslim domination) to ensure their survival, coherence, and unity.[1] Indeed, virtually every member of the Sikh community resident in what became Pakistan in 1947 chose to migrate to India, where both Sikhs and Hindus began to aggressively displace Muslims from their lands and homes. Fearing for their lives, the vast majority of the Muslims in East Punjab (in India) quickly opted for Pakistan, where they proceeded to forcibly evict both Sikhs and the entire Hindu community of West Pakistan. This exchange of refugees in the Northwest was accompanied by massive communal violence and murder on a scale the world will not soon forget, but it was a relatively even exchange and it was virtually over by the end of 1947.

Because there was a relatively even exchange of populations in the Northwest, those refugees that came from West Pakistan to India in 1947 were able to benefit from a compensation pool of land and other properties that had been left behind by the Muslim refugees going to West Pakistan (the Muslims who traveled to West Pakistan in turn gained land and property from the Hindus and Sikhs who had left for India). The government of India estimates that approximately three million acres of land, 700,000 village houses, and 287,000 houses, shops, and other properties in urban areas were distributed to 1,063,000 refugee *families* from West Pakistan after 1947.[2] In addition, the Indian government provided Rs. 65 crores (650 million rupees, or about $130 million at prevailing exchange rates) to build houses and shops for the refugees from West Pakistan, and also made cash payments to the refugees that amounted to more than Rs. 200 crores ($400 million prior to devaluation). This meant that an average of three acres of land was distributed to each of the families from West Pakistan eligible for compensation, and that a good many of the refugees from West Pakistan were provided with homes and business opportunities. If only because they did have access to a compensation pool in the early

1. An excellent discussion of the place of partition in Punjab politics appears in Baldev Raj Nayar, *Minority Politics in the Punjab* (Princeton: Princeton University Press, 1968), Chapter I.

2. Ranajit Roy, "Refugees: West and East," *Hindustan Standard* (Calcutta), July 17, 1970.

years of their migration, these Hindu and Sikh refugees have in most cases been able to improve their economic status; indeed, it is usually argued that the refugees from West Pakistan are now as well-off as almost any other community in India.

The refugee situation in northeastern India has always been different from that in the Northwest. The Hindus who lived in East Bengal prior to 1947 were for the most part from landed families, while the Muslims resident in northeastern India were predominantly landless. East Bengal Hindus, therefore, were reluctant to move to India after 1947, since this would mean that they would have to surrender their lands in East Pakistan, with little or no hope of gaining new lands on the other side of the border. Moreover, India tried to discourage the movement of Hindus from East Pakistan to India by refusing to compensate East Pakistani refugees for land and property abandoned in East Bengal, even though the Compensation Act of 1954 provided such compensation to refugees in India's Northwest. The government of India could justify this dual policy by simply pointing to the fact that there was no land or property to distribute to Pakistani refugees in the east, but an additional justification was the Nehru-Liaquat Ali pact of 1950, which allowed India's East Pakistani refugees to legally claim their abandoned property in East Bengal.

Problems arose in India's Northeast when the Hindus who chose to remain in East Pakistan after 1947 experienced increasingly severe communal pressures, and slowly but surely began to move to India. The pattern of the refugee influx into India after 1947 is illustrated in Table 1, which lists the number of people who registered as refugees in the Indian state of West Bengal during each successive year between 1947 and 1972. From the Table it is clear that the refugee influx into India from East Pakistan was greater in those years when there was widespread communal violence (1950 and 1964 were the worst years before 1971). In some years migration dwindled to almost nothing, but the average number of refugees coming to West Bengal each year during the 25 years *prior to 1971* was nevertheless a considerable 172,462, and the influx was above average in 10 of the 25 years listed in Table 1.

In addition to the refugees that came from East Pakistan to West Bengal, Bengali refugees have also traveled to other Indian States. Table 2 lists the total population figures, as well as the figures for residents born in East Pakistan, residents born in West Bengal, and

Table 1   *Refugees from East Bengal, Registered in West Bengal, 1947–1971*

Year	Number of Refugees
1947	377,899
1948	419,018
1949	275,592
1950	925,185
1951	477,186
1952	
1953	60,647
1954	105,850
1955	211,573
1956	246,840
1957	9,133
1958	4,285
1959	5,539
1960	8,629
1961	10,095
1962	12,804
1963	14,601
1964	667,125
1965	159,989
1966	4,214
1967	6,895
1968	6,589
1969	11,068
1970	248,158
1971	7,094,740
Total	11,363,654

Source: Statistical Officer, Office of the Refugee Rehabilitation Commissioner, Government of West Bengal, quoted in A.K. Sen, *West Bengal: An Analytical Study* (Calcutta: Oxford Publishing Company, 1971), pp. 22–23; and *The Times of India* (New Delhi), February 17, 1972.

Table 2 *Bengali Refugee and Migration Figures for India's Northeastern States, 1961*

State	Total population	Residents born in East Pakistan	Residents born in West Bengal	Total Bengali Speakers
Assam	11,872,772	774,869	55,015	2,061,533
Bihar	46,455,610	100,761	309,232	1,164,041
West Bengal	34,926,279	3,068,750	29,441,400	29,408,246
Orissa	17,548,846	22,698	72,705	125,687
Manipur	780,037	3,056	829	10,011
Tripura	1,142,005	394,883	2,240	722,442
NEFA	38,705	1,299	767	2,253
Nagaland	369,200	1,682	616	3,820
Totals	113,433,454	4,367,998	29,882,804	33,498,033

Source: Census of India, 1961.

resident Bengali speakers for all states in the northeastern region of India, according to the official 1961 census (unfortunately, detailed 1971 census figures will not be available for a number of years). By analyzing this Table, it is possible to gain some idea of the number of Bengalis that had moved from East Pakistan to the various states of northeastern India by 1961, and to contrast these figures with the number of Bengalis that had either migrated to each state from somewhere in India or had been lifelong residents of each state.

As is indicated in Table 2, the greatest concentration of Indian Bengalis relative to non-Bengali state populations (in 1961) was Assam, West Bengal, and Tripura, with a smattering of Bengalis in five other Indian states and territories. In Assam the refugees from East Pakistan accounted for more than a third of the Bengali population in 1961, and the Bengali population accounted for 17.4 per cent of the total population of the state. East Pakistani refugees accounted for more than half of the Bengali population of tiny Tripura by 1961, enough to give the Bengali-speaking community a whopping 63.3 per cent majority in a state that was previously dominated by non-Bengalis. In West Bengal, the Bengali Community is in any case predominant, but the influx of more than three million refugees by 1961 (and more than four million by 1971) has created special problems for West Bengal.

It should be pointed out that there is a considerable difference between the Bengali refugees that moved from East Bengal to India in the years immediately following partition, and those who have come later. Perhaps a majority of refugees in the early years was from the wealthier and better-educated landed Hindu community of East Bengal, which had traditionally dominated Bengal's social structure, but was forced by communal pressure to surrender its land and perquisites in East Bengal after 1947. A study conducted by the University of Calcutta in the 1950s, for example, indicated that East Bengal refugees living in Calcutta at that time were far better educated than either the older residents of Calcutta or the migrants that had come to Calcutta from other Indian states.[3] A more recent study, conducted by Professor Satyesh Chakravarty of Burdwan University in 1971, reveals that more than 90 per cent of the present faculty members in the five major universities of West Bengal have been recruited from East Bengal refugee families. In law, in medicine, in engineering, in other professions, and especially in the state bureaucracies, one finds a similar pattern, with refugees from East Bengal dominating the competition for coveted professional and governmental positions in West Bengal and Tripura, and at least holding their own in Assam.

In recent years, however, the character of the refugee influx into India has changed considerably. Since most of the traditional Hindu elite families of East Bengal had crossed over to India by the mid–1950s, the Hindu community that remained in Pakistan became increasingly a poor and depressed minority, its condition made worse by the almost constant decline in the economy of East Pakistan. By the late 1950s it was clear that the refugees who were traveling to India were no longer coming from elitist backgrounds. By 1964–65, when almost a million people trekked from East Bengal to India, the West Bengal government estimated that the

3. S.N. Sen, *The City of Calcutta: A Socio-Economic Survey, 1954–55 to 1957–58* (Calcutta: Bookland Private Limited, 1960), pp. 207–208.

vast majority of these new refugees were artisans, landless laborers, small shopkeepers, or poor cultivators, even though the catalyst for their movement was still the communal tension between Hindus and Muslims. It should also be pointed out that economic opportunities for the lower classes have been even less satisfactory in East Bengal than in West Bengal during the last 25 years, while communal relations in West Bengal have been relatively better, which means that few West Bengalis have migrated to East Bengal during this period. Indeed the major migration from India to East Pakistan prior to 1971 was the Bihari Muslim community (now numbering 700,000 to 800,000), which is drawn from Bihar and other non-Bengali areas of India.

Changes in the nature of the refugee influx into India's Northeast has led to speculation that there may eventually occur a massive "overflow" or "spillover" of Bengalis into non-Bengali areas, with all of the communal, political, and social problems that this would entail. The potential for such a spillover can be illustrated in the manner of Figure 1, which contrasts population density for the Bengali homeland (West Bengal and Bangladesh) with density figures for those states to the north and east of Bengal. Since the average population density in the districts of Bengal (East and West) is three to four times that of Assam and Tripura, and more than eight times that of any of the other tiny states in the extreme Northeast, it is little wonder that the peoples of the Northeast have feared Bengali migration into less densely populated areas.

In both Assam and Tripura, a number of political leaders have argued that the Bengali spillover has already started. The population of Assam, for example, has increased from 3.7 million to 14.9 million in this century, an increase of 400 per cent as against 129 per cent for India as a whole, with the difference stemming entirely from Bengali migration. Between 1911 and 1931 more than a third of a million Bengalis migrated from one Bengal district (Mymensingh, now in Bangladesh) to the low density districts of the Brahmaputra Valley in Assam (Goalpara, Kamrup, Nowgong, Darrang, and Lakhimpur), and by 1951 more than a half million Bengalis had left East Pakistan for Assam. Even with the rather strict border controls that were in effect between India and East Pakistan after 1947, this influx continued into the 1950s and 1960s. Because of this influx, Assam's population increased by 35.1 per cent between 1951 and 1961 (compared with an all-India decennial growth rate of 21.6 per cent); between 1961 and 1971—according to provisional 1971 census figures—Assam's increase was 34.4 per cent (compared to an all-India average of 24.6 per cent).

Migration of Bengalis into Assam has led to a number of physical and political clashes between Bengalis and Assamese, most of which have revolved around language and land. The first major outbreak of violence between Bengalis and Assamese occurred shortly after Independence, when Assamese Hindus protested against the continuing encroachment of Bengali Muslims in search of land in the Brahmaputra Valley. Prior to India's Independence, the Muslim League Ministry that had governed Assam had permitted settlement by Muslims on government lands, grazing areas, and forest preserves, but after 1947 such settlement was declared illegal. At the time of partition there was also considerable resentment of both Pakistan and the Muslim League among Hindus in Assam, if only because the proponents of Pakistan had at several points claimed the whole of Assam for Pakistan, as part of a larger "Muslim Bengal." When Independence finally came, and Assam was included in India, major communal disturbances broke out between Assamese Hindus and Bengali Muslims, with the result that the Indian Parliament passed the Immigrants (Expulsion from Assam) Act of 1950, aimed at the removal of post-Independence Muslim immigrants from East Bengal (since 1950 Bengali Muslim immigrants in Assam have been popularly known as "infiltrators").

A second series of clashes between Assamese and the Bengalis occured in July 1960, shortly after the Assamese government decided to adopt Assamese as the official state language. This outburst was commonly described in Assam as the "Bengali *kheda*" (*kheda* translates as "round-up," a term commonly used to refer to the herding of elephants). Seizing on the accumulated resentment of Assamese against the Bengali Hindu middle classes who occupied competitive positions in government and in the professions, a number of Assamese political leaders encouraged young men to set fire and loot Bengali homes in the early 1960s, while demanding that all non-Assamese publicly establish their reasons for taking up residence in Assam. A similar movement was launched against the Marwari community in Assam in the late 1960s, led by an underground group (the *Latchit Sena*) which has as its declared goal the ejection of all non-Assamese from Assam.

Resentment against Bengalis in Tripura has led to even greater

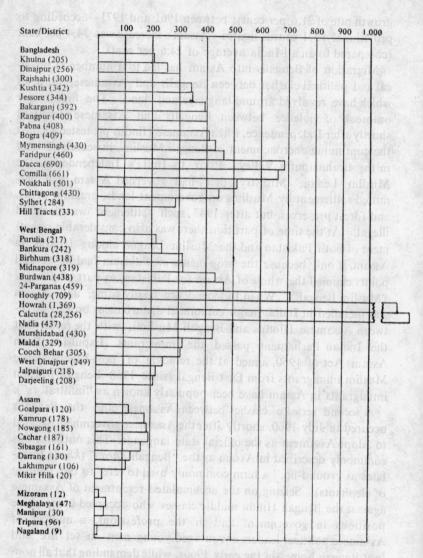

State/District

Bangladesh
Khulna (205)
Dinajpur (256)
Rajshahi (300)
Kushtia (342)
Jessore (344)
Bakarganj (392)
Rangpur (400)
Pabna (408)
Bogra (409)
Mymensingh (430)
Faridpur (460)
Dacca (690)
Comilla (661)
Noakhali (501)
Chittagong (430)
Sylhet (284)
Hill Tracts (33)

West Bengal
Purulia (217)
Bankura (242)
Birbhum (318)
Midnapore (319)
Burdwan (438)
24-Parganas (459)
Hooghly (709)
Howrah (1,369)
Calcutta (28,256)
Nadia (437)
Murshidabad (430)
Malda (329)
Cooch Behar (305)
West Dinajpur (249)
Jalpaiguri (218)
Darjeeling (208)

Assam
Goalpara (120)
Kamrup (178)
Nowgong (185)
Cachar (187)
Sibsagar (161)
Darrang (130)
Lakhimpur (106)
Mikir Hills (20)

Mizoram (12)
Meghalaya (47)
Manipur (30)
Tripura (96)
Nagaland (9)

Figure 1. Population density in Bangladesh and India's Northeastern States, by district (1961). Bangladesh: Average density 360 people per sq. km; West Bengal: Average density 399 people per sq km; Assam: Average density 97 people per sq km; Northeastern states: Average density 43 people per sq km.

violence than in Assam, perhaps because of the fact that the original tribal population of Tripura has now been reduced to a minority. Throughout the 1950s and 1960s a number of tribal groups sought to prevent Bengali immigrants from settling in Tripura by staging terrorist attacks against refugee settlements, and in 1968 a number of these diverse terrorist bands—recruited primarily from the Reang, Noatia, and Lushai tribes—joined together in the *Sangkrak* party (*Sangkrak* in Lushai means "strong arm"). In November 1968, members of the *Sangkrak* party attacked Hejachera, a Bengali village in northeastern Tripura, burned a Bengali market at Chailengeta, and looted Bengali property in a number of other Bengali areas. Since then the *Sangkrak* party has joined with the Mizo National Front, which has advocated secession from India, acquired small arms and ammunition, and is pursuing a guerrilla strategy directed against the Bengali majority and the state government.

THE "MOVEMENT OF TEN MILLION"

In this atmosphere it is little wonder that Mrs. Gandhi became concerned when almost ten million refugees flooded into India's northeastern states in a nine-month period in 1971 (the map indicates the number of refugees that were accommodated in each of India's states, and contrasts refugee figures with those of the regular state populations). If the refugees had been allowed to remain in India as residents, the population of West Bengal (using provisional 1971 census figures) would have jumped from 44.4 million to 51.5 million, an increase of 16 per cent in a single year. Similarly, the population of Tripura would have increased by 82 per cent and the new state of Meghalaya by 70 per cent, with Meghalaya suddenly being inundated by a Bengali population that would have accounted for almost half (46 per cent) of the total state population. In short, there was a distinct danger that the previous gradual spillover of Bengalis into less densely populated areas might have reached floodtide proportions if the 1971 refugee influx had not been reversed.

When one considers the highly charged political and communal atmosphere in which the 1971 influx took place, it is simply astounding that India was able to accommodate such a vast number of refugees without large-scale incidents, and perhaps even more

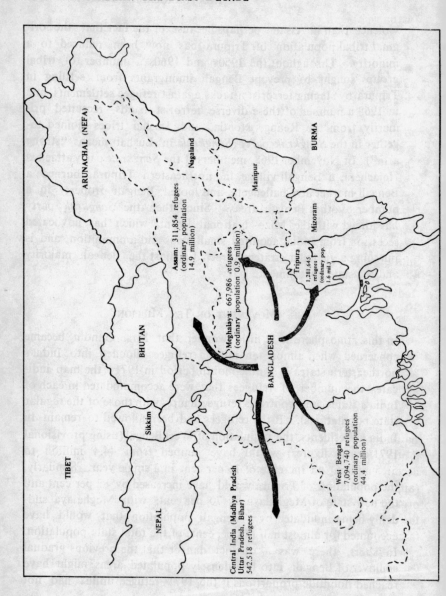

astonishing that India was able to return the bulk of the refugees to Bangladesh after the surrender of Pakistani troops. Much of the credit for the orderly manner in which the refugees were accommodated and returned should go to Prime Minister Indira Gandhi, who made two crucial decisions almost as soon as the refugees started coming. First, during a series of public meetings with the refugees and Bangladesh freedom fighters in the border areas in the summer, Mrs. Gandhi made it clear that the 1971 refugees would not be allowed to remain in India as permanent residents, even though East Bengal refugees that had come to India before 1971 had been granted citizenship. Second, Mrs. Gandhi established a special organization within the Union Ministry of Relief and Rehabilitation, charged with the task of establishing and maintaining temporary camps for the refugees. By insisting from the beginning that the 1971 refugee influx was different from previous refugee movements, Mrs. Gandhi immediately dampened the expectations of many Bengalis that might otherwise have tried to settle in India. At the same time, the decision to place the vast majority of the refugees in temporary camps facilitated relief work, made it easier for the Indian government to maintain order, and eventually simplified the task of returning the refugees to their homes.

The massive organization that actually established the camps and coordinated relief programs for the refugees was headed by Colonel P.N. Luthra.[4] Working in conjunction with seven state governments, 24 Indian voluntary organizations, and 12 international agencies, Colonel Luthra established 896 refugee camps in a little less than nine months, and these camps eventually provided accommodation for 6.8 million refugees. The remaining refugees (approximately three million) were registered by Colonel Luthra's organization and provided with rations and medical assistance from the camps, but were able to find shelter with friends and relatives rather than being confined to camp life. Although Pakistani press releases have occasionally questioned the official refugee figures

4.   Figures on the refugee influx into India in 1971 and the repatriation of refugees to Bangladesh in 1972 are drawn primarily from interviews with relief officials in India and Bangladesh in January–February 1972. I am especially grateful to Mr. A.K. Sengupta of the Ministry of Relief and Rehabilitation in West Bengal, and to Mr. A.H.M. Kamaruzzaman, Minister of Relief and Rehabilitation of Bangladesh, for their assistance.

released by the Indian government, every reporter or analyst who has traveled to India has argued that India's figures are deadly accurate, and a good many random checks by international agencies and reporters have confirmed their accuracy.

Colonel Luthra's organization was made up of 29,522 government employees, a majority of whom were hired on a temporary basis solely to assist in the administration of the relief operation. In addition, countless volunteers from a large number of different nations worked feverishly and selflessly to keep the relief machinery going. The majority of the camps were set up in West Bengal and Tripura, states that already had a majority Bengali population, but camps were also established in Assam, Meghalaya, Bihar, Uttar Pradesh, and Madhya Pradesh. Camps in central India were designed by the Indian government to relieve crowded conditions in West Bengal and Tripura, and to diminish the number of refugees in Assam. It should be pointed out, however, that the relatively small number of refugees in Assam was only partly a result of a conscious decision to discourage refugee movement there, since it was also related to the difficulties that refugees experienced when traveling to Assam during the monsoon months. (Assam has a higher volume of rainfall during the monsoon than any other part of India.)

Government sensitivity with regard to the establishment of refugee camps in Assam stemmed primarily from the fear that communal clashes between Assamese Hindus and Bengali Muslims might result from a large-scale influx. In April 1971, when the first wave of refugees began to travel to India, there were a number of violent communal outbursts in Assam and Meghalaya, with Assamese Hindus pitted against Bengali Muslims. Although these communal clashes were quickly brought under control by the Indian army and the police, it was clear that the actions of the Pakistan army in East Bengal had roused communal passions, and that this had created a particularly explosive situation in Assam, where many Hindus had been conditioned to think of all Muslim Bengalis from Pakistan as "infiltrators." Under these circumstances, Colonel Luthra's organization made a conscious decision to move most of the Bengali Muslim refugees from Assam to refugee camps in other states, and to keep the total number of refugees in Assam to a minimum.

Precise figures on the religious background of the refugees are not available but it is estimated that somewhere between 80 to 90 per cent of the 1971 refugees were Hindus.   Within Bangladesh the Hindu community had been singled out for massacre by the Pakistan army, along with intellectuals, students, members of the Awami League, and later, guerrilla fighters.   Some observers have argued that the West Pakistanis were attempting to rid East Bengal of all Hindus, which would have meant a drop of 12 per cent or so in the size of the East Bengal population, thus making the two wings of the erstwhile Pakistan relatively equal.   Others have argued that severe repression of Hindus stemmed from the notion that the Hindu community had fomented the conditions leading to the secession of East Pakistan, since many of the radical Muslim students who had championed secession had also rejected Islam, espoused Hinduism, and glorified "Calcutta culture."   For whatever reason, it is clear that the Pakistan army made little effort to disguise its determined and brutal attempt to search out and annihilate Bengali Hindus: Hindu shops and homes were smashed and burned throughout East Bengal, temples were blown to pieces, large numbers of cows (sacred to Hindus) were destroyed or maimed, and countless numbers of Hindu men were found with their penises cut off, a symbolic reminder of the principal physical difference between Hindus and Muslims (who practice circumcision).   In the words of Simon Dring, an American correspondent who covered the Bangladesh crisis, there is no doubt that the army crackdown on East Bengal in 1971 was carried out "in the name of Allah and a United Pakistan."[5]

The communal nature of the Bangladesh crisis made it all the more imperative that both the Awami League Leadership of the secessionist movement and the Indian government do everything in their power to dampen religious animosities, since both had declared their unreserved commitment to secularism.   Special arrangements were therefore made in the camps to keep political parties and other "agitators" away, senior citizens and other influential people in the camps were encouraged to promote communal harmony, and all religious ceremonies and functions (Hindu, Muslim, Christian, and

5.   Simon Dring, "The Sack of Dacca," in *Dateline Bangladesh*, edited by Ajit Bhattacharjea (Bombay: Jaico Publishing House, 1971), p. 67.   This volume is an excellent collection of reports from journalists filed in Bangladesh during 1971.

others) were allowed. Despite the heat of a scorching summer, and
the inconvenience of a heavy monsoon, communal conflicts in the
camps were kept to a minimum, a sharp contrast to the situation
across the border.

By far the greatest task of Colonel Luthra's organization, however, was the necessity to provide the refugees with shelter, water,
food, and medical assistance, and it was here that India's effort in
coping with the refugee influx received the acclamation of peoples
around the world. Colonel Luthra requisitioned whatever indigenous materials he could find that could be used for roofing—thatch,
shon grass, *hogla*, and other leaves—combining these with plastic
sheeting, tents, tarpaulins, and bamboo sticks to build more than
two million temporary shelters. In the beginning stages of the influx, refugees were also housed in public buildings—schools, colleges,
libraries, community halls, railway stations, government offices,
parks, compounds of private buildings, institutes, post offices, and
museums—causing considerable inconvenience to the local population, but, nevertheless, providing temporary shelter for the refugees.
During the monsoon months Colonel Luthra's organization also
used such ingenious devices as large concrete drainage and sewage
pipes for temporary refugee shelters, until such time that something
more adequate could be constructed.

In the beginning stages, cooked food was given to the refugees in the
camps, but centralized cooking facilities proved too costly (and too
disruptive of camp life) when the refugees began to number in the
millions, with the result that a decision was made in early May to
supply only dry rations, vitamins, and warm milk. This decision
had the advantage of providing camp residents with something to
do, since a good many of them had brought cooking pots, plates,
and mugs, while others were issued such utensils by both government
and voluntary organizations. Recreational facilities also relieved
the strain of camp life, as did the educational programs that were
conducted primarily by refugee group leaders and teachers (children
were usually taught Bengali, simple arithmetic, health, hygiene,
sanitation, and welfare work). A corps of 800 doctors, 2,100
paramedical personnel, and 72 medical students provided medical
relief to the undernourished and the injured, while inoculating more
than six million people and vaccinating another 4.7 million. By
the end of 1971 more than 2.4 million people had been treated in

the camps for various ailments (including a cholera epidemic), and yet deaths totaled a remarkably low 6,349.

The cost of maintaining the camps through late November 1971 was estimated by Colonel Luthra at two billion rupees ($275 million), but this figure is expected to almost double by the time the refugees have returned to their homes (the government of India is planning on the basis of a total cost for the camps of 3.6 billion rupees [$500 million] to be expended by the end of March 1972). While international agencies and foreign governments have promised relief assistance totaling 1.98 billion rupees ($271 million), less than half of that (.87 billion rupees, or $119 million) had been received from foreign sources by late January 1972. Clearly, the ten million refugees that came to India in 1971 owe their survival primarily to the generosity of Indian citizens, the dedication of Indian relief workers, and the resources of the Indian government.

PROBLEMS OF REPATRIATION

India's strategy for repatriation of the refugees is quite simple to outline, although it involves formidable logistical problems. First, transportation has been provided for all refugees requiring it, which has meant a massive mobilization of transport facilities on the part of the Indian government. Soon after the surrender of Pakistani troops on December 16, 1972, the Indian army re-established the five major railway lines that had linked India with East Bengal before the creation of Pakistan; each of these lines has since been used to move two trainloads of refugees to Bangladesh every day. In addition, a fleet of more than 5,000 trucks and buses— drawn from all over eastern India—have been pressed into daily service, along with a vast flotilla of barges that have carried refugees into the remote villages of riverine East Bengal. Many of the refugees that were camped on the border of Bangladesh have returned home on foot, some have hitched rides on bullock carts, and some of those camped in central India have been returned on Indian ships from southern ports, but the vast majority of the ten million have been returned to their homes by road, rail, or river barge.

Beginning in early January 1972, a certain portion of the refugees has been selected by camp officials for repatriation each day, with numbers depending on the space available in transport vehicles.

While still in India, each refugee has been given a "journey allow-ance" (the amount varies with the distance the refugee is expected to travel) and two weeks worth of food rations, before being loaded onto trucks and buses that eventually bring him (or her) to one of 237 transit camps in Bangladesh. Once back in Bangladesh, each of the refugees is then given an additional cash allowance (the funds being provided by the Indian government) which is calculated to last a full month. Since neither rations nor other facilities are available in the transit camps in Bangladesh, most of the refugees have left these camps for their homes within 24-48 hours of their arrival.

This strategy has worked amazingly well in bringing about the rapid repatriation of a large number of people. Each refugee has been given a positive inducement (the cash grants, rations, travel allowances), along with a nudge (the closing of camps, withdrawal of ration cards, and other facilities), and provided with free trans-portation home. In addition, the refugees have been promised—by Prime Minister Sheikh Mujibur Rahman of Bangladesh himself— that any property, which they may have been forced to "sell" under duress, will be returned to them and they will be given govern-ment assistance to reconstruct their homes and businesses, or to acquire new tools, implements, seeds, fertilizer, and cattle. Along with the refugees, India has sent to Bangladesh much of the equip-ment that was used in the camps, including the tents, tarpaulins, blankets, utensils, and medical supplies. In this manner, India expects to close down all of its refugee camps by March 25, 1972, exactly a year after the beginning of the army crackdown on East Bengal.

There is little doubt that virtually all of the refugees who have been living in Indian camps can and will be returned to Bangladesh, along with the bulk of those that had taken shelter with Indian friends and relatives. By early March 1972, Colonel Luthra's organization estimated that there were only about 200,000 refugees left in the camps, while another 817,000 were staying with friends and relatives. This means that almost nine million refugees had already been repatriated in a period of slightly more than two months. The obvious problem for the Indian government is that a good many of the refugees who chose to stay on with relatives and friends until March are likely to want to stay longer, so that the last million may turn out to be much more difficult to repatriate than the first nine million. Anticipating that this might be the case, Colonel Luthra has requested the various state authorities to "take necessary action as early as possible," but thus far the meaning of the phrase "necessary action" has not been spelled out.

Problems of repatriation would be considerably lessened if the reports on economic conditions in Bangladesh were better than they are. But thus far reconstruction within Bangladesh has not proceeded as quickly as either the Bangladesh or Indian governments had hoped. Mr. A.H.M. Kamaruzzaman, the Bangladesh Minister for Relief and Rehabilitation, argues that his government needs approximately Rs. 2,000 crores ($2.72 billion) in external assistance during the next year if the refugees are to be rehoused, fed, and provided with the same level of economic activity that existed in Bangladesh before 1971, a figure that contrasts sharply with the Rs. 200 crores ($272 million after devaluation) in external assistance that has thus far been provided for 1972. Similarly, Finance Ministry officials in New Delhi say that India (or someone else) would have to provide almost $2.72 billion (Rs. 2,000 crores) annually for the next five years to make the Bangladesh economy viable, and the United Nations Secretary-General Kurt Waldheim has stated in his report to the General Assembly that "additional assistance [additional, that is, to the $300 million already promised] is required in excess of $565 million for the remainder of 1972" in order "to meet but the most immediate needs of the affected area so as to avert the threat of large-scale misery and hunger." In the words of Secretary-General Waldheim, "never in the history of the United Nations has international assistance been needed so urgently and in such great amounts."

Should the Bangladesh government fail to find sufficient external resources to revive its battered economy, the people who will be most affected are the refugees who traveled to India, and the other East Bengalis who lost their homes and means of livelihood during the army crackdown in 1971. But others will suffer too. Shortfalls in external assistance will mean that the Bangladesh transportation network will work even less efficiently than it has worked in the past; port facilities will not be capable of sustaining either imports or exports; materials will not be available for rebuilding homes; and tools, animals, and implements—all necessary for productive agriculture—will be in exremely short supply. Under these circumstances, the struggle for survival in Bangladesh is likely to become

violent, conflict between Hindus and the two Muslim communities
(Bengali and Bihari) could be increasingly difficult to control, and
a number of people, refugees or otherwise, might just decide to
move again.

Hopefully, none of this will happen. But even if the Bangladesh
government is able to contain communal animosities that have
been exacerbated by the events of 1971, and even if it is able to
provide enough food and shelter to keep the repatriated refugees
alive, there will still be pressure on the people of Bangladesh to
move to areas that are less densely populated and more prosperous
than East Bengal. Indeed, with an open border between India and
Bangladesh, it is going to be more difficult than ever before for
India to control the spillover of Bengalis into India's northeastern
states. In this atmosphere, the fears of many non-Bengalis in
northeastern India have been expressed in the manner of an
Assamese correspondent, writing in the *Economic and Political
Weekly*:

> ...it is likely, when once things settle down, and with a compa-
> ratively open border with Bangladesh, that there will be a
> considerable future illicit [Bengali] immigration into Assam,
> particularly into pockets [like the district of Nowgong] where
> there are already concentrations of immigrant communities from
> East Bengal.

> Looking fairly far ahead, can one see here a prospect of the
> real, final disintegration of Assam? There are about 12 million
> of us [Assamese], and just across a rather open border, there are
> over 70 million of them [Bengalis], and the pressure on land
> there is far worse than it is here. Would it be too far-fetched to
> suggest that, despite all the smooth talk that is now going on
> about the eternal friendship between India and Bangladesh, the
> North-Eastern region might prove a potential area of conflict
> between the two countries?[6]

INDIAN PLANNING AND THE NORTHEAST

Conflict between India and Bangladesh is one consequence that is
likely to result from migration patterns in the northeastern region

6. *Economic and Political Weekly* (Bombay), VII: 5-7 (February 1972).
p. 199.

of South Asia. Conflict between the central government of India and the state governments as well as conflict between India's states, are other consequences that can be expected. From the point of view of the Indian government, however, the independence of Bangladesh from West Pakistan is nevertheless desirable, if only because it opens up the possibility of greater cooperation across international boundaries in the Northeast. In contrast to the hostile confrontation of the last 25 years, relations between India and Bangladesh will now be predicated on the assumption that linguistic and religious conflicts can either be accommodated or controlled within nation-states that derive their legitimacy from the ideals of secularism and parliamentary democracy.

This is not to argue that problems of nation-building in South Asia have suddenly disappeared, or that future migration patterns will necessarily be more stabilizing than those of the past, even if India and Bangladesh manage to maintain their parliamentary democratic systems. For the basic dilemma of democratic multi-ethnic societies is that political boundaries can never completely coincide with community boundaries so long as spatial mobility is allowed, and yet unrestrained spatial mobility will inevitably result in interethnic conflict, nativistic reactions, and violent confrontations that ultimately threaten political stability. In the words of Professor Myron Weiner:

> To take no action to either protect local people or to enhance their capacity to compete with migrants is to sit idly by as racial and linguistic conflicts grow. But to cope with the problem by attempting to prevent the immigration of skilled and motivated persons will either fail or, to the extent that such measures do succeed, substantially slow the country's rate of economic growth while simultaneously destroying the many advantages of a common citizenship.[7]

The obvious challenge for both India and Bangladesh in the future will be to provide a framework for spatial mobility, flow of trade, and cooperative development activities, while at the same time playing an active part in the mitigation of inter-community conflict.

7. Myron Weiner, "The Socio-Political Consequences of Inter-State Migration in India," unpublished manuscript, July 1971, p. 45.

While it is still too early for either India or Bangladesh to have settled on long-range policies toward migration flows in the northeastern region in order to meet this challenge, some policy planning goals have already been established, and these point to the likely trend of governmental attitudes in the future.   First and foremost among these is the declared intention of the Indian government to spend more of its resources in the Northeast—in Bangladesh, in West Bengal, and in the other Indian states.   Obviously, most of the resources that have been spent in Bangladesh thus far have gone for repatriation of the refugees, as well as for reconstruction projects in Bangladesh that have facilitated the return and rehabilitation of the refugees.   In the future, however, India is also hoping to promote the integrated development of the entire Ganga-Brahmaputra basin by bringing about greater regional cooperation between Nepal, Bhutan, Sikkim, Bangladesh, and northeastern India.   Integrated development would call for massive transportation and communication projects, flood control measures of a magnitude that boggle the imagination, and a series of highly complex trade agreements—all difficult for a poor country to manage—but Indian planners are hoping that sufficient international assistance can be coupled with a degree of stability in the Northeast to make integrated development possible.

Prime Minister Indira Gandhi has already displayed her good intentions toward the Bengali-speaking area, not only by her assistance to the Bangladesh independence movement but also in her attitudes towards the economy of West Bengal.   In August 1971, Mrs. Gandhi announced a 16-point program for the development of the West Bengal economy, which included plans for a new bridge across the Hooghly River, more rapid development of a new port city at Haldia (complete with a large fertilizer factory and other industries), and a number of projects (including an underground railway) designed to make the city of Calcutta a more livable metropolitan area.   On a smaller but no less important scale, the 16-point development program of August 1971 included a promise to release substantial orders of the Indian wagon-building industry to factories in West Bengal, a target of 2,000 small industrial units to be set up in West Bengal each year, assurances of timely and sufficient supply of credit and raw materials to West Bengal industry, permission to work multiple shifts, and provision of concessional finance for industries to be set up in "backward areas" of the state.

The 16-point program also contained a promise that the Indian government would review its list of incentives to industry, in order to make them more attractive for West Bengal businessmen.

In November 1971 the Indian government released an entirely new list of incentives for West Bengal, which were more or less patterned after those granted previously (with considerable success) to Maharashtra and other Indian states. The incentives that were granted relate primarily to preferences in state purchases, fiscal relief for new industrial units and for the substantial expansion of existing units, availability of land on long-term lease at "growth centers," contributions towards the cost of feasibility studies of development projects, subsidies for power generation, long-term loans and working capital for industries, and industrial exemptions from the payment of water rates. Business organizations in West Bengal have obviously welcomed both the 16-point economic development program and the incentives, but have thus far complained of a lack of implementation, a charge that the Indian government counters by pointing to its burden of expenditures in Bangladesh.

Central to India's new economic initiatives in Bengal and northeastern India is the assumption that the "green revolution" in agriculture will eventually spread to West Bengal, as a result of new gains being made in rice technology. If the new technology does take root in Bengal, and if Bengal follows the patterns that have been exhibited in other states where the new technology has caught on, there is likely to be a surplus of agricultural labor along with an increase in food supplies, and this will mean increasing pressure on the already overcrowded lands of Bengal. Increasing pressure on land will in turn release larger and larger numbers of peasants from the land, either for migration to less densely crowded areas or for absorption in the industrial sector. In the eyes of Indian planners, therefore, one of the most compelling reasons for the development of industry in West Bengal is the need to absorb a burgeoning surplus of rural peasants as industrial laborers, in order to prevent large-scale future migration.

The possibility that India may not be able to raise sufficient resources is one major stumbling block to the realization of its plans for Bengal, but another stems from the fact that industry in West Bengal is so heavily dominated by non-Bengalis from western and central India. Non-Bengali businessmen have traditionally controlled a major portion of industrial capital in West Bengal, and a recent survey of Calcutta (Bengal's largest industrial center) indicated that more than half of Calcutta's total wage earners—in all income categories—were non-Bengalis, even though Bengali-speakers accounted for 85 per cent of the city's population. This means that development of the industrial sector in West Bengal could conceivably work to the relative advantage of non-Bengalis in West Bengal itself, and that non-Bengalis could use their economic power there to gain control of trade between West Bengal and Bangladesh, a possibility that is again enhanced by a more open border. Should this be the case, the tensions that already exist between Bengalis and non-Bengalis would most likely increase, which could in turn lead to the growth of a variety of Bengali radical and millenarian movements.

In this highly complex situation, the Indian government has thus far allowed considerable movement back and forth between Bangladesh and India's northeastern states (including West Bengal), but leaders of both nations have also insisted on a number of restrictions designed to impede certain kinds of traffic. In order to control general movement, all travelers between India and Bangladesh are now required to possess certificates of travel, which can be issued by the Bangladesh government or by one of the state governments in India (under the signature of an Under Secretary in the Indian Home Ministry). At the same time, the Indian and Bangladesh military are cooperating to patrol the border between the two countries, in an attempt to prevent unlawful activities. From newspaper reports it would appear that the Bangladesh border forces have thus far concentrated on a counter-insurgency effort directed against the Mizo National Front, a guerrilla army that has been using the Chittagong Hill Tracts in Bangladesh as a staging area for forays in Tripura and Mizoram in India. Similarly, the Indian Border Security Force (BSF) has focused its attention on the movement of arms and other forms of political collaboration between radical leftist parties in India and Bangladesh. In addition, both Indian and Bangladesh border forces have attempted to prevent a growing private trade between Bangladesh and India that has been established despite the decision of Prime Ministers Indira Gandhi and Mujibur Rahman that all trade between the two countries be conducted on a state-to-state basis.

A strategy that focuses primarily on development activities and peace-keeping has also been formalized in India's northeastern region, with the creation in late 1971 of a North-Eastern Council, to be composed of representatives from each of the states to the north and east of Bengal. While the North-Eastern Council is usually described by Indian government spokesmen as "an instrument for the coordinated development of the region," it is clear that the Council will also play a major role in the maintenance of law and order. The charter of the new Council, for example, states that the Council "shall review, from time to time, the measures taken by the States represented on the Council for the maintenance of security and public order therein and recommend to the governments of the states concerned further measures necessary in this regard."[8]   On the Council itself, the representatives of the states will be joined by four nominees of the central government, drawn from the Ministries of Defense, Home Affairs, Finance, and Planning, again indicating the orientation of the Council toward development and security matters. Finally, the five full-fledged states of the Northeast (Meghalaya, Manipur, Tripura, Nagaland, and Assam) will have a common governor and a common high court, the two institutions most closely connected with security matters, while the two Union territories in the Northeast—Arunachal and Mizoram—will be directly controlled by New Delhi.

Policies designed to promote development and security in the Northeast may have some effect on future migration patterns, but neither government officials nor observers in South Asia are expecting a reversal of present trends. Few countries in the world have had much success in regulating the internal movement of citizens, and democratic societies have generally had less success than others. Since the Indian Constitution guarantees that all of its citizens "shall have the right to move freely throughout the territory of India, and to reside and settle in any part of the territory of India," a massive migration between India's states could only be prevented by either amending or abrogating the Constitution. Moreover, while India and Bangladesh do have a clear legal right to control the flow of traffic across their common international border, much of the force of their legal authority is diminished by the fact that their common border consists of 1,349 miles of jungles, marshes, swamps, rivers, hills, and paddy fields, a most difficult terrain to

8. *Draft Scheme of North Eastern Council*, placed by the Chief Minister of Assam on the table of the Assam Legislative Assembly, November 1, 1971, cf. Items 5 (h) and 10.

patrol. Under these circumstances, both India and Bangladesh are likely to continue to expend their limited resources on development activities and security measures, rather than pursue a far more costly and divisive strategy that would entail strict control of population flows.

SIX

INDO-BANGLADESH
RELATIONS (1975)

One of the major disappointments in subcontinental affairs during the past few years has been the failure of India and Bangladesh to make meaningful progress toward cooperation, and of Pakistan to reconcile itself with either. Indian officials feel that Pakistanis have remained intractable—even though they themselves have acted magnanimously—in the wake of the Bangladesh liberation war in 1971. Bangladesh and India failed to resolve enough of their differences during the years following to make joint development projects or other exchanges viable. However, struggles with inflation, balance of payments deficits, and resource shortages have necessarily preoccupied national leaders in all three countries. Complex issues in international diplomacy complicate the severe domestic problems and inhibit dialogue or trialogue.

All three nations still commit themselves publicly to "normalizing relations on the subcontinent." Should that commitment to cooperation be too weak, however, a rapid return to confrontation is quite possible. For a time in autumn, it even appeared imminent. Indo-Bangladesh relations were strained by the coup in Bangladesh that toppled Sheikh Mujibur Rahman's government on August 15, 1975,[1] since the new leaders appeared to favor Pakistan at India's expense. Pakistan's immediate recognition of the new government and the announcement on Radio Pakistan that the name of Bangladesh had been changed from "The People's Republic of Bangla-

1. See my *The Bangladesh Coup* [MFF-15-'75], Fieldstaff Reports, South Asia Series, Vol, XIX, No. 14, 1975.

2. For a more detailed discussion of Indo-Soviet relations, see my *India and the Soviets* [MFF-5-'75], Fieldstaff Reports, South Asia Series, Vol. XIX, No. 5, 1975.

desh" to "The Islamic Republic of Bangladesh," introduced a third dimension to possible confrontation. The new Bangladesh leaders quickly denied the name change but indicated their desire to restore ties with Pakistan and China. Since the August coup, both India and the Soviet Union believe they have lost influence in Bangladesh.[2]

The recent coup and subsequent political maneuvering have sustained an atmosphere in which confrontation seems as likely as cooperation. In any event, attention in India and Bangladesh will probably be concentrated on a series of problems involving the long border between the two nations, delimitation of a maritime boundary, and the status of the Farakka barrage. Understanding the background of these issues would seem essential for any projection of future trends.

BORDER PROBLEMS

It is impossible to stand anywhere in Bangladesh and be more than 80 miles from India. This fact alone makes India's influence in Bangladesh inevitable. It is countered, however, by intense Bangladesh nationalism, reinforced by 24 years of Pakistani rule in East Bengal and dissatisfaction with Indo-Bangladesh relations since the liberation war in 1971. When issues involving common management of problems along the border are discussed, there are pragmatists on both sides who realize the need for cooperation, but their voices are often drowned in emotional nationalist rhetoric or ignored by petty politicians and traders. Over the past three and a half years, the number of incidents leading to debate has been great, and three major problem areas have emerged: (1) movement of arms and ammunition from Bangladesh into India and collaboration between extremist politicians on both sides; (2) smuggling; and (3) the influx of large numbers of poor people from Bangladesh into India without either government's permission.

The influx of arms from Bangladesh into India was made possible when Mujibur Rahman's government failed to retrieve all the weapons and ammunition accumulated by private armies, political parties, and individuals during the liberation war of 1971. Mujib deeply distrusted the Bangladesh army, for most of the officers had been trained in Pakistan and were associated, in his eyes, with a military regime that had jailed him 11 times. Rather than attempt to win the army over, Mujib proceeded to build his own *Rakhi Bahini* (Security Force), trained by the Indian military. He also created a number of armed political groups under the tutelage of, and loyal to, his family members and close associates. The principal groups were the Jubbo (Youth) League, led by Skeikh Fazlul Huque Moni (Mujib's nephew), and a number of private armies raised by heroes of the liberation war, the most prominent being the collection of *Mukti Bahini* (Freedom Fighters) led by Quadr Siddiqui, the so-called "Tiger of Tangail." Although in theory Jubbo League and private armies were affiliated with Mujib's political party (the Bangladesh Krishak-Sramic Awami League, or BAKSHAL), most observers viewed the bands of armed youth as Mujib's private armed forces.

Opposition parties, of course, attempted to maintain their own armies. The result was a state of almost constant warfare in the Bangladesh countryside, with opposition leaders and Awami Leaguers being killed almost every day. Mujib estimated that in 1974 alone more than 3,000 of his supporters, including six members of Parliament, had been killed by "extremists." Opposition parties vowed revenge when many of their top leaders were assassinated, allegedly by "Mujibadis" (believers in "Mujibism"). Understandably, opposition leaders engaging in this form of guerrilla warfare frequently used India as a refuge. Moreover, they sought to establish contacts with those radical political parties in West Bengal that have for years been convinced of the need for using violence against the Indian government. Thus radical opposition leaders could unite against the governments of both nations.

During the first two years of Bangladesh independence neither Mrs. Gandhi nor Mujib saw the radical combined forces as a serious threat. Each was more concerned with rebels at home; large numbers of Bangladesh and Indian "extremists" were either killed or imprisoned. As attempts to repress such opposition intensified in both countries, however, radical leaders drew closer. Usually coordination efforts across the international border were expressed in Maoist or other pro-Peking ideological terms. While there is no evidence that the Chinese supported such activities, Indian officials became concerned that a genuine guerrilla movement might be developing in Bengal, and this led them to suggest joint Indo-Bangladesh efforts to curb "extremist" activities.[3] In May

3. For a discussion of India's apprehension regarding China, see my *India's*

1974, during talks in New Delhi, Mrs. Gandhi and Mujibur Rahman agreed to establish a joint ministerial committee to explore ways to coordinate administrative and security forces on the border.

The two leaders also had become increasingly alarmed by widespread allegations in Bangladesh that officials in both countries were involved in smuggling relief supplies, jute, rice, and fertilizer, among other items, to India in return for textiles, medicines, and consumer goods. The persistent rumors tended to destroy whatever goodwill India had cultivated in Bangladesh and to undermine Mujib's popularity. Tension escalated rapidly in early 1974 when several Bangladesh military officers (including some who were involved in the August coup) claimed they had been dismissed because they had traced smuggling activities to Mujib's family and friends.

Subsequent negotiations on the border problems were conducted in a rather laconic manner. The talks emphasized formulating ground rules for routine operations of the Indian Border Security Force (BSF) and the Bangladesh Rifles, the two military groups that enforce border regulations. At the end of three days discussion in late April 1975, an Indian spokesman declared that "there are no major border problems as such between the two countries." The only result of the talks was "a program for the establishment of more channels of communication and better liaison between the two countries." Right or wrong, it was widely believed in Bangladesh—and in India—that neither government would take effective action against smuggling because border officials were sharing in its profits.

Shortly afterward, in May and June, mutual concern over the border's permeability was intensified by a rapid increase in the number of destitute migrants from Bangladesh into India. The migration was considerably smaller than the "movement of ten million" in 1971, and it was recognized that it reflected the dreadful state of the Bangladesh economy rather than communal factors. Nevertheless, migration was substantially greater in 1975 than it had been in the three previous years, and officials from both nations were worried.

Northern Border: In the Wake of Bangladesh [MFF–6–'5.7], Fieldstaff Reports, South Asia Service, Vol. XIX, No. 6, 1975.

It is impossible to determine precisely the number of people from Bangladesh who have entered India since Bangladesh achieved independence, but it is certainly several hundred thousand, most of them during the past twelve months. In April 1975, a railway police official estimated that an average of 200 Bangladesh migrants entered Assam daily by train, while many more slipped in via obscure village paths. In May 1975, migration into Tripura was estimated at more than 2,000 per day. While officials in Meghalaya have refused to estimate numbers, they are concerned about what they call "a steady infiltration." According to officials in West Bengal, more than 60,000 Bangladesh migrants illegally entered Nadia district during the first seven months of 1975. Estimates of the migration into the five other border districts of West Bengal are somewhat lower. By May 1975 India's BSF had refused entry to more than 42,000 Bangladesh citizens during the previous seven months, and this number probably represented only "a fraction" of all those who had entered India illegally.

Compelling motives fed the migrants' determination and made the exodus difficult to stop. From the fall of 1974 to the spring of 1975, people in Bangladesh faced famine. Rumors spread that India was willing to open refugee camps similar to those constructed in 1971. Indian studies showing that only 10–30 per cent of the migrants (the figures differed from one district to another) were Muslim led some to believe that Bangladesh Hindus were being pressured to leave. Officials in both countries hastened to point out that there was no evidence of government-inspired communal antipathy, but some migrants did complain about local communal pressures and "agents" that "assisted" Hindus who wanted to migrate.

Bangladesh border guards, whose checkpoints are an average of five miles apart, have been unable to impede the exodus. In May 1975, four squads of river police began patrolling in motorboats on the Indian side. Nevertheless, migrants can cross at unguarded points or collude with border officials to enter India. The usual procedure is to secure lodging in a Bangladesh border village through an "agent," and wait there for an opportunity to be sent across. Once in India, migrants can obtain temporary refuge, usually for a stiff fee. The goal of most migrants is to reach the home of a relative or fellow caste member, where he will be relatively secure.

India has made it known that it will not provide citizenship for the Bangladesh migrants. And Mr. Bipin Pal Das, Indian Deputy Minister for External Affairs, stated unequivocally in May 1975 that "there will be no gruel kitchens or camps." Indian attempts to repatriate hundreds of Bangladesh migrants, however, have met with resistance by Bangladesh border officials, who claim that "some Indians may be trying to send back the refugees who left East Pakistan after 1948." Establishing an individual's citizenship is virtually impossible since the migrants ordinarily do not carry the necessary papers.

Indian officials who were expressing growing concern that the problem had not yet been solved through regular diplomatic channels even before the Bangladesh coup of August 15, 1975, were anxious for Mrs. Gandhi and Sheikh Mujibur Rahman to discuss the problem. Mujib's assassination in the coup not only postponed discussion, but introduced a new dimension to the friction between India and the new Bangladesh government.

THE MARITIME BOUNDARY

The maritime boundary between India and Bangladesh is of vital importance to the exploitation of new oil finds, crucial to both nations since they must import most of their petroleum at great cost. Conflict began in April 1974, when Bangladesh first approached India for talks. Receiving no response Bangladesh proceeded to draw up contracts with foreign oil companies for off-shore drilling based on its own definition of the maritime boundary. Upon discovering—eight months later—that Bangladesh had already signed contracts with seven companies (four American and three others), the Indian government immediately agreed to discuss the issue.[4]

By mid–February 1975, after three meetings, foreign secretaries and technical experts from both sides had agreed only to resolve the issue on the basis of three common points: (1) the boundary would be delimited by mutual agreement; (2) it would be delimited in a manner that was equitable to both; and (3) the

4. A broader perspective on India's oil stakes can be found in my *Oil Exploration in India* [MFF–12–'75], Fieldstaff Reports, South Asia Series, Vol. XIX, No. 12, 1975.

boundary would be drawn in a manner that protected the interests of both India and Bangladesh. While most observers described these platitudes as indicative of a stalemate, Bangladesh and Indian officials continued to call the talks "friendly, cordial and useful." After a fourth set of meetings in early March 1975, India suggested that, "pending delimitation of the boundary, neither side should act in a manner which might prejudice the position of the other," an implication that Bangladesh should desist from surveying and drilling activities in disputed offshore territories. However, the foreign companies had already completed surveys of approximately one-third of the contracted area and Petro-Bangla had already been created to supervise exploration, procurement, supply, and distribution of oil. Since these first surveys had raised hopes of striking oil in the Bay of Bengal, Bangladesh was anxious to complete the rest of the surveys and begin drilling.

By late March 1975 Indian and Bangladesh negotiators were finally willing to admit that their talks had indeed reached a stalemate. In Dacca, the government-controlled press was even speculating that close ties with India might inhibit development of friendship with China and the oil-rich Islamic states. When the Indian press began to report that Bangladesh was committing "transgressions into Indian territorial waters," Mujibur Rahman decided to send his Foreign Minister, Dr. Kamal Hossain, to New Delhi to confer with Indian Foreign Minister Y.B. Chavan.

Before their meeting, Chavan cautioned that both India and Bangladesh had to "remain on guard against the designs and manipulations of those who were unhappy about the growing friendship between the two countries and the process of normalization in the subcontinent." More specifically, Chavan asserted that the United States' February 1975 decision to lift its arms embargo on Pakistan "can only create further tensions, fuel the arms race, and impede the process of normalization."[5]

The real crux of the maritime dispute between India and Bangladesh is similar to conflicts about territorial sea limits elsewhere, especially the West German-Netherlands disagreement of 1974–75,

5. While the interests of the American oil companies under contract with Bangladesh appeared to be limited to commercial profits, Indian critics cited one of the companies' alleged involvement elsewhere with the CIA, an allegation made in the American press at the time of the Congressional investigations of the CIA in mid-1975.

which was refused a hearing in the World Court because there were no binding international covenants for the apportionment of the seabed. The World Court suggested that West Germany and the Netherlands resolve their differences "on the basis of equity," a rather platiudinous formulation that India and Bangladesh both accept.

Where leaders of India and Bangladesh disagree is the method by which the sea boundary should be delineated equitably. The concept of a 200-mile commercial zone stretching from their coasts, acceptable to both sides, is inapplicable in the Bay of Bengal because of its funnel-like shape and the highly irregular configuration of the coastline. Using the 200-mile concept, either India or Bangladesh could claim most of the Bay area. Bangladesh has suggested that a straight line be drawn southward from a point at which Bangladesh and India touch onshore, but India has objected to Bangladesh's choice of a point and to the angle of the line. India has recommended either that a line be drawn parallel to the meridian or in such a way that every point is equidistant from points on the coastline (the so-called "base points"). By early April 1975, Dacca seemed to have accepted the "equidistant line," but talks broke down later over identification of the "base points." International precedents on demarcation of "base points" vary so widely that they offer little help.

Even while the so-called "fifth round" of talks looked promising, optimism evaporated when the Indian navy physically prevented an American oil company vessel from exploring, on behalf of Bangladesh, a disputed area. Shortly after the incident, the Bangladesh government shifted its stance on the boundary issue, claiming even more of the seabed than it had originally. This latest formulation from Dacca, based on advice from American and European legal and technical consultants, claims a territorial boundary following the alignment of what is known as "The Swatch of No No Ground." The "Swatch" is a long and deep crevice in the seabed, extending irregularly southward from a point just south of the mouths of the Malancha and Kunga in Sunderbans area of southern Bengal.

India had accepted Dacca's original 1974 claims to sovereignty over 30,0000 square miles of seabed, but rejected the claim to another 5,000 square miles. Under the "Swatch" formulation, however, India would have to reject a Bangladesh claim to almost

7,000 square miles of seabed. Since the disputed area could potentially have a 10-mile oil-bearing belt and is likely to be rich in minerals from centuries-old Bengal delta sedimentation (10–16 miles in depth), those thousand square miles could make an enormous difference in the future wealth of the two nations. Moreover, India is worried that any concessions it makes to Bangladesh in the Bay of Bengal will be used as precedents by other neighbouring countries—Burma, Pakistan, Thailand, and the Maldives—when delimiting sea boundaries (India has already settled its maritime boundarles with Sri Lanka and Indonesia).

THE FARAKKA BARRAGE

The dispute between India and Bangladesh over construction of a massive barrage at Farakka, in West Bengal, dates back to the early 1960s, when Bangladesh was part of Pakistan. India initiated negotiations with Pakistan to devise a cooperative plan for use of water resources in the Indian Northeast.[6] India has argued that Pakistan dragged its heels in the negotiations in order to create tensions between India and East Pakistan (Bangladesh), hoping to drive the East Bengalis closer to Pakistan. Pakistan has claimed that India sought to escalate tensions by proceeding unilaterally with the construction of the Farakka barrage.

The dispute over the Farakka barrage at times threatened the peace between India and Pakistan. Failing to achieve agreement, India decided in the early 1960s to construct the barrage without Pakistan's consent. Work began and, after the Bangladesh liberation war in 1971, the new government in Dacca was more disposed to cooperate with the Indians in settling the dispute. In 1972 Indira Gandhi and Sheikh Mujibur Rahman established an Indo-Bangladesh Joint Rivers Commission (JRC), which has since met more than a dozen times, seeking to reach a mutually beneficial agreement. December 31, 1947 was set as the deadline for a JRC-designed settlement, in anticipation of the barrage's completion in early 1975. When the deadline passed without agreement, an interim one-year solution was negotiated. A permanent agreement is still being discussed.

6. For background on this issue, see my *Politics and the Use of Water Resources in Bangladesh* [MFF–2–'74], Fieldstaff Reports, South Asia Series, Vol. XVIII, No, 3, 1974.

At least as difficult, and perhaps more important than the political confrontations, are the legal and technical problems encountered in devising a plan for water resource sharing in the Northeast. The region contains portions of six different nations (Nepal, Bhutan, China, India, Bangladesh, and Burma) and ten Indian states and territories (Arunachal, Assam, Nagaland, Mizoram, Meghalaya, Tripura, Manipur, West Bengal, Bihar, and Sikkim),[7] and its topography ranges from the highest peaks of the Nepalese Himalayas to the swampy marshlands and saline coasts of the Bengal delta. A comprehensive plan for water resource development in this region would have to consider the unprecedented harnessing of water in the highest mountains in the world, effects on soil erosion, conservation of wildlife and plants in the Himalayan foothills, and the flood control, power, and irrigation needs of one of the world's most densely populated areas. Any plan which appeared to benefit some more than others would provoke immediate and severe political dispute.

The barrage's principal structure, completed in 1975, is a large dam, built at a cost of $175 million over a 12-year period. Located near the Indo-Bangladesh border a few miles upstream from the junction of the Ganges and the Hooghly rivers, the barrage's purpose is to flush silt and sandbars from the Hooghly downstream by diverting large amounts of water from the Ganges. India believes such flushing will prevent more silting in Calcutta port, already rendered unusable by larger ships because of years of accumulated silt and detritus. Moreover, India hopes the barrage will prevent silting at its newly constructed port of Haldia, 50 miles downstream from Calcutta.

The sticking point for Indo-Bangladesh negotiations is how water from the Ganges is to be shared during the three dry season months (March, April, and May). During the rest of the year there is more than sufficient water for India to divert some of it without depriving Bangladesh, but during the dry season the average minimum discharge below Farakka is estimated at only 55,000 cusecs (cubic feet per second). Indian engineers estimate that 40,000 cusecs of water must be diverted from Farakka, even during the dry months, in order to flush the Hooghly successfully.

7. This region is considered in more detail in my *North-eastern India: In the Wake of Vietnam* [MFF–13–'75], Fieldstaff Reports, South Asia Series, Vol. XIX, 13, 1975.

Bangladesh engineers argue that India should be allowed to divert water only during the nine months of excess flow, because they need all 55,000 cusecs of water during the dry season to flush the Padma river, which flows out of the Ganges further downstream in Bangladesh. A reduced dry season flow would result in further saline encroachment of land in southern Bangladesh, a phenomenon already far advanced. According to studies conducted by the Bangladesh government, something like 4–5,000 square miles of land would become saline were India to divert 40,000 cusecs of water during the dry season. In addition, Dacca, contends that such diversion would aggravate shoaling of Bengali rivers downstream, contribute to Bangladesh flood problems, and adversely affect fishing, conservation, and navigation.

Indian negotiators have suggested a number of compromises, none thus far acceptable to Bangladesh. One proposal would entail building a Brahmaputra-Ganges link canal between Dhubri in Assam and Farakka in West Bengal. Since the Brahmaputra contains far more water than Bangladesh needs (being the source of most flooding in Bangladesh), a canal might benefit Bangladesh by diminishing the size of the Brahmaputra. Dacca objects to this proposal because large numbers of people would be displaced by the scheme, there would be some loss of cultivable land, and construction would be expensive and time-consuming. Some Bangladesh engineers (and foreign experts) have suggested that extensive and costly crossdrainage works would be needed to prevent flooding and waterlogging of the link canal area.

A second suggestion involves storing Ganges water in either India or Nepal during the wet season, for release to India and Bangladesh during the dry months. India is wary of Himalayan storage in Nepal, however, because of the delicate state of Indo-Nepalese relations. And construction of water storage facilities in India raises questions of costs, population displacement, and loss of cultivable land.

Some international experts have suggested establishment of a Himalayan Rivers Commission, with representatives from all major political units concerned, to devise a comprehensive plan for future water resource use in the entire northeastern subcontinent. The Indian, Chinese, and Nepali portions of the Himalayas could constitute an immense natural resource were an arrangement worked out for wet-season water storage for sale later to deficit areas downstream. Such large-scale storage could also provide hydro-electrical power and irrigation water while diminishing the flood and erosion potential of northeastern rivers. That any Himalayan reservoir project must be a transnational endeavor was the conclusion of a 1974 Indian Irrigation Ministry feasibility study for the construction of storage reservoirs in the Subansiri and Siang rivers of Arunachal.

Lacking international initiative and funds for such a comprehensive plan, the most the Indo-Bangladesh JRC could accomplish was a much-flawed interim agreement. Signed on April 17, 1975, it allowed India to open the Farakka barrage on April 20, but it restricted the amount of water for diversion to 11,000 cusecs between April 21 and 30, 12,000 cusecs between May 1 and 10, 15,000 cusecs between May 11 and 20, and 16,000 cusecs between May 21 and 31, figures far below the minimum amount Indian engineers are convinced is necessary.

While both sides hailed the agreement as a "breakthrough," neither Indian nor Bangladesh leaders were happy with it. One West Bengal Minister privately described the amount of water India received as "driblets...in quantities that do not serve our purpose." Dacca apparently wishes to play down the importance of the interim agreement; neither A.R. Serneabad, Bangladesh Minister for Irrigation and Waterways (Mujib's brother-in-law) nor his First Secretary attended the Farakka commisioning ceremony, although Mr. Jagjivan Ram, India's Minister for Agriculture was present.

Indian leaders hoped that under the interim agreement they could collect data to convince Bangladesh that diversion of Ganges water would not be as damaging as Bangladesh engineers had projected. Optimism regarding a permanent agreement was also enhanced by the close personal friendship between Indira Gandhi and Mujibur Rahman, who at several points after 1971 were able to reach agreements when subordinates had failed, but Mujib's death and reported personal differences between Mrs. Gandhi and Mushtaque Ahmed, the new Bangladesh President, have dimmed prospects. Moreover, since one justification for the coup was that Mujib's government had made too many concessions to India, agreement is all the more unlikely.

PROSPECTS FOR COOPERATION AND CONFLICT

The inability of India and Bangladesh to resolve differences on border, maritime, and water diversion issues has been reflected recently in other aspects of their relations. India has been anxious to create a jute cartel similar to OPEC, tentatively called Jute International, a proposal which Bangladesh seemed to have accepted in January 1973. Since early 1973, however, Bangladesh officials have instead sought agreements with Pakistan, China, and Western buyers for jute sales on their own terms. Similarly, India's proposed bilateral trade agreement, exchanging Bangladesh jute for Indian coal, has floundered on pricing the two commodities. Since devaluation of the Bangladesh taka in May 1975, Bangladesh jute exports are far more competitive in international markets than those from India. Greatly concerned, India has expressed a desire to explore ways of eliminating Indo-Bangladesh competition while ensuring jute markets for both nations' exports.

High hopes for substance in Indo-Bangladesh ties—such as new trade prospects, economic collaboration, and cultural exchange—also have been disappointed. The press has cited such obstacles as transport bottlenecks and strikes and raw materials shortages, but most observers blame fundamental differences in both countries. Even Mujib's government at times blamed New Delhi for foul-ups in their relations, justifying such criticism as politically expedient. Both sides, in fact, have avoided admitting their differences publicly. Before the August coup, official statements and handouts emphasized the warm feelings between Prime Minister Indira Gandhi and President Sheikh Mujibur Rahman, the *intention* of finding agreement, and romantic visions of solidarity created in the Bangladesh liberation struggle of 1971. The gap between public posture and reality has hurt relations. While officials were unable to agree on prices for state-controlled trade, illicit trade flourished. As the rhetoric about friendship escalated, negotiators at the Farakka and maritime boundary talks moved furthur and further apart. Indian and Bangladesh officials continued to insist that border problems were "minimal" while refugees streamed into India at alarming rates as the Bangladesh economy steadily deteriorated.

Although conflict between the two nations is likely to become more intense as the new government assumes power in Dacca, many undesirable features of the former relationship should be mitigated. Recognition of the new regime by China (granted on August 31, 1975) should help to diminish opposition to the new government by Maoist groups in the countryside, thus lessening "extremists'" collaboration across the Bangladesh-West Bengal border. If the new government can conclude contracts for jute sales to Pakistan and China, Bangladesh merchants should have less incentive to smuggle jute into India. In any case, Mushtaque's government is unlikely to give as much latitude for jute smuggling as did Mujib's government. In fact, both India and Bangladesh should now have reason to crack down on smuggling. Enlargement of the Indian Border Security Force should flow inevitably from this consideration, and from India's desire to control Bangladesh migration into West Bengal and the northeastern Indian states.

The likelihood of increased conflict between India and Bangladesh stems from a complex set of forces seemingly beyond the control of either side. Anti-Indian feeling in Bangladesh is in large part based on communal and economic factors derived from a long historical process. Regardless of its causes or merits, such feeling can all too easily feed visions of exploitation and dark designs by a powerful neighbor. The intensity of this feeling, now wedded firmly to Bangladesh nationalism, will put pressure on the new Bangladesh government to show no hint of capitulation to India in its official dealings. Should the new Bangladesh government fail to handle communal issues with sensitivity, there could be an exodus of minorities from Bangladesh, which would in turn create intolerable strains on the Indian political system. India cannot push too hard for influence in Dacca without rousing Bangladesh nationalism to dangerous levels. Yet, India must have some influence in Dacca should there be an outbreak of communal violence or an unravelling of the new regime.

The post-coup situation in Bangladesh would test the capabilities of statesmen anywhere in the world. At least for the present—mid-September 1975—cool heads have prevailed, and all parties are still expressing their desire to bring about a "normalization of relations in the subcontinent." Granted the enormous complexity of issues and the seeming inability to control the political process on any one of them for very long, the search for a "normalization of relations" may prove illusive, and dramatic, for many years to come.

PART III POPULATION AND RESOURCES

The major economic problems of Bangladesh have to do with population growth, development of water resources, and growing of enough food to create a measure of self-sufficiency. These are the subjects of the three essays in this section, written in 1973 and 1981. Unfortunately, little has happened in Bangladesh in the 1970s to promise better control of population size or more effective use of water resources. Therefore, almost all of the generalizations developed in the earlier essays in this section still hold for the beginning of the 1980s. Changes with regard to population and resource policies during recent years are discussed in the essays in Part IV of the present volume.

SEVEN

REALISM AND THE DEMOGRAPHIC VARIABLE IN THE FIRST BANGLADESH FIVE-YEAR PLAN (1973)

For a country of almost 80 million people and an overall population growth rate of 3.3 per cent, Bangladesh has a mouse of a population control policy. According to figures furnished by the Department of Family Planning, during the first 16 months of nationhood —from December 16, 1971 until April 30, 1973—only 12,200 intrauterine devices (IUDs) were inserted, 281 vasectomies and 87 tubal ligations performed, and about 1.5 million conventional contraceptives (cycles of pills and condoms by gross) distributed. During the same 16-month period abortions were illegal in Bangladesh, and the practice of marrying women before puberty was still common in the rural areas. The targets of the Family Planning Department of the Bangladesh government for the current year (1973–74) are 16,340 IUDs inserted; 16,340 vasectomies and 6,000 tubal ligations performed; about two million cycles of pills distributed; and about 100 thousand gross of condoms sold. In other words, if the family planning program achieves its goals in Bangladesh this year, it will protect approximately 300,000 married couples, or about 2 per cent of those couples in the reproductive age groups in Bangladesh. This approach is known among its adherents as "the soft sell," with "a high realism content."

Most people in the upper echelons of the Bangladesh Family Planning Department refuse to admit that there is anything in the Muslim historical tradition that inhibits receptivity to family planning in predominantly Muslim societies (Bangladesh is 84 per cent Muslim), despite considerable evidence to the contrary.[1] They argue

---

1. For a short bibliography of published articles on the subject of Muslim involvement in family planning in South Asia, see B.K. Singh, "Attitude of the Two Religious Groups Towards Family Planning," *Psychological Studies*, Vol. XVI, No. 2 (January 1972), pp. 35–38.

that the reason why men and women in Bangladesh are disinclined to accept almost all family planning methods has to do with the family planning program that was initiated by Pakistan in what is now Bangladesh in 1965.[2] That program has been summarized in current Planning Commission documents (prepared by the Family Planning Department) as follows:

> Weaknesses of the programme were obvious. Targets were unrealistic, leading to reporting of inflated performance. Monetary incentive in the absence of strict supervision led to rampant corruption. Conventional contraceptives were almost completely neglected. Complete lack of follow up of IUD insertions left cases of complications without medical help and thus IUD became unpopular. Clients were not really motivated; they were purchased by offers of monetary incentives. The field-level workers, being illiterate and untrained, could not acquire the skills and techniques which are prerequisities for motivational work. Being part-time workers, they were more inclined to earn remuneration rather than to take motivational work seriously. Conflict for power and privileges among the four organizations at headquarters hampered technical and administrative supervision and guidance of the programme. Training programmes were poor. No useful research was done. Evaluation and inspection were perfunctory. The administration was too busy disbursing incentives.[3]

The "soft-sell approach" of the Bangladesh Family Planning Department is a result of an understandable desire to overcome the weaknesses of the Pakistan program. Targets have purposely been lowered to extremely low levels; monetary incentives of all types have been abolished; conventional contraceptives are sold, rather than given away; distribution programs have been closely linked to medical

2. A more complete description of the Pakistan family planning program and the attitudes of Bengalis towards it appears in Marcus F. Franda, *Perceptions of a Population Policy for Bangladesh* [MFF-2-'73], Fieldstaff Reports, South Asia Series, Vol. XVII, No. 2, 1973, reprinted in *Population Perspectives, 1973*, California Institute of Technology, 1974.

3. Government of the People's Republic of Bangladesh, Planning Commission, *Annual Plan, 1973–74* (Dacca: Bangladesh Government Press, 1973), p. 151.

and health clinics, and to training centers for professional field-level workers; and considerable emphasis has been placed on future research. During the First Five-Year Plan (scheduled to begin in April 1974) it is hoped that abortion can be legalized and abortion clinics established, the age of marriage raised, and a core of professional family planning workers trained under a streamlined administrative structure. Moreover, a "climate for family planning acceptance" will hopefully be created by extensive broadcasting of the family planning message on radio, television, and in the press, by a "small family" theme in school and college curricula, and by a series of seminars and workshops held around the country. By the end of the First Five-Year Plan—in 1979—Bangladesh hopes to be, in the words of the Minister of Health and Family Planning, Mr. Abdul Mannan, "at take-off stage for population control."

The core of the new strategy is a motivation program that is now being tested in pilot projects in three Bangladesh cities (Tangail, Khulna, and Noakhali) and their surrounding rural areas. "Couple cards" are to be kept for all couples in reproductive age groups as part of a registration process designed both to secure information and disseminate knowledge. Trained fieldworkers (who will be high school matriculates rather than the illiterate midwives and male "motivators" that dominated the Pakistan program) will be assigned the task of personally visiting every couple in the reproductive age groups in their areas, providing them with information about family planning while securing information about such things as attitudes, size of family, experience with birth control methods, and so forth. By April 1974, when the First Five-Year Plan begins, it is hoped that 525 rural clinics and 22 urban clinics—each attached administratively to hospitals—will be in operation, and motivational fieldworkers will operate out of these clinics. To insure that fieldworkers actually do contact people in their respective areas, regular inspection procedures and periodic evaluation mechanisms will be provided.

The government's pilot projects in Tangail and Khulna, operational now for some 18 months, provide indications of the kinds of problems to be expected with the new strategy, even though official evaluation reports on these projects have yet to be initiated. To begin with, field-level workers associated with both projects are not themselves family planning enthusiasts to anything like the degree which one might expect. Of the 15 men and women that I talked to over the course of two weeks in mid-1973, each was convinced that family planning was necessary for Bangladesh, but many of them also had serious reservations about their ability to convince fellow citizens that this was the case. Ten fieldworkers felt that family planning was in some sense contrary to Islam, even though they thought it necessary to have family planning in Bangladesh for economic reasons. Twelve of the 15 said that they personally would prefer to be part of a large family, even though they intended to limit their own families, again for economic reasons. In short, the family planning motivators that are being trained are themselves still in need of some family planning motivation.

Second, most of the motivators expressed considerable reluctance about interviewing villagers with regard to very private matters, and they articulated a number of attitudes that indicate the great cultural gap between themselves (all of the people I interviewed were matriculates, from elite, non-cultivating families) and the people they were supposed to be motivating. "Peasants are stupid people," one male motivator told me. According to a Lady Family Planning Visitor, "These women do not even know what a menstrual period is."

Third, there is considerable unrest among family planning workers because of what they see as low pay scales, and they particularly resent the administrative changes that have made them a subsidiary part of the Health Ministry. In their view, the Health administrators and clinical technicians look down upon them, and they resent the cessation of all forms of bonuses and incentives for performance. Those who have signed on since the liberation have taken their present positions because of the scarcity of jobs and high rates of unemployment among the educated in Bangladesh; those who are carry-overs from the Pakistan days have remained because they could not get transfers to other parts of the bureaucracy. In the words of the Planning Commission assessment, which readily admits the failures of family planning thus far, these attitudes are summarized as follows: "The main reasons [for failure in 1972–73] appear to be the inadequacies of motivational work and reluctance on the part of fieldworkers to work seriously in the absence of incentives."[4]

4. Ibid., p. 5.

Overcoming these kinds of hurdles in the context of present-day Bangladesh is going to be extremely difficult. The present leadership of Bangladesh has insisted that the constitutional apparatus of the nation will be based on secular principles, in sharp contrast to the ideas that formed the basis of the "Islamic Republic of Pakistan." But secularism is opposed by large numbers of Bengali Muslims (the orthodox Muslim political parties secured almost 20 per cent of the vote even in the 1971 elections, when *the* issue was greater autonomy within Pakistan), and the concept of secularism is hardly understood by the bulk of the population. The result is that discussions of family planning methods are vehemently opposed by orthodox Muslims, while efforts to motivate people for adoption of family planning techniques are resisted and denigrated by a number of organized groups. Attempts on the part of family planning motivators to meet attitudinal resistance head-on are thus discouraged, since discussion of family planning becomes tied to the most delicate kinds of political and personal interrelationships.

Even these obstacles might be surmountable if family planning fieldworkers were themselves totally convinced of the legitimacy of what they are doing, or if they were armed with effective arguments against orthodox Islamic ideas. But their training courses too tend to shy away from detailed discussion of religious or political ideas, either on the plea that there is not enough research, or that fieldworkers should not become involved in heated debate, or that Bangladesh is a secular society and therefore "religion should not enter into it." To be sure, pamphlets quoting passages from the Koran which are favorable to fertility control have been produced, but fieldworkers are not encouraged to disseminate them, and in any case the bulk of the population in Bangladesh does not know how to read or write (effective literacy is estimated to be about 9–10 per cent of the population).

The lack of rapport between middle-class matriculates and peasant-cultivators accentuates communication problems. From the point of view of a peasant-cultivator, the sari-clad woman or the young man dressed in shirt and pants who comes to tell him about family planning is just another in a long line of people sent by the government in Dacca to work in the rural areas in a variety of different kinds of government programs. Family planning workers are classified by the mass of the population along with other government workers as people who are distinguished by their dress, their modes, of transportation (most of them have access to a jeep or car), and their general life styles. Stereotypes about "government workers" abound. They are often associated with the fads and fashions, loose morality, and political wheeling and dealing that takes place in the colleges and high schools; with the corruption and favoritism that characterizes the bureaucracy; and with the perquisites and authority of office that "government servants" command. Family planning fieldworkers complain that the closer they get to their clients the greater the chance that they will be asked to perform bureaucratic favors that have nothing to do with family planning.

The more the fieldworker is known to the village population, the more severe his or her problems tend to become. The vast majority of the matriculates in Bangladesh come from elitist families that either made their money from land or from upwardly mobile families that have benefited from opportunities created by the Pakistan government. In the former case they are associated by family connections with past injustices of the land tenure system; in the latter case they are associated with the colonialism or corruption of the Pakistan regime. Seldom, if ever, are they seen as people dedicated to a particular social cause, such as population control, although it is expected that they will occasionally offer platitudes and "words read in books" in order to draw their salaries. It is simply understood that they took their jobs in order to maintain their connections with the government, which in turn helps them to maintain their elite status.

This is not to argue that family planning fieldworkers are necessarily resented. Indeed, they are often viewed as being useful if they can be won over, at least in the sense that they represent a contact with the elaborate structure of government and the larger world outside. Through their family, friends, government, or college connections they can often influence such things as distribution of relief food or medical supplies, entrance certificates into schools and colleges, the location of tubewells and low-level lift pumps, and other scarce items for which there is an insatiable demand. For this reason alone they are to be tolerated and listened to, in the same manner as all "government servants." If they prove ineffective or unwilling in these matters, they can be neglected, or perhaps a protest movement against them will lead to their replacement by someone who is a more effective "government servant."

From the point of view of the fieldworkers too, there is good reason for them to neglect their assigned bureaucratic functions. They are most interested in rising in the bureaucracy, or in other ways enhancing their status in a particular locality or in society at large. What animates them are such things as pay scales, opportunities for getting themselves into positions where they can become Class I or Class II officers, or chances to obtain certain certificates which will enable them to move to more prestigious or lucrative positions. The proven way to advance in the bureaucracy or to get new opportunities in Bangladesh is to create an elaborate system of contacts at all levels of the government machinery, in order to both keep abreast of opportunities available and have the support of the appropriate backers when there is an opening. Little wonder, then, that most family planning fieldworkers spend most of their time traveling around to visit the various offices in their administrative areas, rather than contacting people to register them on "couple cards."

If field-level workers were highly motivated, however, it would be virtually impossible for them to perform the tasks assigned to them, even with the recently reduced targets. In the 1973–74 Plan, for example, the Family Planning Department is expected to operate 525 rural clinics and 22 urban clinics, four training centers, a postpartum program in four hospitals, and a number of research programs, all within a budget of taka 70 million (about US $9.5 million at official rates). Since only about 20 per cent of the Family Planning Department's total budget is expected to go to the "couple card" program, this means that every "couple card" motivational unit in each of the 547 clinics would be operating with an annual budget of about taka 26,000 (US $3,540). Thus, each clinic could have no more than four motivators, even if salaries and expenses were budgeted at only taka 500 per month (an extremely low figure) and all of the budget were used for the salaries and expenses of fieldworkers (which will not be the case). Using these optimal figures, the Family Planning Department could expect to have 2,188 field-level motivators employed by the end of the year, but this would still be woefully inadequate to the tasks that have been assigned by the Planning Commission. According to the Planning Commission, "It is proposed that at least one-third of the total population of

Bangladesh will be covered by intensive and continuous motivation through couple registration programs...during the year [1973 –74]," meaning that each of the 2,188 field-level workers would be assigned the task of keeping track of more than 12,000 people (or, more than 1,500 couples in the reproductive age groups) on a "continuous and intensive" basis during the year!

In short, while the new strategy of the Bangladesh government may in some respects be an improvement on the Pakistan program, it still exhibits a number of weaknesses that are strikingly similar to those of pre-liberation days. The program is still conceived in an elitist, bureaucratic manner, the basic idea being to train a small core of professionals who will somehow go out and act as brokers between the theoreticians in Dacca (or in international development agencies) and the mass of subjects whose behavior is to be changed. Little consideration has been given to the social dynamics and political sensitivities involved, or to the magnitude of the problem. To be sure, the possibilities for gross corruption and unethical medical practices have been reduced, if only because the massive incentives component in the Pakistan program has been dropped, but this does not mean that the program has gained, or will gain, anywhere near the respect and attention that family planning deserves in Bangladesh.

PRODUCTION POSSIBILITIES AND THE DEMOGRAPHIC EQUATION

Members of the Planning Commission, as well as Ministers in the Bangladesh government, account for the poor performance of the family planning program by pointing to the need for a "large emphasis on rehabilitation and reconstruction after the liberation war."[5] Rather than try to tackle fertility control at this point, the Planning Commission has attempted, in the words of Deputy Planning Commission Chairman Nurul Islam, to "deal first with the production side of the demographic equation." To quote again from the major Plan document:

The major emphasis of the Plan has been on economic "revival" rather than economic "development" in the conventional sense. The Annual Plan [for 1973–74] aims at...increasing domestic

5. Figures and quotes are taken from ibid., pp. 152-153.

production, [in order to] meet the twin challenges of bringing the economy back to the normal production capacity from the postwar level, and to prepare the base for the five-year development programme.[6]

Such thinking reflects perhaps the only sound political and humanitarian strategy that one could pursue, granted the damage that the Bangladesh economy suffered during the civil war, but it also reflects a set of basic ideas about demographic change.   More than ever before, the most popular notion concerning population control—among elites in India and Pakistan as well as in Bangladesh—is that economic growth must *precede* rather than *follow* fertility control.   To quote Mr. M.R. Siddiqui, former Commerce Minister in the Bangladesh government, "We must make it economically with a growing population, regardless of what we do about fertility control in the next 30 years.   Then, if we do make it, the birthrate will most likely come down.   If we don't make it—well, fertility control wouldn't have done us much good in the meantime anyway, would it?"

If such thinking has affected the basic outline of the First and Second Annual Plans (1972–73 and 1973–74), it is also likely to determine both the manner in which the First Five-Year Plan (1974–79) is drafted and the way in which it is revised and implemented. Only incomplete drafts of some portions of the First Five-Year Plan are being circulated—a completed draft document is reportedly being reviewed by the Cabinet—but the thrust of everything that is available would indicate that the only "population policy" being contemplated is one that calls for the meek and mild family planning program outlined earlier, with a heavy emphasis on agricultural and industrial output in an attempt to keep abreast of population growth.   To quote one Planning Department official, "We are thinking both long-range and short-range on agriculture and industrial production, but only long-range on population."

Perhaps the best way to appreciate the predicament of the Bangladesh Planning Commission is to look at the performance of the economy of the country during the First Annual Plan and the projections for the Second Annual Plan. During the former period, Bangladesh suffered four successive

6.   Ibid., p. 11.

rice crop disappointments, as is indicated in Table 1. In December-January, 1971–72—just after the liberation of the country—the *Aman* (Fall) rice crop was 18 per cent below the level of 1969–70, the last year that Bangladesh was not disturbed by floods, cyclones, or political disruption. The *Boro* (Winter) crop in 1971–72 was then beset with a shortage of inputs (owing to the war), and it proved to be 20 per cent less bountiful than in 1969–70. The *Aus* and *Aman* crops in 1972–73 were then affected by drought conditions, resulting in the lowest harvests for these crops in recent years. In short, for one reason or another Bangladesh has been unable to get rice production back to prewar levels.

Table 1. *Rice Production in Bangladesh, 1968–1973 (in tons)**

Year	Aus Rice Crop (harvested August-September)	Aman Rice Crop (harvested December-January)	Boro Rice Crop (harvested March-April)	Total Rice Crop
1968–1969	2,680,000	6,870,000	1,610,000	11,160,000
1969–1970	2,960,000	6,950,000	1,900,000	11,810,000
1970–1971	2,860,000	5,910,000	2,190,000	10,960,000
1971–1972	2,340,000	5,690,000	1,740,000	9,770,000
1972–1973	2,270,000	5,570,000	2,250,000	10,090,000

*Figures are rounded to the nearest 10,000 for easier comparison.
Source: Bangladesh Planning Commission Documents.

The importance of rice in the Bangladesh economy cannot be overstated. In 1971–72 approximately 26.2 million acres of land were under cultivation at some time during the year, of which 23 million acres (88 per cent) were given to rice. Another 1.7 million acres (6.5 per cent) were planted in jute, the principal cash crop, and the rest of the land was given over to minor crops (vegetables, pulses, wheat, etc.). These are the approximate percentages for the various crops each and every year in Bangladesh, indicating the enormous dependence of the cultivators on rice (rice and fish are the traditional staples of the Bengali diet, although dietary habits are changing rapidly). In the last decade, however, rice production has remained relatively static (it was 10,460,000 tons in 1963–64, compared with 10,090,000 tons in the current year) while population has increased more than 25 per cent over this same period.

In the 1960s Bangladesh began to require large quantities of foodgrain imports every year (before this foodgrains had been imported only in years of poor harvests), to the point where it was importing 1–1.5 million tons of foodgrains annually in the period from 1966–67 until the end of the liberation war. During 1972–73, Bangladesh had to import 2.9 million tons of foodgrains, and its own estimated requirements for 1973–74 are another 2.8 million tons. Despite these massive imports—now totaling almost a fifth of what is grown inside the country—people have been eating less (on the average) and they have been forced to change their dietary habits to accommodate large portions of wheat and nutritional mixes of various kinds.

If one looks at this situation from a purely statistical point of view, there should be no reason why Bangladesh cannot feed its present population. Rice output per acre in Bengal is among the lowest in the world; inputs of the new technology in rice (seeds, fertilizers, pesticides, and modern irrigation) have never been applied over an extensive area in an efficient manner; and the vagaries of the weather have combined with political and social unrest to create a situation where planting and harvesting of rice has been constantly disrupted. *If* methods of cultivation that have proven themselves in Japan or the developed world or other parts of Asia could be transferred to Bengal; *if* the new technology could be applied over an extensive area for even a short period of time; *if* the country could have some degree of stability and a few good breaks from the weather—then surely it would be possible to increase the bounty from the rice harvest considerably.

These are big *ifs*. One reason why the weather has affected the rice crop so severely in recent years is that the people of Bangladesh have been unable to maintain or initiate flood control and irrigation programs that would assist them in coping with their climate. The older traditional systems for control of water resources have broken down for lack of authority structures to maintain them, and no one in the society has been able to muster enough authority to put anything in their place. Lack of authority, organization, direction, leadership, management—all of these are also constantly reiterated as the basic reasons for the failure in Bengal to make use of the new technology in agriculture. (For example, the Planning Commission points to such things as untimely supply of seeds, delivery of seeds in poor and rotted condition, lack of sufficient credit, improper use, inadequate supplies, lack of appropriate knowledge of use, and related factors as the kinds of reasons for failure to increase rice production in quantities commensurate with new inputs in 1972–73.) In short, all of these *ifs* boil down to the question of administration, management, control, call it what you will. The basic problem is to find some way to allow or force or entice people into organizing society in such a way that they can gain some degree of control over their own destinies, at least to the degree that they can have some hope of feeding themselves. It is in this light that some observers see in Bangladesh perhaps the ultimate demographic tragedy—so many people on such a small piece of land that they cannot sort out their relationships with one another in any productive way. Perhaps the appropriate analogy here would be to the cage of rats that is so overpopulated that none can survive; perhaps it would be to a form of collective suicide.

The thought of "collective suicide"—or of millions of deaths by starvation, disease, flood, famine, or killing—has prompted a massive international relief effort in Bangladesh. According to official government figures, $432 million in international assistance was spent on relief and reconstruction in 1972–73; another $563 million in international assistance was "in the pipeline" on June 30, 1973; and still another $452 million in international assistance has been committed for future programs. This means that approximately $1,447,000,000 has been or will be made available to Bangladesh over the course of its first three years of independence—in a country where domestic revenue last year (1972–73) was an estimated $330 million, much of which came from the printing of new money (the money supply was increased by an estimated 83 per cent during the year). In addition to international monetary and commodity aid, Bangladesh has attracted the attention of a number of extremely able economists (including the four members of the Planning Commission) who persist in their jobs because they see in this phenomenon one of the more challenging economic problems of the century.

The major goals of the Planning Commission for 1973–74 seem sensible enough. They are to orient the economy in such a way as

(1) to slow or stop the rapidly spiralling inflation that has gripped the country since liberation; (2) to direct development toward labor-intensive employment; (3) to reduce heavy dependence on imports; (4) to promote exports; (5) to complete reconstruction activities; and (6) to promote a more equitable distribution of incomes. "The single most important problem" from the point of view of Planning Commission members is the price situation, which was inevitable granted the general scarcity of things produced but was severely aggravated by a number of other significant factors. Immediately after liberation the Bangladesh taka (replacing the Pakistani rupee) was devalued—from 4.6 to the dollar for the old Pakistani rupee to 7.35 to the dollar for the taka—in order to conform to the official rates being paid for the Indian rupee. Then, since the general price structure in India was much higher than in Bangladesh, and since a decision was made to facilitate commerce with India, prices tended to shoot toward Indian levels. When the Bangladesh government decided to increase the money supply by about 83 per cent during the past year things really got out of hand (the taka is now being sold at 18 and 20 to the dollar in the Bangladesh black market).

The Planning Commission estimates that prices have "at least doubled on the average since liberation" and the price for essential consumption items—rice, edible oil, sugar, kerosene, and cloth—has risen 3–4 times in most parts of the country. General price confusion has resulted from the large-scale smuggling of relief supplies, agricultural produce, and manufactured goods into India (legally only state trading is allowed, but merchants have flagrantly violated the law, as have government officials and enterprising citizens from all walks of life), and such smuggling has recently accelerated in response to more acute scarcity conditions in India in the aftermath of the Indian drought, the general economic crisis in India, and the relatively stronger position of the Indian rupee on international markets. Those who have been hit hardest are the landless poor in the countryside and the poorer sections of the urban population, most of whom are now almost permanently dependent on international relief assistance in one form or another. In every urban center of Bangladesh where relief assistance is available one can see thousands and thousands of rural poor who have migrated from their villages in order to get closer to the communications and transportation networks that are the only things keeping them alive. In Dacca, the capital of Bangladesh, there must be 200–300,000 such people—camped in temporary shelters, sleeping on the pavements, searching for the food, medicine, and clothing that will sustain them until things get better.

But things have not been getting better in Bangladesh. The enormous crash in the expectations of the young *Mukti Bahini* (freedom fighters) of Bangladesh has led to a tremendous upsurge of radical political activity and the growth of nihilism. At last count there were six communist parties, one socialist party, and four other "mass" political parties in opposition to the ruling Awami League, and each of these parties has its subsidiary peasant, labor, youth, and student wings. Every week or so leftist political circles in Bangladesh throb with news of another ideological split, a fresh factional dispute, or a new wave of political killings undertaken by hostile factions of this or that Marxist party. Self-proclaimed potential Mao Tse-tungs, Che Guevaras, and Ho Chi Minhs abound.

The two things that the radical parties of Bangladesh now have in common are a supply of weapons gathered during the liberation war and a series of vendettas against the ruling Awami League. The Prime Minister, Sheikh Mujibur Rahman, purposely and consciously decided to include only his own party people in the governmental structure, the important relief committees, and in the police and army, thereby excluding large numbers of *Mukti Bahini* who had fought in the liberation war under other political party banners. "Mujib" then tried to collect weapons and ammunition from those freedom fighters that had been excluded from the patronage of his party, but Awami League leaders now estimate that only 50–60 per cent of these private arsenals have been surrendered or captured. The Awami League also estimates that at least 20–30 of its party members are being killed each month by rival political groups, and in some months the figures have been considerably higher.

In addition to violent political feuds, there has been a fantastic increase in the number of armed robberies and murders in Bangladesh in the period since liberation. Every day the newspapers report dozens and dozens of instances of armed robbery of banks and post offices; break-ins of homes; the killing and beheading of influentials in the rural areas; attacks on power plants, telephone installations, and industrial plants; armed robbery of trains, river barges, and country boats; highway holdups; rape; armed theft of cars and trucks; looting of government arsenals, police stations and army posts; and the throwing of grenades into government offices. The Bangladesh police force and army, which started almost from scratch at liberation (most police and army personnel were Pakistanis or, if Bengalis, were detained in Pakistan until the September 1973 agreement with India) have been loyal to the government and have performed surprisingly well, but the government campaign to "crush miscreants" has failed to restore a sense of security in any part of Bangladesh.

Insecurity and political tensions have in turn been fed by a series of strikes in almost every sector of Bengali life. During the current year there have been major strikes or slowdowns among college and secondary school teachers, jute workers, government employees of various kinds, and innumerable factory workers in both nationalized and private industries. Responding to massive inflation, workers have quickly formed small but determined unions, propagated a series of demands, and declared strikes. As is usually the case in Bengal, such unions quickly get captured by political parties, and rivalries among unions attached to different political parties lead to demands and a prolongation of strikes. In light of the terrorist tradition of Bengali politics, and the existence of so many weapons in the hands of so many pseudopoliticians, it is not surprising that strikes have frequently led to violent incidents and encounters with the police.

Plagued by massive corruption and an under-current of factionalism in its own ranks, the Awami League has been unable to halt the deterioration of law and order, and this in turn has prevented the evolution of a climate conducive to stable prices and an increase in productive activities. The dependence of everyone in the Awami League on the personal leadership of Sheikh Mujib has prevented an open split in the ruling party, but considerable factionalism nevertheless simmers below the surface. While Mujib was away on an 18-day tour of Europe and Canada in August (the highlight of the tour was his attendance at the Commonwealth Conference in Ottawa) a rumor was circulated within the Awami League linking Mujib's family to a multimillion dollar deal that allegedly ended with a large Swiss bank account in the name of a relative of the Prime Minister. Mujib himself has not commented publicly on the rumor, but he has expressed considerable concern about it in private conversations with a number of people who are close to him.

In the period immediately following the liberation, the attitude of the government toward political violence and civil disorder was somewhat circumscribed. Exhortations were made to surrender weapons, engage in productive activity, and desist from "antisocial behavior." An attempt was even made by the government and the Awami League to develop a set of principles known as "Mujibism" (*Mujjibad* in Bengali) which were intended to inspire the populace in the manner of "Maoism" in China. As the government has established its administrative machinery and put together some semblance of a police force and an army, however, it has exhibited an increasing willingness to use coercion in its attempt to restore civil peace and get the economy moving, while Mujibism has clearly failed to capture the imagination of the populace.

In the last two months the government has resorted increasingly to the practice of imposing surprise day-long curfews in various city neighborhoods, which clears the streets and keeps everyone confined to their homes. During the curfew hours authorities from the water, power, and telephone companies travel door to door collecting old bills, while checking on the legality of installations. Rationing cards are also checked during such curfews, and occasionally the police will use the curfews to track down stores of arms and ammunition or the locations of "miscreants." After a recent meeting of the Cabinet an appeal was issued to all "common citizens" of Bangladesh to "come forward and tell the police in private about the location of miscreants and *dacoits* [armed robbers]," an appeal which has served only to intensify the atmosphere of suspicion and rumor-mongering created by the horrors of the civil war.

The problem of lagging industrial production has recently been tackled in a similar manner. Members of the *Rakhi Bahini* (Mujib's trusted "security force") have been assigned to factories where slowdowns have occurred, so that workers in the factories labor within view of policemen brandishing guns. Absentees are checked by the *Rakhi Bahini* and labor union leaders have been placed under 24-hour surveillance. A number of journalists that have attempted to "expose" the government or to extol the virtues of one or another of the opposition parties have been jailed, as have a number of bureaucrats in the lower and middle echelons of the administration. Sheikh Mujib's nephew, Sheikh Fazlul Haque Moni (known as "nephew of the nation" among Dacca wags) has even formed a Youth League of 100,000 youthful members in order to launch a "purification drive" designed to "weed out from government service elements opposed to the existence of Bangladesh."

Mujib himself has resorted increasingly to threats rather than exhortation in his public pronouncements. In a major speech inaugurating the second national conference of the Bangladesh Chhatra League (the student wing of the Awami League) on August 19, 1973, the Prime Minister asked the students to organize a strong movement to check "miscreants and antisocial elements" as well as "hoarders, smugglers, and black marketeers." He also implored students to "work amongst the people, to embolden them to come forward and tell us who are the corrupt persons and murderers," and then "to make thorough investigation and crush them." At the same time, Mujib told the divided opposition that "this government will not be pulled down by terrorists;...killing under the cover of darkness does not make revolutionaries .. ; secret killings will be treated as criminal [not political] acts." Emphasizing his role in the liberation of Bangladesh, Mujib warned his opponents: "I am steeled in popular movements and I know how to launch movements...if you talk of democracy and at the same time breathe threats against the Government in the language of arms, you must be prepared to face the consequences."

In short, the Awami League government in Bangladesh has come quickly to resemble the stereotype of an opposition nationalist party thrust into power. Thwarted in its attempts to get hold of the administrative machinery, and unable to inspire the populace by example or by "charisma," the government has more frequently relied on coercion and threats. In the elections that were held last spring, Mujib's party did secure 291 of the 300 seats in the National Assembly, while garnering about 90 per cent of the votes, but both the police and members of the Awami League were prominent in their presence at polling booths and reports of widespread ballot-stuffing are almost universal among people of all political suasions (including adherents of the Awami League). Most observers agree that the Awami League would probably have captured a comfortable majority of seats and between 50-60 per cent of the votes even in a totally fair election, and that Mujib himself would unquestionably have received 90 per cent or more of the vote in his own constituency in any case. But the attempt to create a veneer of consensus when a consensus is obviously lacking is now widely resented.

The attempt on the part of planners to deal in a rational manner with the frightening economic situation is, therefore, intimately connected with the future of the political alignments within Bangladesh. If the Awami League can suddenly reverse itself and inspire the confidence of a significant portion of the people; if the coercive movement against "miscreants and antisocial elements" can create some semblance of law and order; if widespread use of the police and army can work in such a way as to restore civil peace and increase production—then perhaps one could begin to set about to actually manage the economy. Alternatively, the emergence of new leadership from among the floundering opposition parties, or perhaps a more cooperative attitude on the part of opposition leaders, might also make a difference. In present-day Bangladesh none of these things seems possible, but then again it is clear that the present situation is a dynamic one, which will change in a variety of unpredictable ways simply because of the existence of so many societal forces that are incompatible with one another.

CONCLUSIONS

It is in light of these kinds of considerations that the Planning Commission considers its work to be of value, despite the seemingly hopeless prospect of its recommendations ever being implemented. The argument of the planners is that they will attempt to devise a set of economic strategies that make sense from the point of view of any ideology, or any government interested in purposefully coping with the challenges of the many possible futures of Bangladesh. The First Five-Year Plan, therefore, is not necessarily intended as the strategy of the present government, although the government is advised to adopt and implement the Plan. The Plan is merely an intelligent blueprint which indicates the directions in which one might move if one were to cope with the massive set of problems facing the nation.

Viewed from this angle, the most important sections of the Plan have to do with the attempt to promote initiative in decision-making and implementation at the local level, and this in turn is intimately bound up with the search for a technology appropriate to Bangladesh. In this sense, the critical element of the Planning Commission's work is their Integrated Rural Development Programme (IRDP), an attempt to establish new institutions of local government in association with a series of co-operatives, which in turn are expected to develop new technological devices for dealing with problems at the village and *thana* levels. The core of the IRDP, the local system of self-government, is described in Plan documents as follows:

> The local government body must be managed by people's elected representatives and the government officials at the local level must serve under them. Under no circumstances should the government bureaucracy be allowed to interfere with the decision making functions of the local government bodies.
>
> At the village level, decisions must be made by peoples' council, i.e., the total body of voters in the village assembled in a mass meeting. Development projects and schemes must be discussed in these meetings before and after execution, and major decisions approved by the people. The peoples' councils should have the authority to call back representatives elected by them to the local government bodies.
>
> ...The co-operative movement cannot become strong and effective without full political support. At the same time, it is important to allow co-operatives to develop as independent autonomous bodies. The practice of controlling the co-operative by the bureaucracy, through, nomination of members in the managing committee and various other devices, must not be allowed to happen. The co-operative laws and acts must be revised to make them consistent with our new ideology and purposes. In order to make the co-operatives truly peoples' organisation the poorest class should be encouraged and helped to organise and manage co-operatives. For this, collective ownership of the means of production should be encouraged.[7]

Bangladesh, of course, is a long way from instituting anything remotely resembling the system described above. In 1972–73 a number of cooperatives were established in 33 of the 414 *thanas*, and plans are in the works to extend the cooperative movement to

7. Ibid., p. 51.

another 56 *thanas* in 1973–74. However, as the Planning Commission itself points out, membership in the cooperatives in 1972–73 was abysmally low (about 25 members in each), landless peasants and sharecroppers "were not attracted to the cooperatives," and "in many cases the cooperatives were dominated by traditional power elites in the villages, who used the cooperatives to expand and consolidate their exploitative roles." (p. 49) The small indigenous tubewell program that was to be launched through the cooperatives in 1972–73 was postponed indefinitely, pending research; the rural credit scheme that was to be worked out through the cooperatives was judged a "failure" and is being revised; while of 1,000 paramedical personnel that were to be trained to work with local self-government bodies (a la the Chinese "barefoot doctor") only 88 were actually given training and this training was considered by the Planning Commission to be "far inferior to what was anticipated."

In this situation, what is realism and what is real? The Planning Commission argues that its plans are as realistic as any that have yet been suggested to meet both short-run and long-range problems, granted at least some leadership capability on the part of the government that intends to implement them.

What is real? Major Jalil, a bearded and long-haried veteran of the freedom movement, now a popular opposition politician, shouts: "Plan! Plan! They have no Plan! All they do is talk platitudes while they line their own pockets. Our children are being maimed, both physically and psychologically. We have no jobs! We have no food! Corruption and inefficiency are everywhere! How can they talk of Plans?"

What is real? Senator William Bart Saxbe, Republican from Ohio, told a press conference in Dacca in mid–August 1973: "The United States has not yet geared itself up to full agricultural production. American farmers can grow enough to feed all of the people of Bangladesh if the right legislation is passed...Bangladesh has many friends in the United States...If Bangladesh can get one good rice harvest, a lot of these problems should begin to straighten themselves out."

What is real? A Russian helicopter pilot, one of more than 200 Soviets serving as consultants to the Bangladesh Air Force (there are far more Soviet consultants acting as "advisors" to the Bangladesh navy and Shipping Corporation) told me just after this Press Conference: "We must assist these people [the Bangladeshis]—they have been exploited for so long."

What is real? A German businessman says casually: "Last year you could make tons of money here. It was floating in the air, and all you had to do was be in the right place at the right time and you could reach up and grab some of it. This year there is still money to be made, but now there are more people getting into the act, and the government is keeping a lot of it for their own people."

What is real? A peasant-cultivator in Comilla that I had interviewed a year ago told me, "Last year there was *hoy-choy* [glorious confusion]. This year there is *golmal* [trouble]. Next year—who knows?—maybe there will be *lorai* [fighting]."

What is real? A British scholar advises me: "You really should go over and see so-and-so at UNICEF. This chap has invented an ingenious rig for drilling tubewells, using parts that can be manufactured here in Bangladesh. Of course, the Bengalis will have to adopt the idea, but that's their problem, isn't it?"

What is real? An AID official who transfered in from Vietnam (three-quarters of US AID personnel in Bangladesh have previously served in Vietnam) tells me: "I like it here. The kids have a fairly good school and lots of interesting friends. They enjoy the pool and the tennis courts, even though they sometimes are a bit bored. And we can travel a lot in India and Asia. The wife is not bogged down in the suburban housewife routine, and we can be together a lot more than we were when I was in Vietnam...Besides, I like Bengalis—they have a sense of humor and a kind of spirit that a lot of people don't have."

Somehow, on the ground in Bangladesh much of this seems very unreal. Sometimes all of it seems unreal. Sometimes all of it seems too, too real. But what is ever-present, and indescribably real, is the tragedy of the suffering of a people who at least for the present have lost control of their own destinies, in large part because they are so many of them in such a small space.

EIGHT

POLITICS AND THE USE OF WATER RESOURCES IN BANGLADESH (1973)

To a greater extent than usual, people in Bangladesh are concerned about the unpredictable nature of their weather and an increasing inability to control their rivers. On the average, annual floods are experienced over a third of the cultivated area of Bangladesh during seven months of the year (approximately April through October), and every fourth or fifth year or so—usually in August or September—the floods become uncontrollable enough to ravage more than half of the land. The last very big floods in Bangladesh occurred in 1970, at about the same time that a series of cyclones devastated the southern coast. In a somewhat exaggerated manner, these two events are now commonly described within Bangladesh as the two greatest natural calamities of this century, and they were of course followed by a year of political disruption in 1971, when Bangladesh fought a successful civil war (with the help of the Indian army) against Pakistan. Paradoxically, parts of Bangladesh last year (1972–73) experienced drought conditions, while the rains during this monsoon season (1973–74) have tended to come in concentrated spurts, causing flash flooding in many areas.

The Bengal Delta is usually divided for analytical purposes into five extensive river systems:

(1) the Ganges (or Padma) and its deltaic streams, the origins of which are to be found in the Himalayan range north of Delhi (the Ganges flows into Bangladesh from the West, meets the Brahmaputra at a point just west of Dacca, and then spills down into the Bay of Bengal through a number of deltaic subsidary rivers and rivulets);

(2) the Brahmaputra's affluents and channels, which originate in Tibet, flow first easterly through China and then westerly through Assam, entering Bangladesh from the north (once the Brahmaputra enters Bangladesh it becomes known as the Jamuna, and it then

proceeds due south until it meets the Ganges, at which point it too disperses into a number of different deltaic rivers and rivulets);

(3) the Meghna and Surma river system, much smaller than either the Ganges or Brahmaputra, consisting exclusively of rain-fed channels that flow out of or through the Sylhet Hills northeast of Dacca;

(4) the rivers of the Chittagong Hill Tracts, similarly confined to the area southeast of Dacca and exclusively rain-fed;

(5) the North Bengal river system—a wide variety of rivers that flow out of the Himalayas in a rather direct route, straight down into Bangladesh and the deltaic portions of West Bengal.

Perhaps nowhere in the world does so much water flow into such a small land area in such a short space of time as is the case in Bangladesh at the end of almost every monsoon season. Much of the water and snow that falls in the Himalayas, and in the Kumaon, Nepal, Bhutan, and Assam Hills finds its way into the rivers that flow into Bangladesh. These rivers are then fed by an average annual rainfall of 75 inches (varying between 67 inches annually in the Northwest to more than 200 inches annually in the Northeast), more than 80 per cent of which occurs during the months from May to October. It has been estimated that the water that flows into Bangladesh would be sufficient to cover every inch of the country to a depth of 34 feet every year if the water dispersed equally over the entire area. People in Bangladesh speak of this enormous volume of water as one of their few natural resources, and they attribute many of the past glories of Bengal to the fact that they have always had an abundance of water. One of the most prominent myths in Bangladesh is that the deltaic soil of this region is more fertile than any other soil in South Asia; another is that the rivers of Bangladesh afford the most complete and easy system of navigation found anywhere in the world; a third is that there is a peculiar Bengali genius in knowing how to cope with large volumes of water. While each of these myths may have been believable at some point in the past, not one of them is now viable as an empirical proposition.

What has happened to Bengal in this century is a function of population growth and population density, political and economic upheavals of the kind one would expect in an area where the demographic situation has become so unfavorable, and a few geographical changes that have worked against the attempt on the part of Bengalis to gain control of their own destinies. At the beginning of this century, when there were approximately 20 million people living on the land that is now Bangladesh, this area had a food surplus. The surplus was never distributed equitably and it was occasionally disrupted by floods and famines, but it was sufficiently large to create a stereotype of Bengal as a land of leisure and ease. These stereotypes were enhanced by the existence of systems of riverine transport and travel that were at least as extensive and efficient as other systems of transport in South Asia at the time, and Bengalis in the nineteenth century did have a reputation throughout India as a people that understood the complexities involved in making use of water resources and controlling the ravages of a monsoon flood. Indeed, it was in large measure the existence of a food surplus in East Bengal that made possible the fantastic growth in population experienced in this century (the other major factor being the introduction of public health schemes that successfully prevented epidemics of common diseases).

Bangladesh today has almost 80 million people, living on a land area just over 55,000 square miles (about the same size as Wisconsin), giving it a population density that is approaching 1,500 people per square mile. This means that Bangladesh is more than three times as crowded on the average as India, more than five times as crowded as China or Indonesia, and almost twice as crowded as Japan. If one took all the people in the entire world and put them in the boundaries of the United States, the United States would still not be as crowded as Bangladesh is today. Yet the population boom in Bangladesh has barely started. More than half the population is now less than 16 years of age, and the most accurate estimates place the rate of annual population growth (births over deaths) at 3.3 per cent per year. At present population growth rates, Bangladesh adds approximately 2.5 million people to its population totals each year (it adds the population of the state of Wisconsin in a little more than two years), meaning that the size of the population can be expected to double at some point in the early 1990s.

Population density has affected the relationship between Bengalis and their use of water resources in a variety of ways. First, Bengalis have moved into areas that were previously considered unfit for human habitation because they were so frequently subjected to the vagaries of the weather and the rivers. Homes and settlements are now constructed in low-lying marshy areas and swamps, in flood-prone river valleys, and in the southern cyclone-prone areas and offshore islands, all of which were very sparsely inhabited or even devoid of human settlements a half-century ago. Moreover, people have moved into these areas without any semblance of a new technology that would enable them to cope with the ravages of the weather. They are kept alive by occasional, massive imported relief efforts. Second, people have begun to do things that they know are harmful to their ecological relationship with the rivers: forests have been cut to such an extent that only 15 per cent of the land of Bangladesh is now classified as forested, and the vegetation of much of this land is such as to seriously call into question the use of the word "forested" to describe it. Erosion is further encouraged by the lack of maintenance of embankments (bundhs), largely a result of a division of landholdings and a subsequent diminution in the authority of the large landholders that used to be responsible for maintaining such embankments. Peasant cultivators today will all point to the lack of maintenance of embankments as a major reason for their increasing vulnerability to the destruction of the rivers and the floods, but few have been willing or able to band together to create social and political institutions capable of exercising enough authority to build, repair, and maintain them.[1]

Third, there is an excessive dependence in Bangladesh on outside agencies and the central government in those matters having to do with flood control and irrigation. The collapse of traditional rural power structures, a remarkable fragmentation of holdings, and the growing aspirations of central government leaders and international development experts to have control of rural development, have combined to produce a situation where people at the local level now feel almost powerless to do things on their own. For example, one of the most effective traditional means of flood control in Bengal was the practice of building human settlements on high ground, generally made higher by earth obtained from the excavation of "tanks" (pukurs) or large ponds, which were in turn used to retain monsoon water for use during the dry season. The

---

1. A fascinating study of the changes that have taken place in one Bangladesh village in this century is S.A. Qadir, "Village Dhanishwar: Three Generations of Man-Land Adjustments in an East Pakistan Village," (Comilla: Academy for Rural Development, 1960).

maintenance of this system—commonly known as *pulbandi*—was the responsibility of local influentials, usually a number of large landholders (*zamindars*) and their tenants. In the latter years of the British raj, when the position of the *zamindars* was undermined considerably, the system began to break down, but this breakdown was rapidly accelerated after East Bengal became Pakistan, if only because most of the *zamindars* (who were Hindus, living in an Islamic Republic) emigrated to India. Land reform measures under the Pakistan government have since made it impossible for anyone to use land as the basis upon which to muster authority sufficient to reinstitute the traditional system, and no other local authority structures have arisen to take the place of those that existed before. The result is that most of the old tanks in Bengal are now covered with silt, to the point where they are totally incapable of retaining enough water to prevent flooding of any kind.

LARGE-SCALE PROJECTS AND POLITICAL CONSTRAINTS

During the period that Bangladesh was part of Pakistan (1947–71), little thought was given to large-scale flood control projects, primarily because of the international political problems that would have been involved in launching them. Bangladesh is remarkably flat. Most of it is between 30 and 40 feet above sea level, the slope of its rivers seldom being more than five inches per mile. The only hills in Bangladesh are the Sylhet Hills and the Chittagong Hill Tracts, but these do not rise to more than about 7,000 feet at their highest point, with the vast majority of the hills being only 2,000 feet or less in elevation. This means that any large-scale attempt to dam up the rivers that flow into Bangladesh, or to build reservoirs, or to initiate schemes for flushing out the silt in the river-beds, would have to be carried out in the mountainous regions where most of the rivers of Bangladesh have their origins—in India, Nepal, Sikkim, Bhutan, or Tibet. Granted the animosity between India and China on the one hand, and India and Pakistan on the other, as well as the dependence of Nepal, Bhutan, and Sikkim on both India and China, it was inconceivable to all but the most romantic optimist that large-scale international flood-control projects could be carried out for the benefit of the erstwhile East Pakistan.

The only large-scale river project affecting Bangladesh that was undertaken while Bangladesh was part of Pakistan was the building of a barrage near Farakka (in West Bengal) by the Indian government, with the barrage being designed in such a way as to flush out the Hooghly River further down stream in India. India's decision to go ahead with this project in the late 1960s, against the wishes of the then Pakistan government, created an enormous stir, and it is still a matter of dispute between India and Bangladesh. Dr. K.L. Rao, India's present Power and Irrigation Minister, has said that the Farakka barrage would divert 40,000 cusecs of water from the Ganges into the Bhagirathi and Hooghly Rivers (both in India) when it is inaugurated later this year, leaving only 25,000 cusecs to flow through Bangladesh during the dry winter months. But the Bangladesh government has argued that the requirements of Bangladesh during these months is 49,000 cusecs, if much of southern Bangladesh is not to become saline for lack of an adequate water flow. From Bangladesh's point of view, the problem is that underground water – the alternative to a flow from the Ganges—becomes increasingly saline in this region as it is pumped from lower and lower depths, so that underground water cannot be considered an alternative in quantities large enough to serve as a substitute for the water India intends to divert. At present the Farakka barrage issue is still being negotiated at the highest levels, with no agreement yet in sight.

Despite the heat that has been generated during the debate over the Farakka barrage, there are a number of leading government officials in both India and Bangladesh who now think it possible to conceive of flood control and multipurpose river development projects that were politically unimaginable during the days when Bangladesh was part of Pakistan. To facilitate such thinking, India has established a Northeast Development Council, which consists of representatives of all of India's northeastern states and is charged with putting forth plans for the integrated development of the northeast in a manner that assures the greatest degree of cooperation with Bangladesh. In addition, India and Bangladesh have established a Joint Rivers Commission, which has been meeting periodically on the Farakka issue and is expected eventually to turn to other areas of potential conflict and cooperation between the two countries.

Then too, the idea of a large-scale flood control and water resources project in the Himalayas is one that is now more appealing to international development agencies than it would have been a few years ago. A number of hydrologists have argued that India and Bangladesh should take advantage of their recent political friendship to at least explore the possibilities of a large-scale project which would work to the advantage of both countries in the long run, but which might not be possible to initiate in a changed international atmosphere. It is this kind of thinking that prompted Bangladesh Finance Minister Tajuddin Ahmed to inquire about the possibility of World Bank financing for an Indo-Bangladesh joint venture, along the lines of the Indus Basin agreement between India and Pakistan, during his August 1973 appearance at a meeting of the Bank's "Committee of 20" in Washington, D.C. According to Mr. Tajuddin's statements upon his return to Dacca, he received an "encouraging response," both from the "Committee of 20" and from World Bank President Robert McNamara (the Bank already has under way a feasibility study for some water control projects in Bangladesh).

A number of water engineers are advancing good technical reasons for focusing on a large-scale flood control and water resources project at this point in time. The Brahmaputra Basin in particular has been singled out in recent years as one area of the world that has been undergoing changes which are likely to seriously affect the lives of those who depend on it for their livelihood, unless something drastic is done fairly quickly. Prior to the great August 1950 earthquake in the Himalayas, the Brahmaputra always carried an enormous amount of silt and sediment (the river is about 1,800 miles long, and is fed by innumerable tributaries that flow down from the more friable hills of the Himalayas). But in 1950 a colossal quantity of detritus was washed down into the river from landslides, and the Brahmaputra has subsequently become extremely restive and unstable. As a result of the great earthquake, the minimum water level at Dibrugarh (in the Indian state of Assam) has risen by over 10 feet, indicating the very considerable general rise of the river bed in the upper reaches as a result of siltation. Moreover, siltation has further increased because of both deforestation and the faulty soil conservation practices of larger and larger numbers of cultivators and entrepreneurs of various kinds in the hilly and mountainous northeastern regions of India. As large quantities of silt and sediment have moved

down the Brahmaputra, it has been attacking its banks more severely each year, causing acute erosion problems downstream, while
siltation has also hampered navigation at several points for longer
and longer periods each year.

In the lower reaches of the Brahmaputra—in both Assam and
Bangladesh—the ravages of the river are further enhanced by the
fact that the land is so level, by the large amounts of rain that are
dumped on the land during each monsoon, and by increasing
human pressure on land. As is typical of all alluvial rivers, the
country in the Brahmaputra valley generally slopes away from the
river banks, and because of population crowding most of the high
ground has now been taken up by forests, tea estates, and towns.
When the Brahamputra spills its banks, it spreads out over the
remaining valleys, which nowadays consist of populated villages
and small cultivated fields, and when much of this is flooded the
problems for the people of Bangladesh become severe.

In the process of building its valley's lower reaches, the Brahmaputra has always shifted laterally from east to west, while moving
in a general southward direction. During the course of such movement, the river has completely and permanently claimed for itself
entire towns (the last town to disappear completely under the river
was Sadiya, in Assam, in 1953); it has eroded large portions of other
towns (Dibrugarh, also in Assam, was so eroded in 1954 that it
received headlines throughout the the world); and it has cut channels
through and across into neighboring tributaries and streams. What
has taken place increasingly in recent years is the formation of spill
channels during periods of high flood, which then flow toward a
neighboring tributary, thus forming over the years a new tributary,
which in turn breaks into neighboring streams. In short, the Brahmaputra and other rivers in Bangladesh have been increasingly subject
to bank erosion, rising river beds as a result of greater deposits of
detritus and silt, more frequent changes in the course of rivers, and
more frequent spilling over of banks. And all of this in an area where
man-land ratios are higher than any comparable area in the world.

In August and September 1973, major erosion was reported in
the Bangladesh towns of Chandpur and Puranbazar, while large
portions of five Bangladesh districts (Rangpur, Faridpur, Tangail,
Pabna, and Mymensingh) were at times almost completely flooded.
In a manner reminiscent of the trek to India of 10 million refugees
in 1971, people moved to higher ground wherever they could find

it or they clung to overcrowded river barges capable of staying afloat in the swirling rivers, or they lived in trees for days on end. Their condition was the more severe because Bangladesh has yet to recover from the terrible disruptions that accompanied its liberation from Pakistan in 1971. Food was already scarce before the floods, the administrative structure is still not geared up to cope with day-to-day happenings even in "normal" times, and the relief effort has merely been keeping people alive without proceeding to the stage where development plans can be initiated.

In this atmosphere, it is little wonder that the Finance Minister, the World Bank, and a number of hydrologists have given serious thought to the possibility of launching a large-scale flood control and water resources project that could conceivably have a major impact on Bangladesh. But the difficulties—both technological and political—involved in even beginning such a project should not be underestimated. On the technological side, accurate historical data on the changing course of the rivers, as well as data for such things as rainfall and erosion patterns, geological formations, and topographical changes over time, are woefully inadequate. Moreover, systemic collection of data would be more difficult and time-consuming in this area than in others, if only because of the plethora of political boundaries and authorities involved and the great distances (usually over difficult terrain) that would have to be covered by those collecting data. Then, too, all of the data that exist at present indicate that control of the rivers of Bangladesh would require engineering and technological feats of an unprecedented nature—not only do many of the rivers have their origins in the highest mountains in the world, they are also woven and braided together in a variety of complex ways, and in many places they flow through mountains and hills that are liable to frequent and severe earthquakes.

On the political side, there are obvious problems in trying to bring together so many different peoples from so many different political entities in a cooperative arrangement (India'a major attempt to bring state governments together in a multipurpose river valley development scheme—the Damodar Valley project—has been universally judged a miserable failure). There are perhaps even more insurmountable political problems, and particularly for India, when assigning relative weights to development priorities. The Indian government is presently giving highest priority among its contemplated big water resources projects to what is known as the Ganges-Cauvery link, a proposed canal that would be almost 2,000 miles long, linking the Ganges River in the north (from a point near Patna, in Bihar) to the Cauvery River in the south. This canal is envisaged as the backbone of a projected national water grid designed to divert flood water from the Ganges during the monsoon months, to areas in western, central, and southern India that are chronically deficient in water and frequently subject to drought.

The Ganges-Cauvery link would take an estimated 30 years to build, and would cost at least $4 billion (at present price levels) over this 30-year period, thus using up much of the credit, foreign exchange, and other resources that India would at least initially be able to invest in large-scale river development programs. Nevertheless, the scheme has widespread support, including the enthusiastic backing of the current Union Minister for Irrigation and Power Dr. K.L. Rao, and the encouragement of a recent study team that was sent to India by the United Nations Development Program (UNDP). According to Dr. Rao's and UNDP'S projections, the Ganges-Cauvery link would make possible the diversion of as much as 20 million acre-feet of floodwater between mid-June and October every year, which in their estimations would not seriously affect the Ganges' annual flow of 400 million acre-feet, three-quarters of which (they argue) "runs to waste" into the sea during this period. The water that would be diverted into the Ganges-Cauvery link canal would be used for a variety of different purposes, including irrigation, flood control, drinking water, and even navigation. According to the UNDP study team, the poor distribution of water in India is primarily a function of the geographical accident that has provided India with no major rivers flowing north to south, and population pressure in future years will make it essential for India to transfer large amounts of water via canals and aqueducts that cut across the major east-west rivers. In this sense, the Ganges-Cauvery link is seen by Dr. Rao and the UNDP team as merely one (albeit the largest and most dramatic) of a number of water development projects designed to benefit the low rainfall areas of India.

For people in Bangladesh, and in the northeastern portions of India, a Ganges-Cauvery link has little appeal, not only because they suspect it would use up resources and international aid commitments that might otherwise be assigned to river development in

India's northeast, but also because they fear the ecological effects in their own areas of a diminished flow of water from the Ganges. Therefore, as the Ganges-Cauvery link assumes greater salience among the many political issues in the sub-continent, one would expect politicians and administrators in India's northeastern states to line up with those environmentalists who are already opposing the link canal on other ecological grounds. As things develop, the issue is likely to become even more complicated, since many foreign experts (including most agricultural economists in such concerned organizations as the Ford Foundation and AID) have argued that the optimum agricultural production strategy for India would be to devote its' major effort to the exploitation (by drilling and tubewells) of the substantial groundwater reserves located at varying depths beneath the Indo-Gangetic plain and the desert and dry lands of Rajasthan and central India. Only a small portion of these resources has been tapped and large quantities of underground water are known to exist in these areas. Moreover, the cost of exploitating these resources is likely to be much less than large-scale river development projects, and the immediate irrigation payoffs from such a strategy are likely to be much greater. All of this means that the people of India's dry land areas will be able to make a good political and technological case for groundwater development schemes in their areas, in a manner that works primarily to their benefit. In this atmosphere, and granted the considerable infighting among the various regions of South Asia for development funds and strategies as they affect water resources, the relatively powerless Bengalis could well be disadvantaged.

THE SEARCH FOR A SMALL-SCALE STRATEGY

In light of these kinds of considerations, planners in Bangladesh as well as officials in the appropriate ministries, are not thinking in terms of large-scale projects in cooperation with India, but are instead trying to devise a series of smaller scale flood control and irrigation schemes that can be carried out within Bangladesh itself. One of the major problems here is that some administrators feel constrained by legacies from the old Pakistan days. The Pakistan government had initiated a number of projects which were all part of a Master Plan for water resource development that had been drawn up by a group of international consultants (under the supervision of the International Engineering Corporation, an American concern, in the 1960s.[2] According to the Bangladesh Planning Commission,

> In most cases, they chose technology and set specifications which suited only the foreign contractors. Agencies like the Planning Department did neither [sic] have the competence nor manpower to criticise their assumptions and recommendations. A study and analysis of some of the multipurpose projects completed so far indicate that the average construction time of these projects was about 11 years and cost overrun factors (ratio of actual cost to estimated cost) was about 300 per cent.[3]

These kinds of feelings, the essence of which is that Pakistan opted for a level of technology that was not suited to Bengal, are shared by some other people in the Bangladesh government, but they are not universally shared in the bureaucracy and they have not yet made a significant impact on the elected political leaders of Bangladesh. As a result, conflicts about the priorities that should be assigned to different flood control and irrigation projects abound.

Those who would like to continue with at least a modified version of the Master Plan argue that flood control should be the principal focus of the Bangladesh government in the future, with irrigation benefits being derived from projects that have as their main target the control of rivers. Mr. Amirul Islam, Commissioner of the Water Development Board, for example, is inclined to favor a strategy that would be built around a number of multipurpose river development projects designed to prevent flooding while providing irrigation and drainage benefits to people in the major river valleys (hydroelectric power is not really feasible in a country without hills or mountains). This strategy calls for the building of a large number of medium-sized flood control embankments along the major rivers of Bangladesh, constructed in conjunction with large pumping stations. These stations would carry water

2.   The modified version of the Master Plan that was being followed just before civil war broke out in 1971 is outlined in *Water Resources Development and Flood Control in East Pakistan* (Dacca: East Pakistan Water and Power Development Authority, 1971).

3.   *Annual Plans*, 1973–74 (Dacca: Planning Commission, Government of the People's Republic of Bangladesh, 1973), p. 53.

from the river itself into the areas from which the river had been excluded and store it in canals for use during the dry season. At the same time, sluice gates are necessarily provided to drain water from the area where flooding occurs. Multipurpose projects of this kind were assigned high priority in the Pakistan Master Plan.

Mr. Islam's argument is that Bengal's water problems are caused not only by an excess of water much of the time, but also by an erratic supply of water throughout the year. During the monsoon season, for example, there will often be periods of two or three weeks when there is little or no rainfall and during these periods the rice crop may be damaged owing to a lack of water. Then too, much of Bengal becomes almost arid when the rivers dry up during the winter months (December–March), with the result that few crops can be planted during these months. If small–and medium-sized floods could be controlled by the building of embankments, and water pumped from the rivers and canals during dry spells, cultivators throughout Bengal could increase their yields considerably, both by decreasing the damage of floods during the monsoon and by increasing their irrigation capabilities during the winter months. If this strategy could be implemented, the only major water crop damage that the cultivator would have to fear would be that which would come from major floods.

As critics of these embankment projects point out, the benefits of such multipurpose projects are considerably less appealing in those areas of Bengal where the rivers dry up completely in the dry winter months. In these areas some benefits would be derived from the building of embankments during the monsoon season, when some flooding would be prevented and irrigation water could be made available during those intermittent periods of the monsoon when the rains are inadequate for the rice crop. During the winter months, however, there would be no water in the rivers to be tapped for irrigation, and experience has shown that water in the canals is usually insufficient.

Even more important, multipurpose projects have been criticized because they involve very large allocations of funds and rely heavily on imports (for the pumping stations, for cement, for sluice gates, and for technology). Granted the heavy costs involved, the Planning Commission has tried to discourage a number of projects of this kind, and at least for the time being has successfully set aside a good portion of the Master Plan. Of a total of 12 major projects in the Master Plan, only four are presently being extended (the Coastal Embankment Project, Phase I; the Chandpur Irrigation and Flood Control Project, Phase I; the Ganges-Kobadak Project, Phase II; and the Karnafuli Irrigation and Flood Control Project), although it is likely that the Bangladesh government will at least try to complete other projects that were started by the Pakistanis.

For many of the same reasons, the Planning Commission has tried to argue against a heavy emphasis on embankment projects designed to protect cities. Indeed, in current Plan documents, the Commission argues that:

> ...urban protective works should be taken up on a selective basis. Only those projects which may be considered essential for protection of life and property should be taken up. Any saving on this account may be diverted towards smaller schemes.[4]

In private conversations Planning Commission members have even argued that, "one alternative to city protection may be to shift an entire city in those cases where the cost of protection from floods becomes prohibitive."

Ideas expressed by members of the Planning Commission reflect their desire to initiate a development pattern that would reduce the dependence of Bangladesh on external assistance, achieve self-sufficiency in foodgrains production, and thrust more and more of the initiative for development activities on people at the local level. In pursuit of these three goals, the Planning Commission has tried to shift the emphasis of water resource development from the costly medium- and large-scale projects envisaged in the Master Plan to extremely small-scale programs that focus on the cultivator. Rather than build large embankments with foreign technology, the Planning Commission has recommended a number of schemes that would try to stir up local initiative for drainage, irrigation, and flood control projects at the village and *thana* level (the *thana* is an administrative unit based on the location of police stations in the rural areas). This is not to argue that the Planning Commission is opposed to all the projects in the Master Plan, since it does admit that "in most cases alternatives [to large-scale projects] simply do not exist," but the preference for small-scale local projects is a

4. Ibid., p. 59.

constant refrain in the writings and converstaions of Planning Commission members.

If the strategy of the Planning Commission is followed, the thrust of water resource development efforts in Bangladesh would be directed at the use of low-lift pumps, tubewells, and manually dug wells for deriving irrigation benefits from groundwater sources, with flood control and drainage projects being undertaken at the local level by the same individuals and cooperative societies that would operate the pumps and drill or dig the tubewells. As members of the Planning Commission point out, what is required for the implementation of this strategy are such things as "full participation by farmers, extension services that teach managerial efficiency at the local level, and technical education for farmers," all of which (the Planning Commission readily admits) are presently lacking in Bangladesh. The views of the Planning Commission, then, represent a vision of what might be possible, granted a considerable change in the skills and attitudes of people at the local level, rather than a blueprint that can be readily implemented. The defense of the Planning Commission position is that it does provide answers to some of the most nagging long-range problems of Bangladesh, since it attempts to come to terms with the excessive aid-dependence of the country while at the same time holding out the possibility of self-sufficiency in foodgrains production and rural development. In a country that is 92 per cent rural, with a burgeoning population and a declining agricultural output, the position of the Planning Commission has won over a number of supporters.

THE PROBLEM OF IMPLEMENTATION

It is doubtful, however, that the Planning Commission will have its way in Bangladesh, at least in the short run, if only because its vision runs counter to almost everything that is happening in the political, economic, and social life of the country since liberation. To be sure, the Ministry of Rural Development has initiated an Integrated Rural Development Programme (IRDP), which did establish a few village cooperative societies in 33 of the 414 *thanas* of Bangladesh in 1972–73, and plans call for the setting up of cooperative societies in 56 additional *thanas* during the current year. But the number of such societies established in each *thana* has been far less than had been originally planned, while the average membership in each cooperative (about 25 people) would indicate that only a fraction of the cultivators are participating in the scheme. In the words of the Planning Commission's own evaluation:

> The landless and share-cropping cultivators were not attracted to these cooperatives. In many cases the cooperatives were dominated by traditional power elites in the villages, who used the cooperatives to expand and consolidate their exploitative roles.

The only local "power elite" (if one can call it that) which has emerged in Bangladesh since the liberation consists of those people who have connections with the Awami League, the political party headed by Bangabandhu Sheikh Mujibur Rahman, the "Father of the Nation." Sheikh Mujib has consciously pursued a strategy of excluding opposition parties from his government, despite a number of appeals that he create a broad "multiparty" front to secure the cooperation of people of all political suasions during the period of postwar reconstruction. Mujib has also insisted that all relief and rehabilitation supplies and funds be channeled through relief committees dominated by Awami League members, with the result that the Awami League has monopolized control of the faucet of foreign relief and aid. Because the period since liberation has been one of rapidly spiraling prices (on the average prices are now at least two or three times what they were in 1971, for all commodities), giving rise to a tremendous amount of corruption (international relief officials estimate that only 30–40 per cent of relief supplies have reached intended recipients), status-conscious elites in Bangladesh have been encouraged to "get a piece of the action" rather than concentrate on development priorities.

With regard to water resources programs, "getting a piece of the action" has entailed a variety of different things. In some cases pumpsets have been diverted from warehouses at the port—by bureaucratic and other means—into the hands of entrepeneurs who disassemble them for their parts. In other cases pumpsets are smuggled into India, or they are diverted from cooperatives to an individual who either has no intention of using them for agricultural purposes or will use them only on a restricted basis. Figures are not available for all pumpset programs in Bangladesh but, in the case of the Bangladesh Agricultural Development Corporation (BADC) more than 30 per cent (2,616 of 8,283) of the new pumpsets procured in early 1972 had still not reached the sites for which they were intended in September 1973.

Even more damaging to the pumpset and tube-well programs has been the tremendous shortage of oil and diesel fuel that has existed in Bangladesh since the liberation. This too has been aggravated by the widespread diversion of oil and fuel and is the most frequently mentioned reason for the miserable failure of the modern tubewell sinking program, which had an established target of 2,400 deep tubewells to be made operable in 1972–73, out of which only 774 were sunk and only 104 were in operating condition at the end of 1972–73 fiscal year. Similarly, only about half of the 2,000 shallow tubewells that were planned for 1972–73 have been drilled, and of these only 153 are presently operable.[5]

The water development program that has failed most miserably, however, is one that calls for the digging of a large number of small wells, using heavy inputs of manual labor and rather crude indigenous implements. Patterned after wells that are apparently being widely used in China, these wells could be drilled or dug to depths ranging from 35 to 100 feet, depending on water levels. One method would employ simple, locally manufactured tripod rigs that could be moved from place to place on handcarts or with large bullock carts. Simply designed centrifugal or propeller pumps could then be used to withdraw water from these wells, which would on the average yield 0.5 cusecs of water each. Preliminary estimates indicate that the cost of constructing one of these wells would range between taka 2,000 and taka 2,500 ($277–$347 at official rates), as compared with costs of taka 60,000–90,000 ($8,310–$12,465) each for 2,900 two-cusec deep tubewells drilled with imported equipment.

There are a number of problems involved in trying to get projects under way for the drilling of indigenous wells of this kind. First, they involve large inputs of manual labor in cooperative ventures if costs are to be kept down. In some cases entire villages would have to work together for weeks on end manually to dig holes six feet in diameter and about 25 to 35 feet deep, in order to get at least 10 feet below the minimum groundwater level. A concrete ring about five feet in diameter would then be lowered into the

5. Ibid., p. 55.

hole, followed by a perforated brick lining as the concrete ring became embedded in the excavation. In short the digging of the well would require large amounts of heavy manual labour, with people willing to work together in a cooperative manner for long periods of time. It is the inability of anyone in society to organize people for such cooperative ventures that has thus far been the downfall of schemes of this kind.

Having grown up in an environment where status accrues to those who can secure imported pumps and drilling equipment, cultivators that are in a position to think about irrigation wells for their lands seek to outmaneuver other peasant groups and local influentials who are also attempting to get technologically advanced devices. Since all of these technologically advanced devices have to be imported, those who succeed are people who have contacts in the ministries in Dacca and in the warehouses at the port in Chittagong. The thrust of people's efforts to climb in status, therefore, is directed at securing such contacts.

The result is a terrific competition for the few devices that can be imported, and a neglect of indigenous means for coming to terms with flood control and irrigation problems. Moreover, because so few devices (relative to need) can be imported, and because these devices depend on complex technological skills that do not exist in Bangladesh, there tends to be enormous wastage of those things that are imported, and competition between those who struggle for these scarce items serves to promote wastage. Pumps and tubewells are fielded on the basis of the political and social clout that a group or individual can muster, often in places that are unsuitable for the fielding of a pump; or they are installed in a manner that ruins their effectiveness and renders them idle most of the time; or they are so inadequately maintained or so subject to sabotage by competing groups and parties that they are virtually out of order on a permanent basis. Some idea of the frequency of such things can be gained from recent statistics of the Water Development Board (WDB) which indicate that of 380 tube wells installed by the WDB in the first 18 months following liberation, seven were ruined during installation, 17 have never discharged enough water to be useful or have discharged only sand, 42 have had consistent electrical mechanical troubles and have therefore failed to function, and 34 are idle because of disruptions to transmission lines.

CONCLUSION

More than ever before, Bangladesh appears to be a society that has lost control of its own destiny, and nowhere is this better illustrated than in its use of water resources. Large-scale projects are not being pursued because they would involve international cooperation that cannot be secured. Medium-sized projects are inadequate to the problems involved, pursued on a sporadic, piecemeal basis, or are mere reactions to immediate crisis situations. Small-scale projects appropriate to levels of technology in Bangladesh have proven to be impossible to implement because of a lack of organizational cooperation among people at the local level. In light of its burgeoning population and declining agricultural output, the only prospect for the immediate future would seem to be a continued reliance on foreign relief and assistance.

NINE

FOOD POLICY AND THE 1980s (1981)

Bangladesh is *sui generis*, if only because it is so poor and so overpopulated relative to food production that it forces one to ask the question, "How can any country get into the predicament of a Bangladesh?" The answer to such a question involves exploration into a number of complexities, including cultural patterns, political realities, economic changes, policy choices, and a multitude of historical events. A useful focus for inquiry is the food distribution system, which lies at the core of the nation's poverty. What are the political determinants of food production? To what extent and in what ways have national political and economic policies affected the nutritional levels of the poorest of the poor? How do present-day food policies compare with those of the past in terms of improving nutritional levels for the poorest segments of the population?

AN HISTORICAL PERSPECTIVE

In a remarkable paper that has, to my knowledge, never been published, Dr. Akhter Hameed Khan has traced the history of the food problem in what is now Bangladesh, from the time of the great famine of 1943 up until the division of Pakistan in 1971.[1] Dr. Khan is in an especially good position to understand the mechanics of famine and food scarcity in Bengal because he was a government officer in the famine areas in 1943, a relief worker in the Khulna famine in 1951, a district officer during the days of community development and land reform in the 1950s and 1960s,

1. Akhter Hameed Khan, "A History of the Food Problem," Unpublished Paper presented at the 16th Conference of the Pakistan Economic Association, Islamabad University, 18–20 February 1973. All references to Dr. Khan's writings are taken from this paper.

and the founder of the heralded Comilla Academy of Rural Development. Dr. Khan argues that the 1943 famine was a major historical turning-point in Bengal because it seriously diminished the Britishers' "proud confidence" in their ability to govern, and it resulted from factors that are "still either patently active or merely dormant." Moreover, Dr. Khan insists, the policies born out of the trauma of 1943 "were scrupulously followed for more than two decades and have not yet been discarded."

Britishers, Bengalis and outside observers now agree that the 1943 famine was entirely man-made, the result of a wartime decision to upset traditional patterns of food production and distribution in order to prevent conquest of India by the Japanese. In early 1942 the Japanese had struck Asia like a "military tornado"—crippling the Royal Navy, overpowering the British in Malaya and Burma, looming like dark clouds over India's eastern borders. As a precaution against a potential enemy landing in the Ganges-Brahmaputra delta, the British decided to pursue what was called a "denial policy"—i.e. to remove carts, boats, rice supplies and other necessities from the southern districts of Bengal in order to "deny" these to the invaders. As Dr. Khan points out, the Japanese escaped the hardships intended for them by not arriving, but unprecedented suffering took place among Bengali farmers, fishermen, carters, boatmen, rice merchants, and, most of all, rice eaters.

The areas of the 1943 "denial policy" were historically surplus rice areas, where grain merchants (*biparis*) purchased surplus rice after the big harvests (in January, February and March) and then sold it to other *biparis* in Dacca during the rainy season (June, July and August). One key variable in the distribution system was the annual flooding of the rivers, which enabled boats to take the rice to markets in Dacca and other overpopulated districts once the monsoon spate had risen high enough. By seizing all boats and carts, the British prevented rice from moving very easily into Dacca, with the result that a scarcity mentality set in, hoarding intensified, and prices soared. Bengali farmers were delighted when they found that prices were moving upward every week, and they quickly decided that they would wait before selling, sell in small quantities, and watch the market. As Dr. Khan points out, "never before had Bengali farmers seen such favourable trends or possessed such holding capacity."

Within a few months, the "denial policy" had brought unprecedented affluence to hundreds of thousands of people—farmers, *biparis*, merchants, or anyone else who could store rice—and pitiful destitution to millions of others. Dr. Khan describes a big farmer who could not tell the police inspector after a 1943 burglary how many currency notes had been stolen because he did not know the extent of his new wealth. On the other side, Dr. Khan says, "I met many buyers—artisans, labourers, tenants—who had sold all their belongings to buy their daily rice."

The 1943 famine was publicly blamed on a series of chronic factors that were undoubtedly present in Bengal but were not the trigger causes of the immediate food scarcity. Production had not kept pace with population growth, the historic Bengali "safety valve" of imported food from Burma during periods of acute scarcity had not been working; and the increasing salinity of previously fertile land in the southern districts was beginning to be a problem. The reaction of the British, and later the Pakistanis, was to invest large amounts in attempts to increase agricultural production, and to intervene on a massive scale in an attempt to rearrange food distribution networks. For the first time in Bengal, five interventionist measures of government became prominent, and all five have remained as salient features of food policy until the present time. These are: 1) control of food prices; 2) control of the foodgrains trade; 3) control of movement of foodgrains; 4) government procurement of food; and 5) rationing.

Since 1943, the State—whether it was under the British, the Pakistanis, or independent Bangladeshi governments—has conceived of itself as the custodian of foodgrain consumers, and especially city-dwellers. Whenever there has been the slightest hint of scarcity, the government has moved in to fix ceiling prices to consumers, to restrict the amount of profits that can be made from foodgrains, and to prevent hoarding. Surplus districts have occasionally been cordoned off by policemen and the military, who are at those times supposed to allow only small handfuls of grain to move legally between districts without government permission. The government itself has undertaken large-scale "procurement" of foodgrains, with the declared intention of supplanting old traders and providing fairer prices. The rationing system has always publicly promised constant prices and stocks, but has blatantly been structured to favor the six largest cities. Unlike the middle-class and rural poor, even low income urban consumers have generally been able to get cheap food, although first priorities for rationed food supplies have gone, by law, to the army, the police and the bureaucracy.

Every available study indicates that government intervention in the distribution of foodgrains in Bengal has not been a force for equality.[2] Rations have gone primarily to the better-off, and for the rest have been unreliable, inadequate and of poor quality. Price controls have generated a black market that has favored the rich. Procurement and price controls have served as disincentives to growers, who have resented the fact that their interests have been sacrificed for the sake of the town-dwellers. Attempts at control of the foodgrains trade has given birth to unprecedented corruption and smuggling, with all records of dishonesty in other sectors of the economy being surpassed by those of government officials and police assigned to control grain movement.

Poverty in Bangladesh has been intensified by a number of other factors. Primary among them is a massive population growth that has resulted from exceptional improvements in public health in this century, with no corresponding improvements in industrial or agricultural productivity. Overall annual population growth rates have risen from an average of just over one per cent in the 1940s to more than two per cent in the 1950s and more than three per cent in the 1970s. A plethora of recent studies indicate that there is some support for control of family size and spacing of children in Bangladesh, and especially among mothers who have already had a number of pregnancies, but that the economics of poverty—essentially, the necessity for large numbers of hands, to improve the likelihood that some of them will be productive enough to sustain the family—still persists.[3]

A second factor intensifying poverty in Bangladesh were the large-scale Hindu-Muslim riots during the years of partition, which,

2. Two excellent studies are: Donald F. McHenry and Kai Bird, "Food Bungle in Bangladesh," *Foreign Policy*, 27 (Summer 1977), pp. 72–88; and F. James Levinson, "The Role of Subsidized Consumption in Reduced Population Growth: The Case of Sri Lanka, Kerala and Bangladesh," Paper presented at the Conference on Nutrition Needs, Laxenbur, Austria May 1978.
3. The best recent study is W. Brian Arthur and Geoffrey McNicoll, "An Analytical Survey of Population and Development in Bangladesh," *Population and Development Review*, IV:1 (March 1978), pp. 23–79.

when coupled with the declaration of Pakistan as an Islamic Republic, led to the exodus of more than 4 million Hindu landlords (*zamindars* and *jotedars*), moneylenders, schoolteachers, government officials, and other elites between 1947 and 1954. These were the people who had run East Bengal—who had built and maintained the embankments (*bheris*) against floods, constructed large tanks (*pukurs*) and lakes for irrigation water, or had financed and supervised the reclamation of old silted riverbeds as the massive rivers of Bengal inexorably shifted course over the years. Without the *zamindars* and *jotedars*, the *bheris* were not maintained, new *pukurs* were not dug, and the silted up rivulets and canals were not re-excavated. Pakistani military and administrative officers during their years in power (1947–1971), tried to take the place of the old authority figures of East Bengal by launching dozens of government programs designed to supply irrigation water, but the Pakistanis ultimately proved illegitimate in the eyes of Bengalis, and Bangladesh was born as a consequence of the only successful civil war in this century.

The liberation war, along with a series of disruptions before and since, have interfered with whatever slight gains may have been made in food production. As is indicated in Table 1, foodgrain output over the past four decades has generally not kept pace with population increases, but there have been certain periods (particularly in the first decade of the 1960s and during the last few years) when there have been spurts of growth. Not surprisingly, these have corresponded with periods of relative calm and stability in the countryside.

During the 1950s, food production was severely hampered by the flight of Hindu landlords and capital to India, and by the resulting insecurity within Bangladesh as the Muslim peasantry fought over tenuous rights to the lands abandoned by the Hindu *zamindars*. Every communal riot in the late 1940s and early 1950s enhanced the nervousness of the elite Hindus of East Bengal, causing them to steadily shift their assets out of Pakistan and into India. The same riots fractured community structures in the villages of East Bengal, making it difficult (and often impossible) for anyone to muster enough authority to maintain the kinds of public works necessary for a productive agriculture. A poorly implemented land reform—ostensibly abolishing all intermediaries, fixing ceilings at 33 acres, and giving occupancy rights to tenants—

Table 1. *Comparisons of foodgrains production (in millions of tons) with population, Bangladesh, 1949–1981*

Population Size	Year	Rice	Wheat	Total Foodgrains
42 million	1949–50	7.5	—	7.5
55 million	1959–60	8.5	0.2	8.7
70 million	1969–70	11.7	0.5	12.2
89 million	1979–80	12.5	0.8	13.3
91 million	1980–81 (projected estimates)	13.9	1.3	15.2

Bracket annotations: 112% (population); 13%, 7% (rice between first rows); 38% (rice); 11% (rice between last rows); 77% (total foodgrains).

Source: Statistics Division, Ministry of Planning, Government of Bangladesh and its predecessors, as quoted in Haroun er Rashid, *Geography of Bangladesh* (Dacca: University Press Limited, 1977), pp. 242, 247; and in interviews with Dr. A.K.M. Ghulam Rabbani, Secretary of the Statistics Division, and with Dr. Charles Antholt and Stephen French of AID-Dacca, all in November/December 1980.

enhanced conflicts within village communities, to the detriment of productive enterprise.[4]

For a short time in the early and mid-1960s, it seemed as though a long-term agricultural boom was underway, in both East and West Pakistan, but this proved to be a temporary phenomenon. Concessional foodgrain imports from the United States emboldened the Pakistan government to relax procurement and controls, and to otherwise remove disincentives to production. Positive incentives were introduced in the shape of subsidies for fertilizer, pesticides, irrigation water, seeds, tubewells and machinery. Ceiling prices for food crops were replaced by floor prices. Counterpart funds were generously provided for rural infrastructure. Large-scale projects

4. See A. Alim, *Land Reforms in Bangladesh: Social Changes, Agricultural Development and Eradication of Poverty* (Dacca: Samina Publishers, 1979).

were initiated for water control, village roads, drainage and irrigation, rural employment, and many other aspects of rural development. But all of these activities were not fully tested during the days of a united Pakistan, if only because they were interrupted by so many occasions of domestic dissension.

These are solid indications that the nascent beginnings of a "green revolution" in Bangladesh have widened the gap between the better-off and worse-off segments of the population, but a more salient feature of the rural scene is the way in which almost all productive activities have been constantly interrupted by the devastations of war and civil strife. The introduction of the new technology in agriculture was seriously retarded in the late 1960s by the build-up to the 1971 civil war, beginning with the general disenchantment (rural and urban) against the rulers of united Pakistan after their embarassment at the hands of India in the 1965 Indo-Pak war. The migration—primarily from rural areas—of 9.7 million political refugees to India in 1971, and then back again to Bangladesh in 1972, was the culmination of a series of upheavals accompanying the independence movement, which seriously affected agricultural production. The gory aftermath of the liberation war has continued through the three coups of 1975 and the unsuccessful coup attempts of the late 1970s and early 1980s.

Not only were crops not sown or maintained or harvested during the years of actual turmoil, the war years have left a legacy of land disputes about who has seized who's land when, or who is entitled to it now that so-and-so has returned from India or West Pakistan and so-and-so remains in India or West Pakistan, or whether such-and-such political party or government was legitimate in promulgating particular pieces of legislation or ordinances to deal with rural conflict and development. In the eyes of many rural dwellers, there has been so much disorder, so much bloodshed and so many changes (or attempted changes) of government during the past decade that it is now impossible to live an harmonious existence. Stories abound of individuals or families gaining vast amounts of wealth from abandoned land or possessions, or from the spillover of the large international relief and development presence in Bangladesh, but these are more than balanced by stories of those who have lost everything—often in the short space of a few minutes, hours or

Table 2. *Size distribution of total owned land in rural Bangladesh*

Number of Acres	Number of Households	Percent of Total	Number of Persons	Percent of Total	Area (Acres)	Percent of Total
Zero	1,767,334	14.69	8,081,266	11.59	—	—
0.01–1.00	5,375,887	44.68	27,561,648	39.54	1,733,223	8.33
1.01–2.00	1,830,170	15.21	10,821,861	15.53	2,660,128	12.78
2.01–3.00	1,045,072	8.69	6,706,826	9.62	2,556,850	12.28
3.01–4.00	621,105	5.16	4,438,188	6.37	2,141,713	10.29
4.01–5.00	370,799	3.08	2,811,716	4.03	1,651,046	7.93
5.01–6.00	253,414	2.11	2,027,653	2.91	1,375,463	6.61
6.01–7.00	173,661	1.44	1,520,481	2.18	1,123,908	5.40
7.01–8.00	110,825	0.92	963,593	1.38	827,971	3.98
8.01–9.00	94,944	0.79	835,505	1.20	803,505	3.86
9.01–10.00	66,979	0.56	581,056	0.83	636,690	3.06
10.01–11.00	60,764	0.51	568,972	0.82	634,253	3.05
11.01–12.00	38,668	0.32	378,394	0.54	444,383	2.14

12.01–13.00	36,251	0.30	358,024	0.51	451,674	2.17
13.01–14.00	25,894	0.22	276,200	0.40	350,779	1 69
14.01–15.00	19,679	0.16	215,091	0.31	285,006	1.37
Over 15.00	95,790	1.16	1,556,732	2.23	3,137,282	15.07
Totals*	12,031,272	100.00	69,703,206	100.00	20,813,879	100.00

*Components may not add to totals due to rounding.

Source: F. Tomasson Jannuzi and James T. Peach, *Bangladesh: A Profile of the Countryside* (Dacca: AID Mission, Bangladesh, 1979), p. 120.

days—through the ravages of civil war and domestic turbulence of the most extreme kind.[5]

WHO ARE THE POOREST?

People are poor for different reasons. The landless in the rural areas and the unemployed squatters in the cities (most of whom are recently migrant landless from the countryside) are unquestionably the most miserable in Bangladesh, but nutritional surveys indicate that 60.8 per cent of the Bangladesh population is undernourished or malnourished, depending on definitions. Smallholding peasants and underemployed urban unskilled laborers are poor by any standards, but they are not always poor in the sense of having nothing. Smallholding peasants have at least a homestead; many day laborers in the cities come from homes in slums rather than straight off the pavement. In general, the urban unemployed tend to be a bit better off than the rural landless because food rations usually reach the poor in the cities long before they get to the most impoverished villagers.

A large percentage of the landless in Bangladesh are from the minority Hindu community (now probably 10 per cent or so of the population), the remnants of the former ruling community of East Bengal. Detailed studies of the Hindu community are not available, but the impression of community leaders and observers is that most Hindus, while woefully poor, are still a cut above the poorest. Perhaps because they are discriminated against, they tend to band together in community solidarity. Although the bulk of the Hindus are landless, they tend to dominate in certain low-level service occupations—as barbers, washermen, fishermen, potmakers, artisans and carpenters. As a community, the tribal population fits much more universally among the poorest than do the Hindus, but the tribal population accounts for less than one per cent of the population (approximately 700,000 people in 1981).

In talking to the poor, one gets the impression that their poverty is caused primarily by changes in family fortunes, flooding and the shifting of rivers. According to Muslim law, each son gets one

5. An excellent study that brings this out is Kamruddin Ahmad, *A Socio-Political History of Bengal and the Birth of Bangladesh* (Dacca: Zahiruddin Mahmud Inside Library, Fourth Edition, 1975), see especially pp. 200 ff.

share and each daughter a half-share of a father's wealth, so that land can become terribly divided in a generation or two. Certain categories of the unfortunate—widows, lepers, the diseased and maimed—tend to be most neglected by families and least employable. Their position in society becomes particularly appalling when a major flood or a shift in the course of a river destroys their home or community, or washes away whatever little wealth they may have accumulated. It is now estimated by government that more than 30 per cent of the people of Bangladesh have had their homes and possessions washed away by floods at some point during the past 10 years, while, during the same period, more than 10 per cent of the population has had their lands seriously rendered less fertile by inundations of sand and silt.

Most studies of poverty in Bangladesh focus on the rural landless, with the percentages of those categorized as landless ranging up to 59 or 60 per cent of the total population if one includes those who claim ownership of less than one acre. The most authoritative recent study, by Jannuzi and Peach in 1977, indicates that 59.4 per cent of the rural population claims ownership rights to less than 1 acre, and 83.3 per cent claims such rights to less than 3 acres. At the same time, the most fortunate 1.16 per cent of the rural population controls just slightly more than 15 per cent of the land, and the wealthiest 16.7 per cent of the population controls exactly two-thirds of the land (see Table 2).[6]

Among villagers themselves, Thorp has found that "the possession and use of 6 acres or more seems indisputably to constitute a person as a 'rich man,' and potentially a 'big man' in rural society."[7] At a step below that, a person owning 3–6 acres is conceived by villagers to be "in a position to improve his situation if the

6. Jannuzi and Peach have published two volumes of findings: (1) *Report on the Hierarchy of Interests in Land in Bangladesh* by F. Tomasson Jannuzi and James T. Peach (Dacca: USAID, 1977) and *Bangladesh: A Profile of the Countryside* (Dacca; USAID, 1979).

7. John P. Thorp, "Socio-Economic Factors and Muslim Cultural Conceptions about Land Ownership in Rural Bangladesh," Unpublished paper presented at the Association for Asian Studies meeting, March 21–23, 1980, Washington, D.C. All quotations used here and in the following paragraphs are from this paper. See also John P. Thorp. "Masters of Earth; Conceptions of 'Power' Among Muslims of Rural Bangladesh," Unpublished Ph.D. dissertation, University of Chicago, 1978.

combination of circumstances involved in producing a crop and marketing it are all in his favor." Thorp also argues, quite appropriately it seems to me, that although it is empirically justifiable to categorize...farmers who possess less than 2/3 acre as functionally landless...this categorization is [not] culturally justifiable." Jannuzi and Peach, like Thorp and other analysts of rural Bengal, distinguish (see Table 3) between those who own no land at all (Landless–I), those who own only a homestead plot (Landless–II), and those who claim ownership to less than a half acre (Landless–III). In Thorp's words, "To possess only a homestead plot makes a considerable difference in the perception a person has of himself and in the perceptions his neighbors have of him...Having been shown these small plots by a number of very proud possessors when I went out to the fields with them, I cannot be satisfied with categorizing them as 'landless'."

Those in the bottom 8–11 per cent of Bangladesh rural society, who have no claim to any land whatsoever, are the truly "landless" in terms of their own cultural conceptions and the perceptions of their peers. In Thorp's terms, they cannot "go out to their fields" because they have no fields. "They do not have even the security of their own green vegetable garden or a fruit bearing tree near their dwelling. Their residence...is at the pleasure of some other householder. They are the powerless in rural Bangladesh society."

While peasants with small homesteads or with plots of less than a half-acre are undoubtedly somewhat better off than those with no land whatsoever, all three of these categories of peasants would be considered by most outsiders to be quite desperately poor. Indeed, estimates of the poor in Bangladesh range up to 80 and 90 per cent of the population, and especially if one includes the unemployed in the towns, unskilled workers, and other city slum dwellers. Urban analysts will often argue that statistics on urban poverty, which invariably show higher per capita incomes and more amenities for the urban poor than for the rural landless, are misleading. In this view, the degrading conditions of city slum living make for a less desirable "quality of life" than one finds in even the most wretched rural conditions. This factor alone provides the basis for the usual explanations of the relatively slow rate of rural-urban migration in Bangladesh, with the urban population still accounting for less than 10 per cent of the total population.

Table 3.   *Landlessness in Rural Bangladesh*

	Number of Households	Per cent of Total	Number of Persons	Per cent of Total
Landless–I	1,311,570	11.07	5,884,927	8.13
Landless–II	3,385,733	32.79	18,703,472	27.10
Landless–III	1,811,276	15.29	9,538,436	13.82

Definitions:

A *Landless–I* household is a rural household that claims ownership of no land, either homestead or other land.

A *Landless–II* household is a rural household that does not claim ownership of any land other than homestead land. Such a household may claim ownership to homestead land.

A *Landless–III* household is a rural household that claims ownership to some land other than the homestead, but no more than 0.5 acres of land other than the homestead. Such a household may claim ownership to homestead land. Thus, the sum of landless–2 and landless–3 households equals the total number of households which claim to own 0.5 acres or less of land other than homestead land.

Source: *Report on the Hierarchy of Interests in Land in Bangladesh*, by F. Tomasson Jannuzi and James T. Peach (Washington: Agency for International Development, 1977), p. xxii.

Perhaps the most important point to be made about the poor in rural Bangladesh is not the extent of their landlessness, but rather the antiquated nature of their agrarian structure. As Jannuzi and Peach have so ably documented, the agrarian structure of Bangladesh "constitutes the major impediment to the implementation of a range of rural development programs that [might otherwise] promote economic growth within an environment of social justice."[8] In this view, even land redistribution in Bangladesh would not be meaningful, either for increased production or redistribution of

8.   *Bangladesh: A Profile of the Countryside*, p. 85. See also A.K. Nazmul Karim. *Changing Society in India, Pakistan and Bangladesh* (Dacca: Nawroze Kitabistan, Third Edition, 1976).

wealth, unless it were accompanied by a change in the agrarian structure. That structure is characterized by landlordism of the type that has prevailed in Bengal for the last few centuries and continues into the 1980s, despite recent attempts at change.

At the heart of Bangladesh's agrarian structure is the *malik* (landlord), whose holdings, rights and prerogatives today are nowhere nearly as great as were those of the old Hindu *zamindars* or *jotedars* of East Bengal. Nonetheless, modern *maliks* are still divorced from direct agricultural operations, and particularly those operations of low status that involve what are perceived to be dirty or menial tasks. To this extent, modern *maliks* are still absentee or non-cultivating landholders, even though several levels of subinfeudation have been abolished and landed estates severely reduced in size.

As landholders, modern *maliks* attempt to minimize the assumption of personal risk in connection with agricultural operations. They typically sublet their lands in order to limit their direct responsibility, either for providing agricultural inputs or for assuming a share of the costs of such inputs used in cultivation by others on their land. In the words of Jannuzi and Peach. "This means in practice that the lessor (sharecropper) has customarily assumed all of the risks and most, if not always all, of the costs of production. No matter how much or how little the sharecropper produces, the *maliks* are guaranteed at least fifty per cent of the product."[9]

Because of the gap between the landed and the non-landed, many scholars, politicians and administrators have tried to conceive of Bangladesh in terms of socio-economic classes, or, in the case of the large number of small Marxist-left parties in Bangladesh, to promote "class solidarity" among the poor. Such attempts have run straight up against what Peter Bertocci calls "structural fragmentation" among the poor—i.e. atomized occupational structures and other factors that stifle the growth of class solidarity and consciousness by virtue of the variation in disparate interests and, therefore, the diverse group identities they engender.[10] One major

9. Ibid., p. 87.
10. Peter Bertocci, "Structural Fragmentation and Peasant Classes in Bangladesh," *Journal of Social Studies* (Dacca), V (October 1979), p. 46. All quotations from Bertocci, plus the general line of the argument, are from this article.

study indicates that, among the lowest 44 per cent of the rural population in terms of landlessness or relative landlessness, 12 per cent—almost a quarter—engages in petty trade as a primary (and 6 per cent as a secondary) source of income, while 8 per cent depends on menial occupations as their basis for subsistence and many others work in non-agricultural food production areas (e.g. fishing, 12 per cent).[11] As Bertocci points out, this "suggests a multiplicity of individual links into the institutional framework of the rural economy, the nature of which has been virtually unstudied."

Even among those landless who depend primarily or secondarily on field labor as their source of income, there are important differences. Migrant laborers—who travel away from their homes in search of work on a seasonal basis—have been shown to drive down agricultural labor wages generally, in direct competition with landless laborers who are locally resident.[12] Further differences exist between landless laborers who have established or maintained traditional patron-client relationships with a *malik*, and other laborers—whether resident or migrant—who are paid strictly on a cash basis and who tend to denigrate patron-client ties.

Among those with land, there are also large numbers of fundamental differences that separate them, including family size, quality of land, efficiency of cultivation, adoption of new techniques, availability of credit and other inputs, and so forth. Jannuzi and Peach found that those farmers who owned the mean or larger amounts of land tended to rent or sharecrop it out *to* others, while those who owned less than the mean tended to rent or sharecrop additional land *from* others in order to make ends meet. Bertocci has identified a number of patterns where *maliks* with amounts of land below the mean will take in land one season and give it out the next, and he has found at least two studies which indicate that rates of indebtedness (including mortgaging of one's land) are higher for "surplus" farmers than for "subsistence" farmers.[13]

11. Abu Andullah, Mosharaf Hossain and Richard Nations, "Agrarian Structure and the IRDP—Preliminary Considerations," *Bangladesh Development Studies*, IC:2 (1976), p. 214, as quoted in Bertocci.

12. Edward Clay, "Institutional Change and Agricultural Wages in Bangladesh," *Bangladesh Development Studies*, IV:4 (1976), pp. 423–440.

13. These are by Ali Akhtar Khan, *Rural Credit in Gazipur Village* (Comilla: Bangladesh Academy for Rural Development, 1964) and Kirsten Westergaard, "Modes of Production in Bangladesh," *Journal of Social Studies* (Dacca), II (1978), pp. 1–26.

Cross-cutting all of these socio-economic divisons are a number of moral precepts and cultural models that promote inter-personal and inter-group factionalism over class conflict. One of these is implicit in the personal struggle between *takdir*, which refers to "the predestined limits and potentialities bestowed by Allah on each individual life," and *takdir*, the "obligation of each individual to realize via maximum effort the fullness of one's given potentialities."[14] In discussing these two moral precepts, Bertocci identifies a "widely accepted belief that one's capacity to maximize attainment of one's (especially economic) goals is intimately linked to the degree one is successful in attaching oneself to persons who are powerful and prestigious." It is not difficult to see how such a belief promotes inter-personal and inter-group factionalism of the type so often identified with the Bangladesh countryside. Bertocci also suggests that the Bengali Muslim peasant's conception of what is "justice" in the distribution of power and prestige, or, conversely, what is "exploitation" or "abuse of power," is radically divergent from the conceptions of Western (or even urban Bangladeshi) class analysts.

In talking with people in Bangladesh, it quickly becomes clear that a majority will classify itself as being among the poorest of the poor, although numerous segments of that majority will seriously question whether other segments should be so classified. This is partly because rewards and subsidies have recently been introduced for those who can qualify for various categories of poverty, but it is also the result of genuine feelings among many people that they have been put upon in recent years, or that their life situation has positively declined relative to what it was before or what it was for their ancestors. It is also clear that there has been a great deal of mobility, both upward and downward, within Bangladeshi society recently, with millions of people losing all or most of their wealth in the succession of floods, famines, wars and civil strife that have battered this part of the world during the last four decades.[15] The contrast between those who have lost and gained is especially

14. The terms are Bertocci's. See pp. 52 ff.
15. For example, see two recent village studies: 1) Anwarullah Chowdhury, *A Bangladesh Village: A Study of Social Stratification* (Dacca: Centre for Social Studies, 1978), especially pp. 141 ff.; and 2) Jenneke Arens and Jos Van Beurden, *Jhagrapur: Poor Peasants and Women in a Village in Bangladesh* (New Delhi: Orient Longman, 1980), especially pp. 190 ff.

striking because the losers have plummeted into the depths of the poorest anywhere in the world, while the gainers have been, almost invariably, poorer Muslims who have, for the first time in the history of this traditionally Hindu-dominated region, acquired considerable degrees of wealth, influence and power.

NUTRITIONAL LEVELS AMONG THE POOR

Perhaps the surest way of identifying the poorest segments of the population is by focussing on nutrition levels. Fortunately, in Bangladesh there have been two excellent nutrition surveys—in 1962-64 and in 1975-76—which make it possible to compare nutrition over time and in great depth.[16] The results of the surveys indicate that both average dietary intake and average calorie intake have decreased for the entire population by an average of 9 per cent each, from levels that were already unsatisfactory at the time of the first survey. The first survey indicated that 45 per cent of all rural families had caloric intakes below a recommended daily minimum of 2,120 calories. In the second survey, this percentage had ballooned to 59 per cent of rural families.

Consumption of foodgrains declined by 9 per cent between 1962 and 1975, even through massive imports of wheat maintained and enhanced consumption levels of the commodity (wheat is the only major category of food that is being consumed in greater quantities now than it was in 1962). Bangladesh is still the fourth largest producer of rice in the world, but rice production has failed to keep up with population growth, with the result that per capita consumption of rice has been steadily declining over the past two decades. Consumption of meat, potatoes, pulses and fish have also declined noticeably during the past twenty years.

The consequences of a lack of proper nutrition are not difficult to see in Bangladesh. More than 80 per cent of children ages 0–5 suffer from malnutrition (a stage of ill health) or undernutrition (meaning that they are less robust or have less vigor, strength or reserve than they would otherwise). A similar percentage of children

16. See *Nutrition Survey of East Pakistan, March 1962–January 1964* (Washington: U.S. Department of Health, Education and Welfare, 1966) and *Nutrition Survey of Rural Bangladesh, 1975–76* (Dacca: Institute of Nutrition and Food Science, Dacca University, December 1977). All figures in this section, unless otherwise noted, are from these two reports.

ages 0–11 are found to be stunted (62 per cent) or wasted (4 per cent) or both stunted and wasted (12 per cent). Almost a million Bangladeshis suffer from night blindness due to vitamin A deficiency, and vitamin A deficiency is also the major cause of total blindness, which has afflicted people in Bangladesh to a greater extent than elsewhere. Seventy per cent of the population—more than 63 million people—are anemic; 82 per cent of the children below 5 years of age do not have the minimum acceptable level of haemoglobin in their blood; and numerous others suffer from such nutrition-deficiency related diseases as Xerosis conjunctivae, Bitot's spot, angular stomatitis, angular scars, marasmus or Kwashiorkor.

Nutritional levels and habits correlate quite positively and strikingly with income. As incomes increase, consumption of all foods other than vegetables—and especially cereals, pulses, fish and milk—increases. The fact that consumption of vegetables does not increase is an indication that vegetables are not a prestigious food item in Bangladesh, a matter of considerable concern to nutritionists in the country. An astounding finding from the 1975–76 nutrition survey is that *every member of every single family owning less than three acres of land was deficient in its intake of calories, calcium, vitamin A, riboflavin and vitamin C.* Overall, the relationships between different indices of socio-economic status with nutrients are more or less the same as their relationships with food groups.

Variations in nutritional levels are often a seasonal phenomenon, and are clearly related to food prices and availability. A major study done over a number of years at a factory town called Companyganj indicated that levels of nutritional status will routinely dip drastically in August, just before the summer rice harvest, but will then bounce back if the harvest is bountiful.[17] The same study also found a correlation between the price of rice and the death rate, with the incidence of death rising rapidly and in quick response to increases in rice prices. A major mapping project by Bruce Currey of the East-West Center in Hawaii has identified areas "liable" and "very liable" to famine, with the major factors contributing to such liability being identified, in order of importance, as flooding, drought, population pressure, food deficit,

17.   *Death Rate, Land and the Price of Rice: 1975–78*, Evaluation Unit Report No. 04, Companyganj Health Project: Noakhali, by Colin W. McCord, Shafiq A. Chowdhury, Abdul Hai Khan and Ali Ashraf (Dacca: Christian Commission for Development in Bangladesh, March 1980).

lack of alternative employment, low crop yields, poor land transport, river erosion, cyclone risk, and maldistribution of agricultural inputs. According to Currey's analysis, the first five factors of those listed above account for over 70 per cent of the composite index of famine liability (see map).[18]

Not all malnutrition or undernutrition, of course, is related to economic status. Indeed, there is a great deal of room in Bangladesh for health education among all socio-economic segments of the population, and especially as regards the rearing of children under 5 years of age. There is a common belief throughout the country that the colosterum—the first milk—is not good for the child, a belief that could not be at greater variance with scientific findings.[19] Because of this belief, parents of newborn babies will commonly withhold milk from the newborn for 24–48 hours. Even health workers will often take the colosterum and dispose of it, while recommending that the baby receive water and honey, a practice that at once exposes children to unsanitary water and deprives them of the nutritional benefits of the first milk.

A second source of undernourishment throughout Bangladesh is the widespread practice of providing supplementary foods only at the age of 15–18 months, at which time a baby is quickly and completely weaned. Some degree of nutrition is assured by the fact that 88 per cent of Bangladesh's mothers breast feed, but tremendous gains in nutritional levels could be made if supplemental foods (simple fruits, vegetables, carbohydrates) were introduced in tiny quantities around 4–6 months of age, progressing to a full diet by 18 months, with a delay in the weaning process until the age of 18–24 months.

A third cultural source of undernourishment is related to treatment of diarrhea, since the common practice in Bangladesh is to withhold food and liquids from sufferers of diarrhea until stools are firm and infrequent. This practice is extremely detrimental—often resulting in death to a diarrheal child—because body fluids are not replaced. Parents argue that they do not want to give food and liquids because this makes stools runny and more frequent, but doctors recommend re-hydration solutions—commonly

18. Bruce Currey et al., *Mapping of Areas Libale to Famine in Bangladesh Final Report, Preliminary Version*), Washington: USAID, September 7, 1978.
19. Cf. *Beliefs and Practices Affecting Food Habits in Rural Bangladesh*, Merlyn Vermuy, Project Director (New York: CARE, April 1980).

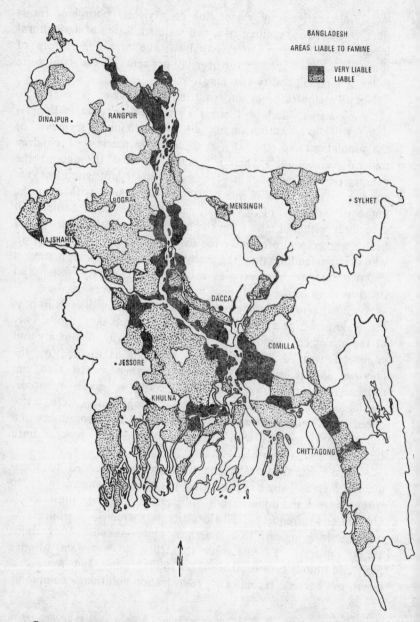

Source and Explanation   Bruce Currey et al., *Mapping of Areas Liable to Famine in Bangladesh* (1978).   The research project which resulted in this map was carried out by a team of researchers from the Johns Hopkins University

a salt, sugar and water mixture—which helps provide nutrition and absorption of needed salts. Health studies in Bangladesh reveal that the major causes of death in the first few years of life are related to neo-natal tetanus, diarrhea, pneumonia, and measles, with all of these becoming the more serious to the extent that a child is malnourished by insufficient food and calorie intake. A series of studies surveyed by Lawrence Marum has suggested that economic factors do outweigh cultural factors in producing malnourishment and undernourishment, but Marum nevertheless concludes that attention to educational and cultural factors might well mitigate some of the harsher effects of economic hardship.[20]

THE PUBLIC FOOD DISTRIBUTION SYSTEM

Throughout the 1970s, Bangladesh never really had a coherent food policy. There was an expansion of the public food distribution system (PFDS), but this was not a planned expansion, nor was it a sign of anything other than a failure to make significant gains in food production. During the latter half of the 1970s, the

20. I am especially indebted to Dr. Marum, an M.D. working for CARE in Bangladesh, for information on which this nutrition section is based. Much of the material is culled from an interview with Dr. Marum in December 1980 in Dacca.

Centre for Medical Research for the Ministry of Relief and Rehabilitation, Government of Bangladesh, with financial support from the United States Agency for International Development (AID). Professor Currey, the principal investigator for the project, is in the School of Social Sciences, Flinders University, Bedford Park, Australia. The map is reproduced here with the permission of Professor Currey and of AID.

Professor Currey cautions users of the map that it only shows areas with a "structural proclivity to famine." It does not say, for example, that the white areas will never suffer from famine, nor does it preclude the possibility that some areas may become more famine-prone because of changes (such as population shifts or activities of war). The principal factors contributing to *structural* liability to famine in Bangladesh were defined by the Johns Hopkins team as follows (in order of importance): flooding, drought, population pressure, food deficit, lack of alternative employment, low crop yields, poor land transport, river erosion, cyclone risk, and maldistribution of agricultural inputs. Taken together, the first five of these factors account for over 70 per cent of the composite index of famine liability.

PFDS handled almost twice as much foodgrain as during the latter half of the 1960s. At present, 13–15 per cent of all foodgrain consumed in the country pass through this system, which employs more people than any other government department. A full quarter of the population (23 million people) is served by it in one form or another, and it requires for its maintenance 1.8 million tons of foodgrain each year.[21] In recent years, 75 per cent of the foodgrains in the system have been imported and financed by concessional aid.

The PFDS in Bangladesh was not designed to feed the poor. Its major purpose is, and has always been, to provide government workers, the police, the military, and other "priority" sectors with payment in kind, as a means of protecting them against the erosive effects on their real income of seasonal and year-to-year fluctuations in food prices. The highest priority within the system is a category called Stautory Rationing (SR), which goes to about two-thirds of the residents of the six major cities (Dacca, Chittagong, Rajshahi, Khulna, Narayanganj and Rangamati). Almost everyone residing in these cities is entitled to a ration card, but food is distributed first to certain "priority categories," in both urban and rural areas, which include members of the armed services, the police, all government employees, students, and employees of large companies. In 1980, these categories (SR, 23 per cent and priority categories, 31 per cent) accounted for a total of 54 per cent of food distribution through the PFDS.[22]

Aside from the six largest cities, the rest of the country is served by what is known as modified rationing (MR), and by Food-For-Work (FFW) and relief programs. Residents in the rural areas are classified into four income categories (A,B,C,D), with those in the lowest, tax-free income category (A) usually being favoured in the administrative rules of distribution. In fact, however, MR, FFW and

21.   Statistics are from the Statistics Division, Ministry of Planning, Government of Bangladesh, and from an interview with its Director, Dr. A.K.M. Ghulam Rabbani.   An excellent summary description of the PFDS appears in Rehman Sobhan, "Politics of Food and Famine in Bangladesh," in *Bangladesh Politics*, ed. Emajuddin Ahamed (Dacca: Centre for Social Studies, 1980), pp. 158–187.

22.   Stated in interviews with Food Ministry officials, Dacca, December 1980.   See also an unpublished paper entitled "Food Policy," Ministry of Food (November 27, 1980).

relief programs are all administered at the local level, and every single study that has been done indicates that much of the grain allotted to local officials for MR, FFW and relief is sold for personal profit.[23] Local Union Council leaders will record that they have distributed a large amount of grain in MR areas when in fact they have distributed much less; they will use faulty scales and weighing methods that err dramatically in their favor; and they will pay workers for moving a small amount of earth under Food-For-Work schemes, but will report to government that much greater amounts have been moved. In addition to these, there are many other ploys that are commonly used to divert PFDS grains into the private sector.

In recent years, Food-For-Work programs have acquired a reputation for greater honesty than some of the older relief schemes, primarily because international agencies have established elaborate procedures for measuring the amount of earth to be moved before the initiation of a canal-digging or road-building project, and then measuring the amount actually moved after the project's completion. FFW projects run by CARE are known to be particularly well-administered, with CARE officials commonly paying local project leaders fewer foodgrains than claimed because of shortfalls in amounts of earth actually moved. This manner of proceeding contrasts sharply with older relief and ration programs in Bangladesh, which are typically viewed as little more than political patronage pure and simple.

There is an anti-corruption wing of the Food Ministry which is supposed to check instances of foodgrain diversion and misuse of ration cards, but it has thus far been ineffective. President Ziaur Rahman himself admits that there is unquestionably more corruption now than when he first came to power five years ago, but he argues that this is a "fact of life" which results from the large-scale influx of foreign food and money.[24] Zia and the major leaders of

23. An excellent study and bibliography of food and other rural issues is B.K. Jahangir, *Differentiation, Polarisation and Confrontation in Rural Bangladesh* (Dacca: Centre for Social Studies, 1979).

24. For an expanded version of Ziaur Rahman's views of the food issue see my "Bangladeshi Nationalism and Ziaur Rahman's Presidency," *AUFS Fieldstaff Reports* (2-part series), 1981. The quotations are from Part I of these reports.

all other political parties in Bangladesh are convinced that the nation needs more rather than less foreign aid.

In a country where filial and fraternal solidarity are highly valued, it is often difficult to distinguish close kinship networks from corruption.[25] Then too, even without considering kinship, identification of corrupt acts is often elusive. There is disagreement, for example, about whether provosts in university dormitories are guilty of corruption when they buy large amounts of wheat with ration cards and then sell wheat on the open market because, they claim, students will not eat wheat products. A well-known story in Dacca involves a case filed by the anti-corruption wing against a prominent social worker who had 50 ration cards. The social worker got the case withdrawn on the argument that so many people came to see her because of her fame as a social worker— this blind man, that beggar, this well-wisher, that friend—that she needed to buy large amounts of food to entertain them. Being a social worker, she successfully argued, she could not afford that much food without ration cards.

Once grain has been diverted from the PFDS into private hands, it will often be held and sold only after scarcity conditions develop and prices rise. In this way, the public distribution system—as it operates on the ground—actually punishes the rural poor rather than helping them. Recent figures also indicate that the rationing system is increasingly being skewed against the urban poor. This is so in large part because the goverment has stopped issuing ration cards to people moving into SR areas after 1974, except in cases of public employees being transferred into these areas. Since the vast majority of the migrants into these 6 large cities are rural poor looking for jobs, the new regulations have effectively increased the proportion of the subsidized ration going to upper income groups.

While there has been a great deal of talk in recent years about the need for food self-sufficiency and rapid agricultural growth in Bangladesh, these priorities have not been reflected in government

25. An extremely well-researched book is K.M. Ashraful Aziz, *Kinship in Bangladesh* (Dacca: International Centre for Diarrhoeal Disease Research, 1979). See also Mohammad Afsaruddin, *Rural Life in Bangladesh: A Study of Five Selected Villages* (Dacca: Nawroze Kitabistan, Second Edition, 1979). Unfortunately, neither of these books is very sensitive to political issues and processes.

budgets. A December 1979 World Bank Report found that the share of agriculture and rural development in Bangladesh plans had declined from 33 per cent to 17 per cent between 1973 and 1979.[26] During the same period, private sector investment in agriculture was practically non-existent. The Bangladesh government itself estimates that less than 20 per cent of total development expenditure has gone to agriculture since independence. It also estimates that the average rural resident receives 28 pounds of foodgrain per year through various forms of public distribution, including Food-For-Work, MR and relief, compared with 321 pounds per year for each ration card holder in the SR cities.

EVOLVING A FOOD STRATEGY

The World Bank, the Aid Bangladesh Consortium and other international donors have exerted increasing pressure on the Bangladesh government in recent years to put more money into agriculture, and to either do away with the rationing system entirely or restructure it in such a way that it favors the poor. These pressures have become the more intense in the early 1980s as world food supplies have failed to keep up with demand, and as traditional concessional suppliers have found new commercial foodgrain markets. In early 1980, American diplomats in Dacca officially told the Bangladesh government that it could not count on American concessional food supplies in the future.

Bangladesh has responded with the formation of a new inner-Cabinet National Committee on Food (NCF), which sits once a fortnight or so and reviews the food situation. The NCF consists of the Ministers of Food, Relief, Agriculture, Shipping, Transport, and so forth, and is chaired by President Ziaur Rahman. There has also been established a Planning and Monitoring unit within the Planning Commission, which deals primarily with food-related issues. Both the NCF and leaders of the Planning Commission Monitoring Unit meet occasionally with an Advisory Committee of the Ministry of Food, which is headed by the Food Minister and includes a number of Members of Parliament. The Advisory Com-

26. This Report, *Bangladesh: Food Policy Issues*, was published for restricted distribution only in December 1979. Nevertheless, its contents have been widely reported in the Bangladesh press and has been fairly widely circulated in Dacca. Figures are from page 7 of this report.

mittee is supposed to represent the interests of farmers, consumers, and other concerned segments of society. Aside from these bureaucratic committees and some political parties (discussed below), the public in Bangladesh is not really represented in decision-making in the food policy area. There are no citizens' committees of any consequence that can reach into the inner councils of government.

In collaboration with aid donors, the NCF formulated (in August 1980) a Food Security Plan, which outlined a number of areas where the government and the aid donors are in substantial agreement. The Plan envisages a gradual reduction in the importance of the ration shops, movement towards an open market system in such a way as to require government intervention only at times of extreme scarcity or surplus, and provision of price supports and other incentives to agricultural producers. Publicly, President Zia has established woefully unrealistic five-year goals to abolish the rationing system entirely and double food production.

Some indication of the sincerity of the government in its efforts to move away from rationing was indicated in May 1980, when a number of measures were promulgated to equalize ration shop prices with those prevailing in the open market. Total shares of food available to any one person in the ration shops was diminished from 3-½ shares to 3 shares, with two-thirds of the new rations being provided in wheat and only one-third in rice (previously, wheat and rice were available on a 50–50 basis; wheat is still considered to be much less desirable than rice). Prices on rationed items (which include salt, sugar, edible oils and other foods, as well as foodgrains) were significantly raised in May 1980, to the point where they then provided only a 15 per cent average subsidy when contrasted with open market prices, as opposed to a 70 per cent subsidy before May 1980.

It is important to point out that the May 1980 tightening of ration shop prices was undertaken at a time when food surpluses in independent Bangladesh were approaching an all-time high, owing largely to a coincidence of large-scale foodgrain imports and several good rice harvests during the year 1980. Foodgrain imports are still plentiful because the government was expecting relatively poor harvests in 1980; the fact that harvests have been so bountiful (primarily because of excellent weather conditions) has left the government with an embarrassing surplus that cannot be adequately stored. In early 1981 large-scale building programs for public food storage warehouses have been undertaken; subsidies are being provided for builders of food storage areas in the private sector; government is renting out schoolbuildings, private homes and numerous other structures for rice storage, and a number of proposals to export rice are being seriously considered.

Both the Bangladesh government and the international agencies are convinced that the only hope for a viable Bangladesh economy is to increase the output of food sufficiently to generate an export surplus and establish a grain reserve within Bangladesh. As Faaland and Parkinson have pointed out, if Bangladesh were routinely exporting food, "a bad crop could be accommodated by reducing exports and the problem moved to other people who ought to be able to buy elsewhere."[27] A reserve of 1–2 million tons of grain would enable the country's leaders to provide their own emergency relief in times of scarcity, would allow them to control prices better and otherwise counter the moves of private hoarders and speculators, and would offer some hope of insulating food prices in Bangladesh from the vagaries of the international market.

In pursuance of an "export and grain reserve" strategy, Ziaur Rahman's government has, for the first time in independent Bangladesh, upped the procurement price of foodgrains to the point where it now constitutes an attractive support price, and the Food Ministry is furiously trying to procure as much grain as possible for government warehouses. The government can presently store about one million tons of grain at a maximum, but the quality of that storage space is highly variable, with perhaps as much as half of it being either temporary or downright inadequate. A crash program is being funded by international donors (led by the Japanese) to provide additional storage for about 200,000 tons of grain by summer 1981, and plans are being made for open-storage —on platforms, covered with plastic and tarps—at eight or nine old World War II airports. Food Ministry officials estimate that they might obtain as much as 300,000 tons of storage capacity from new open-storage plus rental of school buildings and other structures.

On the export front, the Bangladesh government is negotiating

27. Just Faaland and J.R. Parkinson, *Bangladesh: The Test Case of Development* (Boulder, Colorado: Westview Press, 1976), p. 53.

with India to repay a previous loan of 150,000 tons of rice in kind, and is also seriously considering three other export possibilities. One is to export rice and import wheat at cheaper prices. A second is to produce some very high grade aromatic rices which the Gulf and Middle East nations are currently purchasing at $500 per ton, with the idea of exporting these in return for imports of ordinary rice at $200 per ton in bad years. The third possibility is to export low-grade rice, of which Bangladesh has a great deal, primarily to African countries like Senegal, which prefer the low-grades (Senegal, for example, prefers 80 per cent "brokens" when it buys on international markets whereas in the U.S. consumable rice is usually 20 per cent "brokens").

The difficulty with the export market, of course, is that it is a terribly complex business, and one in which Bangladesh has no experience. Saleable rice for international markets has to be maintained at certain standards of moisture content, shipped free from foreign material, exported on schedule, and guarded against pilferage and damage at both ends of a transaction. If rice were exported from Bangladesh today, it would have to go through the big international grain companies, on foreign ships. Even then, it would take at least a few years for the government to restructure its production and marketing habits, its transportation networks, banks and port facilities before it was geared up to any kind of significant amounts of exportable grains.

There are many other pitfalls in the path of an "export and grain reserve" strategy. It is entirely dependent on a high support price to producers and large-scale procurement by the government, but both of these are terribly expensive for the government to maintain over a prolonged period. During the coming year, for example, there is a real question whether the Bangladesh government will have enough currency—and especially in the right places at the right times—to buy the large amounts of grain it intends to purchase. If government falls short of its procurement targets, or fails to maintain high prices to producers, consumer prices will invariably fall below ration shop prices, ration offtakes will dry up completely, and the government will be left with enormous stocks rotting in warehouses. This would throw the market completely out of control and permanently damage the credibility of Zia's government in future foodgrain transactions.

Many of Bangladesh's food strategy problems result from its

lack of insularity from the economies of India and the rest of the world. If Bangladesh were to develop an exportable food surplus and a grain reserve, for example, it would inevitably be tempting for government officials and the private trade to smuggle some of that surplus into food-deficit areas in India at times of scarcity, along time-tested food smuggling routes of the past. There are even greater problems associated with the attempt to get agricultural inputs to Bangladesh farmers, as was demonstrated in 1980, when a major Bangladesh government effort to provide a significant fertilizer subsidy to Bangladesh farmers had to be abandoned because much of the subsidized fertilizer was finding its way into black markets across the border with India.

To the extent that the government does successfully maintain high support prices, procures at unprecedented rates, creates an export surplus, and accumulates a domestic grain reserve, it will most likely favor larger-and medium-sized farmers at the expense of the landless poor.[28] Government spokesmen argue that this is not necessarily the case because more than 80 per cent of the rural population is involved in production of grains and even small farmers are forced to sell rice when the bulk of the paddy comes in during the Aman harvest (December–January). Without adequate storage, and heavily in debt for his agricultural inputs, the small farmer customarily sells much of his crop for much-needed cash immediately after the Aman harvest, and then is forced to buy rice during the "hunger months" preceding the next Aman. If government could enter the market with high support prices immediately after the Aman comes in and then sell it cheaply just before the next Aman, the argument goes, it could undoubtedly benefit the small farmer. Landless or predominantly landless labor would be benefited, government spokesmen say, by a general increase in production and by greater use of high-yielding varieties, which require more labor than the older varieties for productivity.

What makes arguments like those above questionable in the aggregate is the mounting pace of unemployment in the Bangladesh countryside as a consequence of unprecedented population growth and burgeoning age cadres among teenagers. Martin

---

28. The reasons are explored in Mohiuddin Alamgir, *Bangladesh: A Case of Below Poverty Level Equilibrium Trap* (Dacca: Bangladesh Institute of Development Studies, 1978). See also Noazesh Ahmed, *Development Agriculture of Bangladesh* (Dacca: Bangladesh Books International, 1976).

Hanratty, of the Ford Foundation in Dacca, estimates that an increase in agricultural production to 20 million tons of food-grains in five years would produce 1 million new jobs in the agricultural sector, but he also points out that there would still be a net increase of unemployed or underemployed in the rural areas of an additional 3 million people during this five-year period. Under these circumstances, Hanratty and others expect that most of the increases in agricultural production will benefit those with land, that more and more of the smaller landed will become employees of the larger landed, wages will remain low, major returns will go to inputs, and the position of the poorest rural dwellers will continue to recede. This is all the more likely to happen if the Ziaur Rahman government euthusiastically pursues plans to promote a "privatization" of agriculture, permitting the big producers to purchase inputs off the shelf and to otherwise act without the restraints of previous bureaucratic controls.

A number of individuals and organizations have been working with Secretary of Agricultural Obaidullah Khan to initiate experiments that would provide non-land assets to the landless, organized into service cooperatives that could enable their members to earn a decent standard of living.[29] Prototypes of such cooperatives have already been organized by the Bangladesh Rural Advancement Committee (BRAC) and Proshika (a Canadian-funded voluntary association), around tubewell pumps, with cooperatives of the landless operating the pumps and supplying irrigation water (for a fee) to the landed. Hanratty envisages the possibility of 20-30 landless pump cooperatives of this type eventually forming a "union" or "federation", which might in turn generate an agrobusiness, or be used for political purposes and self-protection. Acknowledging the enormous problems involved in sustaining such groups, Hanratty suggests that cooperatives built around non-land assets is a "vision" that provides one of the few real possibilities for absorbing the massive waves of rural unemployment that can be expected in Bangladesh over the next few decades.

President Ziaur Rahman's solution to the rural employment

29. Some of the background thinking to this work appears in Geoffrey D. Wood, "Rural Development in Bangladesh" Whose Framework": *Journal of Social Studies* (Dacca), VIII (April 1980), pp. 1-31 and Geoffrey D. Wood, "The Rural Poor in Bangladesh; A New Framework:," *Journal of Social Studies* (Dacca), X (October 1980), pp. 22-46.

problem has been a series of massive public works projects—building roads and embankments, digging canals, or re-excavating old silted up rivers—in an effort to put people to work in productive activities without enormous government investments. Zia himself travels out to the rural areas (usually by helicopter) at least 15 days a month, with the purpose of most of his visits being the inauguration of a canal-digging project or some other public works effort. In the northern parts of the country, most of these voluntary activities are designed to provide irrigation water, either by digging canals directly to fields or by excavating canals that can be used to store water for low-lift pumps. In the southern regions—and especially in the districts of Noakhali and Purnea—Zia's public works programs have consisted primarily of what is known as "polderization," a Dutch term for reclamation of low-lying lands by the building of embankments and other flood control measures.

What Zia is clearly trying to do is to provide from above the necessary authority and legitimacy structures to generate enough labor for completion of large public works that have been neglected for several decades. The major impact of his large-scale voluntary projects, however, is not to provide paid employment to the poor, since there are no wages involved in these schemes. The immediate beneficiaries of Zia's voluntary canal-digging schemes are the landed, who now get water or flood protection that was not previously available. In some cases the landed will voluntarily provide some food or cash to voluntary laborers involved in these schemes, but in most instances gains for the poor are expected to come solely from the increased agricultural activity that becomes possible once a canal is re-excavated or an embankment built. A reflection of the widespread cynicism about voluntary schemes (which should be distinguished from Food-For-Work and other public works projects where laborers are paid) was a comment by one day laborer in Mymensingh, who told me:

The people who have always dug these canals are the same— they are my ancestors. It is a question of how the others are going to convince us to do the work. My grandfather used to get rice and comfort from the zamindar. I get only a few Taka per day during the harvesting season. This is not enough to buy food for my family. Now the government is asking me to volunteer my labor.   But how are we supposed to work all day when we have no food?

FOOD POLICY AND THE OPPOSITION

The only political parties in Bangladesh that have done any extensive work among the poorest of the poor, or have tried to mobilize them behind a fairly thorough restructuring of society, have been a few relatively minor Marxist-left parties, the most notable among them being the Jatiya Samajtantrik Dal (JSD). But these parties, like all political parties in Bangladesh, are funded by businessmen and led by the educated urban middle-class.[30]   The JSD was perhaps the most prominent party that contained a hard core of dedicated students who frequently went out to rural areas to mobilize the poorest segments of the population, but in late 1980 the party became hopelessly divided on ideological lines, with both factions becoming seriously demoralized about the possibilities of rural change.   Neither faction—nor any other significant Marxist or Communist party in Bangladesh today—believes that the poorest 30 or 40 per cent of the population can lead a future revolution, although they disagree about the extent to which the poorest segments might at some stage be brought in behind other leadership as a revolutionary force.

President Ziaur Rahman is reported to have proposed a substantive agrarian reform when he first came to power in 1975, in hopes that he might be able to build a mass rural base, but this idea was opposed by his key political advisors at the time. Zia's own Bangladesh National Party (BNP) is made up, almost exclusively, of people from middle- and upper-class backgrounds, with ex-military officers and ex-bureaucrats assuming major roles in leadership positions. Since the consolidation of his rule a few years ago, Zia and the BNP have concentrated on the creation of new rural institutions— clustered around *Gram Sarkars* (village councils) and a Village Defence Force—all designed to attract village influentials to the

---

30.   The social backgrounds of political party leadership in Bangladesh are traced out in several essays in Talukder Maniruzzaman, *Group Interests and Political Changes: Studies of Pakistan and Bangladesh* (New Delhi: South Asian Publishers, 1982). For a Marxist perspective see Badruddin Umar, *Imperialism and General Crisis of the Bourgeoisie in Bangladesh* (Dacca: Progoti Prakashani, 1979).

development programs of the BNP while enhancing party and administrative control and influence in the rural areas.[31]

The Awami League—by far the largest opposition party—is also led by middle- and upper-class politicians. It still maintains considerable support among Hindus, some of whom tend to be among the poorest, but otherwise its rural support is mobilized by its own village elites, who are opposed to the BNP's rural elites on the basis of personalistic differences and group factional positions. Rounaq Jahan has pointed out that support from the poor for the Awami League has steadily declined since the liberation war, for a variety of reasons. As she explains it:

> The independence of Bangladesh brought with it great expectation, which later turned into great frustration. The galloping inflation of the early 1970s meant economic hardship for the poor. The high incidence of crime which followed in the aftermath of independence also meant suffering for the poor. As a result, the masses were no longer as enthusiastic about political struggle as they were before independence, when they believed that a political change would necessarily bring about the betterment of their socio-economic conditions. Ziaur Rahman's survival in power, in part, reflects this changed mood of the masses, who are now more cautious about bringing in political change.[32]

Other opposition parties have been no more successful in organizing the poor than have the BNP and Awami League. The Democratic League of former President Khondkar Mushtaque Ahmed is extremely critical of the government on the corruption issue, but its own program for rural development and food policy is essentially the same as the one now being pursued by the government, with

---

31. For an analysis of attempts at institution-building in the countryside before Ziaur Rahman, see Harry W. Blair, *The Elusiveness of Equity: Institutional Approaches to Rural Development in Bangladesh* (Ithaca: Center for International Studies, 1974). For more recent studies see Mohammad Mohiuddin Abdullah, *Rural Development in Bangladesh* (Dacca: Fatema Art Press, 1979) and M. Nurul Haq, *Village Development in Bangladesh* (Comilla: Bangladesh Academy for Rural Development, 2nd Edition, 1978). Ziaur Rahman's attempts at institution-building are analyzed in my 1981 *AUFS Fieldstaff Reports* entitled "Bangladeshi Nationalism and Ziaur Rahman's Presidency."

32. Rounaq Jahan, *Bangladesh Politics: Problems and Issues* (Dacca: University Press Limited, 1980), p. 217.

perhaps a slightly greater emphasis on privatization. Ironically enough, while Mushtaque Ahmed is highly critical of Zia's regime because of its corruption, Mushtaque's own party has suffered organizationally because Mushtaque himself was in the prison for four years, having been convicted on charges of corruption. The other major non-communist party—the Jama'at-i-Islami—is, by the admission of its own leadership, primarily an urban party that appeals to the religiously-minded educated classes. This is so, say its leaders, because "the educated are better trained and equipped than the poor to understand Islam."

Do the nation's political leaders perceive of hunger and malnutrition among the poorest as a critical political issue or a high priority political issue? The answer to that question is clearly no, although there is every fear that, if the middle-class or upper-class is not properly catered to, there will be unrest.[33] Some elite Bangladeshis, as well as many people in the international development agencies, have felt very intensely the normal dilemmas that stem from their enclave existence in the midst of massive hunger and poverty. There are a number of imaginative pilot projects that have attacked the poverty issue head-on in a particular village or group of villages. And yet, these projects are the exceptions, the aberrations, which do not fit with the main thrust of what the Bangladesh government is up to nor with the priority goals of the financial powers that back the international development establishment. As one of Zia's close associates put it, "you do hear about poverty questions from a lot of well-intentioned people in the middle ranks, but anyone involved in the power structure of Bangladesh is interested in other questions—like how Zia will fall, whether there is disaffection in the army, who is getting promoted, who is getting contracts, and these kinds of things."

CONCLUSIONS

In Bangladesh, it is difficult to identify the poorest of the poor. Somewhere between 80 and 90 per cent of the population is poor by anyone's standards, and most people within the country tend to

33. For a detailed analysis of Bangladesh Politics see my two-part 1981 *AUFS Fieldstaff Reports* entitled "Bangladesh Nationalism and Ziaur Rahman's Presidency."

perceive of themselves and their own socio-economic categories as being among the most severely disadvantaged. Those with homestead plots in the rural areas tend to be better off than the completely landless, and perhaps even better off than the urban poorest, who live in more degrading physical conditions. For all of these segments of the population, however, nutritional levels have been steadily declining.

Subsidized food rations have not been intended for the poorest, except in times of acute scarcity when international relief agencies and some domestic programs have successfully strived to prevent famine of the magnitude of 1943. Nevertheless, high population growth rates have combined with economic failure and almost constant civil strife to produce a precipitous decline in purchasing power among the poorest. Since neither agricultural nor rural industrial growth have kept pace with the population spiral, both landlessness and unemployment have rapidly increased. Rural-urban migration has not escalated any more quickly than in other parts of South Asia, but it is growing. More important than rural-urban migration has been the constant influx of Hindus and other low status groups to India, an exodus that has been a growing irritant in Indo-Bangladesh relations.

There is a great deal of rhetoric about poverty whenever Bangladesh is discussed, and most government programs are publicly justified by referring to their poverty-relieving potential. The major concern of government leaders, however, is clearly with political stability, which depends primarily on the support of the bureaucracy, the army, the police, and a number of key middle-class groups. The leadership of Bangladesh would like to do something about bottom-end poverty, if only because it is so degrading to the international image of the country and so demoralizing domestically. But when it comes to actual development programs, there is usually not enough of a surplus to satisfy the pent-up demands of the upper tenth of the Bangladesh population—which is not outrageously wealthy by any outside standards—much less to tackle the food problems of the 80 or 90 per cent of the population that is undernourished or malnourished.

Agricultural production has not kept pace with population growth. Technology in the rural sector is still in the bullock and wooden plow stage, being dependent in the most areas of the country or traditional seeds and other inputs. Where the new seeds and new technology have been introduced, they have unquestionably benefited the larger landowners, thereby contributing to the widening gap between the rich and the poor. In a country where a farmer with unequivocal right to 6 acres is considered well-off, the problem of equity is not one that revolves around large commercial holdings and big estates. Poverty is still associated with an agrarian structure that encourages landholding by *maliks* who do not themselves engage in cultivation, but the poorest of the poor, non-*maliks* and *maliks* alike, are most consistently identified by their inability to master water resources.

Governments have been somewhat helpless in dealing with the pauperization of the Bangladesh countryside because they have not been able to muster enough authority to maintain the large public works—embankments, canals, roads, and so forth—essential to a productive agriculture in this largest deltaic area of the world. The present government of Ziaur Rahman is the most effective that Bangladesh has had, but it is still struggling with long-standing food problems. Excellent weather in 1980–81 produced a bumper harvest which, when coupled with bountiful foodgrain imports, created an embarrassing surplus of food for the first time since independence. The Bangladesh government and international donors are busily constructing new warehouses and storage areas in an attempt to build a foodgrain reserve that could be used by the Food Ministry in its future attempts to gain clout against grain hoarders and speculators. A number of schemes for exporting rice are also being considered.

The Bangladesh government is well aware that surplus world food stocks are dwindling. A new "export and grain reserve" food strategy is a response to this phenomenon. The goals of the government's new food policy are to increase agricultural production by maintaining high price support levels to farmers, all the while using government procurement to initiate rice exports and a grain reserve. Ziaur Rahman's declared intention is to do away with the rationing system entirely, and to double food production in five years, but even his own Food Ministry officials and party leaders remain unconvinced of these possibilities.

Movement towards an open market system and privatization of the foodgrain trade is something that governments in Bangladesh have done whenever there has been a food surplus. Governments can politically afford to go to open market systems when the price of food comes down so low that it approaches the price in ration shops. The question of whether the government is serious or not about going to an open market system while maintaining high support prices to farmers will come when foodstocks dip and the price of foodgrains rise. At that point, a dilemma has always presented itself. If government is unable to maintain large amounts of food in its own warehouses, or is unable to procure by maintaining high support prices, then stocks diminish, prices rise and the government has to go back to its old rationing system in order to satisfy urban elites, the military and the police. If, on the other hand, the government does succeed in maintaining a surplus, keeping procurement prices high, and satisfying rural producers, the benefits of government policies go, almost exclusively, to the better-off in the countryside.

One way to escape from the above dilemma would be by revolution, which might produce collectivization or some other drastic change in the agrarian structure, but all of the available evidence indicates that the poor in the rural areas are either unwilling or unable to support revolutionary political activities. Those political party leaders who did attempt to espouse the interests of the poorest, landless sections of Bangladesh's villages in the 1960s and 1970s are now disillusioned, their parties fragmented. There are no political organizations that effectively represent the interests of the poorest segments of the population, nor is there a single significant political organization that is led by individuals who have come from the most disadvantaged socio-economic groups. Individual mobility, both upward and downward, has been fairly common in modern Bangladesh, but support for revolutionary activities that would overturn newly-formed elite structures has been ineffectual.

Perhaps the most difficult aspects of Bangladesh's food problems stem from the inability of national leaders to insulate the nation's economy from international forces. Bangladesh's vulnerability to Indian economic activity—including smuggling of foodgrains, fertilizers and other agricultural inputs across a sieve-like border—makes it almost impossible to control many of the key variables involved in Bangladesh's domestic food strategy or food policy. The availability and terms of international food shipments to Bangladesh are dependent primarily on political considerations within the United States and other Western nations, such as the extent of food surpluses and foreign policy orientations towards the Soviet Union, China and South Asia.

Unfortunately, the vast bulk of the poor in Bangladesh have been trapped in a terrible bind. They are themselves so powerless and unorganized that they are unable to counter the oppression of the newly-formed elites within the country. They are also unable to take advantage of whatever international moral sentiment might exist for their position because access to their problem is controlled by their own domestic elites and by an international development establishment that is not primarily concerned with the alleviation of bottom-end poverty. Under these circumstances, perhaps the most that one can hope for is the extension of some individual programs for the poorest segments, which have either provided small avenues of mobility or have relieved the conditions of poverty in a local context. Talk of eradicating poverty in Bangladesh is the irresponsible rhetoric of millenarianism. Mankind will be lucky enough if the awful trends of the past three decades can be reversed in the next few years.

PART IV ZIAUR RAHMAN's BANGLADESH

Ziaur Rahman's 5-1/2 year tenure as the de facto ruler of Bangladesh (first as Martial Law Administrator and later as President) is the longest period that anyone has ruled Bangladesh. It was a period characterized in its earlier stages by much political confusion and ruthless suppression of innumerable attempts to destabilize the military. The later years of Zia's regime saw Zia himself blossom into one of the most effective Asian rulers in stirring up interest in development activities, both at home and abroad. Unfortunately, Zia was cut down by the bullets of assassins at the height of his political career, leaving the world to wonder whether he might have gone on to great and unprecedented accomplishments had he lived, or whether his dreams might have turned to dust in his natural lifetime, as many had predicted. The five essays in this section, written over the last two years, explore Zia's life and regime and attempt to assess their impact on Bangladesh as it enters the second decade of its independent existence.

TEN

POLITICAL REALIGNMENTS (1979)

Observers in the subcontinent these days speak of "Zia West" and "Zia East", with "West" referring to Zia ul Huq in Pakistan and "East" to President Ziaur Rahman of Bangladesh. (Customary usage in Bengali dictates that Ziaur Rahman's first name include the letters "ur" when pronounced with Rahman, but not otherwise.) Unlike "Zia West," who has been widely condemned internationally for his medieval interpretations of Islamic law and for his handling of the Bhutto execution, "Zia East" has received a remarkably good press. William Borders of the *New York Times,* for example, describes Ziaur Rahman as "hard-working and apparently incorruptible in his personal life" and as "a soft-spoken, thoughtful man who projects a quiet humility that belies the stern authoritarianism of his martial law regime." As Borders points out, most Western diplomats and development experts in Bangladesh have welcomed Ziaur Rahman "as the best thing that has happened to the country since it broke away from Pakistan."[1]

Ziaur Rahman was born in the northern Bangladesh city of Bogra on January 19, 1936, the son of a government science officer. He joined the Pakistan army at the age of 17 and distinguished himself in the 1965 war against India as the sole Bengali Company Commander at that time. On March 27, 1971—two days after full-scale civil war had erupted in Pakistan—Zia announced in a clandestine radio broadcast that he was President of the new country of Bangladesh, an ambitious self-appointment that has since been bitterly resented (and remembered) by his enemies. Realizing the unpopularity of his action, Zia quickly relinquished his "presidency" to Shiekh Mujibur Rahman in 1971 and subse-

---

1. Quotes are from William Borders, "Bangladesh's Soft-Spoken But Strict President," the *New York Times,* June 7, 1978.

quently distinguished himself in the liberation war as leader of a guerrilla brigade known as the "Z Force,"

In August 1975—three and a half years after the liberation of Bangladesh—Zia watched from the sidelines as "Mujib" was murdered in a bloody military coupled by young army Majors.[2] Those close to Ziaur Rahman say that he knew about the coup and refused to support it physically, but did nothing to prevent it. At the time of the August 1975 coup, Zia was a Major General in the Bangladesh army. Because of his seniority and his known animosity toward Mujib, he was made Army Chief of Staff by Khondakar Mushtaque Ahmed, Mujib's successor as President of Bangladesh. Zia was placed under house arrest on the night of November 3, 1975, by troops loyal to Brigadier Khaled Musharraf, when they staged a short-lived second coup against Mushtaque Ahmed. On November 7, 1975, after a third army coup led by an army faction loyal to Colonel Abu Taher, Ziaur Rahman was released from confinement in his home and installed as Chief Martial Law Administrator of Bangladesh.

Since his assumption of power in 1975, Zia has been trying to move in the direction of civilian rule. On April 21, 1977 he assumed the title of President while retaining his positions as Chief Martial Law Administrator and Commander-in-Chief of the Armed Forces. His opportunity to assume the Presidency came when his own figurehead President, Abu Sadat Mohammed Sayem, was forced to resign on grounds of ill health. Observers of Bangladesh politics argue that Zia's decision to assume the Presidency in April 1977 was the result of a carefully reasoned conclusion that a strong presidential system was the most appropriate vehicle for his own transition to civilian political leadership.

Five weeks after his assumption of the Presidency—on May 30, 1977—Zia claimed electrol legitimacy for the first time when 98.89 per cent of those voting in a national referendum were officially reported to have answered "yes" to the question: "Do you have confidence in President Major General Ziaur Rahman and in the policies and program enunciated by him?" Thirteen months after the referendum—in June 1978—Zia was elected President for a five-year term, securing 76 percent of the total vote against 9 rivals.

2. The anti-Mujib coup is described in Talukder-Maniruzzaman, "Bangladesh in 1975: The Fall of the Mujib Regime and its Aftermath," *Asian Survey*, XVI:2 (February 1976), pp. 119-129.

Staggered on both sides of the Presidential elections were local government elections (March 1977) and national Parliamentary elections (February 1979). The local elections—for municipalities and village councils—were ostensibly nonpartisan but it is widely accepted that most of them were won by local influentials previously loyal to Mujib's political party, the Awami League (AL). Elections to local district offices were subsequently called off when Zia realized that he did not have the political organization to best the Awami League at the local level.[3] In the 1979 Parliamentary elections, Ziaur Rahman's new party, the Bangladesh National Party (BNP), won more than two-thirds of the seats, with a plurality of only 41.2 percent of the vote (see Table 1).

POLITICAL REALIGNMENTS

Zia's BNP government is composed of three distinct strands: (1) his own factional supporters within the Bangladesh military and bureaucracy; (2) the bulk of the leadership and party cadres of the Muslim League and other Islamic fundamentalist parties; and (3) the leadership of the major portion of the Maulana Bhashani faction of the National Awami Party (NAP). Before his death in 1975, Bhashani had advocated an eclectic melding of Marxism and Islam; after Bhashani's death, Mr. Mashiur Rahman, the chairman of Bhashani's NAP, brought the bulk of Bhashani's followers into the BNP with the expectation that Mashiur Rahman would play a major role in Zia's governments. Mashiur Rahman was made "Senior Minister" in Zia's first Cabinet after his assumption of the Presidency, but a fatal heart attack in March 1979 dramatically ended Mashiur Rahman's hopes of becoming Prime Minister.

Like Sheikh Mujibur Rahman, Zia publicly subscribes to democracy, nationalism, and socialism, but he has dropped Mujib's emphasis on secularism as a fundamental feature of the Bangladesh Constitution. Three huge portraits of Bengali politicians—Maulana Bhashani, peasant leader Fazlul Haque, and Mujib's mentor, H.S. Suhrawardy—are hung on the wall behind Zia's desk; Mujib's pic-

3. A large-scale empirical study of the 1977 local elections in Bangladesh is presently being conducted by M. Rashiduzzaman of Glassboro State College. Some preliminary findings appear in M. Rashiduzzaman, "Bangladesh in 1977: Dilemmas of the Military Rulers," *Asian Survey*, XVIII:2 (February 1978), pp. 126–134.

ture has been relegated to an adjoining lounge. Zia describes his political ideals as "absolute faith and trust in the almighty Allah, restoration of democracy, nationalism and socialism, and the ensuring of economic and social justice."

Table 1. *Parliamentary Election Results, February* 1979

Party	No. Seats	% Seats	% Votes
Bangladesh National Party (BNP)	206	68.3	41.2
Awami League (Ukil)	40	13.3	24.4
Muslim League-Islamic Democratic League Alliance (ML-IDL)	19	6.3	10.0
Jatiya Samajtantrik Dal (JSD)	9	3.0	4.9
Awami League (Mizaner)	2	0.7	2.8
Gano Front	2	0.7	0.6
Bangladesh Jatiya Sangram	2	0.7	0.5
NAP (Muzzafar)	1	0.3	2.2
Bangladesh Ganatantrik Andolan	1	0.3	0.2
Jatiya Ekata Party	1	0.3	0.2
Other Parties and Independents	17	6.1	12.9
Total	300	100.0	100.0

Source: Bangladesh Election Commissioner, Sheri Banglar Nagar, Dacca, Bangladesh.

In an attempt to build a nationalist identity, Zia has encouraged use of "Bangladeshi" to describe the people of Bangladesh, rather than "Bengali", the word used during the old Mujib and Pakistan days. Most observers consider it unlikely that people who for centuries have called themselves "Bengalis" could now suddenly start referring to themselves as "Bangladeshis."[4] Nonetheless, Zia

4. A discussion of the identity issue appears in Stephen Oren, "After the Bangladesh Coups," *The World Today* (Chatham House), 32:1 (January 1976), pp. 18–24.

and his followers argue that it is crucial to the future to maintain the distinction between Bangladesh's culture, way of life, and religion and similar cultures found on the other side of the Indian border in West Bengal. Maintenance of the distinction is all the more difficult because Bengali is the near-universal language on both sides of the border.

Secular-minded opponents of Ziaur Rahman worry that the attempt to develop a distinct Bangladeshi nationalism could eventually force Zia's regime into an excessive reliance on fundamentalist Islam as a unifying ideology. His leftist opponents question both his commitment to socialism and his ability to contain extremist Islamic forces. Perhaps most observers are convinced that Zia's attempt to institute in Bangladesh a truly democratic presidential system will make little progress beyond that achieved by military leaders who have made similar attempts after staging coups in Burma, Indonesia, and other developing countries.

Zia's decision to drop secularism as a constitutional principle was one of the conditions necessary for obtaining the support of the Muslim League and other Islamic-based political parties. Some Muslim League leaders have also suggested that Zia change the national flag (because it has no Islamic symbolism) and the national anthem (written by Rabindranath Tagore, a non-Muslim), but he has refused to meet such extremist demands so far. Zia has also refused to grant a Muslim League demand for separate electorates for Hindus and Muslims.

The most controversial aspects of Zia's regime have involved his manipulation of the electoral process and a series of political executions and purges within the military. In the June 1978 presidential poll, Zia gave his opponents only 40 days notice of the election and 23 days in which to campaign. For three years prior to that election, political parties were not allowed to undertake any kind of open political activity and many opposition leaders were in jail. At the time of the 1978 elections, the General Secretary of the Awami League, the principal opposition party, estimated that 5,000 AL members and workers were in jail, most of them already having been there for periods of 2 years or more without trial. Because of martial law regulations, which were still in effect when the 1978 elections took place, processions were banned. Dacca city was under curfew from 11:30 P.M. until 5 A.M. every night, and vehicles were routinely stopped and searched. The ability of anyone to challenge either the election results or conduct of the poll was discouraged by Zia's powers to appoint or remove any judge, his immunity from court proceedings, and the fact that any advice he tendered to his Council of Advisers was beyond the jurisdiction of any court.

During the 1978 election campaign, Zia used the state administrative apparatus for support and continued to hold the positions of President, Commander-in-Chief of the Armed forces, Chief of Staff, and Chief Martial Law Administrator, right through the balloting. General M.A.G. Osmani, the principal opposition candidate for President, produced a number of leaflets issued by district administrative officials instructing people to attend President Zia's meetings, but pleas by Osmani for investigation of such "irregularities" were rejected by the Election Commission. After the elections, Osmani admitted that he had not been able to print posters to cover more than five cities, or even to buy the voters' lists from the Election Commission (total price: $60,000), because he had not had time to raise sufficient funds.[5] In contrast, the Ministry of Information and Broadcasting blanketed the country with pro-Zia posters, news handouts, and photographs of the President's election meetings.

Martial law restrictions on the independent press and on political party activity severely hampered the opposition in its attempts to raise funds, travel in rural areas, or even to hold meeting in major cities during the 1978 campaign. General Osmani was particularly bitter about Zia's refusal of his request to postpone the elections by 90 days, with the result that Osmani had to try and cover the country in a jeep during the beginning of the monsoon season while Zia traveled much more comfortably and quickly by government helicopter. Osmani also expressed his frustration that he had no means to counter the government news media, in which, he claimed, his views had been "distorted" and "baseless stories about (him) published again and again."[6] When Zia did offer

5. For a discussion of the 1978 election campaign see Manash Ghosh, "Mujib's Coup Helped Zia" *The Statesman* (Calcutta) June 21, 1978. The election is analyzed in M. Rashiduzzaman, "Bangladesh in 1978: Search for a Political Party," *Asian Survey*, XIX:2 (February 1979), pp. 181–197.

6. Quoted in Rajendra Sareen, "Poll Rigging to do Zia Harm," *The Tribune* (Chandigarh), June 1, 1978.

limited government facilities to General Osmani, 12 days before the polling, Osmani refused to accept it on grounds that it had come too late.

Most observers are convinced that Zia would have been elected President in 1978 in any case, but most also agree that there was considerable vote fraud on the day of polling. William Borders reported instances where he personally witnessed fraud, including one case in which opposition observers were barred by Zia's supporters from exercising their legal right to watch the balloting.[7] General Osmani refused to say that the election was "rigged," but he argued publicly that it was "grossly unfree and unfair." Osmani, who as Zia's commanding officer had led the Bengali freedom fighters during the liberation war against Pakistan, alleged that 40 of his volunteers had been killed during the 1978 election campaign. He also detailed more than 200 instances where armed men had walked into polling booths to drive out polling officers and anti-government observers ("scrutineers").

Just before the 1979 Parliamentary elections, Zia made a number of concessions to the major opposition parties when they unanimously threatened to boycott the poll. Two months before the elections, the government announced it was releasing more than 10,000 political prisoners who, the government admitted, had been detained without specific charges against them. Fundamental rights, which had been in suspension since 1974, were restored by Presidential order in late 1978 and Zia announced that martial law would be lifted during the first session of the elected Parliament in 1979, if the opposition participated (he later kept his promise). Press freedoms were theoretically restored, although the actions of the government since then have indicated that effective criticism of the regime is still not tolerated.

In late December 1978, Zia decreed a fifth amendment to the 1972 Constitution—in what he called the "second proclamation" of his martial law period—laying down the broad outlines of what will presumably be his regime for the immediate future. Veteran observers of Bangladesh politics describe it as a combination of Mujibur Rahman's BAKSHAL scheme of 1975 and Ayub Khan's "Basic Democracies" of the 1960s. Unlike Mujib's intended one-

---

7. William Borders, "President Far Ahead in Bangladesh Vote," the *New York Times*, June 4, 1978.

party system, Zia's fifth amendment provides for a multiparty polity with an overpowering emphasis on a strong presidency. Zia's supporters argue that his model when drafting the fifth amendment was DeGaulle's France.[8] According to the "second proclamation," the President will appoint the Prime Minister on the basis of the President's understanding as to which of the 300 elected members of Parliament "appears to him" to be commanding the support of a majority of the MPs. To assure further control of the Prime Minister, the fifth amendment states that the President is not obliged to appoint as Prime Minister the leader of the party that wins a majority of the seats in Parliament.

The subservience of the Bangladesh courts to the President is guaranteed in the "second proclamation" by a clause dictating that "the question whether any, and if so, what advice was tendered by the Council of Ministers or a Minister to the President, shall not be inquired into by any court." Control of Parliament is assured by three clauses, providing: (1) that the President can appoint up to one-fifth of his Cabinet from among people who are not Members of Parliament; (2) that the President may enter into treaties with foreign governments without informing Parliament if he considers such action "in the national interest"; and (3) that the President may withhold his assent from any Bill passed by Parliament, in which case he can be made to assent only if a national referendum on the issue is organized and passed. The "second proclamation" has met with widespread protest by the opposition parties on the ground that it does not provide an independent role to Parliament or the courts. General Osmani expressed the sentiments of most opposition leaders when he said: "With the complete concentration of powers in the hands of the President, he will be a virtual dictator."

Primarily because of Zia's promise to lift martial law during the first session of an elected Parliament, and because they feared even greater repression if they refused to contest, most of the opposition leaders agreed to participate in the 1979 Parliamentary elections. The two major parties that did boycott the polls were the Janata Party of General Osmani and the Democratic League of Khondakar

---

8. See Talukder Maniruzzaman, *The Bangladesh Revolution and Its Aftermath* (Dacca Bangladesh Books International, 1981). Maniruzzaman also analyzes both the BAKSHAL scheme and Ayub Khan's "Basic Democracies."

Mushtaque Ahmed. Democratic League leaders argued that they would not contest the elections unless Mushtaque Ahmed were released from prison; Osmani's boycott was an expression of protest against his treatment in the 1978 presidential campaign. The Jatiya Samajtantrik Dal (JSD), a party of young leftists that many see as the party of the future in Bangladesh, agreed to contest the elections—despite continued imprisonment of its three principal leaders, Major M.A. Jalil, A.S.M. Abdur Rab, and Sirajul Alam Khan—after working out a deal with Ziaur Rahman that provided for the release from prison of 300 JSD workers and restoration of the party's printing press and newspaper (*Ganakantha*), both of which had been previously seized by the government.

In the 1979 Parliamentary elections, Zia's BNP secured more than two-thirds (206 to 300) of the seats, with only 41.2 percent of the vote. Like Zia's triumph in the 1978 presidential poll, this victory too was hollow. Most observers were surprised by the small BNP vote, given the enormous advantages it had under martial law. Moreover, a number of major opposition leaders in 1979 made effective charges of vote fraud and electoral unfairness, as had General Osmani in 1978. The most serious allegations of electoral rigging in 1979 revolved around retired Major General Khalilur Rahman, a former Army Chief of Staff and an Awami League candidate, who was originally declared a victor in his constituency by more than 1,200 votes but, two days later, was declared the loser by less than 200 votes. The "recount" on which this reversal was based took place without Rahman's knowledge or consent. When appeals for investigations of such electoral irregularities went unheeded, even the Muslim League vice-president, who had been allied during the campaign with Zia's BNP, charged "massive rigging" and stated that the Awami League would have won an absolute majority in a "free and fair poll."[9]

The principal opposition to the BNP in 1979 was provided by the majority faction of the Awami League, led by Abdul Malek Ukil, the former speaker of Parliament under Sheikh Mujib. The Awami League (Ukil), the more left-oriented of the two AL factions, secured 40 seats with 24.4 percent of the vote. Its failure to

9. Quoted in Kirit Bhaumik, "Zia is up Against Pressure Politics in Bangladesh," *Times of India*, March 4, 1979. See also *The Statesman* (Calcutta), March 8, 1979.

appeal to the mass of Muslim voters in Bangladesh was indicated by the fact that 23 of its 40 seats came from Hindu-majority constituencies and most of the remaining 17 seats were in constituencies bordering on India. The rival faction, led by Mizaner Rahman Chowdhury, secured only two seats with 2.8 percent of the vote, but, unlike the Ukil faction, the Mizaner faction was able to elect its leader. Abdul Malek Ukil was defeated in both of the constituencies that he contested in 1979, the first electoral defeats in his political career.

ISLAM AND INDIA

Perhaps the most remarkable facet of the 1979 Parliamentary elections was the prominence within the new BNP government of men who had previously been charged with, or convicted of, collaboration with Pakistan during the liberation war. More than 400 of the nearly 2,000 Parliamentary candidates in 1979 had been accused or convicted of collaboration by Mujib's Awami League regime, including 3 Ministers in Zia's government and 4 BNP candidates who had previously been Ministers in Ayub Khan's or Yahya Khan's governments of the 1960s. Pro-Pakistanis who had been convicted under the Collaborators Act of 1972 were not allowed to participate in the 1973 elections, but this restriction was removed when Zia repealed the Collaborators Act in 1977. The importance of the so-called collaborators to Zia's BNP party is indicated by the fact that more than three-fourths of the BNP's victorious MPs in 1979 are said by Awami League leaders to be in this category, including Shah Azizur Rahman, the man Zia appointed as his first Prime Minister after the death of Mashiur Rahman.

Mashiur Rahman was himself charged with collaboration by Sheikh Mujib, but was never tried under the 1972 Act. Shah Azizur Rahman was actually tried and jailed for collaboration, primarily because he had at one point agreed to go to the United Nations on behalf of Pakistan to argue against Bangladesh's right to secede. Shah Aziz now claims that he agreed to represent Pakistan under threat of force but feigned illness at the United Nations so he would not have to speak against Bangladesh. His new government is reported to be working on a compilation of "genuine freedom fighters," including some of those charged by Mujib with collaboration, to be published in official gazettes.[10]

Zia's civilian Cabinets have thus far been weighted in favor of bureaucrats and technocrats but have also included representatives from Mashiur Rahman's NAP, the Muslim League, and other parties that have either joined the BNP or supported Zia's presidency. When the BNP was formed, on September 1, 1978, a 29-man Cabinet was chosen, in which former die-hard loyalists to Pakistan sat side by side with heroic leaders of the Bangladesh liberation struggle. Prominent among the former were lawyer-politician Abdul Aleem, a loyal and trusted political ally of Field Marshall Ayub Khan, and Abdul Momem, a member of the Bengal Civil Service who remained with the Pakistan administration throughout 1971 and the liberation war. Among the latter was A.Z.M. Enayetullah Khan, former editor of the weekly *Holiday*, who has since resigned from the Cabinet. One Cabinet Minister, Mr. K.M. Obaidur Rahman, was distinguished by his inclusion in three governments—those of Sheikh Mujibur Rahman, Khondakar Mushtaque Ahmed, and Ziaur Rahman—even though each represented fundamentally different factional interests within Bangladesh.

In his public pronouncements, Zia argues that he is essentially a consensus-builder. He speaks in general terms and usually avoids naming individuals or parties. The tone of his speech is not accusing and he speaks with pride of including in his Cabinet a variety of Bangladesh factional interests.

Nonetheless, it seems almost inevitable that Zia's heavy reliance on the Muslim League, and on former collaborators with Pakistan, will inevitably heighten animosities between his BNP and other parties. Anti-BNP feeling is especially bitter among followers of the Awami League, the JSD, and a number of smaller leftist parties. Zia has not succumbed to pressures from his more extremist, religiously oriented followers that he adopt fundamentalist policies and practices like those currently in vogue in Pakistan and Iran. Indeed, he has constantly called on the people of Bangladesh to adopt a spirit of "peace and tolerance, shunning disputes, hatred and conflict." At the same time, however, a number of his

10. A short biography of Shah Azizur Rahman appears in Saeed Naqvi, "Shah Aziz Calls for Ghalib-Nazrul Day," *Indian Express*, April 19, 1979. The freedom fighter compilation proposal was first mooted in January 1978; see Rajendra Sareen, "Zia's Proposed Political Front Delayed," *The Tribune* (Chandigarh), January 16, 1978.

followers have stirred up communal controversies and Zia has himself spoken favorably of the Muslim League political line, which portrays the Awami League as "indisciplined" and "irreligious" and the JSD as an "underground party" with "antinational leaders and policies."[11]

Awami League leaders are convinced that they are the exclusive targets of a martial law regulation requiring submission to the government of details regarding any acquisition of property between December 16, 1971 (the end of the liberation war) and November 7, 1975 (the beginning of Zia's regime). They were also miffed by Zia's decision in 1978 to release Muslim League and Islamic Democratic League (IDL) funds that had been frozen by Mujib's regime, and to do so just in time for them to be used in the 1979 Parliamentary elections. In the elections, the ML-IDL alliance contested under the slogan "defeat the Awami League and keep Islam safe in the hands of President Zia." Such sentiments, of course, run directly counter to Awami League secularism.

The greatest ill will between Zia and the Awami League stems from Zia's treatment of the young army Majors who staged the August 1975 coup, in which Mujib and his entire family (with the exception of his two daughters, who were in West Germany, and his two sisters, still in their village homes), were killed. The Awami League has demanded an inquiry into the coup, punishment of those who staged it, and a further inquiry into the chaotic events of November 3–7, 1975, when Zia was brought to power. Awami League leaders are convinced, to a man, that either Zia or his followers played a role in allowing the 1975 coup leaders to murder Mujib's four principal lieutenants and potential successors—Syed Nazrul Islam, Mansur Ali, Tajuddin Ahmed, and A.H.M. Kamaruzzaman —in the jails, and then to escape abroad. Such theories were given credence in mid-1979 by Zia's adamant refusal to discipline the young Majors, or to hold meaningful inquiries into any of the events of 1975. In April 1979, one of the Majors was a consultant to the Libyan government, one was a member of Bangladesh's diplomatic representation in Pakistan, and a third was in the Bangladesh diplomatic mission to China.

11. The quotes are from Zia's campaign speeches; see Asim Mukhopadhyay, "Farcical Election," *Economic and Political Weekly* (Bombay), June 3, 1978, pp. 904–906.

Zia's animosity toward the Awami League is partly a function of his lack of respect (and occasional contempt) for Mujib, partly based on his treatment at the hands of the Awami League and India during the liberation war, and partly a consequence of the martial law experience and the present electoral rivalry. Zia had been known to criticize Mujib's tolerance of irreligiosity and lack of discipline, and his inability to stem corruption or get development programs moving in the period prior to 1975. That Zia was the first Bangladesh leader to declare the nation independent in 1971 indicates his impatience at that time with Awami League leaders, whom Zia saw as lacking in courage. Zia's feelings of isolation from the Awami League during the 1971 struggle were detailed in an interview with Manash Ghosh in June 1978, in which Zia suggested that Mujib had been far too dependent on India and excessively indulgent with corrupt Bangladesh and Indian business-men.[12]

In a nation that has never been as religiously fundamentalist as the Islamic countries of the Middle East, it is perhaps not surpris-ing that Zia has moved toward an Islamic polity with caution. He had established close working relationships with major Islamic countries, and especially with Saudi Arabia, Egypt, and Libya, but he has also improved Bangladesh's relations with secular India. Huge billboards with quotations from the Koran—in Arabic and Bengali—can be seen at many intersections in major cities and quotations from scriptures are also frequently posted on Secretariat walls to remind people of such mundane things as basic demands of cleanliness in the Islamic religion. As noted, however, there has been no hint that Zia would institute fundamentalist Islamic policies like those in Pakistan or Iran, which routinely use medieval punishments such as lashes with a whip or the cutting off of limbs to punish offenders of Muslim law.[13]

Nonetheless, it is clear that Zia's followers are determined to move the nation away from the wide degrees of tolerance associated with Mujib's secularism. Their orthodox attitudes toward women,

12. Manash Ghosh, "Zia's Stress on Stability and Progress," *The States-man* (Calcutta), June 15, 1978.

13. The orientation of Zia's government toward Islam is analyzed in M. Rashiduzzaman, "Changing Political Patterns in Bangladesh: Internal Constraints and External Fears," *Asian Survey*, XVII:9 (September 1977), pp. 793–808.

for example, are revealed in the BNP's selection of candidates for Parliament in 1979—not one of the 300 was a female. Indeed, of the almost 2,000 candidates for Parliament, only 19 were women, with most of these contesting on Awami League tickets. Zia himself explains this absence of women candidates by arguing that "women do not want to contest the elections." His fifth constitutional amendment provides for 30 reserved seats for women in the new Parliament, to be filled by a special election in which balloting is restricted to already elected (and, coincidentally, all male) Members of Parliament.[14]

Improvement in Indo-Bangladesh relations has been rather steady since the election of the Janata government in India in March 1977. After the assassination of Mujibur Rahman in the August 1975 coup, Indira Gandhi became distrustful of Bangladesh governments and severely contentious in her behavior toward them. During her last few years as Prime Minister, she gave support and asylum to Bangladesh rebels based in India and refused to make concessions in negotiations with Bangladesh on such matters as the sharing of river waters, demarcation of maritime boundaries, and trade terms. Meanwhile, her government used both police and the military to cope with the nagging problems of smuggling and illegal movement of people across the Indo-Bangladesh border.

Morarji Desai's government has stopped supporting Bangladesh rebels based in India, although it has allowed some of them to remain in India as exiles.[15] It has concluded a five-year agreement on the sharing of waters from the Farakka Barrage by making concessions to Bangladesh that had been refused for the previous 11 years. Concessions have also been made in some trade matters and a number of Indo-Bangladesh committees have been established to sort out questions relating to trade, the establishment of joint industrial ventures, the integration of transport and communications systems, the maritime boundary, and the continuing influx of Bangladesh refugees into India. Mr. T.N. Kaul, a former Foreign Secretary under Indira Gandhi, has publicly opposed the Farakka agreement, labeling it part of India's "appeasement policy" toward Bangladesh. Without being specific, Kaul states that Desai's

---

14. Analyses of the 1979 elections appear in the *New York Times*, February 19, 20, and 22, 1979.

15. See D. Sen, "Bangla Tiger Happy After Talks with PM," *Hindustan Times*, November 26, 1977.

government has "given away part of her vital interests without getting anything concrete in return."[16]

The most intractable problem in Indo-Bangladesh relations continues to be the inexorable movement of poor Bangladesh refugees across the 2,521-mile border into India. Most of the influx has gone into the Indian states of West Bengal, Assam, and Tripura, but all the northeastern states have felt its effects. In early 1979 it was estimated that more than half the total population of three million in Nadia district of West Bengal were refugees from Bangladesh. Of the other seven West Bengal districts that border on Bangladesh, more than a third of the population of each is estimated to be refugees. As security measures on West Bengal's borders tightened during the Indira Gandhi years, migration into Assam, Tripura, Meghalaya, and other northeastern states accelerated. The number of immigrants into Assam since 1971 is estimated at more than 600,000; to Meghalaya more than 300,000; to Tripura, more than 200,000.[17] In 1979, a new migration of Magh and Chakma tribals from the Chittagong Hill Tracts in Bangladesh, numbering in the thousands, began filtering into the Indian state of Mizoram.[18]

Both Indian and Bangladesh officials are now willing to acknowledge publicly the extent of the migration, something that was not always admitted during the Indira Gandhi years. Both sets of officials are also convinced that the movement of migrants is a result of severe economic hardship in Bangladesh as well as occasional flare-ups of communal tension. A majority of the refugees are Hindus—as is attested to by the decline of Bangladesh's Hindu population from 18 to 10 percent of the total over the past three decades—but at least a quarter of them (and especially those going to Goalpara and Cachar districts in Assam) are Muslims. The boundary is now extensively marked with little conical concrete blocks and small T-shaped iron plates, and is guarded

16. T.N. Kaul, *Diplomacy in Peace and War* (New Delhi: Vikas Publishers 1979), pp. 237 ff.

17. Quoted from government sources in *The Hindu* (Madras), March 19, 1979. For an excellent analysis of the migration in historical perspective, see Myron Weiner, *Sons of the Soil: Migration and Ethnic Conflict in India* (Princeton: Princeton University Press, 1978), pp. 75–144.

18. *Tha Statesman* (Calcutta), March 20, 1979. India's approach toward its insurgency problem in the northeast is traced in Onkar Marwah, "Northeastern India: New Delhi Confronts the Insurgents," *Orbis*, 21:2 (Summer 1977), pp. 353–374.

at intervals averaging 500 yards or so by border policemen and bureaucrats. Nonetheless, the difficult terrain, together with the gap between the miserable economic conditions of Bangladesh and the relative affluence of India, has made it impossible to stem the constant daily movement of refugees.

One measure that is being considered is the issuance of identity cards to people along the border, with such cards being required for employment in the tea gardens, oils fields, railways, and industries of India.[19] Another proposal, which was adopted by the two governments when Morarji Desai visited Dacca in April 1979, calls for more regular conferences and communications between the Border Security Forces of Bangladesh and the Indian states, for purposes of sorting out details of how human border traffic could be better regulated. In the final analysis, however, both the Zia and Desai governments are agreed that the refugee problem in the northeast can be effectively tackled only if problems relating to communal tensions and economic disparities are squarely faced.

Ziaur Rahman has gained the respect of most Hindu leaders of Bangladesh for his cool-headed views on the communal issue, but many of the people in his party continue to exacerbate communal tensions. During the 1978 and 1979 election campaigns, some Zia supporters were reported to have told Hindus that they would either lose their property or be forced to go to India if they voted for the Awami League. In other cases, local Hindu leaders were accused of being subversives working for India. Election posters in the 1978 campaign depicted General Zia as "the one who saved Bangladesh from the evil designs of India" and cautioned voters to elect Zia, "lest you turn Bangladesh into Sikkim or Bhutan."[20]

On the Indian side, too, government spokesmen have been highly conscious of the need for discretion on communal issues, but private Indian citizens and local political party functionaries have occasionally stirred up communal passions. Some of the most irresponsible and unfounded charges—of massive electoral rigging, forcible conversion, and other atrocities—have come from Mr.

19. Kuldip Nayar, "Government Concerned Over Bangla Infiltrators," *The Indian Express,* April 16, 1979.

20. P.B. Sinha, "Zia's Post-Poll Problems," *The Tribune* (Chandigarh), June 15, 1978; see also *The Times af India,* April 20, 1979.

Samar Guha, a Janata Member of Parliament from West Bengal.[21]
Leaders of the Jana Sangh Party, which has a reputation for militant
Hinduism, have shown remarkable balance and poise in their
handling of Indo-Bangladesh relations, even though the words or
actions of a handful of their members have occasionally disrupted
communal harmony.[22]

CONCLUSIONS

The ability of Ziaur Rahman to stay in power for three and a half
years has lent a degree of stability to Bangladesh that had not been
there for at least the past decade Since 1969, the only government
to stay in power for more than three years was the Awami League
regime of Sheikh Mujib, but that government was plagued by the
disorder, inflation, and corruption that followed in the wake of the
liberation war. Zia's transition to civilian rule has thus far been
characterized by manipulation of electoral alliances and a highly
undemocratic process of governance. This has produced a new
constitutional order which combines features of Mujib's BAKSHAL
Scheme and the Ayub Khan regime, both of which were highly
authoritarian and unsuccessful.

Zia's BNP regime has as its primary constituencies the military
and bureaucratic factions loyal to Ziaur Rahman himself and the
Islamic parties that previously provided the opposition to Sheikh
Mujib. Zia has made a genuine effort to dampen the communal
inclinations of some of his more extremist supporters, but his increasing reliance on pro-Islamic elements in the population has
strained his relations with some secular-minded enthusiasts in
Bangladesh and India. Indo-Bangladesh relations have noticeably
improved since the Janata government came to power in March 1977,
despite the inability of the two governments to find lasting solutions
to any of their nagging problems. It is generally agreed that Zia's
future success or failures will depend on his ability to promote
economic development and to affect some degree of reconciliation
on highly emotional religious and political issues. His efforts in
these directions will be the subject of the next essay in this volume.

21. See, for example, *The Hindustan Times*, April 11, 1979.
22. An excellent analysis of the Jana Sangh's role in the Janata government appears in K.R. Sundar Rajan, "The RSS Connection," *The Hindustan
Times*, April 20, 1979.

ELEVEN

POVERTY AND DISCONTENT (1979)

Ziaur Rahman has enemies within Bangladesh. Many of these are in the army or other branches of the military. Most of Zia's enemies in the army owe their loyalties to the ghost of Colonel Abu Taher, the man who, more than any other, helped install Zia in power on the morning of November 7, 1975 and was executed by Zia in the jails on the night of July 21, 1976. Zia's perfidy in trying and executing Abu Taher has been invoked by most of the soldiers that have taken part in several attempted coups since November 7, 1975.[1]

Supporters of Ziaur Rahman suggest that Abu Taher's role in the November 7, 1975 coup has been exaggerated in Western press reports. It is generally acknowledged that Taher and his political party, the Jatio Samajtantrik Dal (JSD) did play the major role, but other leftist pro-Chinese parties (the Sammobadi Dal and Sarbohara Party were the most prominent) were instrumental in mobilizing *jawans* (common soldiers). Muslim League leaders claim they played a part in contacting and activating West Pakistan-returned *jawans* and officers. In general, it is agreed that the principal dynamic of the Novermber 7 coup was an upsurge of anti-Indian emotion directed against Khaled Musharraf because it was widely felt that he had taken Indian assistance in staging his coup four days earlier.

From Taher's point of view, however, the coup that installed Ziaur Rahman in power was a revolutionary soldiers' mutiny. Taher argued that all previous coups and political changes in Bangladesh had been carried out to advance the narrow, competing interests of factional elites, and especially the upper echelons of the

1 The record of coups is traced, and a highly complimentary view of Ziaur Rahman provided, in Denis Warner, "Bangladesh: Is There Anything to Look Forward to?" *The Atlantic Monthly*, 242:5 (November 1978), pp. 6–13.

officer corps. Taher's coup was intended to place power in the hands of common soldiers and nonelite segments of the general population. Taher inspired his troops to revolt by calling for the abolition of British colonial rules and regulations within the army and for the establishment of a "classless army." Selection of officers was to be from among the ranks, rather than from privileged classes attending special schools. Common soldiers were no longer to be allowed to serve as household servants of officers. Pay scales and the quality of housing for the rank and file were to be considerably upgraded.[2]

Once Ziaur Rahman was installed in power, Taher issued a declaration in which he tried to reorganize the structure of military authority. The declaration fixed final control of the army in a Central Organisation, made up of common soldiers and officers. It specifically stated that "Only after consultation will General Zia be able to take any final decision." According to Taher's conception, the Central Organisation was to be linked to committees of peasants, workers, students, and "other progressive revolutionaries" in a grand coalition of national interests that would govern the country. As Lawrence Lifschultz has pointed out, this was the first time that a powerful *radical* force had emerged within an organized military establishment in South Asia.[3]

Taher's coup recalled the glorious days of the liberation war. Soldiers loyal to Taher moved on Dacca—from Rangpur, Chittagong, Comilla, and Jessore—taking over all strategic points in the capital city and freeing political prisoners (including Ziaur Rahman). People poured into the streets shouting slogans. Zia was reported to have embraced Taher while in his nightshirt and, in front of a number of witnesses, thanked Taher for saving his life. Zia recalled at the time that he and Taher had always taken the same side on important military issues, including the need for a people's army. Zia and Taher had fought in the same (Eleventh) sector during the liberation war and Zia had supported Taher when the latter's

2. Taher's "12 demands" and his political strategy are described in Talukder Maniruzzaman, *The Bangladesh Revolution and Its Aftermath*: (Dacca Bangladesh Books International, 1981).

3. Lawrence Lifschultz, "Abu Taher's Last Testament: Bangladesh: The Unfinished Revolution," *The Economic and Political Weekly* (Bombay), August 1977, p. 1309. I am indebted to Lifschultz for most of the material on Abu Taher in this *AUFS Report*.

leftist views led Mujibur Rahman to force him out of the army. It was a telephone call from Zia to Taher on November 4, 1975 that had led Taher to stage the coup against Khaled Musharraf. On the evening of November, 1975, Zia signed a document committing himself to the implementation of Taher's ideas.[4]

At the root of Taher's ideas was the conviction that Bangladesh had to choose a revolutionary socialist path of austere self-reliance rather than what Lifschultz had called," "a path of capitalist development based on the largesse of the Americans and the plans of the World Bank."[5] Taher had been especially appalled by the gross scale of corruption under Mujib, including one scandal in which the World Bank had knowingly paid $4 million in bribes to promote some of its irrigation projects and another where a multimillion dollar black market had been established in Dacca with relief supplies.[6] Taher and his closest friend, Colonel Mohammad Ziauddin, had already acquired reputations within the Bangladesh military for scrupulous honesty and for opposition to lifestyles that relied heavily on imported luxury goods. In 1973, both Taher and Ziauddin had ordered all officers under their command to surrender any property they had acquired illegally during and after the liberation war. In a fit of rage that is still discussed in Dacca military circles today, Ziauddin built a vast bonfire of the loot collected from his officers and ordered an entire brigade to stand at attention while television sets, refrigerators, radios, and cameras went up in flames.

Taher's ideas were not to be implemented. During Mujib's time, radical elements within the military who opposed foreign aid and argued for an austere and self-reliant approach to reconstruction were purged. When Taher and Ziauddin were dismissed from the army by Mujib, Taher helped found an armed wing of the Jatiya Samajtantrik Dal (JSD), designed to provide an organizational focus for soldiers within the army. Ziauddin joined a smaller leftist party (Sarbohara), which was also committed to violence, and has

4. Lifschultz, p. 1310.
5. Ibid.
6. The incidents are detailed in two articles in the *Far Eastern Economic Review*: "Bangladesh: Playground for Opportunists," September 6, 1974 and "Letter from London," February 7, 1975. See also my "The Bangladesh Coup" (MF-15-'75], *AUFS Reports*, South Asia Series, Vol. XIX, No. 15, 1976, and Lifschultz, p. 1331.

since assumed leadership of a small band of guerrillas fighting for the autonomy of the Chittagong Hill Tracts. After the November 7 coup, Zia at first released leaders and members of the JSD who had been jailed without trial by Sheikh Mujib. On the night of November 23, however, he rounded up the JSD leaders and clamped them back in prison. On November 24 he arrested Taher.

Taher and 32 others were tried in Dacca Central Jail, the first trial behind bars in the history of either Bangladesh or East Pakistan. The charges ranged from treason to mutiny to "propagation of political ideology and disaffection among the officers and other members of the Defence Services." Twenty-two of the defendants were members of the armed forces; the other 11 were leading figures in the JSD. Two of the JSD leaders were sentenced to life imprisonment and their property confiscated; 14 were given sentences of 5-10 years and fined; 16 of the defendants were acquitted. Colonel Abu Taher was sentenced to death by hanging and hanged inside Dacca Central Jail on July 21, 1976.

POLITICAL EXECUTIONS

Since the execution of Abu Taher, the Bangladesh government has tried hundreds of soldiers before Martial Law Tribunals and has continued a policy of executing those convicted of the most serious crimes. The major wave of executions came in October 1977 when some sections of the army and the bulk of the air force attempted a coup while Zia's government was negotiating with hijackers of a Japanese Airlines plane that had landed at Dacca airport. Eleven senior air force officers, 10 army officers, and an estimated 200 other soldiers were killed in the attempted coup at the airport on October 2; hundreds of others were said to have been killed during an earlier attempted coup at Bogra on September 30. Zia himself announced that 460 people were tried for participation in the October coup, of whom only 63 were acquitted. On October 15, 1977 he announced that 37 members of the army and air force had been executed and indicated that some death sentences were still "being carried out."[7]

Throughout late 1977 and early 1978 there were major shakeups in the Bangladesh military, while executions continued. Peter Gill,

7. *New York Times*, October 20, 1977 and *The Hindu*, October 16, 1977.

of the London *Daily Telegraph* (January 10, 1978), was told by senior military officers in Bangladesh in January 1978 that 150 members of the air force had either been hanged or shot by firing squads. By mid-January it was estimated that only 11 officers were left in the entire air force, of which only 3 were capable of piloting an aircraft. A number of the remaining senior officers were reported to have resigned in protest when 28-year-old Group Captain M. Sadruddin was appointed Air Chief of Staff.

The principal reason for the October 1977 coup was the presence in Bangladesh of an eight-man British military advisory team commanded by Colonel T.A. Gibson. The ostensible purpose of the Gibson mission was to set up a military Staff College at Savar, outside Dacca, but an additional object was rumored to be the preparation of dossiers for Western intelligence on the entire officer corps in Bangladesh. Rumors were fed by the fact that Gibson and his men were part of Britain's Special Air Services Brigade, the most respected counterinsurgency intelligence outfit in the British army. The British had also given Dacca a grant for £720,000 to develop Bangladesh's police telecommunications, replacing in that capacity an American Office of Public Safety (OPS) AID program that had created East Pakistan's police telecommunications grid in the 1960s. Caught off guard by the coups and executions of 1975, 1976, and 1977, Western intelligence began to realize in 1977 the extent to which it had previously been dependent on West Pakistani intelligence sources. As one well-informed Bengali explained the Gibson mission:

They want to know when Zia falls, who can be the next pro-Western Ayub Khan. But they also want to be able to spot any Marxists like Abu Taher. They want to know who is politically reliable. You can't do that sitting in London or in an office in the Pentagon. Computers will not tell you. Personal contact might.[8]

Followers of Abu Taher were outraged by the Gibson mission. Having placed Zia in power after a coup that called for the "complete abolition of British colonial practices within the armed forces," soldiers and officers now found that, a year and a half later, the

---

8. The quote is from an excellent article by NMJ (pseudonym), "Murder in Dacca: Ziaur Rahman's Second Round," *The Economic and Political Weekly* (Bombay) March 25, 1978, p. 555. Most of my material on The Gibson mission is from this article. See also Simon Winchester, "Implications of British Aid to Bangladesh," *The Guardian* (London), January 1, 1978.

British were being asked to set up a permanent military training program. In two ill-planned moves, the coup leaders struck at Bogra on September 30, and at Dacca on October 2, 1977. Most of them were killed in clashes with troops loyal to Zia. Many of the others have since been executed.

In a February 1978 report, Amnesty International (AI) estimated that "at least 130, and perhaps several hundred military men" had been executed for their alleged involvement in the September/October 1977 coup attempts.[9] AI officials admitted privately that this was a conservative figure, based on a list of 129 names that was supplied to them and verified by independent sources. The U.S. Embassy officially quoted the government's announcement that only 37 rebels had been executed, but a confidential cable to the State Department, leaked to the *Washington Post* (February 10, 1978), said: "our best estimate, drawn from sources available to the Embassy as a whole, is that 217 military personnel were executed in the aftermath of the coup attempt." On March 5, 1978, *The Times* of London concluded, on the basis of conversations with senior officers in Bangladesh, that more than 800 servicemen had been convicted by military tribunals and about 600, mostly from the air force, had been executed by firing squads or by hanging.

The Amnesty International report focused in large part on the operations of Bangladesh's Martial Law Tribunals, which were not only ordering executions but were also handing out lesser sentences. Two types of Martial Law Courts (MLCs) were in existence, the first (Special MLCs) consisting of two armed forces officers and a magistrate, the second (Summary MLCs) having only one member who was either a magistrate or an army officer. Special MLCs had the power to award the death sentence. Summary MLCs did not. In neither case did a prisoner have the right to *habeas corpus* or to an appeal. AI has concluded that the executions of Abu Taher and other military men during Zia's regime have been "held under the most unsatisfactory circumstances" and that those accused "could never have been convicted if their trials had taken place before an ordinary criminal court."[10]

Repression of radical elements within the military has taken place simultaneously with the increasing involvement of the pro-Zia

9. The Report is excerpted in *The Times of India*, February 28, 1978.
10. Quoted in "Murder in Dacca...," op. cit., p. 553.

military faction in politics. In the 1979 elections, 17 retired army men contested for Parliament, including 10 from Zia's BNP, 5 of whom were Ministers in Zia's Cabinet. In the 1978 elections, retired General Khalilur Rahman of the Awami League provided details, never refuted by the government, of a meeting at Dacca cantonment where a senior army general addressed senior police officers and asked them to insure that President Zia won the elections "at any cost," but that Zia should not be shown to have polled more than 70 per cent of the votes.[11]

Since the publication of the Amnesty International report, more shake-ups of the military have taken place amid continuing rumors of more executions. AI estimated in January 1978 that there were 10,000-15,000 political prisoners in Bangladesh jails, but other informed sources place the figures much higher. In December 1978 the government announced it was releasing more than 10,000 political prisoners who had been held without trial, including 300 JSD members. Leaders of all the opposition parties claimed in early 1979 that several hundred of their members were still behind bars; both the JSD and Awami League claimed that thousands of their people were still in prison.

AUTHORITARIANISM AND THE ECONOMY

Zia's justification for executions and electoral manipulations is similar to that of many authoritarian figures in other developing nations. He argues that the country is so in need of a period of stability and discipline that displays of raw force and undemocratic measures are warranted. One of his closest advisers said in an interview in early 1979 that Zia seriously considered the ideas of Abu Taher but, once in office, decided that they would so divide and polarize the nation that they could not form the basis for a successful regime. In an interview with Kevin Rafferty in September 1978, Zia echoed this line of reasoning when he said: "I do not want to do radical things. We must keep this people together."[12]

As is the case with so many other authoritarian figures, Zia himself is an extremely hard-working person who is not personally

11. D. Sen, "Zia is Heading for Sweeping Victory," *The Hindustan Times*, June 5, 1978. See also *Times of India*.
12. Kevin Rafferty, "'Lucky' in Bangladesh," *The Washington Post*, September 3, 1978.

associated with corruption. He spends considerable time traveling—
by helicopter, by jeep, and on foot—to every nook and cranny of
Bangladesh. At the end of the 1979 elections he boasted that he
had been in villages in all 414 *thanas* (administrative units roughly
equivalent to counties in the West). When he was a senior
military officer, he insisted on taking loans to purchase furniture
and domestic appliances; as President and Chief Martial Law
Administrator he insists on a $17 monthly deduction from his
salary to pay for personal use of his official car.

In direct contradiction to Abu Taher's ideas, however, Zia has
increased Bangladesh's dependence on aid and relief supplies from
the West. He now argues that it is the "moral duty" of nations
friendly to Bangladesh to step up their assistance and insists that
the nations's capacity for absorbing aid has "increased greatly."
Since 1971, Bangladesh has received more than $7 billion in aid.
More than 50 percent of the current national budget and more
than 70 per cent of planned public sector outlays in the current Two-
Year Plan (1978–1980) are expected to come from foreign donors.
Zia has suggested that his government could utilize as much as $2
billion in aid per year, as compared with a current level of just
over $1 billion. "We hope," he has said,

*that friendly countries will come forward with an open hand and give
us a one-time big push—lots of aid and assistance—so that we can
pick up ourselves in a short time and we won't have to depend on
others as we have.*[13]

Heavy aid inputs and an emphasis on law and order have changed
the face of Dacca and, to a lesser extent, other Bangladesh cities.
More than 10,000 Westerners, representing 193 relief and development agencies, now live in the capital city, a sharp contrast to the few
hundred that were there prior to the liberation war of 1971. In
the modern parts of Dacca, streets have been widened, neat rows of
green verges have been constructed between traffic lanes, trees have
been planted throughout the city, impressive overhead pedestrian
walkways have been built across major arteries, old buildings have

13. Quoted in William Borders, "Bangladesh Leader Calls Vote Fair,
Asks For More Aid," the *New York Times*, June 6, 1978. See also Manash
Ghosh, "Zia Appeals for More Economic Aid," *The Statesman* (Calcutta) June
6, 1978.

been painted and large numbers of multistoried buildings have been constructed. City policemen and policewomen in smart blue, white, and khaki uniforms keep watch at most intersections, occasionally using microphones to tell erring drivers and pedestrians to correct themselves. Traffic rules, including those requiring cars to pull to the side of the road when the President or Vice-President passes by, are enforced. Beggars and illegal squatters have been removed from the sidewalks and sent out to colonies on the outskirts of Dacca.

Perhaps the most frequent sight in Dacca these days is that of road crews, paving and repaving streets in the modern parts of the city. Some members of the crews are crushing bricks or rocks to provide a roadbed, others are heating bitumen, laying sand, or rolling out the pavement. Most of the work relies heavily on manual labor and is part of Zia's foreign-aided program of large-scale public works and food-for-work projects. Streets and parks in modern sections of Dacca city are lit with beautiful lights, neon signs glow from every tall building, and the roads are filled with foreign cars and scooters. The stores are now packed with foreign goods, with most of them (including the cars and scooters) coming from Japan and Europe rather than from India.

This urban enclave economy is driven, exclusively, by a small, affluent, upper-middle class that is as conspicuous and as willing to engage in ostentatious living as any such class anywhere in the world. Much of this class works, in one way or another, for the foreign agencies active in Bangladesh. It gets much of its foreign money from what is known as the "indenting trade," which means essentially the cut that Bengali businessmen and contractors secure from commodity orders under aid and import-export agreements.[14] Foreign exchange and foreign goods have also been earned under the so-called "wage-earners' scheme," which allows imports to be made with the earnings of the 200,000 Bangladesh families living abroad. This scheme has not only met the demands of the affluent class—for foreign cars, electronic gadgets, and superior textiles —but it has also at times met some basic requirements of the not-so-affluent. For example, when textile prices shot up beyond the reach of most Bangladeshis in 1978 and 1979, second-hand garments

14. An excellent discussion of the "indenting trade" appears in Kirit Bhaumik, "Prosperity Noted in Dacca: But Prices Soaring," *Times of India,* March 6, 1979.

were allowed to be imported from abroad through foreign "wage-earners," to the point where sale of foreign second-hand garments has now become a thriving business.[15]

Much of Dacca's affluence also comes from the plane loads of Bangladeshis working in the Gulf states, who arrive several times each week with television sets, stereo tape recorders, and innumerable other gadgets and luxury items. Getting off the same planes are Arabs in search of more labor, or some who are simply in the country to "feel the monsoon." There are an estimated 50,000 Bangladeshis in the Gulf now and the numbers are climbing steadily each month. Arabic language schools are flourishing, bookshops routinely stock Bengali-Arabic dictionaries, and travel agents devote most of their time to arrangements for job-seekers going to the Near and Middle East.

The presence of foreign development and relief agencies, particularly when combined with the exodus to the Gulf, has created a boom in the establishment of schools and institutes that provide skills and training to members of the elite classes. Training for secretaries, drivers, bookkeepers, clerks, hairdressers, barbers, mechanics, nurses, paramedics, waiters, and a variety of other jobs is routinely available from both government and private agencies in the city. Mobility is so great for those who have skills or a profession that foreign development organizations complain they often have to hire a foreigner to do a job they have trained several Bengalis to do, simply because the Bengalis, once trained, have moved on to the Gulf or elsewhere.

Side by side with new professionals and skilled workers is a rising class of private businessmen and entrepreneurs that has been encouraged by a liberalization of rules governing private enterprise. Zia has not only denationalized many businesses and restored many industrial units to their original owners, he has also provided for liberal financial backing to new enterprises by government banks and credit institutions and has granted tax incentives to both old and new businesses. Budding young Bangladesh businessmen now routinely make weekend trips to Hong Kong, Bangkok, and Singapore, for shopping and pleasure as well as business. They

15. Ibid. An analysis of goverhment intervention in the Bangladesh economy appears in A.M.A. Rahim, "A Review of Industrial Investment Policy in Bangladesh, 1971–1977," *Asian Survey*, XVIII:11 (November 1978), pp. 1181–1190.

have also contributed their share to a tremendous construction boom in the more fashionable residential areas of Dacca, where large, modern homes are being constructed at the rate of several per week.[16]

Bangladesh's new elites speak frequently of a Japanese model of development, or conjure up futuristic visions of Bangladesh cities built along the lines of Singapore or Hong Kong. In hopes of attracting some Singapore-style trade and export industries, a free port is being constructed near Chittagong. The usual argument for such activities is that the rural sector in Bangladesh cannot be expected to raise the capital or provide the employment necessary for development, which means that a heavy emphasis must be placed on the industrial and trade sectors. Bangladeshi elites, including Zia's government, are also convinced that the major push for industrial development has to come from private enterprise, and must necessarily entail a great deal of penetration by foreign multinationals.

Total direct foreign investment in Bangladesh is now estimated at roughly $200 million, most of which dates from the pre-1947 period. Zia's government has offered liberal tax holidays and even more liberal terms for repatriation of profits and salaries. Bangladesh businessmen emphasize the cheap and plentiful labor supply and their own eagerness to collaborate as further incentives for foreign investors. They prefer joint ventures in which the foreign partner provides the foreign exchange, but are willing to undertake management contracts, licensing, and third party arrangements. Pharmaceuticals is currently the fastest growing area for foreign investment, but there has also been some activity in export industries like seafood, electronics, garments, processed foods, and other labor-intensive products. A number of foreign firms have been successful in discovering vast reserves of high-quality natural gas and have been granted lucrative production-sharing contracts by the Bangladesh government. The 46 oil wells that have been drilled by foreign companies (mostly offshore) have failed to turn up any significant reserves of crude petroleum.

While there has not yet been any significant breakthrough in

16. Descriptions of Dacca's new class of nouveau riche appear in two articles by Manash Ghosh: "Dacca Resplendent with New Affluence," *The Statesman*, May 30, 1978 and "The Young Bangladesh Professionals," *The Statesman*, February 14, 1979.

employment-producing industrial growth, Bangladesh businessmen insist this is not the fault of the government's basic economic strategy. Indeed, they suggest that the government must disinvest itself of state-owned units at a still faster pace, and that even more concessions (like compensation for assets seized during previous regimes) must be granted. For many foreign and domestic businessmen, however, memories of the instability and bureaucratic socialist measures of the pre-1975 era dictate caution.

Nevertheless, authoritarian control of the foreign-related portions of the economy by a small elite class of nouveau riche has made possible a dual economy of the most extreme kind, with the modern enclave centered on Dacca becoming increasingly affluent and the fetid rural sector continuing to grow and rot. Those who are part of the modern economy work in airconditioned offices, have access to imported cars and luxury goods, aspire to travel abroad, and invariably watch television (*The Waltons*, *Persuaders*, *Hawaii Five-O*, and *I Love Lucy* are representative of Bangladesh's daily fare, which consists primarily of imported canned programs). The latest craze among the most mod Dacca families is to have a video cassette recorder, which enables the family and its friends to watch imported movies (including Hindi movies from India) and to record favorite programs.

Were it not for the sea of suffering humanity in which this island of affluence operates, such a bourgeois existence might not be worthy of mention. Questions about the legitimacy of the modern economy arise in part because it is being imposed with such authoritarian brutality, but also because it mercilessly accentuates the gap between rich and poor, to the advantage of those who run the authoritarian structures. Zia, the government, the foreign development and relief agencies, and every other representative of the elite classes in Dacca will argue strenuously, and often very eloquently, that programs must be designed to benefit the poorest of the poor. The government's next five-year plan is supposed to have a "rural bias." But somehow, the vast majority of the programs that have been designed by Western experts and Dacca bureaucrats have ended up contributing, almost exclusively, to the riches of the affluent nouveau riche.

A number of well-documented empirical studies have shown that landlessness has been increasing at ever more rapid rates during the past eight years, while the dependence of sharecroppers and tenants on landlords has also been increasing.[17]   Real agricultural wages are about two-thirds what they were in 1970![18] As the potential rural work force has expanded by about 800,000 per year, without finding work, production per acre of most crops has remained relatively constant.[19]   The introduction of the new technology in agriculture, even at a place like Comilla (where smaller farmers were truly benefiting from programs in the 1960s), has unquestionably redounded to the benefit of the bigger farmers in the 1970s.[20] Distress sales of land by those with the smallest holdings and the partition of holdings into fragments have both accentuated.[21]

Foreign development agencies have admittedly been unable to make much progress in family planning or other population control programs, primarily because they have been unable to inspire a corps of educators or health workers to undertake the difficult tasks of working and persuading at the local level.   With its population of 84 million growing at the rate of 2.6 percent per year, unemployment in Bangladesh continues to spread like a flame on a dry thatched roof, and yet the present economic pattern is probably creating jobs for no more than a quarter or so of the new entrants to the labor force each year.[22]   Inflation levels were officially 11.3 percent in 1977 and 12.33 percent in 1978, but people on the ground scoff at such figures and state that there is no doubt in their minds that most inflation statistics are "cooked up."   As Kirit Bhaumik pointed out in the *Times of India* (March 6, 1979), prices of everything but rice and second-hand garments are now higher than at any time in the history of Bangladesh.

17.   For a bibliography on landlessness, see Shapan Adnan and associates, "Review of Landlessness in Rural Bangladesh" (Chittagong: Department of Economics, Chittagong University, 1979).

18.   Edward J. Clay, "Institutional Change and Agricultural Wages in Bangladesh," Staff Paper 76–5 (New York: Agricultural Development Council, 1979), p. 424.

19.   See *The Year Book of Agricultural Statistics of Bangladesh* (Dacca: Bangladesh Bureau of Statistics, Ministry of Planning, 1978).

20.   Harry W. Blair, "Rural Development, Class Structure and Bureaucracy in Bangladesh," *World Development*, VI:1 (1978), pp. 65–82.

21.   A.R. Khan, *Poverty and Inequality in Rural Bangladesh*, World Employment Programme Research Working Paper (Geneva: International Labour Organisation, 1976).

22.   Statistics in this paragraph were quoted to me in March 1979 by Dr. A.K.M. Ghulam Rabbani, Director-General of the Bangladesh Bureau of Statistics and Secretary, Statistics Division, Ministry of Planning.

Zia's government has tried to hold prices down by offering rice and other foodgrains in ration shops at subsidized rates; as mentioned previously, second-hand garments have been imported in large quantities under the "foreign wage-earners scheme." But detailed studies show that neither the second-hand garments nor rationed foodgrains are reaching the poorest sections of the Bangladesh population. They, too, are being used to maintain a satisfactory standard of living for urban elites and followers of the current regime. In the words of AID economist F. James Levinson:

In Bangladesh, the ration system, which provides rice and wheat at roughly two-thirds of their open market prices, reaches less than 25 percent of the country's population and less than 15 percent of the rural populace. Rural food distribution (the so-called "modified ration system") is highly sporadic, and rarely exceeds one kilogram of foodgrain per adult per month. Two-thirds of the food in the ration system is allotted to residents of the six largest cities, plus such special target categories as government employees (the military—author), and "large employers." Much of the food in the ration system is imported, and its sale through this vehicle provides a healthy share of the government's operating expenditure.....Clearly the system is oriented not toward the basic needs of the poor but rather toward those whose political support is most essential for government survival.[23]

As a consequence of accelerating impoverishment all around, the nutritional status of the vast bulk of the population has plummeted. While in 1963 only 10 percent of the households consumed less than 80 percent of caloric needs, the figure is now 30 percent. Levinson points out that

Second and third degree malnutrition among children below the age of three (using weight-for-age standards) increased from 50 percent in 1964 to an astounding 75 percent in 1976. This figure

---

23. Quoted from F. James Levinson, "The Role of Subsidized Consumption in Reduced Population Growth: The Cases of Sri Lanka, Kerala and Bangladesh." Paper presented at the Conference on Nutrition Needs, Laxenbur, Austria, May 1978.

compares with less than 20 percent in most of Latin America and less than 4 percent in Chile.[24]

Soaring prices and declining nutritional levels have created a severe crisis for fixed-income lower-class groups and wage-earners, which has been reflected in a spate of wildcat strikes and demonstrations. Like the crushing of attempted coups, Zia's government has ruthlessly put down strikes with force and has continued to ban demonstrations in the cities. Indeed, Zia's first act after the 1979 elections was to ban strikes by ordinance, and to forbid redress to the courts on any mattter relating to strikes or demonstrations.[25] During the first Parliamentary session of 1979, Zia did lift martial law, but only after he had used his two-thirds majority to ratify all the martial law proclamations, regulations, and ordinances that had been issued during the previous 43 months. This act was intended to provide a degree of Parliamentary legitimacy to a political system which still has many of the same characteristics as the martial law regime. Not surprisingly, the major opposition parties walked out of Parliament in protest and would have nothing to do with the constitutional ratification.[26]

FOREIGN PRESSURES AND ALTERNATIVES

There have been a number of food aid scandals in Bangladesh, in which both Bangladeshi elites and American farmers and businessmen have been accused of profiteering.[27] The most serious charge

24. Ibid. Discussion of the Political ramifications of the present pattern of political development appears in Emajuddin Ahamed, "Development Strategy in Bangladesh: Probable Political Consequences," *Asian Survey* XVIII:11 (November 1978), pp. 1168–1180.

25. Kirit Bhaumik, "Strikes Banned in Bangladesh," *Times of India*, February 25, 1979.

26. *The Hindu* (Madras), April 7, 1979.

27. The major scandals are discussed in Donald F. McHenry and Kai Bird, "Food Bungle in Bangladesh," *Foreign Policy*, 27 (Summer 1977), pp. 72–107. See also M.V. Kamath, "A Case of Dual Duplicity: U.S. Food for Bangladesh," *Times of India*, September 2, 1977; Warren Unna, "Bangladesh Troublesome for U.S. Food Aid," *The Statesman* (Calcutta), November 25, 1977; Laurence Marks, "The Great Food Aid Swindle," *The Tribune* (Chandigarh), July 7, 1978; and James K. Boyce and Betsy Hartmann, "U.S. Aid for the Rich: View from a Bangladesh Village," *The Nation*, 226:8 (March 4, 1978), pp.

is that the American foodgrain lobby has encouraged more food aid than is good for Bangladesh because U.S. farmers need foreign markets for their surpluses. Bangladesh economists argue that they should have a secure market for their jute—to the detriment of the U.S. synthetic carpet-backing industry—in exchange for being a dumping-ground for American wheat. Americans complain that most of their food aid never reaches the poor or the rural areas, although it is intended by law to do so, and that much of the imported food which is said to go into ration shops actually ends up on the open market or is smuggled for sale into India. U.S. Embassy personnel in Dacca admit they have tried to convince the Bangladesh government that it should tax the wealthy in the agricultural sector more than it does (only 0.7 percent of total revenue currently comes from rural residents).

In early 1979 the United States began to delay shipments of its food supplies to Bangladesh after serious differences developed over their utilization by the Zia regime.[28] Zia responded by getting 200,000 tons of foodgrains from India, requesting more food from the European Economic Community, and slightly readjusting internal supply patterns. Previous attempts by the United States to withhold food (from November 1975 to March 1976) did persuade the Bangladesh government to raise ration shop prices at America's behest, but there are obvious limits to U.S. pressure. Bangladesh is not high on America's list of priorities, but there are a small number of influential Americans who are concerned with their investments there. American farmers do have an interest in selling their wheat. A famine in Bangladesh could quite easily touch the humanitarian instincts of the U.S. public, in which case Congressmen who voted against food aid might be blamed for a catastrophe. No American interest, therefore, would be served by encouraging widespread instability in Bangladesh. Nothing could destabilize Zia's regime more than skyrocketing food prices brought on by an American embargo on food shipments.

Under these circumstances, the Americans and other foreigners in Dacca occasionally resemble a previous generation of Americans

---

239-242. The article by Boyce and Hartmann is especially valuable since the authors spent more than nine months in Bangladesh villages from 1974 to 1976.

28. Sayeed Naqvi, "US Food Assistance Delay Deepens Bangladesh Crisis," *The Indian Express*, April 23, 1979.

in Vietnam. They sustain massive backing for a regime that is not doing what it says it is doing, is widely preceived internally to be inhumanly authoritarian, and does not seem to be accomplishing much for anyone beyond a narrow coterie of elites. Some members of the international development establishment keep hoping there will be "light at the end of the tunnel" if certain administrative changes are made, lacuna are plugged, or sufficient pressure is applied to the right Bengali elites to alter their behavior.[29] The more one sees of the consequences of the present pattern, however, the more convincing are arguments that there is something inherently counterproductive and illegitimate about the entire thrust of the foreign presence there, despite the undisputed fact that it has saved millions of lives over the past eight years.

Ziaur Rahman himself seems to be walking a number of tightropes simultaneously. One relates to questions of secularism and relations with India. His dilemma in this regard was underscored in April 1979 when he sought and received a promise of 200,000 tons of badly needed foodgrains from India but was unwilling to acknowledge publicly that he had done so because he feared charges from his own party that he was becoming dependent on his giant neighbor.

The importance of cooperative relationships with India can hardly be overestimated. In order to make any progress on control of water resources—an absolute necessity for rural development—arrangements must be worked out primarily with India, from which most of Bangladesh's rivers flow. The Bangladesh government is preparing a 20-year river development plan that would involve India, Nepal, Bhutan, and China, to be financed primarily by the World Bank and other international agencies. India, however, has rejected this "Mekong Delta approach," preferring instead a less grandiose series of bilateral projects involving only Bangladesh and India.[30] Bangladesh

---

29. Orientations on this question are traced out in Steve Jones, "Rural Development in Bangladesh." Paper presented to a conference on Basic Needs, Appropriate Technology and Agrarian Reform, Dacca, March 1979, pp. 27–28. For an especially incisive analysis of the aid dilemma from the Bangladesh point of view, see Nurul Islam, *Development Planning in Bangladesh*: *A Study in Political Economy* (London: C. Hurst and Co., 1977).

30. Dieter Braun, "Changes in South Asian Intra-Regional and External Relationships," *The World Today* (Chatham House), 34:10 (October 1978), pp.

engineers fear they will be outmaneuvered by their wealthier neighbors in bilateral projects; Indian engineers feel they will lose control of "internationalized" projects.

India and Bangladesh have also reached an impasse on the question of defining a maritime boundary. India invokes the same principle that it has used to define ocean boundaries with Sri Lanka, the Maldives, Indonesia, and Thailand. Bangladesh is arguing for a lateral baseline that would tilt the maritime boundary several thousand kilometers toward the Indian coast.[31] Lack of definition of the boundary line has already seriously retarded Bangladesh's oil-drilling efforts in the Bay of Bengal.

Similar differences exist in matters of trade. Bangladesh government agencies have been purchasing from non-Indian sources such things as locomotives, railway coaches and wagons, transport vehicles, farm inputs and machinery, steel, cement, cycles, and a variety of consumer goods, despite quite competitive quality goods available from India at far cheaper prices. At the same time, Indian government and business circles have been less than enthusiastic in responding to Bangladesh proposals to transport goods from the Indian northeast across Bangladesh to Calcutta, a route that would save millions of rupees in freight charges each year. Indian interests argue that transport and shipping charges should be paid to Indian firms rather than Bangladesh railways and steamers, even if the cost to the Indian consumer is two to three times higher.

The major hurdle to be overcome in Indo-Bangladesh trade relations is a lopsided imbalance in favor of India. Indian exports to Bangladesh in 1975–76 were worth $84.5 million while Bangladesh exports to India were worth only $7.5 million during the same period.[32] Two years later the corresponding figures were $77.3 million and $2.6 million. India has proposed to narrow this trade deficit by

390–400. An imaginative proposal by a prominent Indian which differs considerably from official proposals is B.G. Verghese, *Gift of the Greater Ganga: An Approach to the Integrated Development of the Ganga-Brahmaputra Basin* (Few Delhi: Corromandel Lecture Series, 1977).

31. The issue is discussed in Robert S. Anderson, "Impressions of Bangladesh: The Rule of Arms and the Politics of Exhortation," *Pacific Affairs*, 49:3 (Fall 1976), pp. 443–475. See also Ataus Samad, "U.S. Firms to Hunt Bangladesh Oil and Gas," *Christian Science Monitor*, July 21, 1977.

32. Kirit Bhaumik, "Steady Rise in Trade With Bangladesh," *Times of India*, March 18, 1979.

establishing a number of joint ventures in Bangladesh (for the manufacture of cement, sponge iron, urea fertilizers, and other products), with the intention of exporting much of the production to India. If the trade gap can be reduced—by the establishment of joint ventures or by any other means—there is no question that both India and Bangladesh would benefit enormously. A prerequisite for either joint ventures or enhanced trade, however, is greater receptivity to India and Indians than exists in Bangladesh at present. To the extent that Zia moves away from secularism and becomes dependent on pro-Islamic elements of the population, possibilities for greater receptivity could diminish.

A second of Zia's tightropes involves, on the one hand, his increasing dependence on the class of urban nouveau riche, which is obviously benefiting from his regime, and, on the other, his desire to build a broader rural base of support. Both his frequent trips to the countryside and his rhetoric would indicate that he would like to come down solidly on the side of rural interests, but his heavy dependence on a strategy of modern urban industrial growth has made that impossible. In a country where 92 percent of the people live in rural areas and agriculture accounts for 56 percent of GNP and 75 percent of the labor force, Zia's government is still investing only 26 percent of its developmental resources in the rural sector!

Zia's most severe dilemma has to do with his position vis-a-vis the army, and the consequences of that position for his move toward civilian rule. If he does not leave the army, he reneges on a promise and fails to meet a widespread expectation, thereby virtually assuring his failure to become the civilian president that he wants to be. If he does leave the army, he loses his place in the command structure of his principal institutional base in society.

Despite the purges and executions of the past eight years, most military men agree that large numbers of *jawans*, and especially those who fought in the liberation war, still have loyalties to radical leaders like Abu Taher. Those opposed to Taher's ideas tend to come from among the Pakistan-returned soldiers and the officer corps, although some officers have attempted to curry favor with the men under them by speaking privately in defense of Abu Taher. With rapid expansion of the army (it is now estimated to be approaching 100,000 men), possibilities for both dissatisfaction and for infiltration by civilian-led political parties have increased.

Major sections of the army's officer corps are already dissatisfied with Zia for bringing the Awami League and other parties back to positions of respectability in 1979, and for reinstituting what they see as the sordid process of politics. At the same time, same officers who have been involved in politics either do not want to go back to the barracks, or their fellow officers do not want them back. Intense personal rivalries exist among military men who became officers at the same time as Ziaur Rahman and who have parallel careers. Meanwhile, lurking in the background are the living ghosts of Major M.A Jalil and Khondakar Mushtaque Ahmed, both of whom are still imprisoned and both of whom still have some troops loyal to them. Towering above them all is the ghost of Abu Taher.

TWELVE

DOMESTIC ORDER (1981)

For the first time in the near-decade of its independent existence, Bangladesh has an effective government. President Ziaur Rahman has at several key points been ruthless in suppressing his opponents, he is still struggling to create solid party and governmental institutions, and he has barely managed to jostle the languorous Bangladesh economy, but he has been able to restore a modicum of law and order to a nation that had become increasingly anarchistic in the early 1970s and he has provided more coherent political and economic development strategies for Bangladesh than had either of his predecessors. While his regime exhibits some similarities with Ayub Khan's Pakistan of the 1960s, or to Marcos' Philippines and Suharto's Indonesia of the 1970s, the mainsprings of Zia's thought and actions are indigenously Bangladeshi and uniquely his own. Zia's successes or failures in the future will depend in large measure on his ability to become identified with a new Bangladeshi nationalism that he has championed but has still not precisely defined.

Ziaur Rahman first came to power in Bangladesh in November 1975, after the third of three bloody military coups that started with the killing of Sheikh Mujibur Rahman and most of his family in August 1975.[1] During the first 18 months of his regime, Zia governed solely as a military man, through a rather severe Martial Law Administration. On April 21, 1977, he began to move towards civilianization by assuming the title of President, all the while retaining his position as Chief Martial Law Administrator and Supreme Commander of the Armed Forces. In June 1978 he was elected President for a five-year term; in February 1979 elections his new

---

1. See the author's "The Bangladesh Coup," *AUFS Fieldstaff Reports*, South Asia Series, XIX:15 (September 1975) and his two-part series "Ziaur Rahman's Bangladesh," 1979/Nos. 25 and 26.

political party (the Bangladesh National Party, or BNP) secured 206 of 300 seats in Parliament with 41.2 per cent of the popular vote. While Zia still retains his title as Supreme Commander of the Armed Forces and continues to live in a rented home in the military cantonment (where he has resided since 1972), he has moved a considerable distance towards civilian rule during the last two years. In recent months the outlines of his intended political and economic reforms have begun to acquire some clarity and focus.

Perhaps the most remarkable feature of Zia's regime is the extent of his own personal travel around the country and the degree of his exuberance and enthusiasm for development programs. In most months he will be out of Dacca for at least 15 days, usually leaving the capital by helicopter after an early breakfast and returning just before dark. Bangladesh is small enough that the President can get to any part of the country within two hours. Zia travels so often now that his security people have developed a routine which enables them to move him—with only a second helicopter as escort and with relatively light security—to virtually any village in the country. On some occasions he will travel by jeep, van or car, and there have been times when he has set off for considerable distances on foot, but on most days he can be counted on to be in his army helicopter, making six to eight stops in the countryside.

Why does the President travel so much and so relentlessly? A major part of the answer is that he is trying to build party and governmental institutions that can be instruments of his will, keep him in power, and perhaps result in long-term developmental gains. It is also clear that he enjoys politics and uses his jaunts out of Dacca to breathe some country air and escape from the boorish sycophants and hangers-on who adorn the bureaucracy and political halls of the capital. Finally, his trips outside the city enable him to stay in touch with what village people are thinking, keep tabs on party cadres and local administrators, and provide innumerable opportunities for excellent public relations work and press copy. In an age when all political leaders are forced to do a considerable amount of travel, Ziaur Rahman may well be the most widely-travelled leader of them all.

There is little in Zia's early childhood to indicate that he would pursue a political career. He was born in the northern Bangladesh city of Bogra on January 19, 1936, the son of a government chemist. Educated in Calcutta for a short time in the 1940s, he moved with his family to Karachi when Pakistan was created in 1947. In 1953, at the age of 17, he joined the Pakistan army. Like other Bengalis, he felt discriminated against by his senior military officers, but he distinguished himself as a soldier and moved up through the ranks fairly quickly. In the 1965 war against India, Zia was the only Bengali Company Commander in the Pakistan army, having been promoted on the battlefield in the Lahore sector after fighting as a captain and, later, as a major. Zia himself states unequivocally that he never considered any career other than the military, although he is not certain what exactly attracted him to it. As he puts is, "I never really thought about other things—you see, I got into war very early in life and I had a very busy career. I did most of the courses that one can do, I fought in the 1965 war in the front lines— we had the worst type of fighting in our area—and then, in 1971, I had a brigade of thousands of guerrillas."[2]

Zia first betrayed his interest in politics on March 27, 1971— two days after full-scale civil war had erupted in Pakistan—when he announced in a clandestine radio broadcast that he was President of the new country of Bangladesh, an ambitious self-appointment that has since been bitterly resented (and remembered) by his enemies. Realizing the unpopularity of his action, Zia quickly relinquished his "presidency" to Sheikh Mujibur Rahman in 1971 and subsequently distinguished himself in the liberation war as leader of a guerrilla brigade known as the "Z Force." Now he recalls those days with zest. "Ahhh!," he says, "I had many thousands of men—I just didn't know how many men I had! It must have run into three, four or five thousand—perhaps many more. My battalions were very big! And I could have raised another three battalions!"

Not surprisingly, Zia argues that his liberation war experience was the major determinant of his present attitude toward life. The principal impact of the war was to convince him that he could command large numbers of men, and that goals which seemed unattainable could be realized if one persisted with determination and effort. "In "71," he says, "when we got started with the war, we were told that we should not do all these things because we would not succeed. But the question was not of success or failure—we had to start

2. All quotations from Ziaur Rahman and other political leaders in this article are, unless otherwise cited, from personal interviews conducted in November/December 1980.

and try." Having won the war in 1971, Zia was disappointed with the way in which Sheikh Mujibur Rahman ran the country during the first three-and-a-half years of Independence, although Zia now refuses, for political reasons, to mention Mujib's name in a negative context. Speaking of Bangladesh's post-liberation army, however, Zia says, "Oh, it was crazy. We wanted to keep the army absolutely professional, but politics was introduced at all levels...the army was too small...it was disorganized...it was not allowed to get organized...it was nothing...there was a lot of pressure on us not to have a big army...we did not even have uniforms or clothes for the soldiers."

Zia's version of his entry into politics partakes in large measure of the diffidence usually voiced by South Asian leaders. He admits that he was disappointed in 1972 when he was passed over for the post of head of the army, and he claims that he would have quit the army then if his friends had not insisted that he stay on. In his words, "everyone in the army said, you can't leave, you've got to stay on. How can you leave? So, I said, alright, let's stay on." Most observers are agreed that Zia cautioned his officers against participation in the coups of August 15, 1975 and November 3, 1975, even though he was informed about them in advance and did nothing to stop them. Ironically enough, he has shown considerable leniency towards all of the surviving officers of those first two coups—neither of which benefited him and in the second of which he and his family were placed under house arrest—but he gave the orders that resulted in the execution of Colonel Abu Taher, the man most responsible for installing him in power after the third coup on November 7, 1975.

Taher is now described by Zia as a courageous but "simplehearted man." Zia still speaks of Taher as "my officer in the 1971 war—I gave him weapons, I gave him troops to fight with when he escaped from Pakistan"—but, according to Zia's version, Taher became a "changed man" after he was booted out of the army by Sheikh Mujibur Rahman in 1973. In 1974 Taher was taken into a leftist political party called the Jatiya Samajtantrik Dal (JSD), and later raised an underground JSD political cadre with unauthorized arms.[3] "They made him the chief," Zia says, "and

---

3. Taher's side of the story is best told by Lawrence Lifschultz in *Bangladesh: The Unfinished Revolution* (London: Zed Press, 1979), see especially pp. 1–98.

he just debased the law of the land...He defied the law of the land, and his underground forces killed many people. So the law of the land had to come into effect, and the court gave him the punishment of execution, as was deserved."

Zia himself refuses to talk about his personal relationship with Taher, which apparently was at one time quite intimate, but a number of people close to Zia have argued that the decision to execute Taher was by far the most difficult the President has ever had to make. According to most versions, Zia called his top 47 officers together and polled them as to what should be done with Taher, shortly before Taher was hanged in the jails on July 21, 1976. Zia reportedly agreed to Taher's execution only after all 47 officers voted for it with considerable conviction, their fear being that failure to execute Taher would leave him a living martyr and irrevocably undermine discipline within the army.

NEW VILLAGE INSTITUTIONS

At the core of Zia's political and economic philosophy since he has come to power is a military man's belief in organizational discipline and an almost naive faith in the powers of positive thinking and hard work. The people of Bangladesh, he says, "have been wasting their time...they have got to be organized and put to work." He has put them to work, in thousands of earth-moving operations...building embankments, excavating and re-excavating canals, and constructing or repairing roads—in teams of hundreds and thousands, all carrying dirt from one place to another, one basketful at a time. Some of the work is done on a voluntary basis, some is done under Food-for-Work programs, and some is done in return for cash payments. Zia himself is convinced that, "...wherever people have worked, they are a different lot...a different lot of people. They now know that they can work with their own hands and do the job."

Working with one's hands is something that has traditionally been associated with low status in Bengal. Ziaur Rahman is trying to change that attitude, along with several others. He is the first Bangladesh President to speak often and publicly about the need to limit family size to two children by practising family planning, something that is still not popular or widely accepted as legitimate in most Bangladeshi villages. He implores cultivators to get rid of the earthen boundaries (*ayals*, pronounced "isles") between their small plots of land, which have for centuries been used by Bengali peasants as boundary markers and as footpaths, even though all of the *ayals* taken together account for the equivalent of an extra district of cultivable land if one totals up the space they occupy in Bangladesh. Zia also sends shivers up and down the spines of urban middle-class Bengalis when he says that he will tax the well-off, abolish food rationing, and undertake long overdue reforms of the educational system.

How does Ziaur Rahman plan to bring about a restructuring of Bangladesh society? He himself points to the creation of a number of new village-level institutions which he has introduced in the last three years, and especially what he calls *Gram Sarkars* (village governments), a Village Defence Force, and his own local BNP party units. Most of the *Gram Sarkars* have been chosen by a "consensus" evolved at village meetings, with the nature of that "consensus" being determined by Thana Circle officers (the Thana is roughly equivalent in size to an American county) representing the central government. In some instances where it has not been possible to determine a consensus behind the appropriate number of *Gram Sarkar* candidates, on-the-spot elections have been held, with villagers physically lining up behind the candidates of their choice and their bodies being tallied as votes by the Circle officer. Observers who have watched the selection process in several villages suggest that Members of Parliament and District Officers frequently play a major role in choosing "consensual" candidates.

The *Gram Sarkars* are distinguished by the unique basis of representation within them, since two of their 11 members must be from the landless classes, two from among women, two from the landed peasantry, two from shopkeepers, and two from among fishermen and artisans (the eleventh member is the chairman, chosen and coopted by the other 10 members). As of mid-December 1980, *Gram Sarkars* had been chosen in approximately two-thirds of Bangladesh's estimated 68,000 villages, with an expectation on the part of the President that the remainder would be selected by February.

It is not yet clear whether Bangladesh's *Gram Sarkars* will be given enough power and money to actually accomplish a great deal, but it is significant that they are the first village-level governments to be established in what is now Bangladesh. It could also be significant that the *Gram Sarkars* are being given judicial as well as administrative powers. Under Ayub Khan's "Guided Democracy," there were Union-level governments, with the Union consisting of several villages banded together for administrative purposes, but there were no administrative or judicial units linked to the center at the village level. Unfortunately, the Union Councils became nests of corruption and favoritism for Ayub Khan's political parties and the Pakistan military, with the result that they fell into considerable disrepute.

The Village Defence Force (VDF) that Ziaur Rahman is creating is theoretically an entirely voluntary organization, even though it is being organized out of the Home Ministry. Zia himself traces, its origins to 1976, when, he says, "the law and order situation in the villages was hopeless." The VDF consists of approximately 150 people in each village, who are expected to play leadership roles in maintaining law and order, supervising adult education and family planning programs, and raising volunteers for development activities like canal-digging and road-building. In order to interest villagers in the initial establishment of a VDF, the Home Ministry provides radios, newspapers, books, and small rewards—like umbrellas or briefcases—for outstanding activities. A special newsletter, published and distributed by the Home Ministry, details the achievements and activities of model VDF units, in order that other parts of the country might emulate them. Although the Village Defence Parties are theoretically non-partisan voluntary associations, reports from a number of villages indicate that Zia's BNP has often acted as a catalyst in organizing them.

Administrative links between the central government and the Village Defence Force is perhaps best described in the words of the Home Minister, Mustafizur Rahman, who is directly responsible for organizing them. In his words, "I have got, at various tiers, one officer dealing with them. Then, I personally, or my staff, visit them, plus I make other Ministers go and attend their rallies... They [the Village Defence Parties] are not armed. They patrol the village area at night by rotation. In the village, they know who is a bad chap...they keep a watch on him. If they find someone, for example, stealing food-for-work grains, they pick him up, take him to the Thana and hand him over to the police. Then it becomes a police matter...They also do development work, family planning work, and adult education, and we give them motivation and rewards. Time and again we go there to motivate them, and once in a while we hold a national rally for four or five days also."

Both the Home Minister and the President speak of a system of checks and balances at the local level when describing Bangladesh's new village-based institutions. Theoretically, local Village Defence Parties should be able to expose corrupt activities that are taking place in the *Gram Sarkars* or within the regular police, the administrative network or the ruling BNP. Similarly, the *Gram Sarkars*, police, administrators and party members should be able to check on one another to expose any wrong-doing or any shirking of responsibility. In practice, of course, it is entirely possible that a single family or caste group or other set of elites might capture all meaningful local government institutions in a particular village and confine central government patronage and local developmental benefits to their own circle of followers. It is also possible that Zia himself or some of his followers might try to use Bangladesh's newly-created village institutions to build centers of influence and patronage with loyalties only to the BNP, in much the same manner that Ayub Khan sought to use the Union Councils in the 1960s.[4]

Zia has indicated that he is less concerned about possibilities of corruption and patronage than he is with the need to get development activities going. In fact, he readily admits that there is more corruption in Bangladesh now than there was when he first came to power five years ago, something which he attributes to sheer increases in the size of the domestic economy and increased contact with the international world. In the early stages of development, he argues, "it is bound to happen like this...corruption is a fact of life."

One of the reasons that Ziaur Rahman can speak so blithely about corruption is his personal reputation for scrupulous honesty where his own family is concerned. Indeed, there has not been the slightest hint of the kind of familial corruption that surrounded Mujibur Rahman when he was alive, or of the charges that have tainted most leading politicians in Bangladesh. Zia himself owns no known property, and he has semi-publicly discouraged attempts

4. For comparisons of Zia's regime to that of Ayub Khan, see Rounaq Jahan, *Bangladesh Politics:. Problems and Issues* (Dacca: University Press Limited, 1980), see especially pp. 197 ff.

by his wife to acquire a small plot of land as a future house site in Dacca. Three of Zia's four brothers have lived outside Bangladesh for the last 15 years, and none of them have any known financial ties of any consequence back in Dacca. A fourth brother previously lived with the President and his family but decided to move out of the cantonment a few years ago, lest there be conflict of interest or nepotism charges raised in the press.

Zia is known to have dismissed Ministers and other lesser officials for corrupt activities, but only after detailed cases have been compiled, documented and presented to the President himself. Opposition politicians argue that all but a handful of the 40 Ministers in Zia's Cabinet are known to engage in corrupt activities, but that Zia is reluctant to dismiss them because he is either highly dependent on them politically or unable to muster sufficient evidence to confront them. There is an anti-corruption investigation system within the President's Secretariat, and Zia is also attempting to organize what he calls a "check-up system" in the rural areas, which will theoretically enable local institutions to exercise some degree of control over corrupt activities or inefficiency at the village level. During recent months, for example, Zia's government has required family planning workers to obtain a certificate from local governments, attesting that the family planning worker has been doing his or her work properly, under threat that salaries will be withheld if such certificates cannot be obtained.

Once new village-level institutions have been created, Zia has promised to decentralize powers and fun ing in major areas, even in cases where such decentralization may run counter to significant interests. One such area already blocked out for decentralization is primary education, which Zia sees as "a legacy of the colonial system—something terrible and unfit for the present time." Zia's principal objection is with the attempt to run the primary schools from Dacca. "That is silly!" he says. "We can't control these thousands and thousands of government schools. The teachers are not teaching and yet they are getting salaries. I am not in favour of it." Over the next few years, Zia plans to turn primary schools over to local bodies, with funds being granted from the central government on a matching basis. He and his educational advisers expect that there will be strikes and demonstrations by teachers and educational administrators, who fear that standards may become parochialized and that funds may either not be forthcoming from local areas or swallowed by local elites. He is also aware that" no one can change the educational system overnight." Nonetheless, he is determined to proceed with educational reform in an effort to "gradually change the system."

Gradualism and caution are words that occur frequently in Zia's conversations, but they are balanced, at least equally, by references to the need to move faster and more efficiently. With regard to the rationing system, for example, Zia states flatly that "there is a lot of food politics in this country [Bangladesh]...a lot of realities ...we have to face them." Nevertheless, his plans are to drastically increase agricultural production over the next five years by maintaining high prices for agricultural products through subsidies and exports, all the while reducing quotas in the ration shops and eventually getting rid of the rationing system itself.[5] He describes this ambitious scenario as "a delicate balance" and suggests that "we don't want to do anything so drastic so quickly...we have to be very careful. At other times, however, he likens his developmental approach to the flight of an aircraft. In his words, "If the speed of the aircraft falls below a certain level, you know it will fall. So, we've got to keep the party and the government moving very fast, and the same is the case with the whole people. That's why we go out so much to mobilize them."

PARTY POLITICS AND THE BUREAUCRACY

Most observers are agreed that Zia has little to fear, at least for the present, from opposition political parties. During the first three years of his regime, political parties were not allowed to undertake any open political activity and many opposition leaders were in jail.[6] Since the June 1978 presidential election, all of the major opposition leaders have been released and party activity has flourished, although one major leader of the Communist Party—Mohammad Farhad—was jailed in mid-1980 when he openly predicted

---

5. An analysis of Zia's food policy appears in the author's "The Very Poor in Bangladesh: Food Policy and Politics," *India Quarterly*, XXXVII: 2 (Apri -June 1981), pp. 165-193.

6. Zia's first four years are analyzed in Jahan, op. cit. and in several essays appearing in *Politics and Bureaucracy in a New Nation*, edited by Mohammad Mohabbat Khan and Habib Mohammad Zafarullah (Dacca: Centre for Administrative Studies, 1980).

(and some say, advocated) an Afghan–style revolution for Bangladesh. Zia admits that there are a number of other political prisoners in Bangladesh, but argues that this is because "politics in our country has many sides." Zia contends that most of the political prisoners in Bangladesh at present are "criminals who were trained by various political parties to be with them."

The principal opposition party is still the Awami League (AL), now led by Abdul Malek Ukil, a leading figure in the AL since the days of Mujibur Rahman. A small breakaway faction of the Awami League is led by Mizaner Rahman Choudhury, who opposed Mujib's attempts to establish a one-party government towards the end of his (Mujib's) life, but a number of leaders from the Mizaner faction of the AL joined Zia's BNP in December 1980. The Ukil Awami League is also seriously divided into two major factions: the largest, led by General–Secretary Abdur Razzak, is usually identified as pro-Soviet and pro-India, advocating nationalization of industries and banks, the establishment of agricultural cooperatives, and other "socialist" measures; the rival (Tofael Ahmad) faction of the AL is often branded as pro-American, although its leaders insist that it is simply more nationalistic, less pro-Soviet and less pro-Indian than its rival.

The Awami League demonstrated its strength in March 1977 elections to municipalities and Union Councils when it bested Zia's first attempt at a political party (the so-called JAGODAL party) in what were ostensibly non-partisan polls. Indeed, it is commonly assumed now that it was that experience which led Ziaur Rahman to form his second political party (the BNP) and to pursue his schemes for *Gram Sarkars* and a Village Defence Force. In 1980, factional rivalry within the Ukil Awami League became so great that the party was unable to hold a national convention, and calls for greater militancy and discipline among party cadres have generally failed to rouse party members to anything resembling party activity during the days of Mujib. The party still has considerable support among Bangladesh Hindus (about 10 per cent of the population) and some sizable pockets of support elsewhere. It appeals primarily to a broad spectrum of people who identified strongly with Mujib, to a number of businessmen who would gain from closer ties with India, and to urban middle- and lower-class clerks and laborers who advocate a centrist type of socialism. Since trade unions in Bangladesh generally support the ruling party, it is not surprising that the AL suffered major defeats in recent trade union elections in industrial areas, with Zia's BNP unions registering significant gains.

Next to the Awami League, the largest party in Bangladesh is the Muslim League, which contested the February 1979 elections as part of the Islamic Democratic League Alliance (the IDLA won 19 seats in Parliament and 10 per cent of the vote in 1979). The organizational backbone of the IDL is the Jamaat-i-Islami, which did not contest the 1979 election but is probably the best-organized party in the country—its members hold regular weekly meetings and are required to submit weekly progress reports on their personal development, readings of the Koran and party work—but the appeal of their Islamic fundamentalist ideology has not been spreading in Bangladesh at a rapid pace. Moreover, Ziaur Rahman has managed to pick up considerable support from Islamic-minded segments of the population by establishing a Ministry of Religion, making religious studies compulsory in all schools, introducing modern education into the *madrassahs* (traditional centers of Islamic learning), maintaining good relations with the Arabs, and dropping references to secularism in the Constitution.

A second major party that did not contest the 1978 elections is the Democratic League of Khondakar Mushtaque Ahmed, who succeeded Mujib as president in the aftermath of the August 15, 1975 coup. With a program remarkably like Zia's, Mushtaque says he is for democracy, free enterprise and religion, but his only really severe differences with Zia are a greater emphasis on de-national-ization and a preference for a parliamentary rather than a presi-dential system. Mushtaque accuses Zia's regime of greater corruption and inefficiency than existed under his own 3-month government, although, ironically, the reason the Democratic League did not contest the 1978 elections was its lack of readiness, with Mushtaque in the midst of a four-year stint in jail on charges of corruption. If and when the next elections are held, Mushtaque's party is expected to do fairly well, although it cannot at this point present any serious electoral challenge to the President. The party is also taken seriously because Mushtaque is said to have some support within the military.

The parties that have been most severely affected by Ziaur Rahman's regime have been the small Marxist-left parties that have provided much of the dynamism of Bengali politics in the past.

Many of these were pro-Chinese parties that began to crumble when Peking supported Pakistan in 1971, and at least one of them (the JSD) was decimated when Abu Taher and his associates were executed in the jails in 1976.[7] The largest of the Marxist-left parties, Maulana Bhashani's National Awami Party (NAP), has joined the BNP en masse, as have a number of lesser leftist groups. The JSD—now the largest leftist party in Parliament, with eight members—split into two parts in November 1980, with the break-away Bangladesh Samajtantrik Dal (BSD) claiming that the older JSD leadership had pursued an opportunistic tactical line designed to secure its release from prison.

The JSD was founded by a group of young people—Abdur Rab, M.A. Jalil, Serajul Alam Khan, and others—who came out of the Awami League in 1972. Abu Taher was recruited to the JSD in 1974, after Mujib had dropped him from the army, and Taher subsequently headed an armed wing of the JSD, called the *Gono Bahini* (People's Army), which remained intact from March 1974 until Taher was hanged in the jails in July 1976. The JSD disbanded its armed wing in October 1976 and has since admitted that its attempts to politicize the army were a miserable failure. Taher is still described by both the JSD and BSD as "our beloved leader," and party members are told that "his sacrifice should be honored," but the official line now is that Taher was misguided by the party.

In recent student elections at Dacca University, the BSD demonstrated that it has more student support than the JSD, a crucial factor in a country where students form the hard core of all leftist political groups. The BSD is headed by Kaliquaman Bhuiya, Abdullah Sarkar, and A.F.M. Mahbubul Huq, all former leaders of the JSD and all now in their 40s. The BSD sees itself as being less pro-Soviet and less pro-Indian than the JSD. Its leadership says that it will contest elections, but only to convince people that revolution is necessary and possible, and that the present system is unworkable. The principal emphasis of the BSD will be on the

7. The most comprehensive analysis of the left in Bangladesh is Talukder Maniruzzaman, *Radical Politics and the Emergence of Bangladesh* (Dacca: Bangladesh Books, 1976). For an excellent current analysis of the problems of the left, by Bangladesh's most prominent Marxist theoretician, see Badruddin Umar, *Imperialism and General Crisis of the Bourgeoisie in Bangladesh* (Dacca: Progoti Prakashani, 1979).

organization of urban workers and students, with the hope of
becoming, in the words of Mahbubul Huq, "the embryo of a pro-
letarian party" and "a platform of action." The primary activities
of the BSD will be strikes, demonstrations, processions and hartals,
designed to build militancy within its own ranks and to stir up
revolutionary discontent among the general populace.

Since his assumption of the presidency in 1978, Zia has allowed
a considerable amount of dissent and has genuinely encouraged
criticism of his programs, but all within limits. He clearly dis-
likes yes-men and yes-women and will usually promote someone
who is slightly critical of him over someone who has a tendency to
always agree. At the same time, he does not pretend to be a full
blown liberal democrat. He has been quoted as complaining, in
soldier's language, that the opposition parties, while they were in
power, "took the pants off democracy and raped her thousands of
times, and now they criticize me for not being a virgin." He says
that he would like to encourage strong and responsible opposition
parties, and his actions indicate that he enjoys political discussion,
political debates, and political campaigning. At the same time,
however, he has never hesitated to use his official positions—first
as a military man, then as a martial law administrator and now as
an authoritarian president—to place his rivals at a considerabe dis-
advantage in elections and other political battles.[8] He prides
himself on being "patient with politicians" but "ruthless when
necessary." Those close to him suggest that, as in the past, he is
likely in the future to be most ruthless where disloyalty or indiscipline within the army is concerned.

When Zia first came to power, in 1975, he tended to rely heavily
on members of the old Civil Service of Pakistan (CSP) and other
bureaucrats who had been shunted aside by Mujib, and on ex-army
people, professionals and technocrats who Mujib had similarly
alienated. Mujib created near-chaos within the bureaucracy when
he selected, largely on a political basis, more than 500 top administrators from among people with little or no experience, as part of a
special "freedom-fighters" pool, a concession that made it possible
for these 500 people to get into the bureaucracy without training and
with only perfunctory exams. Zia was originally quite popular with

8.   For details, see my two-part series "Ziaur Rahman's Bangladesh,"
op. cit.

senior bureaucrats because he purged the administration of most of Mujib's appointees, was rigorous about exams and training, and, by rationalizing promotion and retirement policies, restored some semblance of order within the ranks.

During the last two years, however, Zia pushed through a major reform of the administrative apparatus which has been quite unpopular with senior bureaucrats, and he has threatened to take away some of the bureaucracy's perquisites (like heavily-subsidized food rations and exemptions from income tax). He has also increasingly tried to by-pass regular administrative channels to get things done. In his own conversations, Zia expresses a general feeling of exasperation with administrative delays and bottlenecks. He states flatly that he would like to do away with "letter-writing" and "note-passing," and that he would either "like files to move or not to have files at all."

Zia also states openly that he would like to promote a General's conception of a small, streamlined structure of command in which the person at the top can simply "pick up the telephone and get things done." But several top bureaucrats have become furious at him because he will by-pass people at the top and go down below and order something done, or because he will suddenly get enthusiastic about a second matter, quickly abandoning without warning the first idea and everyone involved in it. One bureaucrat complains bitterly of the time he received constant praise and kudos from Zia as he bravely resisted a strike against government workers, only to find to his dismay that Zia had meanwhile gone behind his back and made a deal with the strikers. Other leading administrators object to the way Zia constantly picks up people from outside the bureaucracy and assigns them positions of responsibility. Still others say that Zia has no loyalties to those who are trying most to help him (in the words of one of his ex-aides, "you cannot try to get too close to him because he'll simply use you and then discard you").

During the last few years, Zia has seemed to attach more and more importance to his political party, the BNP, to the point where a number of observers are convinced that he would like to work primarily through the party rather than the bureaucracy. Zia himself conceives of several diverse channels of decision-making, depending on the complexity and importance of the matter under consideration. "Whenever there is a difficult problem," he says, "I call the Cabinet or I call the Executive Committee of the party or the Standing Committee, depending on the nature of the problem...I try to keep away as much as possible, but in the early stages of something I have to get involved. Once we take a decision, then we leave it to the committees for detailed work and execution."

The BNP's Secretary-General, Budradoza Chowdhury, has tried to promote the practice of having all of Zia's policies discussed and approved by the BNP Executive Council, and he has criticized the President at least twice at inner-party meetings for failing to do so. Zia, who often uses the royal "we" to refer to himself, explains his tendency to act alone as follows: "sometimes it happens that we have to take a quick decision. In that case, we call the Standing Committee. Sometimes the whole lot of the Standing Committee is not present, so we take the decision and get it okayed later on by the Executive Committee or the full Standing Committee." On some matters, Zia admits, decision-making is confined to "a very small level—I take the personal responsibility." This is the case, for example, with his canal-digging program, which many people in the party and government privately criticize. It is also the case for all major decisions concerning the command structure of the army and other services.

Zia's pre-eminent position in the government, party and army is a consequence of his Constitutional prerogative to hire and fire or veto almost at will. All executive authority rests in him, since the Cabinet is appointed by him, holds office at his pleasure, and has only advisory powers. As Chairman of the BNP and Supreme Commander of the Armed Forces, he holds similar positions in the party and army. Parliament is elected under conditions and terms set by the President, and can be summoned, prorogued and dissolved by him at will, subject only to the constitutional provision that it must meet twice a year and Zia's personal pledge (given publicly after an opposition boycott) that it would remain in session at least six months each year. The President appoints the Chief Justice of the Supreme Court and all other judges, including those in the Appellate Courts, the High Courts, and in special administrative and military tribunals. Constitutionally, the only way the President can be removed during his five-year term is on grounds of incapacity, and then only if a motion to that affect is passed by three-fourths of the total members of Parliament. His election takes place at times and on terms he sets; it need not be held simultaneously with elections to Parliament.

Constitutional prerogatives are enhanced in Zia's case by his lack of hesitancy to shift his principal advisors and course of action rather drastically from time to time. When Zia first came to power as Deputy Martial Law Administrator (MLA) in November 1975, he kept Justice A.M. Sayem as President and ruled as head of the army in a purely military regime. The major reason he stayed on as head of the army was to restructure it, a process that took approximately two years. Once the army was reorganized, he shuffled Sayem out of the Presidency (on public grounds of ill-health), rewrote the Constitution to provide for his own presidency, and got himself elected. He then dropped two of the three principal political advisors who had propelled him that far—Maudud Ahmed and Nurul Islam (the third, Mashiur Rahman, died of a heart attack in 1979)—replacing them with another set of advisors who have since been changed a number of times.

The three man who served Zia as Deputy MLAs in 1975–77—former Chiefs respectively of the Army, Navy and Air Force—are all out of power now and all are said to be supporters of Mushtaque Ahmed's Democratic League. In 1978, when Zia's first Parliament was elected, he used the occasion to undertake a thorough house-cleaning of his Cabinet, which had at that point been with him for less than three years. In his present Cabinet, Finance Minister Saiful Rahman is the only person who has managed to stay on continuously through all of Zia's governments.

THE ARMY AND THE POLICE

In the army, change has been at least as drastic as in the government and party. Major purges took place in late 1976, following the execution of Abu Taher and the conviction of some of Taher's army supporters on charges of "propagating disaffection among the officers and other members of the Defence Services." Zia was reported to have been shattered, and to have become visibly nervous in public for the only time in his life, in October 1977 when some sections of the army and the bulk of the air force attempted a coup. Eleven senior air force officers, 10 army officers and an estimated 200 other soldiers were killed in the abortive October coup, while hundreds of others were said to have been killed during an earlier coup attempt at Bogra on September 30, 1977. Zia himself announced that 460 people were tried for participation in the October coup, of whom only 63 were acquitted. On October 15, 1977 he announced that 37 members of the army and air force had been executed, and he indicated that some death sentences were still "being carried out."[9]

Since 1977 there have been several smaller coup attempts and petty mutinies within the military, the last one in mid–1980 when Zia was out of the country. Zia himself now seems quite relaxed about the military, although he complains of a lack of officers. He says that he is technically not supposed to wear a military uniform anymore because he is now a civilian President, but he still puts it on in public occasionally because he simply likes wearing it. He also dons uniforms of the para-military Ansars and Village Defence Force at ceremonial functions and usually salutes his old officers (and is saluted in return) as though he were still a General. "I was in the army," he says, "so I know everybody— virtually everybody in the Armed Forces—Army, Navy, Air Force." He claims that he continues to live in his rented home in the cantonment because the official President's home in Dacca is "too big and too air-conditioned," but most people insist the arrangement stems from his desire to keep close tabs on his old military associates.

Shortages in the ranks of officers are a consequence of the lack of representation of Bengalis in the old Pakistan army, a heavy log of resignations during Mujib's time, the absorption of officers into the bureaucracy and public corporations under Zia, and finally, the decimation of officer ranks (especially in the Air Force) in the wake of several coups and abortive coups. Zia says that he still receives frequent requests from public corporations and government agencies for the transfer or assignment of an army officer and he now gives a flat "no" to everyone. To speed up the process of building an officer cadre, he has established additional courses at the Military Academy and Staff College and is sending officers for training to Malaysia, China, Indonesia, France, Italy, Britain and the United States.

Starting with an organization that literally did not have enough uniforms, Zia has infused considerable discipline and has given to

9.   Ibid.

the military (to the army especially) an unprecedented respectability. He has raised salaries, been quick with promotions to people of merit, purged the ranks of political ideologues and radicals, stabilized the military academy and staff college, provided modern weapons and equipment, and established quite impressive training and recreational facilities. The restoration of Islam, in place of secularism, has been popular with his officer corps, which is overwhelmingly drawn from former officers of the old Pakistan army. Zia's economic strategy—favoring the upper-class peasantry and urban middle—and upper-class families—is fully supported by the vast bulk of the military officers and *jawans* (soldiers), who are drawn almost exclusively from these sectors of society.[10]

Some idea of Zia's dependence on former Pakistan military officers can be gleaned from the fact that only two of the 50 Major-Generals and Brigadiers at present are men who fought in the liberation war. The other 48 are all officers who were in Pakistan during 1971 and were later repatriated to Bangladesh. Of the original eight sector commanders who led the Bangladesh liberation struggle, none are now in the Bangladesh military. Zia was one of the eight—the others have all been retired, civilianized, killed, or executed. The Commander-in-Chief of the army now is H.M. Ershad, a man much older than Zia, who was trapped in Pakistan in 1971 and returned to Bangladesh in 1973. The only two leading officers who fought for Bangladesh in the liberation war are Major-General Shaukat Ali, who has been stripped of his operational command and is now Principal Staff Officer of the President, and Major-General Manzoor, who has been moved out of Dacca and placed in charge of a Division of soldiers based in Chittagong.

Zia himself is guarded by his own old Division, most of which has been with him for many years. He says that the army should now be able to stay in the barracks, without getting involved in politics at all, but most people doubt that this will be the case. The army thus far has not played a role in development activities, but Zia is contemplating some dam-building projects and other activities that might keep them busy and bring them into closer

10. The Development strategy is traced out in Emajuddin Ahamed, "Development Strategy in Bangladesh: Probable Political Consequences," in *Bangladesh Politics*, ed. Emajuddin Ahamed (Dacca: Centre for Social Studies, 1980), pp. 98–116.

contact with rural problems. There have been enormous pressures from the younger ranks of the army to induct more of them into the civil service, although Zia has resisted this strenuously and with considerable success. At one point he did bring a number of army officials and ex-officers into the police service, but he argues that this was a one-time exception, necessitated by the need for disciplined men in the police ranks, and that this will not set a precedent for the future.

The police force has witnessed a more thoroughgoing reform than any such force in the whole of South Asia. It has been given higher salaries, new uniforms and equipment, better training and recreational facilities, and more powers. Its size has expanded considerably, as has its sense of prestige and worth. Much the same is true of the Ansars, a para-military force of reserves created by the Pakistan government and, like the Village Defence Force, organized by the Home Ministry. The Ansars, who are paid only when they are mobilized for a few weeks each year, have now acquired new training facilities and weapons. Zia estimates their strength at 40 batallions, as compared to 20 batallions in the past. Zia himself argues that the Ansars are much better organized than the Village Defence Force, and emphasizes that they could now be mobilized in a period of 24 hours if needed, something that was clearly not the case during the days of Pakistan.

Opposition politicians complain that Zia's regime is essentially military rule despite the trappings, with ex-policemen and ex-soldiers dominating the bureaucracy and ex-military men dominating the police. There is something to this—six of 20 First Secretaries are ex-police officers, 14 of 20 Superintendents of police are ex-army majors and captains, and 10 of the 20 heads of the top public corporations are ex-military—despite Zia's attempts to move towards greater civilianization. The dilemma he has confronted in trying to recruit non-military people to government was perhaps best summarized by one of his former close associates as follows: "he makes every effort to recruit people of talent from every sector of society, but in the end he finds himself trusting army officers personally, and he also probably sees them as, on the average, greater nationalists...Army officers are not necessarily tougher, but they have usually picked up certain strengths, and that pays off...He [Zia] is aware that, when you want democratic rule, you cannot show toughness all the time, but he has got to have people who will stick with him and see it through when the going gets tough."

A number of observers have likened Zia's regime to that of Suharto's Indonesia, where military and ex-military officers are in charge of strategic bureaucratic and economic positions in an ostensibly non-military regime, and where corruption has become institutionalized.   There is also something to this, in the sense that military and ex-military officers do predominate in Bangladesh and are expected to demand their personal share of the spoils—even though the system is not nearly as well-developed in Dacca as it is in Djakarta.   Indeed, if Ziaur Rahman does have an Achilles heel, it is the disaffection that is there in the younger ranks of the army, among men who see their superior officers benefiting greatly from a private enclave economy that is often illegal and under-the-table.   Part of Zia's problem is that the ranks of the army tend to have different ideals than those of their senior officers—often closer to Abu Taher's than Ziaur Rahman's—with the younger officers more easily influenced by the appeals of political leaders who champion those ideals.   Part of the problem, too, is the inability of Ziaur Rahman to provide enough spoils for enough officers far enough down into the ranks.

CONCLUSION

Regardless of whether one is fully supportive of him or not, it is clear that Ziaur Rahman has gained greater control of the Bangladesh polity and economy than anyone in the past. He is essentially a practical, military man who argues that "If you go by academic means, you will not find any answer." He sees himself as an institution-builder—building roads, canals and monuments, local government institutions, reforming the army and police—and as an enthusiast for development. He is aware of his inadequacies. He has said, for example, that when he came to power he had to start from the beginning to learn something about Finance because "I just didn't know anything about it!" He gets exceptionally high mark from everyone for being willing to learn and willing to admit when he is wrong. His stated goal is to create a civilian regime in which party and governmental institutions can eventually provide a democratic framework for the future.

For the time being, however, Zia has survived and prospered

because he has been willing to use the instruments of coercion he commands. He has been known to sack without warning Secretaries who left meetings too often or failed to attend, to fire on the spot engineers who could not meet construction deadlines, and to order the execution of hundreds of soldiers who violated fundamental rules of discipline. It would be unfair to say that he believes only in violence and military order, since, on a number of occasions he has backed away from coercive remedies to problems. In one of the most famous of these, he was actually struck by a student at Dacca University some years ago and simply walked away without punishing the student and without allowing his police and military bodyguards to strike back.

Zia's principal problem is the age-old one of giving over a military regime to civilians. The problem is compounded in his case by the miserable state of the Bangladesh economy, the volatile nature of Bengali politics, and an increasingly threatening international environment. International factors will be analyzed in the next essay in this volume.

THIRTEEN

INTERNATIONAL ENTANGLEMENTS
(1981)

Ziaur Rahman conceives of himself as an international person, and of his country as interdependent with the rest of the world. During the last year or so he has attended meetings of the Islamic Conference in Morocco, addressed a United Nations session in New York, met with President Jimmie Carter in Washington, appeared at the funeral of Prime Minister Ohira of Japan, engaged in trade negotiations in Djakarta, Singapore and Beijing, contracted for a nuclear power plant with Giscard D'estaing in Paris, discussed bilateral relations with Indira Gandhi in New Delhi, and bargained for oil and money in the Persian Gulf. His principal appeal is for massive amounts of aid, primarily from the United States and other Western aid donors, but also from OPEC and the Socialist bloc. His major international concerns are to find financial and material support sufficient to prevent further deterioration of the Bangladesh economy and, beyond that, to establish development and trade patterns that might make it possible for Bangladesh to begin to operate on its own steam. His concept of Bangladeshi nationalism is directed in part at the attempt to provide positive goals and values for his people. It is also directed at the overriding fear of most of his countrymen that India might achieve such a position of predominance as to render meaningless Bangladesh's status as an independent and sovereign nation.

RELATIONSHIPS WITH AID DONORS

Despite his admission that corruption has increased significantly during his five years in power, and his realization that this increase is due precisely to the massive amounts of international aid flowing into the country, Zia is convinced that "aid from all countries should be increased." As pointed out in the previous essay in this volume, Zia sees corruption as "a fact of life" that is "bound to happen." He has never been personally involved in the kinds of familial scandals that surround most public figures in Bangladesh and he has on a number of occasions taken legal action or sacked people at the highest levels on corruption charges. Nevertheless, he is criticized on the corruption issue because he has done more to institutionalize what are commonly viewed as corrupt activities than has any previous Bangladesh ruler. In the words of one of his principal political opponents, "There used to be blatant instances of corruption under Mujib, but those were spectacular cases involving certain individuals who were out to build their own private fortunes. What Zia has done is to regularize corruption and make it almost necessary for everyone to become involved in it."

One does not have to remain long in Bangladesh to figure out that most of what is called corruption stems from a dual or enclave economy of the most exaggerated sort. Between $1 billion and $1.5 billion in international assistance has been going into Bangladesh *every year* for the last eight years, in a country that could, at a maximum, raise a twentieth of that amount from its own resources.[1] People who have access to foreign money routinely stay in hotels that cost $50 to $60 per day, eat meals that cost $8 to $10 each, import cars at costs of $12,000 to $15,000 or more—and all of this in a nation where *annual* per capita incomes are less than the *per diem* allowances of most businessmen and the price of a gallon of petrol more than the average family earns in a week. The only ways for Bangladesh is to support daily consumption within the enclave economy are to secure foreign contracts at foreign wage rates or engage in under-the-table transactions. Both are often considered illegitimate. The alternative is to throw oneself back on the economy of the masses, which is more miserable than almost any economy anywhere in the world.

"I know all about the enclave economy," Zia says. "There is nothing abnormal about it." Zia also articulates an awareness of

1. An analysis of Bangladesh's aid-dependence appears in the author's "Aid-Dependence and the Many Futures of Bangladesh," *AUFS Fieldstaff Reports*, South Asia Series, XVI:12 (October 1972). See also Abu Mahmood, "Are Foreign Aid and Loans Indispensable for the Socio-Economic Development of Bangladesh," *Asian Affairs* (Dacca), I:1 (January–June 1980), pp. 5–29.

the various ways in which aid-dependence is being promoted in
Bangladesh, but suggests "We've got to go through it [a stage of aid-
dependence]! Otherwise, we'll never pick up!" He says that he
will "take measures" against corruption, through legal and coercive
channels—"we cannot keep quiet about it," he asserts time and
again—but he also makes it clear that he sees the political costs of
constant vigilance against corruption as being too formidable. In
his view, there is "rich man's corruption" and "poor man's
corruption," with one feeding upon the other. If poverty is attacked
directly, says one of his aides, society can rid itself of aid-dependence, achieve some balance between the enclave and the mass
economy, and diminish the susceptibility of both rich and poor to
engage in corrupt activities. But this aide—like Zia's other associates, and Zia himself—sees poverty as a function primarily of
international factors. So long as there are severe international
imbalances between rich and poor, says the same aide, "we can
try to keep corruption in check, but we certainly can't put a stop
to it."

With these bumptious attitudes towards enclave-style development, Zia has embarked on an unprecedented quest to woo aid
donors. During Robert McNamara's last year at the World Bank,
Zia managed to get McNamara out to Bangladesh for two days,
where, after some heavy courting, the old Work Bank president
agreed to $1 billion in additional funding for Bangladesh over the
next three years. While in the U.S. for the UN session and his
meeting with Carter, Zia is reported to have impressed every person
he met—including some of Ronald Reagan's people—with his
arguments for bilateral aid, although the pay-offs from that
performance are not yet visible. Zia and his associates talk of
desirable levels of funding in terms that would account for most of
the Second Five-Year Development Plan—now in its first year—
totaling more than $15 billion. "The rich nations of the world,"
Zia says, "are not doing enough. They must do more."

Those who have discussed the subject with him say that Zia can
find a thousand reasons why the wealthy nations of the world
should pour money, personnel, technology and material into
Bangladesh. Zia himself talks of plans to increase the number of
sterilizations by tubectomy and vasectomy from the present level of
25,000 per month to levels of 100,000 per month, or even 200,000
per month, and swears that "our people want to do it, but we don't

have the capacity to sterilize." He talks of vast reserves of coal and limestone waiting to be developed, and of 800,000 acres that could be planted to cotton. For these and numerous other developmental projects to take place he sees a need for Western technology of the most sophisticated type. "Oil!" he enthuses. "We have got the oil—we just have to drill it up. There is oil here—we already have samples of crude oil.. our drilling in the Bay of Bengal shows that there are very rich structures for oil. We are now setting up our capability for offshore drilling."

Hard-nosed analysts of agriculture, family planning, the oil industry and other aspects of development are convinced that Zia's exuberance either betrays a soldier's naivete about the complexities of modern economic life in the poor nations of the world, or, much more likely, is the civilian equivalent of a former General's peptalk to his troops. The odds against Zia's stated goal of doubling food production in the next five years—particularly if he is going to take 800,000 acres out to plant to cotton—is at least a million to one. Sterilizations on the scale that Zia talks about led to the political demise of Ayub Khan in the 1960s and contributed mightily to the growth of the intense anti-Pakistan sentiment that culminated in the bloody civil war of 1971. Most family planning workers agree that there is a significant reservoir of unspoken support for limiting family size, particularly among women who already have several children, but they are also aware that Bangladesh (and especially its male segment) is still overwhelmingly opposed to population control and that a large section of Bangladesh society could be roused to a fever pitch of violent opposition to the government—as happened in India during the emergency —by anything resembling a coercive or crash family planning program.

The big oil companies have known for some time now—in fact, long before Zia came to power—that there is a lot of natural gas in Bangladesh, including a considerable quantity offshore. While many petroleum experts are convinced that there should be large deposits of oil in the Bay of Bengal, attempts to find it have not yet produced a bonanza. In any case, major problems of an international legal nature will have to be overcome before Bangladesh can systematically start tapping any oil that has been discovered. This is so if only because there is still no agreement on the disputed Indo-Bangladesh maritime boundary and the multinationals have thus far been unwilling to invest more than routine amounts for exploration.

"Yes, we will have shortfalls," Zia predicts. "So what?" "Does that mean we should give up, that we should not make the effort?" He brushes aside people whom he calls "complainers...the ones who always bring in theory and say it can't be done." He talks animatedly about the time in 1979, when he went out on the world markets to commercially buy foodgrains to prevent a famine in Bangladesh. "They said we would not be able to procure food or pay for it. When we did, they said we would not be able to un- load. When we unloaded, they said we would not be able to get it inland. And I told them, you are right, such things happened before, but we've got to make it this time, otherwise people will die. And we did it, and at the end of the thing many of them came and said, we are sorry for thinking that you would not be able to do it."

Zia is popular with aid donors because he shares many of their values, in just the right amounts and in the right ways to be accept- able to people across a wide spectrum of viewpoints. He is for family planning, for example, but he is cautious about the way he introduces it. His description of his entreaties at a public meet- ing is as follows: "I told them that you have got to do family plan- ning—two children—and I told them, raise your hands. And all the men, women and children raised their hands. Now many people necessarily did not understand what I said. But they raised their hands. When they go back, they will ask their friends, why did I raise hand?...and they will want to do it...You see, now we have motivated the people..."

In other areas—land reform, woman's rights, participation, decentralization, private sector development, education, removal of illiteracy, as well as family planning—Zia spouts the rhetoric of the international development establishment but remains both a pragmatist about implementation and, in many ways, a rather conservative Bengali Muslim. He wants massive educational re- form "in a spirit of harmony," land reform "based on a national consensus," and "responsible growth" of the private sector. He has done more for women's rights than any other male leader of Bangladesh, even counting the period when it was part of Pakistan, and yet he takes a rather traditional attitude towards his own family ("my kids are small," he says, "and my wife is my wife, and she looks after the house...If she is not going to look after

the house, then I can't do my job..."). While many of these attitudes are criticized by one or another segment of society within
Bangladesh, they strike a remarkable balance between such diverse
forces as Islamic fundamentalism, radical Marxism, and the bourgeois ethics of the international community. As one of Zia's opponents described his approach, "he says with great enthusiasm that
he is going to do what can't be done, but then he doesn't really
push the matter beyond a certain point because he knows it would
get him into trouble...In that respect, he shares the contradictions
between the radical and conservative stances of the international
funding agencies."

Critics of the President argue that a combination of radical
rhetoric and conservative implementation, particularly when coupled
with the burgeoning growth of an enclave economy, will eventually
produce insurmountable dilemmas for Zia, in both urban and rural
areas.[2] In the cities, the enclave economy is propelling an intolerable inflation of 20–25 per cent per year, which is especially
resented by those on the periphery or outside the enclave. To the
extent that Zia presses for genuine reforms affecting urban dwellers—women's rights, family planning, or abolition of the ration
shops, for example—he could trigger off large-scale opposition
movements that might be fueled—a la Iran—by inflation, a large
foreign presence, resentment against authoritarian actions, and by a
societal cause that appeals to the primodial sentiments of a
disgruntled population.

In the rural areas, the above dilemma is compounded by another.
To the extent that Zia continues to press for land reform, increased
participation of poorer segments of the population and a decentralization of power down into the villages, he raises seemingly uncontrollable expectations of fundamental change, but a failure to
push effectively for a devolution of participation and power puts
him at odds with many of his international benefactors and some
sectors of his political support-base. Perhaps the greatest potential stumbling-block in this regard is the possibility that new
village-level institutions will not become centers of dynamism for
development, but will instead bring within eyesight and earshot of

2. Possible political consequences of Zia's development strategy are
analyzed in Emajuddin Ahamed, "Development Strategy in Bangladesh:
Probable Political Consequences," in *Bangladesh Politics*, ed. Emajuddin
Ahamed (Dacca: Centre for Social Studies, 1980), pp. 98–116.

villagers—on their own turf—the extent to which Zia's regime is dependent on patronage networks that feed on external funding.

"This is not Iran," Zia states flatly. "Iran's problem was different. I went to Iran just two or three months before the Shah left, and I have seen the whole thing. That's a completely different situation as compared to ours. It is different in many respects. They had too much easy money from the oil. They have a lesser number of people, and they had lots of money. We have too many people..." Zia speaks of his regime as "a delicate balance," in which he, his advisors, the opposition, and people in newly-created local institutions "push on each other a lot." He articulates with passion his commitment to build rural power-bases: "We cannot keep the village people befooled and illiterate and out of strength and expect that the rest of the few people in the cities will be good. It can't be. So we are taking the society from the grass-roots level. Politics! We start with politics at the grass-roots level, organizing the society at the grass-roots level—the local government—voluntary bodies at the grass-roots level—so that there is a challenge from the people against our party, a challenge from the people against the government. So the whole democratic society is, in a circular manner, kind of balanced up."

The one key variable for development, in Zia's view, is international aid. He speaks of aid as giving a "kick" to development and ticks off his needs without effort: "agricultural inputs, pumps, tubewells, fertilizer, machineries, oil and gas development and exploration, mining, coalmines, limestone, hard rock, construction of roads, railway systems—these are the main ones." He argues that Bangladesh deserves more aid because it has the capacity to absorb more than other poor nations (this is so, he says, in part because of its size, in part because he now has "a system for working on projects," and in part because Bangladesh has more skilled manpower and experience with experimental developmental projects than any other country). After a number of caveats and amidst much confusion, Zia even argues that the Western nations should enhance aid flows because that would help him raise more domestic resources.

Most of Zia's comments on aid follow the familiar scripts of Third World leaders engaged in the so-called North-South dialogue. He is particularly opposed to tied loans, or aid with strings, because, he argues, such arrangements are a major source of corruption. "When you have to take the machinery only from one country, manipulation is bound to creep in. Your officer comes to our officer and says, look, you give me this or that and I will give you half a per cent or, say $200,000...that's how a lot of corruption takes place... when it is an open loan, my officer can tell the chap to go to hell and get his goods somewhere else...one can exercise more judgement in looking where to purchase."

In response to the suggestion that many Western nations might find it difficult to give large amounts of economic aid because they are themselves reeling under the economic problems of the 1980s, Zia finds it difficult to hide his disgust. "Awrrr! That is too little, that is hardly to be compared with our suffering," he says. "That is nothing—you can absorb it! The rich countries should give more, he says, because Bangladesh was exploited longer than other developing countries, because it achieved its independence later, and because "there will be imbalance and confusion all over the world and...you will be sucked into it...the people of America will not cherish it." But most of his appeal is for positive cooperation: "What we find," he goes on, "is that people from the developed countries, they're always inclined to say, you can't do it, you can't do it, you can't do it. But some of you must encourage us and come and stand by our side. You see, anything can be done. Organization is required. A man is required. Money is required. Technology is required. What you can do, you can put the money and technology. We can put the organization and the man and the plan. We are doing it!"

RELATIONS WITH INDIA

One of the reasons why Zia has been willing to invite Western nations into his country, with very few reservations or constraints, has to do with the widespread fear within Bangladesh that India and the Soviet Union will somehow combine to topple Zia's regime and render Bangladesh independence meaningless. Zia himself is extremely careful never to say anything negative about India or its leaders, nor will he criticize Mujibur Rahman by name, but he does speak out against what he calls "a Moscow-type of socialism," "foreignism," and BAKSHALISM, in contexts that clearly imply associations with Delhi and Moscow. In Zia's vocabulary, the term BAKSHALITES refers to the one-party authoritarian regime that Mujib established in 1974—with full backing from both India and the USSR—when Mujib banned all political parties and commanded them to merge with his Bangladesh Krishak Sramik Awami League (BAKSHAL). After Mujib's assassination, BAKSHAL disintegrated, but Zia labels as BAKSHALITES all members of its surviving core, now clustered together in the pro-India and pro-Moscow Malek faction of the Awami League and in the Communist Party of Bangladesh (CPB).

When asked about the role of socialism in Bangladesh, Zia says that "we ourselves are doing it [socialism], but we cannot do the way they do in Russia. It is not acceptable. We can't do it. Conditions are different here." Both in public and in private he has genuinely and assiduously sought cooperative relationships with India. At the same time, however, he states openly that large-scale cooperation with India cannot play all that large a role in Bangladesh's development "because India itself is poor."

Ziaur Rahman's distrust of India dates back to the early 1970s, when Sheikh Mujibur Rahman and the Awami League were in power, fully supported by Delhi and Moscow.[3] Zia was not given the top position in the army under Mujib, even though Zia was senior to the man Mujib appointed, and Zia was extremely critical of Mujib's treatment of the military. India's leadership was visibly shaken when Mujib was killed in the August 1975 coup, with Zia apparently knowing about the coup in advance but refusing to do anything to prevent it. Indian leaders do not blame Ziaur Rahman for either the August 15th or November 3rd coups in 1975, but a number of Indian diplomats consider him culpable and untrustworthy because he apparently had prior knowledge of the coups and, in both instances, refused to initiate actions that might have saved India-backed Bangladesh leaders (Mujib in the case of the first coup and Khaled Musharraf in the second).

Indo-Bangladesh relations improved noticably under the Janata government, which wrested power from Indira Gandhi in March

3. See Talukder Maniruzzaman, *The Bangladesh Revolution and Its Aftermath* (Dacca: Bangladesh Books International, 1981). This book by Maniruzzaman, along with a second book by A.M.A. Muhith, *Bangladesh: Emergence of a Nation* (Dacca; Bangladesh Books International, 1978) are the two most comprehensive and authentic accounts of the liberation struggle.

1977 and surrendered it back to her in January 1980. Since the return of Gandhi, relationships have at times been testy, with widespread rumors circulating in Bangladesh that the Indian government is, at the very least, adopting an unreasonably assertive attitude towards its smaller neighbors. Rumors have also circulated widely that India is prepared for armed intervention in Bangladesh's domestic politics should it be deemed necessary. Zia himself has fed some of these rumors by occasionally making impassioned speeches throughout the country, in which he never mentions specific acts or specific countries by name but, nonetheless, leaves little doubt about the butt of his intended references. In one case, for example, he told a Bangladesh audience that the BAKSHALITES are "pursuing a politics of weapons" and are "suported by foreign funds."[4] Zia called on his audience to "wipe out foreignism from the soil," and then added: "If the BAKSHALITES want to migrate to the land of their foreign masters, we would bear the passage money."

In an atmosphere of such considerable distrust, it is not surprising that little or no headway has been made in tackling the wide variety of issues outstanding between Delhi and Dacca. Indeed, a number of new issues have been added to previous lists, largely as a consequence of changes in the international environment as the world enters the 1980s. Heading the list of new issues have been serious differences with regard to the Soviet and Vietnamese interventions in Afghanistan and Kampuchea respectively, with India taking an equivocal stance and Bangladesh favoring a straightforward condemnation of the Soviets and Vietnamese. From New Delhi's perspective, Bangladesh's strategic location and its susceptibility to foreign influence have become all the more important at a time when India is faced with major political upheavals in its northeastern region.

The troubles in India's northeast are related primarily to demands by the Assamese and other small linguistic groups, that all Bangladeshis who have migrated to Assam since 1971 (or some xenophobic groups would say even before 1971) be considered "foreigners" and sent back to Bangladesh. The "anti-foreign" agitation has been so great in 1980 that the Indian army had to be called in to

4. Quoted in the government newspaper *Bangladesh Observer*, November 25, 1980.

run oil rigs and maintain law and order. Even then, hundreds of lives were lost, the economy of Assam was riddled with problems, and both transportation and communication links between Assam and the rest of India were severely disrupted because of the nearly constant violent demonstrations throughout the year. In late October 1980, Prime Minister Gandhi tried to pacify the Assamese by stating in Parliament that any Bangladeshi "detected as a foreigner in Assam...will have to go back to Bangladesh, unless they can go to some other country." Mrs. Gandhi estimated that the number of such persons would be "in the thousands" and not "in the millions." She said that she had not "formally" talked to Ziaur Rahman about this policy, "but I think he is aware of the situation."[5]

Mrs. Gandhi's Parliamentary statement ran directly counter to Ziaur Rahman's assertion in New Delhi in September that "there are no Bangladeshi refugees in India any more. There is no question of our taking any people back. It is an internal problem of the government of India."[6] Zia's Foreign Minister later told the Bangladesh Parliament that Zia's government would "under no circumstances accept any of the evicted persons from the Assam region" and further stated that questions concerning the eviction of Bangladeshis from Assam had never been raised officially with the Bangladesh government at any level.[7]

The number of intricate problems associated with any attempt to define a Bangladeshi "foreigner" in Assam are legion. Only 57 per cent of the 15 million people of Assam speak Assamese, with another 17.4 per cent speaking Bengali and most of the rest (16 per cent) speaking local tribal languages that in some instances spill over into Bangladesh.[8] Of the 17.4 per cent Bengali speakers, many, if not most, have come from what is now the state of West Bengal, in India, and the majority of them came to Assam before 1971. More than 30 per cent of the Assamese population is Muslim,

5. *The Statesman* (Calcutta), October 22, 1980.
6. *Times of India* (Bombay), September 20, 1980.
7. *Hindustan Times* (New Delhi), December 30, 1980.
8. The figures are from the 1971 Indian Census. For a detailed analysis see my "Refugees and Migration Patterns in Northeastern India and Bangladesh," *AUFS Fieldstaff Reports*, South Asia Series, XVI:3 (May 1972) and my "Northeastern India: In the Wake of Vietnam," *AUFS Fieldstaff Reports*, Southeast Asia Series, XIX:13 (August 1975).

with figures ranging from 24 per cent in the Brahmaputra valley to 43 per cent in the district of Goalpara, but, as Myron Weiner has pointed out, the Indian census does not cross-tabulate religion and migration, with the result that "there is no way of knowing how many Muslims in Assam are migrants or of migrant origin."[9]

Estimates by Indians of the number of Bangladeshi "foreigners" in Assam range from 50,000 to 5 million, but the issue is now so surcharged with emotion that anything resembling an accurate count is unthinkable. Most of the people involved are landless and illiterate, the Bangladesh-India border is not sharply defined geophysically, and neither country has In the past maintained detailed records of its citizens or required them to keep certificates of citizenship.

Border disputes have been complicated in recent years by the growing emotional intensity and violence of Assamese political campaigns against Bengalis, by a number of "harvesting clashes" in which nationals from one country have claimed land from the other (usually arising after a river has shifted course), and a continuation of large-scale smuggling in both directions. There have been frequent reports in both the Indian and Bangladesh press of firing across the border, with Indian journalists usually accusing the Bangladesh Rifles of being "trigger-happy" and the Bangladesh press countering with similar charges against the Indian Border Security Force (BSF). Both sides have also issued constant and conflicting stories about the number of migrants who have been forcibly sent across the border at gunpoint by one army or the other.

Although Delhi and Dacca have entered into a number of agreements to demarcate their land boundary, mark it in great detail, and police it in a more efficient manner, implementation of the agreements has been beset with constant difficulties. In one case, Bangladesh ratified an agreement providing for the exchange of two tiny disputed enclaves (Berubari and Daharam), but New Delhi was unable to ratify the agreement because the West Bengal

---

9. Myron Weiner, *Sons of the Soil: Migration and Ethnic Conflict in India* (Princeton: Princeton University Press, 1978), p. 102. Weiner's case study of the Assam ethnic conflict (pp. 75–144 in this book) is by far the best work on the subject. An excellent more recent work is Nirmal Nibedon, *Northeast India: The Ethnic Explosion* (New Delhi: Lancers Publishers, 1981).

state government refused to cede a strip of land granting Bangladesh access to the enclave it was to receive from India. There are 12 other small enclaves in dispute, but attempts to survey them, draw up maps, and determine the legal rights of citizens, businesses and local governments—who are presumably to be exchanged between the two nations eventually—all have raised hornets' nests of problems.

Both nations have also had difficulty maintaining the morale and integrity of their border police and armies. The Indian Border Security Force (BSF) was founded in 1965 as a force of a few thousand, but now numbers more than 100,000 men and women. It is involved in anti-guerrilla operations in Assam, political operations against rural Maoists in West Bengal and Bihar, and several other military, para-military and civilian operations in different parts of India. Over the years, the BSF has become increasingly controversial, as it has been used in more and more civilian affairs away from the border areas, including activity in putting down Hindu-Muslim communal riots in several cities in Uttar Pradesh in 1980.

BSF personnel assigned to the Bangladesh border generally lead difficult and lonely lives, in border posts and colonies that are usually without electric power and lights, contain few other amenities, and offer virtually no entertainment. In recent years, BSF personnel on the Bangladesh border have provided medical aid and books for students, built schools and jetties, established fisheries, pigstyes, goateries and poultry farms, and engaged in a number of social welfare projects, all with a view to becoming more involved in "constructive work" that might bring them closer to villagers. They have also been given updated equipment, including several speedboats and motorboats, satellite-linked communications gear, and a number of modern gadgets used for controlling crowds.

Despite its attempts to appear closer to the people, however, the BSF still has a reputation for bribe-taking and complicity in the illegal migration and trade that continues across the border. The Bangladesh Rifles, on the other side, have a reputation that is about the same, if not worse. In both cases, salaries and perquisites, never much to begin with, have failed to keep up with inflation, and on both sides of the border the amounts to be made from smuggling have increased enormously.

The main items in the smugglers' inventory of late have been used ready-made garments, collected free or for a pittance from Bangladeshi well-wishers in the U.S. or Europe and shipped legally and duty-free into Bangladesh under a special scheme designed to help the poor. The smuggling-in of readymade garments from Bangladesh to India is now big business. A large number of markets have sprung up in the Dharamtullah-Chowringee area of Calcutta, and in numerous smaller cities in Eastern India, in which vast amounts of such smuggled clothing are sold openly. Other items that have come into India in large quantities in 1980 include fertilizers (which were for a time selling at subsidized rates in Bangladesh but are notoriously scarce in India), sugar (there has been a severe shortage in India this year), fish, and a wide assortment of electronic gadgets, watches, cameras and other items that have far less prohibitive duties in Bangladesh than in India. Goods smuggled back to Bangladesh include consumer and light industry products that India has learned to produce on a mass basis in recent years, ranging from saris and cosmetics to tubewell pumps and processed foods.

Delhi and Dacca did manage to sign a two-year cultural agreement and a three-year trade accord in 1980. In addition, a joint business council was established in the private sector by the Federation of Indian Chambers of Commerce and its counterpart in Dacca. The two governments also reached agreement on "a working formula" for the establishment of a rail link and railway transit facilities for India across Bangladesh. Veteran observers of Indo-Bangladesh relations saw all of these agreements as similar to the dozens of agreements that have been reached and never implemented or, in some cases, only half-heartedly implemented in the past. Perhaps the most encouraging thing that can be said about the accumulation of such agreements is that it has brought Indian and Bangladesh officials together fairly regularly, and has usually resulted in declarations of good intentions and promises of cooperation at several points each year. It has also forced officials from both countries to think through the difficulties involved in realizing proposed cooperative endeavors.

BANGLADESHI NATIONALISM

The thorniest issues in Indo-Bangladesh relations result from seemingly intractable differences over water resources, the sharing of the waters of the two great river systems (the Ganges and the Brahmaputra) which flow from India into Bangladesh, and similar differences over the delineation of a maritime boundary. Both of these disputes have been detailed in previous Fieldstaff Reports and both seem as far away from a solution today as they were when Bangladesh became independent a decade ago.[10] A third controversy of immeasurable dimensions has arisen during the last two years as a consequence of the discovery (from satellite pictures) that one (or perhaps two) islands are being created in the Bay of Bengal by the increasingly heavy silt deposits flowing down from the Himalayas in this century.

India's Foreign Minister told the Indian Parliament in December 1980 that the new island (which the Indians call New Moore island or Purbasha and the Bangladeshis call South Talapatty) belongs to India, but the Bangladesh government immediately objected to the statement and accused New Delhi of renegging on a previous commitment to jointly survey what Dacca says are two islands before making unilateral public claims. Since both of the islands are still slowly being formed, their eventual or potential size is not yet clear. Indian diplomats who want to minimize the rashness of their seizure say they are infinitesimal while, one Bangladeshi geographer suggests that the two islands together may some day account for land space as large as 25,000 square miles, the equivalent of about 45 per cent of present-day Bangladesh. In the near future, ownership claims to the islands will be most significant in delineating the maritime boundary between Bangladesh and India, since they could change the location of the baselines on which the boundary is drawn. Presumably, it was with this in mind that New Delhi so bluntly staked its claim in 1980.

The most emotive issue in Indo-Bangladesh relations in 1980 was a proposal by Ziaur Rahman that Bangladesh sell natural gas to India, at twice the usual international market rates, which would equate the price of gas with current prices for petroleum. Bangladesh is reported to have 10 trillion cubic feet of natural gas reserves, and Zia's proposal is to sell one-tenth of that to India over the next decade. For India, this would be the equivalent of getting half a million barrels of oil a day. From the perspective of Bangladesh,

10. See my "Indo Bangladesh Relations," *AUFS Fieldstaff Reports*, South Asia Series, XIX:16 (September 1975).

natural gas sales would immediately swing the balance-of-payments between Delhi and Dacca radically in Dacca's favor, since Bangladesh is currently exporting only $2.5 million worth of goods per year to India while importing $36 million per year. Natural gas sales alone could account for hundreds of millions of dollars annually.

Zia's proposal to sell natural gas to India roused Bangladeshi anti-Indian sentiments to fever pitch in 1980. Former President Khondakar Mushtaque Ahmed threatened a fast unto death if Zia went through with the deal, while other opposition leaders adopted the slogan: "we will give blood, but not natural gas." There have been financial and physical problems as well in trying to implement Zia's proposal. A scheme to construct a 175-mile pipeline from the Bangladesh gas fields at Bakhrabad to a receiving station in Calcutta carries with it an estimated price tag of $300 million, a figure far beyond anything the Indians or Bangladeshis could afford by themselves. Both countries are exploring the possibility of World Bank support for the proposed pipeline, and Bangladesh is simultaneously probing possibilities of selling liquefied natural gas (LNG) to Japan or the United States, with the cost of the facilities being paid by the purchaser in return for exclusive rights to buy the entire reserves. The major problems with the LNG proposal are: 1) that it is prohibitively expensive (estimated costs of the LNG plant in Bangladesh range up to $1.5 billion); 2) it would tie the interests of Bangladesh irrevocably to the Western nations that agreed to it; and 3) it would entail enormous risks for the purchasing country because of the potential political instability of Bangladesh.

In January 1981, Bangladesh Petroleum Minister Akbar Hossain told the Bangladesh Parliament that Zia's government would sell natural gas to India only if Dacca could get an equivalent amount of petroleum products from abroad. This statement was intended to blunt widespread criticism within Bangladesh of proposed gas sales to India, by opposition leaders who argue that the government should use reserves of natural gas to alleviate poverty and get development going at home before exporting gas abroad. Even within Zia's own party, he has encountered enormous opposition to his gas sales proposal, with some major BNP party leaders suggesting that this single issue has caused the President more political damage than any other. One of Zia's aides even stated flatly his private opinion, that "gas sales to India are politically not possible."

Appreciation of the depths of Bangladeshi sentiments regarding water resources and natural gas is essential to an understanding of Zia's concept of Bangladeshi nationalism, which is intended to simultaneously consolidate feelings of nationhood, provide a series of symbols for unifying the country, contribute to the enthusiasm with which nation-building activities are pursued, and, ultimately, maintain the identity and integrity of Bangladesh as a nation-state independent of India. In contrast to the xenophobic nationalisms of many newly independent countries, Zia's Bangladeshi nationalism provides for a remarkable degree of accommodation to foreigners, and even to Indians, although it does occasionally play on anti-Indian and anti-Soviet sentiments that have accumulated in Bangladesh over the years. While it differs markedly from the secular nationalism of modern India, it is also far from the Islamic fundamentalist nationalisms of Pakistan, Iran and the Gulf states. Opposition politicians frequently try to pooh-pooh Zia's sorties into nationalist symbol-creation, even though many of them will admit privately that his ultimate success or failure as a leader could well depend on his manipulation of nationalist sentiments and values.

Zia himself defines his concept of Bangladeshi nationalism as something positive, intended to take advantage of emotions within the country to create institutions of self-help, self-reliance, the ability to stand on one's own feet, and a commitment to develop one's own resources. At political rallies, for example, he tells his audiences: "We are all Bangladeshis! This is our soil! This is our water! This is our air! These are our plants! We will take this soil and this water and this air, and we will make our plants grow faster and better! We will improve the soil and we will dig canals for the water. We will grow more rice and wheat! We must! We are all Bangladeshis now!"

Zia does not use the possessive "my" to refer to anything in Bangladesh, as Mujibur Rahman used to do (Mujib always, and sometimes comically, would describe people and institutions within Bangladesh as my women, my workers, my universities, my factories, my army, my programs, etc.). Zia always emphasizes that "this is our country, this is our land." In private conversations he says, "This soil has been polluted by so many conquerors. Now is the opportunity. We dig this soil and make it more productive. We build up industries and raise our heads with dignity." He tries to communicate these feelings to people. Usually, he comes across with conviction. "Now the time has come to build our nation, our country, our soil," he says. "We must rely on our strengths— no foreignism. If Bangladesh has its own destiny, it must develop in its own way. You can give this message to the whole world: it will develop in its own way."

Prior to Ziaur Rahman, observers used to talk about an upsurge of Bengali nationalism as the force that drove the Bangladesh liberation movement in the late 1960s and early 1970s. By 1975, however, it was clear that Bengali nationalism was far too ambiguous a concept for the new nation of Bangladesh. The term "Bengali" describes a linguistic group of 140 million people or so—90 million in Bangladesh and 50 million in the state of West Bengal in India— two-thirds of whom are Muslims.[11] If one considers the Bengalis as a single entity, it could be called—as Richard V. Weekes has labelled it—"the second largest Muslim ethnic group after the Arabs," but this would be misleading.[12] Bengalis have historically been so divided by caste and community that a common sense of Bengali nationhood never evolved.[13]

Linguistic and cultural affinities were important in securing the support of Bengali-speakers in the Indian state of West Bengal for the 1971 Bangladesh liberation struggle, and this in turn helped cement Indian support against Pakistan. After 1971, however, questions about possible domination of Bangladesh by Indians led many Bangladeshis to reject the old symbols of Bengali nationalism and to set off in search of new symbols. Questions about whether Bengali culture or Muslim culture had been more important in moldin₅ Bangladeshis became prominent. Differences between East

11. Scholarly explorations of Bengali and Bangladeshi nationalisms appear in *Reflections on the Bengal Renaissance*, ed. David Kopf and Safiuddin Joarder (Rajshahi: Institute of Bangladesh Studies, 1977), and in an essay entitled "Bangladesh Nationalism," in M. Anisuzzaman, *Bangladesh: Public Administration and Society* (Dacca: Bangladesh Books International, 1979).

12. Cf. Richard V. Weekes, "Bengali," in *Muslim Peoples: A World Ethnographic Survey* (Westport, Connecticut: Greenwood Press, 1978), pp. 89–99.

13. For details see Kamruddin Ahmad, *A Socio-Political History of Bengal and the Birth of Bangladesh*, Fourth Revised Edition (Dacca: Zahiruddin Mahmud Inside Library, 1975). See also A.K. Nazmul Karim, *Changing Society in India, Pakistan and Bangladesh*, Third Edition (Dacca: Nawroze Kitabistan), see esp. pp. 107–140.

and West Bengalis—in dress, food, eating habits, ceremonial customs, and even language—were emphasized rather than downplayed by Bangladeshis after 1971. From the very inception of Bangladesh there was an almost universal rejection of the possibility that the Bengalis of West Bengal and Bangladesh might come together to demand a single nation-state which could provide a homeland for all Bengalis.

In retrospect, it is surprising how quickly Bengali nationalism dissipated once Bangladesh had been created. Indeed, most analysts now suggest that Sheikh Mujibur Rahman missed a golden opportunity to consolidate his own position as a leader by not paying more attention to the formulation of his own brand of nationalism once independence was achieved. At least part of the reason for this might well have been his close ties to India, which prevented him from framing a full-blown independent position. His critics now argue that he alienated many people in Bangladesh by constantly thanking India in his speeches for the role that the Indian army played in the 1971 war, and by his adoption of national symbols and ideals—a secular Constitution, a "mixed economy," and a "socialist pattern of society"—all remarkably similar to those of India.

Ziaur Rahman is still struggling to define the contours of his concept of Bangladeshi nationalism, but he is fully convinced that the concept lies at the heart of future developments. "We don't have any such problem like India," he says. "We have one language for the whole country, right from north to south, east to west. We don't have regionalism, or minorities of that type. But this is a new country. This has been colonized for many years, many centuries. So it is only correct to develop the spirit of nationalism, to consolidate the nationhood."

Unlike India, which does not have a majority linguistic-religious community, almost 90 per cent of Bangladesh is Bengali Muslim. The area that is now Bangladesh was almost 20 per cent Hindu in 1947, and the Hindus had historically dominated East Bengal—as landlords, moneylenders, college professors, government officials, and so forth. More than 4 million Hindus, most of them from the wealthiest and dominant ruling families of East Bengal, migrated to India in the years 1947–1954. The vast majority of the Hindus who have stayed on in Bangladesh are in the lower-middle or poorer classes of society—as cultivators, cobblers, sweets makers, and schoolteachers—but Hindus now own little land and seldom are found in positions of great authority.

While Zia's government has dropped the word "secular" from the Bangladesh Constitution, it has not consciously tried to discriminate against Hindus. "Absolute Trust and Faith in the Almighty Allah as the basis of all actions" is a Fundamental Principle of State Policy, but "no discrimination against any citizen on grounds of religion, race, caste, sex or place of birth" is a Fundamental Right. Muslim, Hindu, Christian and Buddhist holidays are observed and the ceremonies of all four of these religious communities are shown on national television. A number of Indian journalists have commended the Bangladesh press for showing admirable restraint in reporting on Hindu-Muslim riots in India—something that Ziaur Rahman has insisted on—and more than one Indian journalist has observed that the independent nation of Bangladesh has not yet had "a single major communal eruption in which people have lost their lives."[14]

At least part of the explanation for Bangladesh's relative communal harmony has to do with two factors that are not entirely positive: 1) since there was so much communal killing in the periods surrounding the partition of 1947 and just preceding the civil war in 1971, much of the current calm stems more from fear and disgust with bloodshed than from a new spirit of harmony; 2) much of what passes for communal harmony today is simply a function of the minority Hindu community having been cowed down by the predominance and aggressiveness of the majority Muslims. Many Bangladesh Hindus do feel discriminated against and many feel insecure. Some Bangladesh Hindus consciously refuse to acquire property or many material goods because they feel they should remain mobile in case they are forced to move to India. Others have property claims against Muslims who, they allege, illegally acquired property that rightfully belonged to them or to their community.

Ziaur Rahman does not wear secularism on his sleeve, as Mujib often did, but he has gone out of his way to promote communal harmony. In 1980 he established a committee to inquire into the difficulties faced by the Hindus, and to sort out their claims to

14. Kirit Bhaumik, "Dacca Restraint on Riots," *Times of India* (Bombay) September 15, 1980.

property rights. Throughout his five years in power, Zia has presided at a number of Hindu functions and conferences and has encouraged cultural events in which both Muslims and Hindus participate. When speaking to Hindus, he now asks them "to spread the message of Bangladeshi nationalism," although he is still quite vague about how precisely Hindus might fit into that message.[15]

On those occasions where Zia has backed away from a secular-minded position, it has often seemed to be at the instigation of the Arabs or with Arab leaders in mind. It is commonly assumed, for example, that insertion of the clause "Faith in the Almighty Allah" as a Fundamental Principle of the Constitution, plus a Constitutional commitment to pursue friendly relations with Islamic countries, were prerequisites for Bangladesh admission to the Islamic Conference, a 42–member world organization based in Saudi Arabia that has already supplied Bangladesh with large amounts of petrodollars. The Arabs are also funding an Islamic University in Bangladesh, which Zia was somewhat reluctant to build but has agreed to—in the face of considerable opposition within his own party and from several opposition parties—presumably because he needs the money for higher education. At one point Zia put policewomen on the road into Dacca from the airport, but he quickly withdrew them when a Sheikh from one of the Gulf states objected to their presence. Zia also compromised with an initial resistance to declare Friday a holiday, at the instigation of a Sheikh, and instead declared it a half-holiday for those who wish to take it.

Zia himself says simply that "Islam is encouraged by the government." Recitations from the Koran are a regular part of his public meetings, and the BNP party song clearly evokes religious sentiments and postures of prayer. Zia is especially anxious that modern subjects be introduced into the *madrassahs* and taught in the new Islamic University. To the extent that he exhibits a deep commitment to Islam, it carries with it a resolve to update the religion and adapt it to the world of the future.

Many of the opposition parties, and especially the pro-India Awami League, criticize Zia for not being more secular, and for

15. The quote is from the *Hindustan Times* (New Delhi), August 29, 1980.

his frequent disregard of human rights and dignity, particularly where those opposed to him are concerned. The Awami League is especially anxious that respectability and legitimacy be restored to Sheikh Mujibur Rahman and his followers, since Zia has tended to indirectly (although never by name) denigrate them and link them to conspirational activities. The AL was irate when Zia renamed "Independence Day"—March 26, 1971—"National Day", a change that the AL saw as an attempt to cater to pro-Pakistan sentiment and blot out memories of Mujib's sacrifices (it was on that day that Mujib was arrested by the Pakistanis and the 1971 civil war began). The AL has generally been campaigning for a restoration of Mujib to a position of public prominence and has vowed that if it ever returns to power it will bring Mujib's body from its present location—a grave in Mujib's home village in Faridpur—to a site of honor in the Dacca mausoleum being built by Ziaur Rahman. The absence of Mujib from that mausoleum is a striking symbol of Zia's intentions to downplay Mujib's role as a nationalist leader.

The entire opposition walked out of Parliament in December 1980 in protest against the introduction of Zia's Disturbed Areas Bill, which enables the government to assume extensive and autocratic powers. Under the provisions of the bill, even a police sub-inspector or constable can shoot a person or arrest him on "reasonable suspicion" in areas where the government simply declares that law and order has broken down. Government spokesmen argue that they need such powers to cope with an insurrection of Buddhist, Hindu and Christian tribals in the Chakma region of the Chittagong Hill Tracts in south eastern Bangladesh, where the Chakma rebels are demanding self-determination, preservation of their national identity, and an end to persecution. Opposition leaders (and some members of Zia's party as well) are fearful that the bill will be subject to misuse throughout Bangladesh. A number of Zia's followers have argued that it was poor political judgement on Zia's part to insist on the bill, since there were other emergency powers that could be and are already being used in the Chakma Hills.

Zia's government has made it clear that it will not tolerate rebel activities on its borders, and it has stepped up considerably a policy that began with the establishment of Pakistan, to colonize the tribal regions with Bengalis from the plains.[16]   Resettlement colonies have been established by the Bangladesh government in the sparsely-populated tribal regions, with migrant families from the plains being provided with a few acres of land, a period of free rations, and a small amount of cash.   The Bengali population in the Chittagong Hill Tracts (the total population of the district is only a few hundred thousand) went from 9 per cent in 1951 to 11.6 per cent in 1974, but it has since skyrocketed to 27.5 per cent under Ziaur Rahman.

At current rates of settlement, Bengalis will easily gain a majority in the Chittagong Hills district in the next decade.   Hindus are understandably concerned because the vast bulk of the settlers going into the Hills are Muslims.   Moreover, government settlement activities have not been carried out with much feeling for the sensitivities, rights and property of the tribals, nor have government troops hesitated to put down insurgents with gruesome repression. One Hindu expressed her fears as follows: "If Zia's government can so ruthlessly and systematically move in on the tribal population today, what is to prevent them from doing the same to Hindus tomorrow?"

Because of the possibility that communal tensions in Bangladesh might someday result in a massive influx of Hindu refugees to India, as happened in 1971, and because of the present migration of Bangladeshis into Assam and northeastern India, the Indian government is deeply concerned with Bangladesh's policies towards its minorities.   The Chinese are also involved with tribals in north-eastern India and Bangladesh, if only because they are heavily supporting tribal groups in Burma who occasionally spill over into these areas.[17]

16.   Figures are from official Bangladesh statistics as quoted in Urmula Phadnis, "Woes of Tribals in Bangladesh," *Times of India* (Bombay), January 5, 1981.   An excellent analysis of the tribal agitation appears in Kazi Montu, "Tribal Insurgency in Chittagong Hill Tracts," *Economic amd Political Weekly* (Bombay), XV:36 (September 6, 1980), pp. 1510–1512.   See also B.K. Joshi, "Terror Campaign in Chittagong," *Times of India* (Bombay), December 17, 1980 and Manabendra Narayan Larma, "Genocide in Chittagong Hill Tracts," *Amrita Bazaar Patrika* (Calcutta), September 19, 1980.

17.   For a recent account of Chinese activities in Burma and Bangladesh see Rahul Burman, "Insurgency in Burma," *Indian Express* (New Delhi), December 9, 1980.   Interesting background is provided by Shamsuddin Ahmed, *Glimpses into the History of the Burmese and Chinese Muslims* (1936–1978) (Chittagong: Begum Sakina Shamsuddin Ahmed, 1978).

But the cordiality of Zia's relationships with China is indicated by the fact that Beijing is by far the largest supplier of arms and ammunition to Bangladesh.

Zia has tried to contain any Hindu extremist attitudes or movements that might develop against him—in India or Bangladesh—by his tolerant attitude towards Hindus domestically, and by steering a middle course between India and Pakistan in international affairs. He has taken a very tough bargaining position with Pakistan on the two issues still outstanding in Bangladesh-Pakistan relations: 1) the sharing of assets and liabilities from the old united Pakistan days; and 2) the unwillingness of Pakistan to repatriate approximately 300,000 non-Bengali Muslims from Bangladesh (the so-called "Biharis") who desperately want to leave Bangladesh and settle in Pakistan. Differences between Bangladesh and Pakistan also became evident in August 1980, when Ziaur Rahman proposed the establishment of a regional organization for economic cooperation in South Asia—it would have included India, Pakistan, Sri Lanka, Bangladesh, Nepal and Bhutan—but Pakistan opposed the move on grounds that India would dominate the organization.

In international affairs, Zia refers to Bangladesh as non-aligned, but he does not link non-alignment to Bangladeshi nationalism, as Nehru and Indira Gandhi have done in the case of Indian nationalism.[18] Zia says that "communism is not our way," but he will not identify totally with capitalism either. He would like to find a new identity for Bangladesh in international affairs—as "a bridge to Southeast Asia" or as a "bridge to Islam in Asia," for example —but he admits that he has not been entirely successful in promoting this image. For the present, he continues to search for a new international symbolism for Bangladesh and continues to be non-aligned, even though, he insists, non-alignment is not what makes Bangladesh distinctive and different.

CONCLUSIONS

Ziaur Rahman is an historic figure in Bangladesh, in part because he has established the nation's first effective government, but

18. Bangladesh's international relationships are traced out in Marcus Franda and Ataur Rahman, "Dacca, Delhi and the Powers," in *The Moscow-Beifing-Washington Triangle: Security Implications for Asian States*, ed. Raju G.C. Thomas (Ithaca: Cornell University Press, 1982).

primarily because of his efforts to build institutions that can carry forward a new concept of Bangladeshi nationalism. Like a lot of military men, Ziaur Rahman has taken a great interest in building things. He has created new village institutions and a new political party; reformed the bureaucracy, the military and the police; built parks, city squares, a new Parliament complex, and a huge new international airport; he has widened boulevards and repaved roads, dug canals, and contracted for nuclear power plants and oil rigs. With an eye to establishing visible symbols of Bangladeshi nationalism, Zia is constructing a massive mausoleum, which will be dedicated to H.S. Suhrawardy, Khawaja Nazimuddin, and A.K. Fazlul Haque—three great leaders of Bangladesh's past.

There is a lot of pipe-dream in what Zia is doing, and many fundamental problems as well. Perhaps the most that can be said is that he is grasping for something important as he tries to work out what Bangladeshi nationalism can be. But major questions remain unanswered. Is it really possible that flamboyant but still rather routine development programs—like population control, canal digging and literacy campaigns—might form the basis of a nationalism strong enough for Bangladesh to stand up to India and achieve a degree of self-reliance? Are Zia's Village Defence Parties aimed solely at development activities, or are they designed to provide Zia with storm troopers in the rural areas? To what extent might they be used as an ultimate reserve force against India in military or para-military campaigns? How does Zia expect to bring along with him the sizable portion of the Bangladesh population that still has enormous respect for Sheikh Mujibur Rahman—"the father of the nation"—when Zia refuses to mention Mujib's name in public and indirectly accuses Mujib's party of armed conspiracies?

Perhaps the greatest obstacle to building Bangladeshi nationalism is that Bangladesh is a country that cannot stand on its own feet. Almost everyone—including every major leader in the opposition —agrees that Bangladesh cannot get rid of foreign aid. If only for this reason, Ziaur Rahman has to evolve a nationalism that includes a great deal of internationalism and is not directed too aggressively at India: he is too vulnerable to do otherwise; a withdrawal or cutback of Western aid would be economically disastrous; India would pay an enormous price but it could topple governments in Bangladesh if it was determined. For all of these reasons, and more, Bangladeshi nationalism has to be a balanced nationalism. It cannot be xenophobic.

A lot of Zia's formulations are directed at international development agencies and the Arabs. He tries to satisfy foreigners that Bangladesh is doing something. In that sense, his Bangladeshi nationalism is a compromise with nationalism as many others conceive of it. It contrasts particularly with populism and the populist rhetoric of Marxist theoreticians.

Perhaps more important, however, are the aspirations behind Zia's nationalism, rather than the inability to immediately realize them. Zia wants his people to feel strongly and emotionally that they are Bangladeshis. He wants people to be enthusiastic about building up the country. He wants them to be vigilant and prepared to resist, militarily if necessary, pressures from outside. He wants people to have confidence that they can grow things themselves and do things themselves, without relying on foreigners. He wants them to have pride in their religion, and to have no problems with minority communities. None of these things are yet there, nor are they likely to be there in Zia's lifetime. But Zia's aspirations could well be the nascent beginnings of a set of ideals which will eventually guide Bangladesh, as a nation, into the future.

FOURTEEN

THE DEATH OF
ZIAUR RAHMAN (1982)

Ziaur Rahman's violent death on May 30, 1981 was the height of tragedy, in part because of its seeming inevitability—almost predictability—in part because it dramatized the many ironies of Zia's life and political career. He was the fourth President of Bangladesh and the third Bangladesh ruler to die in a hail of gunfire (the other two were Sheikh Mujibur Rahman, the "Father of the Nation" who was killed in August 1975, and Major-General Khaled Musharraf, mastermind of a coup that kept him in power—as a de facto military ruler rather than President—for 3 days in November 1975). Zia had been in power in Bangladesh for $5\frac{1}{2}$ years, during which time, by his own admission, 406 Bangladesh military officers were executed at his orders. And yet he was killed by a General and a group of young officers whom he had refused to discipline despite persistent recommendations from senior military advisors that the dissident officers be disciplined or even retired. Zia was most frequently criticized by his opponents for being brutal, ruthless, cold and authoritarian, but his death was intimately related to a self-imposed relaxation of the security apparatus around him and to an almost naive belief in his powers of persuasion. In the vast majority of the new nations of Asia and Africa leaders become more autocratic and less accessible the longer their regimes last. The great difference, the great drama, the great tragedy of Ziaur Rahman was that his own regime was cut short at the zenith of his personal physical and political powers precisely because he was moving significantly towards civilianization and democratization.

Death came instantaneously. Zia left Dacca, the capital of Bangladesh, at 9 A.M. on Friday the 29th and flew to the southern port city of Chittagong on Air Force One, a Fokker F-27 gifted to Bangladesh by the Dutch government. His trip had been planned and had taken shape during the previous few days. He was originally supposed to come back to Dacca on the same day, as was his usual practice, but decided instead to stay overnight in order to meet more party leaders and perhaps to convince a recalcitrant General to accept a transfer. Since most of his meetings were downtown, Zia had decided to spend the night in Chittagong Circuit House, a two-storey rambling Victorian structure located on a hill in the heart of the city. Zia had stayed in Circuit House many times before, whenever he was meeting politicians. His reasoning was that it was inappropriate for army men to meet him outside the cantonment or for politicians to meet him in the cantonment.

During the day of the 29th, the President met some politicos and civic leaders, talked to his wife in Dacca by telephone, said his prayers late at night, did some paperwork, and went to bed at 2.00 A.M. A little less than two hours later—at 3.55 A.M.—he was awakened by the sounds of shelling and gunfire, got up, yelled for his aides, opened the door of his suite (No. 4), either to see what was happening or to fight his attackers, and walked into a sheet of submachinegun bullets that knocked out his right eye and almost cut him in two. Witnesses who saw him after the shooting was over say that his body was crumpled, head on toes, in a pool of blood.

The great puzzle surrounding Ziaur Rahman's death was how he managed to get himself stuck in Chittagong without sufficient security to protect him from army officers who had been increasingly hostile over the previous year. Zia had taken only 15 personal bodyguards with him to Chittagong; neither these people nor a few dozen policemen guarding Circuit House were armed with anything more sophisticated than common pistols or rifles. Most of Zia's security and intelligence officers had been cautioning him for months to be more careful, but Zia, who had been trained in intelligence by the Pakistan army, seemed to prefer less and less security as his regime wore on. Foreign correspondents, diplomats and government officials were seldom if ever checked when they entered Zia's home, office, airport lounge or aircraft; the President traveled to the most remote villages by helicopter, with only one other helicopter as escort and with only two or three bodyguards accompanying him.[1] Once in the villages on these day-long trips,

---

1. A description of the casual security that characterized Zia's encounters

Zia would charge out into the crowds, Kennedy-style, much to the chagrin of local police officers, whose men assigned to guard him were often armed only with bamboo-sticks (*lathis*) and perhaps a few cannisters of tear gas.

Many of the top brass in the Bangladesh army saw the relaxation of security around Zia as part of a dramatic attempt on the President's part to become a truly civilian politician. After Zia came to power in November 1975 he governed as a General through a rather severe Martial Law Administration for 18 months and then began to move toward civilian rule by assuming the title of President in April 1977. During this period the security around Zia was formidable and two major coup attempts against him—in June 1976 and September/October 1977—were brutally suppressed. Continual dissension within the army convinced Zia that he needed a powerful civilian political base if he were to govern effectively, but, perhaps more important, he began to enjoy immensely the give-and-take of Bangladesh politics once he decided to become a civilian leader. In June 1978 he was elected President for a five-year term and in February 1979 his new political party (the Bangladesh National Party, or BNP) secured 206 of 300 seats in Parliament with 41.2 per cent of the popular vote. After his "civilianization," Zia continued to live in a rented home in the Dacca Military Cantonment, where he had resided since 1972, but he stopped wearing his military uniform in public and insisted on being called "President Zia" rather than "General Zia."

A number of Military leaders in Bangladesh were wary of Zia's attempts to build a political base independent of the military. They tended to denigrate the President's frequent trips to the country-side, his faith in highly participatry programs like canal digging, and his attention to the development of new village governments (Gram Sarkars). Local Units of the BNP were distrusted by army men and were frequently singled out as "nests of corruption." On May 20th, ten days before Zia went to Chittagong, several Major-Generals in the army met with Zia in Dacca and criticized him severely for "over-democratizing" the political system. They were especially critical of Zia's economic policies, which had begun to favor the rural sector and pinch the urban middle-class, including

---

with newsmen and diplomats appears in Chanchal Sarkar, "Zia: Journey on Razor's Edge," *Hindustan Times* (New Delhi), June 2, 1981.

the military and the bureaucracy.[2] They argued that inflation and the law and order situation were both careening out of control, that Zia had been so concerned with his international image that he had neglected domestic politics, that there was rampant corruption within the BNP, and that Zia had not been strong enough in his dealings with India. They criticized the President for trying, in the words of one General, to "play politics too much," or, in the words of another, for "being too clever in balancing off all the political factions." The overwhelming demand of the military leaders at this May 20th meeting was for a re-imposition of martial law, to be accompanied by press censorship, restrictions on political activities, and denial of some judicial rights.

GENERAL MANZOOR

The most vocal and outspoken person at the May 20th meeting was Major-General Mohammad Abul Manzoor, Commander of a Division in Chittagong, who was reported to have pounded on the table and shouted at Zia during the course of the discussion. The other officers present did not necessarily support Manzoor, but their sullenness and milder expressions of discontent made it clear to everyone that they were unhappy with the directions in which Zia was leading the country. Manzoor flew back to Chittagong after the May 23rd meeting and apparently started planning the attempted coup that cost Zia his life. Some reporters speculate that Manzoor might have believed that the May 20th meeting had sealed "an unwritten covenant between him and the rest of the army" were he to attempt a coup.[3] The gossip mills in Dacca had spread rumors—even before Zia's death—that Manzoor and others were planning to lead a coup in July or August 1981, prompting other reporters to speculate that Manzoor and his associates in Chittagong had simply hastened their plans once they found the President unguarded in their territory and felt threatened by his

2. For a discussion of these policies see Marcus Franda, "Food Policy and Politics in Bangladesh," *India Quarterly*, XXXVII:2 (April–June 1981), pp. 165–193.

3. Gautam Adhikari, "Zia and Manzur: Were Two Killed with One Stone?" *The Hindu* (Madras), June 20, 1981.

movements against them.[4]

Were it not for the gross inaccuracies and pure fabrication found in most of the reporting of the coup attempt—especially in the Indian press—the ordinary citizen might have been in a better position to sort fact from fiction. As it is, there has been so much misreporting of the event that it would take years of diligent investigative work and full cooperation from the Bangladesh government for a historian to sort out what precisely happened on the morning of May 30th. What follows is a somewhat cautious account, based on information that has been corroborated from a number of sources representing many different shades of partisan opinion and observation.

Rivalry between Manzoor and Zia, like most cases of factional conflict in South Asia, had a long past. Manzoor was born on January 24, 1940—four years after Zia—in Krishnanagar, West Bengal, to a relatively poor family originally from Noakhali district. His father was a clerk and his mother died at an early age. Manzoor received an Intermediate degree from the Air Force Cadet College at Sarghoda in West Pakistan and attended Dacca University for a year before joining the military. He distinguished himself as a brilliant student at the Pakistan Military Academy, attended the Defence Service Staff College in Canada, and subsequently built a reputation as a bright and able officer after his return to Pakistan. During the liberation war in 1971, Manzoor was one of the few Bangladeshi officers to escape from West Pakistan, making a dramatic entry into India in the Rajasthan desert. He soon found himself as one of 8 Sector Commanders (Ziaur Rahman was another) fighting the Pakistanis in Bangladesh.

Manzoor, like Zia, had something of a falling out with Sheikh Mujibur Rahman after independence, with the result that Manzoor was sent by Mujib to New Delhi as military attache in the Bangladesh High Commission in 1973. Ziaur Rahman rescued Manzoor from that ignominious exile when he came to power in 1975 by bringing Manzoor back to Dacca as Chief of the General Staff, relying on him as one of his leading Generals while promoting him rapidly up the ladder. Manzoor at first cooperated fully with Zia and in fact saved Zia's regime and life by helping to put down

---

4. Manash Ghosh, "Manzoor Was a Victim, Not the Villain," *The Statesman* (Calcutta), June 17, 1981.

an attempted coup on October 2, 1977.[5] Manzoor's role in quashing that coup attempt intensified his quest to become Chief of Staff, the top spot in the army, which Zia gave to Lieutenant-General H.M. Ershad after Zia became a civilian Commander-in-Chief and President in April 1977. To be sure, Ershad was older and had more seniority than Manzoor (Ershad was born on February 1, 1930 and was commissioned in 1952; Manzoor was the youngest General in the Bangladesh army and was commissioned only in 1960), but Manzoor saw Ershad as an unimaginative desk-bound General who had blotted his copybook by remaining loyal to the Pakistan army in 1971.

Zia's decision to name Ershad over Manzoor as Chief of Staff reflected his overall strategy for building a disciplined army, which placed a heavy reliance on repatriated officers and *jawans* (soldiers) from Pakistan plus new recruits who had not fought in the liberation war. At the time of Zia's death only 3 of the top 50 Major-Generals and Brigadiers in the Bangladesh army were men who had fought for Bangladesh in 1971; of these three, only Manzoor had troops under his command. The other "freedom-fighters" were Major-General Mir Shaukat Ali, who had previously been stripped of his command by Zia and was (at the time of Zia's death) Principal Staff Officer to the President, and Major-General Moin Chowdhury. Of the 11 men who had served at various times as Sector Commanders during the liberation war, none are now in the Bangladesh army. Most of them—like Manzoor and Zia—are dead, having been executed or killed in coup attempts; the others, including Shaukat Ali, have been retired from the military.

With the death of Manzoor and a wave of executions and forced retirements following Court Martial proceedings against Manzoor's surviving co-conspirators, the percentage of "freedom-fighters" in the Bangladesh army will almost certainly fall below 10 per cent. At the time of Zia's death the percentage was estimated at 15 per cent, with another 25 per cent being *jawans* repatriated from Pakistan after 1971 and 60 per cent new recruits of the later 1970s. Zia and other senior officers in the Bangladesh army felt strongly that the repatriates and new recruits were

5. The incident is detailed in Ziullr Rahman Khan, *Leadership in the Least Developed Country: Bangladesh*, Unpublished Manuscript scheduled for publication in 1982, p. 214.

much better and more disciplined soldiers than the freedom-fighters, primarily because their training had been more thorough and the circumstances of their promotions within the army less politicized. Most of the freedom-fighters were heady with the heroism of the liberation war, trained hastily in guerrilla warfare in India during the 1971 fracas, and then quickly promoted by Sheikh Mujibur Rahman in order to give them seniority over the Pakistan repatriates. Some of the freedom-fighters, and especially the unit known as the Rakhi Bahini (which was formed specifically to protect Mujib and his government), were little more than extensions of political parties.

As Talukder Maniruzzaman has explained it, the freedom-fighters in the Bangladesh army were mostly students who joined the guerrilla forces in 1971 or they were deserters from Pakistan's conventional army who were called upon to learn guerrilla warfare in 1971.[6] Participation in guerrilla warfare, side-by-side with political activists and politically conscious students, served to radicalize the freedom fighters, to the point where they demanded a restructuring of the armed forces into what they called a "democratic and productive" army after the liberation war was over. They also demanded their own advancement over those older military officers who had stayed on in Pakistan, and did not hesitate to take up arms in guerrilla style operations against their commanding officers, or even against the head-of-state. Maniruzzaman estimates that there had been 19 army attempts to seize power in Bangladesh prior to the 1981 Chittagong *putsch*, almost all of them led by participants in the 1971 guerrilla war.

Zia did make some attempts to integrate the freedom fighters into the Bangladesh military, but for the most part he conceived of himself as being "ruthless" towards anyone in the army who was guilty of indiscipline. He expanded the army from 5 divisions when he took over in 1975 to 8 when he was killed in 1981 (there are two divisions in Dacca, two in Chittagong and the Chittagong Hill Tracts, and one each in Rangpur, Bogra, Comilla and Jessore), with the idea that this would bring in so many new

6. Talukder Maniruzzaman, "Ziaur Rahman and Bangladesh," in *Group Interests and Political Changes: Studies of Pakistan and Bangladesh* (New Delhi: South Asian Publishers, 1982).

recruits that the freedom fighters would be greatly outnumbered. When Colonel Abu Taher, a leading freedom fighter, joined a political party and began to call for a revolution against Zia's government in 1976, Zia had Taher arrested, tried, and hanged in the jails, despite the fact that Taher had been one of Zia's best friends, had been a Sector Commander in 1971, and had played a major role in staging the coup that brought Zia to power. Zia later—in 1977—had hundreds of officers and politicians tried and executed for plotting against the government within the army. Almost every one of those executed came from among the freedom fighters.

In this atmosphere, it is all the more surprising that Zia failed to discipline Manzoor, right up until the very end. Manzoor's contempt for Ershad and his criticisms of Zia were widely known. Like Taher, Manzoor conceived of himself as a socialist, who wanted less corruption, less reliance on international development aid, and fewer international ties than Zia was willing to countenance or promote. Manzoor, like Taher, has often been associated in press reports with a pro-Chinese position, but it might be fairer to say that both Manzoor and Taher were more anti-Indian, anti-Russian and anti-American than they were pro-Chinese. Taher was far more intimately involved in politics than Manzoor, since he was a member and leader of an underground unit of the *Jatio Samajtantrik Dal* (JSD), a Marxist-left group that at one time advocated an armed revolution to be led by the *jawans*. Manzoor was reported to have met JSD leaders on occasion—against the wishes of other military officers, including Zia—and he was also reportedly a friend of Mohammad Toaha, the Bangladesh politician who is probably closest to the Chinese. But there is no evidence that Manzoor ever acted on behalf of either a political party or a foreign power.

While Zia had preferred Ershad to Manzoor because Ershad was loyal, believed in a constitutional process and had the confidence of the repatriate Generals, it was also widely assumed that Manzoor was a bit too independent, arrogant, ambitious and revolutionary to warrant Zia's complete trust. Moreover, once Zia had opted for Ershad over Manzoor, relations between Zia and Manzoor steadily deteriorated. In 1978 Zia transferred Manzoor to Chittagong, presumably to get him out of the center of power in Dacca; in 1980 Zia told Manzoor he was being transferred to Bogra. When Manzoor refused to move to Bogra, Zia tried to strip him of his command and transfer him to Dacca as a Principal Staff Officer, but Manzoor simply tore up this transfer order and refused to budge. Throughout early 1981 Zia then tried to negotiate with Manzoor by offering him an ambassadorship in any West European nation; Manzoor responded with intensified criticism of Zia's regime. On the morning of May 27th, two days before he flew off to Chittagong, Zia had issued orders to Manzoor to report as Commandant of the Military Staff College in Dacca "with effect from June 1." Unlike previous orders, this one had specified a date and copies of it were sent around to all other army units on May 29th. At last it appeared that Zia had decided to discipline Manzoor.

But then Zia went down to Chittagong with inadequate security and was killed by officers in the command of Manzoor. Senior Bangladesh officers now claim that they had warned Zia not to go to Chittagong at all, but instead to simply have Manzoor arrested and brought back to Dacca for a military trial. The Defence Forces Intelligence (DFI) had been irked for some time because Zia had been gradually shifting his security affairs to the non-military National Security Intelligence (NSI) and the Special Branch of the Home Ministry. NSI was in charge of the President's trip to Chittagong after Zia himself sent Major-General Mahabbatjan Chowdhury, the Chief of DFI, back to Dacca on the evening of the 29th. A number of BNP leaders had told Zia during the previous week that there was no need for him to travel to Chittagong on party business, since the party dispute that he was going to patch up had its roots in a personality clash between Deputy Prime Minister Jamaluddin Ahmed and Deputy Speaker Sultan Ahmed Chowdhury, both of whom were in Dacca.

Zia is reported to have told some Generals that he did not fear a coup from Manzoor because Manzoor "could not make it stick" and "would have everything to lose." In the end, Zia was right on both counts, but that did not prevent younger officers in Manzoor's command from killing the President. One of Zia's relatives has suggested that Zia was so close to Manzoor that he felt he could persuade him to move to Dacca on a personal basis, a sentiment supported by the disbelief exhibited when Zia's widow and children were told that Manzoor (whom the children called "uncle") was somehow responsible for Zia's death. Two of the party leaders who went with Zia to Chittagong and survived the killings on the morning of the 30th suggest that Zia had adopted a somewhat fatalistic attitude towards potential assassins, reasoning that he could be an effective civilian President only if he took risks with his own life. Intelligence people estimate that they had uncovered more than two dozen genuine attempts on Zia's life during the course of his five years in power, including one in Chittagong just 20 days previous to the assassination when explosives were found in a switch that Zia was to throw open while inaugurating a dry dock (the inauguration was postponed when the explosives were discovered; the dry dock was formally opened by Jamaluddin Ahmed after Zia's death).

Whatever the reasons for Zia's inadequate security, the main events of May 29th and 30th are fairly well-established. Zia arrived in Chittagong at 10.10 A. M., held meetings with BNP leaders throughout the day, and addressed a group of civic leaders. Manzoor had been offended because Zia had told him that it was not necessary for anyone from the cantonment to meet him at the airport. There were numerous reports that Zia and Manzoor met on the 29th—either in the cantonment or at Circuit House—but witnesses present in Chittagong recall no such meeting. While Zia may have had plans to meet Manzoor on the 30th, his ostensible purpose for going to Chittagong was to iron out a political party dispute. He had not even told many of his top security people that he had issued orders transferring Manzoor to Dacca.

Manzoor may have been planning a coup for some time, but it seems more likely that he and a group of young officers had put the assassination effort together within the space of a few days. The people who came to kill Zia, by all accounts, were 20 officers (Brigadiers, Colonels, Majors, Captains and one Lieutenant); Manzoor was not among them. They arrived in the midst of a torrential downpour that had started shortly after midnight, in two vehicles (a van and a jeep), without supporting soldiers. Zia's security offered little resistance. Fifteen of the attackers shelled the Circuit House from a distance with two rockets that hit below Zia's room, engulfing that portion of the building in smoke, while the other five machine-gunned their way up to the second floor and killed the President. Forty or fifty armed police on the grounds of the Circuit House had taken shelter from the rain by the time the military officers arrived. A few reacted quickly to the shelling and offered immediate resistance to the attackers; the others were reportedly unsure whether the army jeep coming up the driveway contained soldiers who were trying to help or kill the President. Zia exposed himself to his attackers by leaving his room to personally confront them. Had he remained in his suite or locked himself in his bathroom, he might have given his bodyguards and the police the additional increment of time that would have been necessary to repel the attack. Some security people have speculated that Zia may have come out of his room to lead the attack because he had mistakenly thought that his attackers were still out on the driveway rather than on the stairs leading up to his suite. Most people close to Zia explain his actions as being his natural instincts, which were to charge headlong into a fight rather than run or hide from it.

Only two of Zia's bodyguards were reported to have resisted the attacking officers and two of the attackers were injured. Seven of the people in Circuit House—including three of Zia's bodyguards, two aides, an electrician and a telephone operator—were killed. On the grounds of Circuit House, one policeman was killed and 8 other policemen injured. An autopsy indicated that at least 21 and perhaps as many as 27 bullets entered Zia's body, primarily in his face and chest. Several other people in Zia's party were unharmed; no attempt was made to search out and kill anyone but Zia. The entire operation lasted less than 20 minutes.

CONSPIRACY THEORIES

In a country where theorizing about conspiracies is a national pasttime, there has been widespread speculation about the role of Manzoor and his younger officers in the coup attempt. Most of the evidence suggests that Manzoor was concerned that he would no longer be able to resist a transfer to Dacca, which meant that he, like Shaukat, would be stripped of his command. This would have been terribly humiliating for Manzoor, since he saw himself as deserving of Ershad's position and as a future President. His younger officers realized that they might be subjected to forced retirement from the military or some form of discipline if they lost the protection of Manzoor. They all knew that any hopes they might have had for staging a coup would be dissipated once Zia returned to Dacca. Disciplinary measures against junior officers had been prominent in military circles because more than a hundred officers had just been purged from the army in the month before

Zia's death. In addition, only a few days before Zia's trip to Chittagong, two army officers and a civilian had been sentenced to terms of up to 10 years rigorous imprisonment on charges of plotting the abortive coup of June 17, 1980. One of the officers involved in that coup attempt—Deedarul Alam—had become a fugitive and was ultimately arrested in Chittagong, where he was thought to have had connections with some of Manzoor's subordinates.

Manzoor must have expected support from military and civilian leaders in Dacca, as happened in 1975 when Sheikh Mujib was killed. But Zia was far more popular than Mujib at the time of his assassination, and Manzoor foolishly—madly—tried to stage a coup from a peripheral area like Chittagong without any semblance of a base in the capital city of Dacca. Unlike 1975, when most Awami League Ministers crossed over and supported the young majors who killed Mujib, Ershad and every other officer outside Chittagong responded to news of Zia's death by swearing allegiance to the Constitutional government in Dacca. Vice-President Abdus Sattar was dragged out of his bed at Combined Military Hospital in Dacca at 6 A.M. and taken straight to the President's palace (Bangabhawan), where he was sworn in as Acting President. Ershad and several Cabinet Ministers were present at the swearing-in ceremony; Prime Minister Shah Azizur Rahman was in Kushtia but returned to Dacca within a half-hour after receiving news of the assassination. The Cabinet assembled at 9 A.M. on the 30th, initiating the post-Zia phase of Bangladesh politics.

Within a few hours of Zia's death it was clear that the coup attempt was going to fail. If Manzoor and his men had any understanding with officers in the other cantonments, they never materialized. General Manzoor made only one radio broadcast in Chittagong during the 48 hours that the rebels controlled the port city and that was on the evening of May 31st, shortly before the coup attempt was abandoned. Most of the broadcasts from Chittagong Radio were made in the name of Manzoor, who was described as the head of a 7–member Revolutionary Council (*Biplabi Parishad*), but Manzoor never introduced himself as head of a new government. He pointedly described himself in his radio broadcast as GOC (General Office in Charge) of the Chittagong Division or as Commander of the 24th Division and suggested that the Revolutionary Council had "requested" him to speak. Speculation that Manzoor was not the man behind the coup attempt was encouraged by a 5-hour delay between the time Ziaur Rahman was killed and the announcement on Chittagong radio declaring a new government. Dacca Radio did not blame Manzoor until its noon broadcast on the 30th. Nowhere did Manzoor condone the murder of Zia or try to justify it, although in some broadcasts made in Manzoor's name the Revolutionary Council had called Zia "autocratic" and had invoked the ghost of Abu Taher.

When he appeared at a "cross-section" meeting of Chittagong bureaucrats, journalists, bank managers and police officials on the morning of May 31st, Manzoor was already a defeated man. A Chittagong journalist who attended the meeting described his appearance as follows:

The man was a bundle of nerves. He said he was committed to die. He raved and ranted against everything. He invoked Islam. The next moment he talked of secularism. He spoke against corruption and pointed fingers at the bank managers, describing them as the fountainhead of corruption. He said he had prohibited drinking, gambling and the flesh trade. He talked of socialism. In the same breath, he reposed his trust in Allah. As he wobbled out of the room, he looked like a stuffed soldier, already dead.[7]

Manzoor and 150 of his followers—including Manzoor's and other officers' wives and children—fled Chittagong around midnight on May 31/June 1st in six disparate groups that went in six different directions. Their exit had been prompted by the surrender to Dacca of a trusted platoon that Manzoor had dispatched towards Noakhali (the platoon simply said goodbye to the rebels over the radio and voluntarily gave itself up to the government). Manzoor and his group were arrested in the Fatekchari forest, 30 miles or so north of Chittagong, at around 9 A.M. on June 1st. When he was taken to the Fatekchari police station, Manzoor pleaded with his captors not to send him back to the cantonment but instead to imprison him in Chittagong central jail; he was especially anxious that the police tape-record his statement immediately. The police officer-in-charge apparently recorded Manzoor's lengthy statement,

7.   Quoted in Sumit Mitra, "An Ominous Void," *India Today* (New Delhi fortnightly), VI:12 (June 16-30, 1981), p. 31.

which has not been released to the public and may have been lost or destroyed. Manzoor and two of his officers were sent back to the cantonment in mid-afternoon. The police originally stated that they had returned Manzoor to the cantonment, where he and two of his officers were subsequently killed by vengeful army men. The official Bangladesh government version of Manzoor's death is that he was killed by angry mobs on the way to the cantonment.

Some conspiracy theories since Manzoor's death are based on speculation that a clack of repatriate Generals and politicians in Dacca may have set Manzoor up to kill Zia, leading Manzoor to believe they would support him once the deed was done.[8] By first encouraging Manzoor—and later abandoning him after he had carried out the assassination—they were able to get rid of the last three freedom-fighter Generals who stood in the way of the repatriates claiming power exclusively for themselves. This theory accounts for the lack of security around Zia as something designed by the conspirators. Zia's decision to stay the night in the extremely vulnerable Circuit House (it is located on a hill and has no place for cover) is similarly explained as being arranged by Zia's security men as part of the plot. The death of Manzoor before he could be put on trial and the disappearance of Manzoor's tape-recorded statement are viewed as the logical culmination of a scheme that was carried out with cold-blooded efficiency.

In a vain effort to put rumors at rest, the Bangladesh government named three tribunals to investigate Ziaur Rahman's assassination. One was a civilian Supreme Court Commission, headed by Justice Ruhul Islam and composed of a second Supreme Court Judge (A.T.M. Afzal) and a District and Sessions Judge from Khulna (Syed Serajuddin). The second was a Military Inquiry Tribunal, under Major-General Mizzamil Hussain. The third was a 7–man Field General Court Martial directed by Major-General Abdur Rahman. More than two dozen rebel officers were arrested and tried in Chittagong or Dacca; two others fled to the Chittagong Hill Tracts and are still being pursued by the Bangladesh army. The Bangladesh government did not arrest all of the officers named as co-conspirators by the Revolutionary Council, since in most

8. This theory is developed in detail in Jyoti Sen Gupta, *Bangladesh: In Blood and Tears* (New Delhi: Nayaprakash Publishers, 1981). Sen Gupta is a former Indian newspaper correspondent in Dacca who wrote this book on the basis of materials published in India and interviews conducted in India.

instances it was quite clear that the Council was simply appealing for national support by appointing officers or claiming the loyalties of army men in other cantonments. Shaukat Ali, who was named Acting Chief of Staff by the Revolutionary Council, was not arrested by the government in Dacca but was instead promoted, retired and sent to Egypt as Ambassador. Major-General Moin Chowdhury, the only remaining freedom fighter with the rank of General, retained his military rank but was sent as Ambassador to the Philippines.

There were hundreds of forced retirements from the army in the wake of the assassination. Twelve officers—including 10 who had been distinguished for gallantry in the liberation war—were convicted of being directly involved in the assassination and hanged on September 23, 1981. The government's own conspiracy theory is laid out in a five-part White Paper published in August 1981.[9] Aside from Manzoor and the Junior officers in Chittagong, the White Paper implicated retired Colonel Mahfuzzar Rahman, Zia's personal military secretary, who was arrested shortly after the coup attempt. "Mahfuz," as he was known, is alleged to have sent Zia's two closest bodyguards downstairs from Zia's room just prior to the attack on May 30th and to have later showed up in the Chittagong cantonment. The announcement of the death of Ziaur Rahman on Chittagong Radio was made in the name of "Mahfuz." Mahfuz and Lieutenant-Colonel Matiar Rahman, who was named in the White Paper as the most brutal of Zia's assassins, were among those officers hanged on September 23rd.

THE NEW POLITICS

The new government is headed by 75–year-old Abdus Sattar, who was appointed Vice-President by Ziaur Rahman in 1979, became the constitutional Acting President immediately after Zia's death, and was elected President in his own right on November 15, 1981. Sattar had been in the hospital, suffering from high blood pressure and diabetes, but he rallied remarkably on May 30th and quickly took control of the machinery of government. In his first speech as Acting President, Sattar paused to wipe away tears and then

9. The white Paper was reprinted in *The Bangladesh Observer*, (Dacca daily). August 5–9, 1981.

said of Zia, "He was a very dear thing. I loved him like a son. We must find out how and why this happened." Sattar promised that he would hold elections within the 180 days prescribed by the constitution and at first declared that he would not be a candidate. Within a few weeks, however, Sattar was coopted by the BNP as its compromise candidate when the party was threatened with a split between two factions that wanted different nominees. Sattar not only accepted the BNP nomination but helped put through a constitutional amendment that made him eligible to contest.

In the November election, Sattar received an impressive two-thirds of the vote (see Table 6) with 55 per cent of the eligible electorate casting ballots. The Awami League candidate, Kamal Hossain, a renowned lawyer and former Minister in the Cabinets of Sheikh Mujibur Rahman, turned out to be the only real challenger to Sattar and the BNP. All other party candidates forfeited their deposits because they received less than one-eighth of the vote. Dr. Hossain and the Awami League rejected the election results as a "farce" and charged the BNP with massive electoral fraud; most outside observers were chagrined at electoral procedures that made it possible for the government to rig the elections, even though the announced results seemed to reflect mass sentiments.[10] India's

Table 6. *Presidential Election Results, November 1981*

Candidate	Party	Votes Received	% Votes
Abdus Sattar	BNP	14,285,621	66.0%
Kamal Hossain	Awami League	5,690,758	26.3%
Maulana Hafizji Huzur	Independent	387,215	1.8%
M.A.G. Osmany	Citizen's Committee	302,003	1.4%
M.A. Jalil	JSD	249,340	1.2%
Muzaffar Ahmed	NAP (Pro-Moscow)	224,766	1.0%
Others	Others	465,324	2.3%
	Totals	21,605,027	100.0%

SOURCE: Indian newspapers, November 16–18, 1981.

10. See "A Country Near the Bottom of the Barrel, "*The Economist* (London), Vol. 281, No. 7212 (November 21, 1981), pp. 51–52.

highly respected news analyst Ajit Bhattacharjea echoed the arguments of most editorials, in India and elsewhere, when he said that Kamal Hossain "would be well-advised to accept Mr. Sattar's advice to promote the stability and integrity of Bangladesh by functioning as the leader of a constitutional opposition party."[11]

While Zia was alive, Sattar was generally viewed as a figurehead Vice-President who posed no threat whatsoever to the President. Originally from Birbhum district in West Bengal (now in India) Sattar had been trained as a lawyer and had been associated with A.K. Fazlul Haque, H.S. Suhrawardy and other great Muslim politicians of Bengal during the nationalist movement against the British. Sattar practiced law before the Alipore High Court in Calcutta prior to the partition of India, served for a brief time as Home Minister in one of the many Pakistan governments of the mid-1950s, became a High Court Judge in Dacca in the late 1950s and was eventually appointed to the Supreme Court by Ayub Khan. He resigned from the Supreme Court to become Yahya Khan's Chief Election Commissioner in 1969 and presided over the momentous 1970 elections that resulted in a massive mandate for Sheikh Mujibur Rahman and the Awami League. Mujib appointed Sattar to a number of Commissions in the early 1970s and President A.S.M. Sayem appointed him as a Special Presidential Assistant in 1975. Sattar continued as a Presidential Assistant under Ziaur Rahman until he was appointed Vice-President in 1979.

As Vice-President, Sattar saw an incredible number of people every day, despite his ill health. He conceived of his job as taking pressure off the President by receiving people who did not necessarily need to spend time with the President but who had to be heard or evaluated. Zia trusted Sattar's political judgement, admired his sharp legal mind, and respected his cool-headed, shrewd approach to problem-solving. Perhaps Sattar's greatest strength is his reputation as a pious Muslim who is secular-minded. He is best known as a good listener and raconteur, capable of establishing rapport with people across religions and ideologies. From the time that Sattar and Ziaur Rahman started working intimately together in 1975 Sattar conceived of Zia as a son who was in need of

---

11. Ajit Bhattacharjea, "Bangladesh Election and After," *Indian Express* (New Delhi daily), November 21, 1981, p. 6.

a gentle political education; Zia reciprocated that sentiment by frequently speaking of Sattar as a father-figure.

Were it not for his advanced age and poor health, Sattar might be considered an ideal successor to Ziaur Rahman. Zia himself had not named nor provided for a successor; the BNP party constitution had not even set down a procedure by which a new party leader might be chosen. In the Bangladesh Constitution, which was originally drafted by Mujib in 1972 and amended by Zia in 1977, the Vice-President becomes Acting President at the death of the President and is required by law to hold new Presidential elections within 6 months. Strangely enough, according to the constitution, the Acting President was not allowed to contest those elections because his office could be interpreted in another constitutional clause as "an office of profit." Consternation about the "office of profit" clause has been expressed by almost everyone who has read it after Zia's death (and apparently very few had read it carefully prior to Zia's death) since the constitution explicitly stated that the clause did not apply to the Prime Minister and Members of Parliament but was binding on everyone else, including, presumably, an incumbent President, Vice-President or Acting President. If this clause had been allowed to remain in the constitution, Zia himself would not have been eligible for re-election (had he lived) without first resigning his Presidency.

Zia's closest associates have stated that the anomalies of the "office of profit" clause had been pointed out to Zia while he was alive and that he had chosen not to pursue a constitutional amendment to change it. Some say that Zia opted for this course because he did not want to make his second term a political issue until it became necessary; others suggest that Zia may have been thinking of stepping down from the Presidency to stage a dramatic election campaign, limiting himself to one term in the spirit of Mexico's politics, or changing the political system entirely. In any event, Sattar's government moved quickly to amend the constitution after the BNP had decided that Sattar should be its nominee. The new 6th amendment, which was passed in parliament on July 8, 1981, enables an incumbent President, Acting President or Vice-President to contest elections without resigning their "office of profit."

Most of the opposition parties boycotted the Parliamentary session in which the 6th amendment was passed, contending that the amendment had been drafted solely to suit the needs of the ruling party. The four major opposition groups—led respectively by the Awami League of Mujib's daughter, Hasina Wajed, the Democratic League of ex-President Khondakar Mushtaque Ahmed, the JSD of M.A. Jalil and the pro-Moscow National Awami Party (NAP) of Professor Muzaffar Ahmed—would have preferred a constitutional amendment re-establishing a Parliamentary rather than a Presidential system, but none of the opposition parties except the Awami League had many votes in Parliament and they were incapable of uniting against the BNP. Leaders of many parties expressed serious doubts that free and fair elections would be possible with the BNP in control of the electoral machinery.[12] Several of them, including the Awami League, set down conditions for their participation in the elections, which included: 1) withdrawal of the emergency that had been declared after Zia's death; 2) release of all political prisoners; 3) an end to political harassment; 4) the shifting of the election date from September to November; 5) revision of the electoral rolls on the basis of the 1981 census: 6) freedom of the press and equal access by all candidates to the media; and 7) regulations prohibiting the government from using official transport or administrative machinery for electioneering.

Sattar surprised most of the opposition parties by withdrawing the emergency, releasing large numbers of political prisoners, shifting the election date from September to November, and revising electoral rolls, all before the elections took place. He was clearly advantaged during the election campaign because he was the incumbent, but the obvious reason for his overwhelming victory was his identification with Ziaur Rahman. Zia had gained considerable popularity throughout the country as a result of his travels to thousands of villages; his personal reputation was enhanced by his martyrdom, which occurred at a point when things had started to go sour but had not yet deteriorated. While the BNP is not all that well-established in the country-side and is divided into a number of warring factions, it is the party in power and its members are anxious to rally behind a popular and dynamic leader. For the time being at least, Sattar has demonstrated remarkable vigor and resolve in filling the shoes of the deceased President.

12. The opposition boycott and doubts about the fairness of the 1981 elections are explained in Mainul Hosein, "A Custom-Tailored Constitution," *The New Nation* (Dacca Weekly), IV:51 (July 12, 1981), pp. 1, 8.

In the 1981 elections, one of Sattar's most formidable potential opponents, Mushtaque Ahmed, was declared ineligible because he had served a 3-1/2 year jail sentence after a 1976 conviction on charges of corruption.[13] Mushtaque contended that he was exempt from a constitutional clause barring anyone convicted of "crimes of moral turpitude" contesting for the Presidency for 5 years after the end of the jail sentence, since he had been convicted by a Martial Law court that, he claimed, had no authority to try an ex-President. Just before the election campaign, however, the Dacca High Court decided against Mushtaque, with the result that he was forced to sit out the election. Most of his followers presumably voted for Abdus Sattar.

The other towering opposition leader who might have run well against Sattar is Hasina Wajed, Mujib's daughter, who escaped death in 1975 when she was in Germany with her physicist husband on the day of the assassination of Mujib and most of his family. Amidst much confusion about her age (she claimed to be 35-years-old, the constitutional minimum, on September 28, 1981, but this was disputed by the BNP), the Awami League decided against Hasina as a presidential candidate. Although she proved herself an extremely capable campaigner, she had several political liabilities in 1981. She had been living in India for more than 5 years prior to her return to Bangladesh in May 1981, and this exile, particularly when coupled with some of her public statements and her father's legacies, identified her with an unreserved pro-Indian position. This was reflected in 1981 campaign posters depicting her as "Indira Wajed."

The Awami League party, which Hasina now heads, is seriously divided into pro- and anti-Moscow factions, with Hasina being the only glue holding them together. She was elected president of the Awami League on February 16, 1981 and chose to hold her first meetings with her party people in New Delhi rather than Dacca. When she did finally return to Dacca—on May 17, 1981—she was immediately embarassed by her unwillingness to condemn outright India's claims to the newly-formed island in the Bay of Bengal that the Bangladeshis call South Talapatty (it is known as New Moore Island in New Delhi and Purbasha in Calcutta), claimed by both Bangladesh and India. Bangladeshis were reminded of the corrup-

13. Mushtaque's political career is traced out in detail in Zillur Rahman Khan, op. cit., pp. 190 ff.

tion and violence of the Awami League years when Mujib's house and 2.7 million Taka worth of currency notes and jewellery found in it were handed over to Hasina by the Bangladesh government shortly after her return to Dacca. At the same time, government officials pointedly refused to surrender to Hasina several dozen unlicensed firearms and weapons found in Mujib's house at the time of his assassination.

Hasina's great strengths are her symbolic importance as the daughter of Mujib, whose memory still evokes positive emotions among many Bangladeshis, and the network of local Awami League units that continue to exhibit strength in the countryside. The AL is not as disciplined or as well-organized as the Jamaat-i-Islami, the principal fundamentalist Islamic party in Bangladesh, but the AL is far more broadly-based and considerably larger than the Jamaat. Moreover, the Jamaat has not contested the last two Presidential elections in Bangladesh. Hasina's return to Dacca in May 1981 demonstrated the strength of the Awami League when the party turned out 3,000 truckloads of people to meet her, in a driving rain, on one of the darkest and stormiest days of the year. Since then, Hasina has attracted large crowds wherever she has appeared. She elicited tears from the eyes of most Bengalis by visiting her father's grave, speaking eloquently of her mother, and vowing to take revenge against the killers of her family. The determination of the government to prevent her from becoming a martyr was demonstrated when she was provided with an Intelligence and police shield during the uncertain days following Ziaur Rahman's assassination.

Granted the upsurge of pro-Islamic and anti-Indian sentiment in Bangladesh in recent years, it is not surprising that the Awami League could garner only 26 per cent of the vote in 1981. Indeed, what has been surprising is the ability of the party to maintain its nationwide organization by contesting local and national elections, staging demonstrations, and otherwise sustaining its front organizations among students, workers, women and peasants. Awami Leaguers who made money during the 3-1/2 years when the party was in power have continued to provide financial support, since many of them view the party as a form of political protection against their rivals and find themselves unable to cross over to any of the other parties. Most of Bangladesh's Hindus (10 per cent of the population) and many businessmen interested in expanded commercial relationships with India are supporters of the AL because of its close connections and historical links with New Delhi. It is widely assumed that both India and the Soviet Union provide funds to the Awami League, but no concrete evidence of such funding has ever been made public.

With the Awami League out of power for the near future, factionalism within the party is expected to sharpen. The pro-Moscow section of the party is headed by Abdur Razzak and was opposed to participation in the 1981 elections. The anti-Moscow faction, led by Kamal Hossain, initially wanted to back retired General M.A.G. Osmany but settled on Hossain as a compromise candidate when the Razzak group refused to countenance Osmany.[14] The Razzak group has also been critical of Hasina Wajed, a consensual choice for the party presidency, and Razzak remains in control of party machinery despite Hasina's formal ascendancy to the top of the organizational ladder. During the election campaign there were several instances of physical clashes between supporters of the two Awami League factions. Kamal Hossain's followers have since blamed the party's defeat on Razzak's obstinacy; pro-Razzak people see the disastrous election results as legitimation of their advocacy of an electoral boycott. Independent observers fear that the inclination of both factions will now be toward greater militancy, with each group trying to prove its bonafides in the crucible of extremist political struggles.

PROSPECTS FOR THE FUTURE

The orderly transition that has taken place since the death of Ziaur Rahman has led to considerable optimism that Bangladesh may be able to maintain an electoral democracy under its present constitution.[15] The major impediments to such a scenario are likely to come from militant sections of the Awami League and, to a lesser extent, other opposition parties, or from sections of the army that are bent on asserting themselves in politics. Awami League leaders, including Kamal Hossain and Hasina Wajed, have pledged

14. An excellent discussion of Awami League factionalism appears in "Bangladesh: Eyes on the Army," Economic and Political Weekly (Bombay), XVI:47 (November 21, 1981), pp. 1880–1881.

15. See, for example, the editorial in The Guardian (London), November 20, 1981.

that they will act constitutionally, but they have also promised major protest demonstrations and a series of legal actions against the government because of what they describe as "massive rigging" of the 1981 elections. Some extremist sections of the Awami League have advocated a strategy of militant agitation against the government, in hopes that the constitution might be rendered unworkable, the army forced to intervene and subsequently embarrassed, and the Awami League ultimately elevated to power as a final viable alternative.

Hopes of building a militant opposition are fueled by the current economic crisis in Bangladesh, which has been exacerbated by a mid-1981 decision of the International Monetary Fund (IMF) to suspend nearly $1 billion in credits, on grounds that the heavy losses in Bangladesh public sector corporations are a result of mismanagement of those credits that have been given in the past. Suspension of the IMF credits has reduced Bangladesh's foreign exchange reserves to an all-time low and forced the government to halt all but the most essential imports. Awami League leaders are hoping to reap the whirlwind of discontent resulting from economic hardships, and to rally such discontent behind a series of political slogans that it has been trumpeting since Mujib's death.

By themselves, the opposition parties are unlikely to post a threat to the government in the immediate future, but many observers fear that they might be able to create conditions of seeming instability, thereby providing the military with an excuse to involve itself increasingly in the political process. Such fears were heightened during and after the 1981 election campaign when Lieutenant-General H M. Ershad, the Chief of Staff of the Bangladesh army, called on politicians to consider important constitutional changes which would actively involve the military in the country's affairs and, in his view, would ward off the possibility of future coup attempts. In an interview with Peter Nieswand of *The Guardian* (London), Ershad expressed his strong feeling that "the army should be directly associated with the governance of the country," in order that soldiers "feel their commitment" and "to arrest the tendency of uprising, at least to fulfill the ambition or the lust for power."[16]

Ershad denied that his proposals were at variance with those of

16. Ibid., October 7, 1981.

President Sattar, even though Sattar was quick to state, after his election, that "the army has a role to protect the sovereignty of the country and I don't think any other role is possible."[17] Highly reliable sources confirm that General Ershad had proposed to Sattar a suggestion for a military takeover that had been discussed by army leaders when it appeared that the Awami League would do much better in the 1981 elections than had originally been anticipated.[18] Ershad was also forced to retract a series of statements made during an interview with a Dacca weekly (*Holiday*) in which Ershad cast doubts on both Kamal Hossain and Osmany as candidates acceptable to the military.[19] Sattar quashed the army's bid for a military coup by threatening to immediately retire to his house in Dacca in the event of open army intervention. Major-General Mohabbatjan Chowdhury. Director-General of Military Intelligence, provided valuable support to Sattar when he conducted a secret nation-wide poll that showed Sattar running well ahead of all other Presidential candidates.

A major power behind Abdus Sattar has been Prime Minister Shah Azizur Rahman, 54, a renowned lawyer originally from West Bengal, who was General-Secretary of the Awami League in the 1950s, General Secretary of the East Pakistan Muslim League in the 1960s, leader of the opposition in Parliament during the last years of Ayub Khan, and a supporter of the idea of a united Pakistan throughout the period of the Bangladesh liberation movement. Shah Aziz, as he is known, is a brilliant orator and a superb politician, but he has been so crippled by widespread resentment of his support for Pakistan in 1971 that his ascendancy to a position of dominance within the party and government has threatened to produce a party split. Most BNP leaders feel that Shah Aziz lacks the personality and breadth to eventually succeed Sattar; his gruff manner and lack of knowledge of external affairs are viewed as fatal shortcomings. The position of Shah Aziz and his supporters has also been clouded by the fact that Zia had been

17. D. Sen, "Bangla Army Chief Insists on Role in Government," *Hindustan Times*, November 22, 1981. For an elaboration of Ershad's views see Tyler Marshall, "Dacca: Military Short Circuits," *International Herald Tribune*, August 27, 1981.

18. Michael T. Kaufman, "Sattar Reportedly Thwarted Plan for Military Takeover, "*International Herald Tribune*, November 18, 1981.

19. See *Holiday*, November 7, 1981.

considering a purge of "bad elements" within the BNP who had been guilty of corrupt activities, and Shah Aziz had frequently been listed as a prime target of Zia's contemplated reshuffle.

One possible successor to Zia under other circumstances might have been Budradozza Choudhury, General-Secretary of the BNP and a man whom Zia appeared to be promoting as a possible successor. Choudhury, who is still in his 40s, is often regarded as the best physician in Bangladesh and has established a prominent reputation with a nationwide television program in which he gives medical advice and answers questions from viewers. Unfortunately, rivalry between Choudhury and Shah Aziz is so deep-rooted that the candidacy of either one of them for President would undoubtedly have split the party in June 1981. It is to the credit of the political acumen of both men that they agreed to unanimously back the nomination of Sattar. While Choudhury is suave, sophisticated and brilliant, he is disadvantaged relative to Shah Aziz and others because he lacks any semblance of a political base and is a fairly recent newcomer to politics, having been personally recruited by Ziaur Rahman in 1977. Immediately after Zia's death, Budradozza sided with Shah Aziz in order to fend off a challenge from a third dissident faction of the BNP.

The most formidable opposition to Shah Aziz within the BNP has come from this third faction, which consists of men in their early 40s who, unlike Shah Aziz, are identified with the liberation movement. The principal leaders of this third group—which is sometimes known as the "gang of 70," reflecting its probable strength in Parliament—are: 1) Moudud Ahmed, who was Deputy Prime Minister under Zia until 1979 when he was relieved of office for trying to "democratize" the BNP. Moudud went to Harvard University and to Germany after his innings as Deputy Prime Minister, where he finished a book on Bangladesh politics.[20] He is reported to have the support of at least 20 Members of Parliament, including six ex-Ministers who were dropped from the Cabinet at the time of his dismissal by Zia; 2) Moudud has joined forces with Nurul Islam Shishu from Barisal, a major in the Bangladesh liberation army in 1971, who was rapidly promoted by Zia, retired from

---

20.   Ahmed's earlier book is *Bangladesh: Constitutional Quest for Autonomy, 1950-1971* (Dacca: University Press Ltd., 1979).

the army as a Major-General at the age of 40, and made Agricultural Minister in the last of Zia's Cabinets.

Shishu has the advantages of personality, vigor, connections in the military, among businessmen and in international development circles, plus his record as a freedom-fighter. His major liabilities stem from his reputation as a modern jet-setter who drinks and enjoys the company of women, these being personal characteristics that tend to alienate the Muslim rightists in the BNP and in the army. Shortly after Zia's death, Shishu and Akbar Hossain were dropped from Sattar's Cabinet, allegedly because they were politicking in the cantonment; many observers viewed the dismissals as a sure sign that Shishu is considered forever unacceptable to both the Shah Aziz faction of the BNP and the Generals. Since then, Shishu has become a leader of the dissidents within the BNP. 3) The third dissident leader is Akbar Hossain, a retired Lieutenant Colonel, also in his 40s, who fought in the liberation war, joined the BNP while Zia was alive, and was Petroleum Minister during the last year of Zia's life. Hossain was dismissed from Sattar's Cabinet along with Shishu. It is estimated that Shishu and Hossain together have a group of 30 to 50 Members of Parliament who are loyal to them.

When Moudud, Shishu and Hossain accepted Sattar's nomination for President, they tried to extract a promise as a condition of their support that the Vice-President would be "elected." Sattar, however, eventually appointed his own choice for Vice-President, Dr. M.N. Huda, a former Professor of Economics at Dacca University and Presidential Advisor to both Zia and Sattar. Huda had been a member of the old Civil Service of Pakistan, the elite corps of Pakistan bureaucrats, with long experience in the Planning Ministry. He had been preeminently responsible for the economic development strategy devised by Ziaur Rahman, which moved Bangladesh away from the watered-down socialism of Mujibur Rahman to a more free-swinging laissez-faire economy somewhat on the Indonesian model. Considering the poor state of Sattar's health and the awesome powers of the Presidency, it is understandable that Huda's appointment was considered a prize plum. Prior to that appointment, the constitutional successor to Sattar was Mirza Gholam Hafiz, the Speaker of the Parliament, president of the Chinese-Bangladesh Friendship Society and a long-time rival of Shah Aziz.

Civilian and army leaders agree that the best future scenario for Bangladesh would be one in which the army would remain united, disciplined and supportive of an elected constitutional government. One difficulty in establishing such a scenario is that the present government is still struggling for electoral legitimacy, even after the 1981 election, and the BNP is seriously divided by intense personalistic factionalism. Judging from the experience of Bangladesh's past, an alternative scenario might be an eventual break-up of the BNP and a shifting of coalitions between and within parties, with governments coming and going and changing their spots fairly often. Bangladesh does not have the innumerable linguistic, religious and caste divisions found in India, but personalistic conflicts—between repatriates and freedom-fighters, West Bengalis and East Bengalis. Muslim fundamentalists and modernizers, leftists, rightists and innumerable others—have often proven to be far more intractable than straight-out ethnic divisions that pit different races, religions or castes against one another.

Factional conflict in Bangladesh has become even more dysfunctional since 1971 because of the propensity of some factional groups to pursue the heroic, guerrilla style of the liberation war. As Maniruzzaman has pointed out, there has been a patterned structure to much of the violence that has occurred in Bangladesh over the last decade: "a group of armed men make a sudden and surprise appearance, liquidate their target with volleys from automatic weapons and run away out of sight, all with lightning speed."[21] This was a principal tactic of the Bangladesh guerrillas in the 1971 war, when Pakistani military officers and administrators were liquidated in their homes and offices. It has become a tactic that is now widely used in the universities, in political parties and labor unions, in the army, and in attacks on national leaders. Police statistics indicate that more than 23,000 persons (an average of 210 a month or 7 a day) have been murdered in Bangladesh since it became independent, with most of these murders allegedly having political motives.[22] Zia's death—and the other violent deaths that have preceded and followed it—raises the spectre, not of a political system in which there might be countless numbers of successful coups, but rather, and more frighteningly, the prospect of innumerable abortive coup attempts and lightning raids on authority figures,

21. Maniruzzaman, p. 4.
22. *Ittefaq* (Dacca daily), June 13, 1981.

which could render life unbearably insecure for anyone who tries to assume responsibility for getting things done.

There is another side to Bangladesh, which has perhaps not received as much attention as it should. The army is now united at the top, behind repatriate Generals and Brigadiers who have a deep-seated interest in maintaining unity among themselves. This group of officers has demonstrated that it can work effectively together and has proven—on many occasions—that it can thwart coup attempts directed against the civilian governments it has supported. Indiscipline within the army might lead to many raids and murders by commandoes in the night, but, for the near future, the only possibility of a successful coup d' etat would be one led by the Generals themselves.

While the Generals might intervene directly at some point in the future, their clear preference is to allow a civilian government to exist, with the army leadership having disproportionate influence relative to other groups in the functioning of government and in the distribution of patronage. This was Zia's conception of civil-military relations, particularly in his early years of martial law, and it is one that could remain viable for at least a few years into the future. Zia's re-institution of the bureaucratic elite that had first been created by the Pakistanis in the 1950s and 1960s has made it possible for the military to conceptualize a situation where the upper echelons of the bureaucracy and the army form the bedrock of a stable political core in Bangladesh, with party politicians and the lower ranks of the military and bureaucracy stirring in a state of constant flux around them. Zia had a similar conception during his first two years in power, but he was clearly trying to move towards greater democratization, decentralization and civilianization in the two or three years immediately before he was killed.

The dilemmas confronting the Bangladesh military now are the same as those faced by Ziaur Rahman. Rule by the military-bureaucratic elite may produce a political process that looks quite orderly, but it tends to cover up problems and suppress discontent in such a way as to produce a pressure cooker effect that can suddenly result in dramatic spurts of massive opposition against it. The strength of the bureaucratic establishment in Bangladesh is not that it can get things done, but that it can protect its own interests and the interests of those it serves by sustaining an environment of inertia and lethargy that has existed for a number of decades. Similarly, the military has historically been able to suppress the opposition, but not to inspire the population to produce more or to distribute it more equitably, both of these being necessary if problems are to be solved in the future. Zia's great accomplishment was the generation of an unprecedented enthusiasm for development among large segments of the population, and among international aid donors, while keeping political factionalism and meaneuvering within reasonable bounds. He often likened his efforts to the flight of an aircraft. "If the speed of the aircraft falls below a certain level," he once said, "you know it will fall. So, we've got to keep the party and the government moving very fast, and the same is the case with the whole people. That's why we go out so much to mobilize them."[23]

It may be that someone in Bangladesh—from the army or perhaps even a civilian—will find similar pressures pushing him or her in directions that Zia was headed. It may even be that some-one can muster the boundless energy, will and enthusiasm that Zia brought to the Presidency. If a new charismat comes to Bangla-desh, he or she would be well-advised to follow more effectively Zia's advice that "politics must be met with politics; firepower with firepower." Zia was struggling somewhat successfully to meet Bangladesh politicians on their own terms; he failed just once—but fatally—to have sufficient firepower at his command when a group of young officers were determined to murder him.

The immediate question for Bangladesh now is, who will do all of the things that Ziaur Rahman was doing? Who will raise massive amounts of international development funds in a world where aid donors are becoming increasingly bearish? Can anyone keep the lid on the politicking, the intrigues and recriminations of Bangladesh's innumerable politicians and bureaucrats without suppressing them so much that they explode in uncontrolled and unproductive outbursts against the government? Is it possible for anyone to accomplish what Ziaur Rahman seemed to be moving towards in the far reaches of the countryside—i.e. a situation where food production was increasing rapidly while rural development activities were slowly chipping away at old-fashioned practices and

23. The quote is from my "Ziaur Rahman and Bangladeshi Nationalism," *Economic and Political Weekly*, XVI:10-12 (Annual Number, March 1981), p. 361.

structures that have kept Bangladesh dependent on foreign aid despite its fertile soil?

In a country of 90 million people, which has faced the challenges that Bangladesh has had to confront over the past decade, the betting has to be that adequate leadership exists somewhere. As one member of the Bangladesh Parliament pointed out in the week following Zia's death, the nation could be proud that it had made the transition to a post-Zia leadership in a manner that "lived up to the democratic ideals of our martyred leader."[24] The great imponderables now are where leadership will come from and whether it will be up to the unprecedented challenges confronting this seemingly illfated nation as it enters the second decade of its independent existence.

24. Quoted in William Borders, "In Bangladesh, Peace For Now," *The New York Times*, June 5, 1981.

SUBJECT INDEX

Jolossard S. Farozui